To our friends

and families.

Contents

Section I   Navigation and Steering

Section II   Editing and Realism

Section III   Evaluation

Section IV   Applications

Section V   Conclusions

List of Figures

List of Tables

Preface

We are delighted to introduce this book *Simulating Heterogeneous Crowds with Interactive Behaviors*. This book project was started after a Eurographics Tutorial, which the editors organized in 2014. The original tutorial was extended by inviting renowned researchers in the crowd simulation field to contribute their latest work to the book.

Although many of the topics covered in this book already appear in published papers, they are spread over many different journals and conferences. This volume consolidates many of those fundamental topics and approaches in one place that are important when trying to simulate crowds that demonstrate a certain level of heterogeneity.

This book is divided into four major sections: navigation and steering, editing and realism, evaluation, and applications. There is a final 5th section with conclusions from the editors.

The chapters on *navigation and steering* introduce a variety of methods that have been used over the past decade to move groups of virtual people toward individual goals while avoiding collisions between agents and with the environment. Some of the methods described in the first chapter include a variety of parameters that can help introduce heterogeneity in the crowd. In order to have agents navigating complex or large spaces, steering alone is not enough; the second chapter gives an overview of methods that can create abstract representations of the environments to perform higher-level tasks such as path finding. Finally, in order to enhance heterogeneity, the third chapter introduces methods for data-driven simulation that exploit heterogeneity in behaviors extracted from examples in the real world.

In the second section, *editing and realism* play a role in providing some control over the final look of the simulation. For example, we may want to observe certain formations among agent groups, or have specific densities or flows in different parts of the environment. In order to achieve heterogeneity, it is important to explore effective methods for editing and authoring in order to allow the user to orchestrate overall crowd movement. For example, crowds may have a global "personality," which is evident in their collective behavioral choices. The inclusion of models of personality and emotion to drive the simulation can also greatly enhance realism and heterogeneity. For realism and rendering speed, one chapter provides an overview of graphics display techniques, focusing on two methods that are based on graphical impostors per body part. These techniques enhance the overall realism of the crowd by adding variety in appearance.

One of the most important issues when doing research in crowd simulation is addressed in the third section on *evaluation*. Here, we cover a number of methods for performing quantitative evaluation of crowds in terms of measurable features such as densities or flows. Evaluation may also compare simulations with agent decisions based on available real data.

Finally, the fourth section of this volume documents some examples of *applications* where crowd simulation is required. The first chapter in this section provides a very entertaining view of how this field has evolved in the animation industry from a Pixar point of view. The second chapter covers a completely different industrial and societally important application in safety and evacuation dynamics.

The editors of this book have made notable contributions to and have a comprehensive history in the crowd simulation research field. Norman Badler became interested in computational modeling of humans and their movements in the mid-1970s as he was completing his PhD dissertation at the University of Toronto. After taking an academic position at the University of Pennsylvania, he worked with a variety of geometric and animation methods for human modeling. Eventually, he and his students developed an interactive human software system for ergonomic applications: "Jack." After successfully spinning this software to a start-up, he began to look into animating groups of virtual human models. The primary drivers of these investigations were Jan Allbeck and Nuria Pelechano. Allbeck was particularly interested in agent heterogeneity, action variety, scheduling, and reactive behaviors. Pelechano examined agent communication, high-density crowds, and geometric extensions to social forces models. Their achievements were documented in the 2008 book *Virtual Crowds: Methods, Simulation, and Control*. Subsequently, Mubbasir Kapadia became a postdoctoral researcher for 2 years in Badler's Center for Human Modeling and Simulation at Penn and produced considerable new approaches to various issues in human crowd simulation ranging from steering behaviors to story-telling planning systems.

Nuria Pelechano continued her work with Allbeck and Badler during her postdoc to explore the field of presence for the evaluation of crowd simulation methods, as an alternative to the quantitative approaches presented in this book. They also investigated the inclusion of psychological models to add heterogeneity into the overall simulation. In 2007, Pelechano joined the Universitat Politècnica de Catalunya, and since then she has been working on developing rendering techniques that can handle a variety of animations for crowds in real time. Part of her recent work in collaboration with Kapadia and Badler has focused on animation techniques to accurately following footstep trajectories and simulation of groups of agents with different granularities.

Jan Allbeck's interest since joining George Mason University has focused on developing purposeful agents. Allbeck and her students have looked at ways to increase virtual human's understanding of their environment, including attention and memory models and most recently automated generation of action and object semantics.

After his postdoctorate, Mubbasir Kapadia joined the animation group at Disney Research, Zurich. Since 2015, Kapadia is an assistant professor at Rutgers University where he conducts research in humanoid character animation, crowd simulation, and digital storytelling.

It is the editors' collective hope that this volume will continue to motivate research and applications in heterogeneous crowd simulation. Realistic spatial environments supporting real-life situations and populated by multiple individuals have been an inspiration to us. We hope you will find them just as fascinating.

Editors

Nuria Pelechano is an associate professor at the Universitat Politècnica de Catalunya. She earned a BS in computer science engineering at the Universitat de València in 2001, an MSc at the University College London in 2002, and a PhD at the University of Pennsylvania (UPenn) in 2006 as a Fulbright Scholar, under the supervision of Professor Norman I. Badler. During her postdoc, she worked at the Architecture Department at UPenn in technology transfer projects on crowd evacuation. She is a coauthor of two books on virtual crowds with Morgan & Claypool Publishers (2008 and 2015). She has over 35 publications in journals and international conferences on computer graphics and animation, and she has also been a reviewer for many conferences and journals. She has participated in projects funded by the EU, the Spanish government, and U.S. institutions. Her research interests include simulation, animation, and rendering of crowds, generation of navigation meshes, real-time 3D graphics, and human–avatar interaction in virtual environments.

Jan M. Allbeck is an associate professor in the Department of Computer Science at George Mason University, where she is also the faculty advisor for the undergraduate concentration in computer game design and director of the games and intelligent animation laboratory. She earned a PhD in computer and information science at the University of Pennsylvania in 2009. She has more than 50 publications in international journals and conference proceedings and has served as a reviewer for over 40 journals, conferences, and workshops. She has had the great opportunity to explore many aspects of computer graphics, but is most drawn to research at the crossroads of animation, artificial intelligence, and psychology in the simulation of virtual humans.

Mubbasir Kapadia is an assistant professor in the Computer Science Department at Rutgers University. Previously, he was an associate research scientist at Disney Research Zurich. He was a postdoctoral researcher and assistant director at the Center for Human Modeling and Simulation at the University of Pennsylvania, under the directorship of Professor Norman I. Badler. He earned a PhD in computer science at the University of California, Los Angeles under the advisement of Professor Petros Faloutsos. Kapadia's research interests include developing computational models of virtual humans with applications in crowd modeling and digital storytelling.

Norman I. Badler is Rachleff Professor of Computer and Information Science at the University of Pennsylvania. He earned a BA in creative studies mathematics at the University of California, Santa Barbara in 1970, an MSc in mathematics at the University of Toronto in 1971, and a PhD in computer science at the University of Toronto in 1975. He served as the senior coeditor for the journal *Graphical Models* for 20 years and presently serves on the editorial boards of several other journals, including *Presence*. His research involves software development to acquire, simulate, animate, and control 3D computer graphics of human body, face, gesture, locomotion, and manual task motions, both individually and for heterogeneous groups. He has supervised or cosupervised 62 PhD students, many of whom have become academics or researchers in movie visual effects and game industries. He is the founding director of the SIG Center for Computer Graphics, the Center for Human Modeling and Simulation, and the ViDi Center for Digital Visualization at the University of Pennsylvania (UPenn). He has served UPenn as chair of the Computer Information Science Department (1990–1994) and as an associate dean of the School of Engineering and Applied Science (2001–2005).

Contributors

Aytek Aman earned a BS and an MS in computer engineering at Bilkent University, Ankara, Turkey, in 2011 and 2014, respectively. He is working on a PhD in computer engineering at Bilkent University. His research interests include virtual and augmented reality, crowd simulation, and computer vision.

Carlos Andújar is an associate professor of computer science at the Universitat Politècnica de Catalunya (UPC-BarcelonaTech). His research interests include 3D user interfaces, virtual and augmented reality, large model visualization, and real-time rendering. He earned a degree in computer science in 1994 at the Barcelona School of Informatics and a PhD summa cum laude in software engineering in 1999 at UPC. In 2000, his PhD was honored with the university's extraordinary doctorate award in informatics. He is a member of the university's modeling, visualization, interaction, and virtual reality research group. He has been a research visitor at the Georgia Institute of Technology (1998) and the University of Genoa (2000–2001).

Muhammad Baqui is a PhD candidate at the Center for Computational Fluid Dynamics at George Mason University. He earned a BSc in mechanical engineering at Bangladesh University of Engineering and Technology and an MSc in mechanical engineering from North Dakota State University. His research work focuses on understanding high-density pedestrian flows through image processing and computational methods.

Alejandro Beacco earned a PhD in computer science at the Universitat Politècnica de Catalunya, under the supervision of Dr. Nuria Pelechano. His research focuses on improving simulation, animation, and visualization of crowds in real time. He has extensive knowledge in crowd animation and visualization, 3D character animation, and 3D rendering techniques for dynamic objects or characters. He is working as a postdoc at the Experimental Virtual Environments (EVENT) Lab for Neuroscience and Technology at the Universitat de Barcelona.

Glen Berseth is a PhD student in the Department of Computer Science at the University of British Columbia. He earned a BSc in computer science at York University in 2012 and an MSc at York University under the supervision of Petros Faloutsos in 2014. His research interests include character animation, crowd simulation, machine learning, and cognitive agents.

Britto is project engineer at SL-Rasch GmbH, which is well known for its unique architectural and high-end engineering tasks related to Hajj, especially the world-class projects done for Mecca and Madinah. As a graduate in mechanical engineering, Britto worked in different engineering disciplines, and executed projects related to machinery design, plant layouts, lightweight membrane structures, CFD aerodynamic wind simulations, CFD climatic simulations, and crowd management simulations. His recent work focuses on Hajj-specific research topics, such as comfort analysis for the high-density pilgrimage crowd, fundamental behavior analysis of high-density crowds (performing Tawaf), crowd pressure studies, and crowd management scenarios for the Hajj pilgrimage.

Vinicius J. Cassol earned a PhD in computer science at Pontifícia Universidade Católica do Rio Grande do Sul, Brazil, in 2016, supervised by Professor Soraia Musse. He was a visiting scholar at the University of Pennsylvania under the supervision of Professor Norman Badler in 2013. His research focuses on crowd simulation and analysis of evacuation process. Dr. Cassol is currently a lecturer in computer graphics and games at the University of Vale do Rio dos Sinos (Unisinos), Brazil.

Panayiotis Charalambous is a postdoctoral fellow at the Mimetic Team in INRIA Rennes, France, where he is working on novel algorithms for crowd authoring and simulation. He earned a PhD in 2014 at the University of Cyprus under the supervision of Yiorgos Chrysanthou. Before that, he studied at the National and Kapodistrian University of Athens, where he earned a BSc and an MSc in computer science and telecommunications. His research interests include data-driven methods for crowd simulation and analysis, computer animation, motion analysis, and applications of machine learning techniques on computer graphics.

Yiorgos L. Chrysanthou is an associate professor at the Computer Science Department of the University of Cyprus, where he is heading the graphics and hypermedia lab. He earned a PhD at Queen Mary and Westfield College and worked as a lecturer at University College London. He has published over 75 papers in journals and international conferences on computer graphics and virtual reality and is the coauthor of the book *Computer Graphics and Virtual Environments: From Realism to Real-Time* (Addison-Wesley 2001 + China Machine Press 2004). His research interests are in the general area of 3D computer graphics, including crowd simulation, motion capture and animation, high dynamic range (HDR) lighting, and applications to serious games and cultural heritage.

Funda Durupınar earned a PhD in 2010 from the Department of Computer Engineering at Bilkent University, Ankara, Turkey. She earned a BS at Middle East Technical University, Ankara, Turkey, and an MS at Bilkent University, both in computer engineering in 2002 and 2004, respectively. She conducted research as a postdoctoral fellow at the Center for Human Modeling and Simulation, the University of Pennsylvania, from 2011 to 2015. She is a research software engineer at the Oregon Health and Science University, Portland, Oregon. Her research interests include crowd simulation, intelligent and emotional virtual agents, physically based simulation, cloth modeling, and rendering.

Petros Faloutsos is a professor in the Department of Electrical Engineering and Computer Science at York University. He earned a PhD (2002) and an MSc in computer science at the University of Toronto, Canada, and a BEng in electrical engineering at the National Technical University of Athens, Greece. Faloutsos's research focuses on digital media, computer graphics, virtual humans, and health informatics. He is the coauthor of a frequently cited paper on the topology of the Internet that earned an ACM SIGCOMM Test of Time Award in 2010. Faloutsos is an associate editor of the *Journal of the Visual Computer* and a member of the editorial board of the *Journal of Virtual Worlds*. He is also a member of ACM and the Technical Chamber of Greece.

Uğur Güdükbay earned a BS in computer engineering at the Middle East Technical University, Ankara, Turkey, in 1987 and an MS and PhD in computer engineering and information science at Bilkent University, Ankara, Turkey, in 1989 and 1994, respectively. He conducted research as a postdoctoral fellow at the Human Modeling and Simulation Laboratory at the

University of Pennsylvania. He is a professor in the Department of Computer Engineering at Bilkent University. His research interests are different aspects of computer graphics, including human modeling and animation, crowd simulation, physically based modeling, rendering, and visualization.

Stephen J. Guy is an assistant professor in the Department of Computer Science and Engineering at the University of Minnesota. His research focuses on interactive computer graphics (real-time crowd simulation, path planning, intelligent virtual characters) and multi-robot coordination (collision avoidance, sensor fusion, path planning under uncertainty). His work on motion planning has been used in a variety of AAA games, including those by Relic Entertainment, EA, Digital Extremes, and Monolith Productions. His work in crowd simulation has been recognized by best paper awards at international conferences. His research has garnered broad interest in industry, academia, and the press, with coverage of his work ranging from the *Boston Globe* to *Nature* to the Game Developer's Conference. He earned a PhD in computer science at the University of North Carolina at Chapel Hill with fellowships from Google, Intel, and the UNCF. He earned a BS in computer engineering with honors at the University of Virginia.

Eberhard Haug is one of the founding members of the ESI Group, the well-known virtual prototyping company, where he held the position of scientific director. He now acts as a consultant. He graduated from the University of Stuttgart in civil engineering and earned a PhD in structural engineering at the University of California, Berkeley, where he wrote a program for the large displacement finite element stress-controlled shape finding and analysis of lightweight structures. He was a research associate at the University of Stuttgart with Professors Frei Otto and J. Argyris. At ESI, he was the driving force behind the development of various industrial nonlinear FE analysis programs and material model developments, and he is the principal inceptor of the world's premier crash, occupant safety, and stamping simulation codes. He has published many papers on the theory and industrial application of modern numerical simulation techniques. His recent work focuses on biomechanics, pedestrian crowd management, and lightweight structures engineering design and analysis.

Brandon Haworth is a PhD student in the Department of Electrical Engineering and Computer Science at York University. He earned a BSc and an MSc in computer science at York University in 2013 and 2016, respectively. His research interests include crowd steering behaviors, crowd simulation, architectural optimization, assistive technologies, rehabilitative technologies, digital game design, and serious games.

Cláudio Rosito Jung earned BS and MS degrees in applied mathematics and a PhD in computer sciences at Universidade Federal do Rio Grande do Sul (UFRGS), Brazil, in 1993, 1995, and 2002, respectively. He is a faculty member at UFRGS in the Computer Science Department. His research interests include several aspects in image processing, computer vision and pattern recognition, such as medical imaging, multiscale image analysis, intelligent vehicles, multimedia applications, human motion synthesis and analysis, audiovisual signal processing, and stereo/multiview matching.

Marcelo Kallmann is a founding faculty and associate professor of computer science at the School of Engineering of the University of California, Merced (UC Merced). He earned a PhD at the Swiss Federal Institute of Technology in Lausanne (EPFL), was a research faculty at the University of Southern California (USC) and a scientist at the USC Institute for Creative Technologies (ICT), before moving to UC Merced in 2005. His areas of research include computer animation, virtual reality, and motion planning. At UC Merced, he established and leads the computer graphics research group. His research work has been supported by several awards from the U.S. National Science Foundation, and his work on triangulations for path planning has been adopted by *The Sims 4*, the latest installment of one of a best-selling video game series.

Paul Kanyuk is a second unit and crowds technical supervisor at Pixar Animation Studios with credits on *Cars, Ratatouille, WALL·E, Up, Cars 2, Brave, Monster's University, Lava, The Good Dinosaur*, and *Finding Dory*. His specialty is crowd simulation, shading, and rendering, and he is responsible for the procedural animation and rendering of numerous crowd spectacles, including the hordes of rats in *Ratatouille*, the deluge of falling passengers in *WALL·E*, and the vicious pack of talking dogs in *Up*. He earned a BSE in digital media design at the University of Pennsylvania and teaches courses in RenderMan and Crowd Simulation at the Academy of Art University in San Francisco. He is an avid musician and plays bass guitar in Bay Area rock bands.

Ioannis Karamouzas is a postdoctoral researcher in the Department of Computer Science and Engineering at the University of Minnesota. His research focuses on the development of motion planning algorithms for autonomous agents, robots, and crowds of virtual characters. He earned a PhD in computer science at Utrecht University with the support of the Netherlands Organization for Scientific Research. His work has been published in top-tier graphics, robotics, and physics venues. He has also contributed to crowd simulation and AI game development books, and his research has been integrated into commercial applications, including computer games, driving simulators, and pedestrian simulation suites.

Jongmin Kim earned a BS in EECS at KAIST, Daejeon, Korea, in 2006, and a PhD in EECS at Seoul National University, Seoul, Korea, in 2014. He was a research professor at the Institute for Embedded Software at Hanyang University in 2015. Since 2016, he has been a mocap software developer at Weta Digital. His research interests include computer graphics, character animation, deep learning, and numerical optimization.

Jehee Lee earned a PhD in computer science at the Korean Advanced Institute of Science and Technology. He is a professor of computer science and engineering at Seoul National University. His research interests include computer graphics, animation, biomechanics, and robotics. He is interested in developing new ways of understanding, representing, planning, and simulating human and animal movements. This involves full-body motion analysis and synthesis, biped control and simulation, clinical gait analysis, motion capture, motion planning, data-driven and physically based techniques, interactive avatar control, crowd simulation, and controller design. He cochaired the ACM/EG Symposium on Computer Animation in 2012 and served on numerous program committees, including ACM SIGGRAPH, ACM SIGGRAPH Asia, ACM/EG Symposium on Computer Animation, Pacific Graphics, CGI, and CASA. He is an associate editor of *IEEE Transactions on Visualization and Computer Graphics*. He leads the SNU Movement Research Laboratory.

Ming C. Lin earned a BS, an MS, and a PhD in electrical engineering and computer science at the University of California, Berkeley. She is the John R. Louise S. Parker Distinguished Professor of Computer Science at the University of North Carolina (UNC), Chapel Hill and an honorary distinguished professor (Yangtze Scholar) at Tsinghua University in China. She has received several honors and awards, including the NSF Young Faculty Career Award in 1995, UNC Hettleman Award for Scholarly Achievements in 2002, Beverly W. Long Distinguished Term Professor 2007–2010, IEEE VGTC VR Technical Achievement Award 2010, and 10 best paper awards. She is a fellow of ACM and IEEE. Her research interests include computer graphics, robotics, and human–computer interaction, with focuses on physically based modeling, sound rendering, haptics, algorithmic robotics, virtual environments, interactive techniques, geometric computing, and distributed interactive simulation. She has coauthored and authored more than 250 refereed scientific publications and coedited and authored four books. She has cochaired over 25 international conferences and workshops. She is a former editor-in-chief of *IEEE Transactions on Visualization and Computer Graphics* (TVCG) from 2011 to 2014. She has served on the editorial boards of several journals. She is currently a member of the IEEE Computer Society (CS) board of governors and a member of Computing Research Association—Women (CRAW) board of directors. She has also served on the steering or executive committees of several conferences and technical advisory boards for government agencies, industry, and the international scientific research community.

Rainald Löhner is the head of the CFD center at the College of Sciences of George Mason University in Fairfax, Virginia. He earned an MSc in mechanical engineering at the Technische Universität Braunschweig, Germany, as well as a PhD and DSc in civil engineering at the University College of Swansea, Wales, where he studied under Professors Ken Morgan and Olgierd Zienkiewicz. His areas of interest include numerical methods, solvers, grid generation, parallel computing, visualization, preprocessing, fluid–structure interaction, shape and process optimization, as well as pedestrian and crowd modeling. His codes and methods have been applied in many fields, including aerodynamics or airplanes, cars and trains, hydrodynamics of ships, submarines and UAVs, shock–structure interaction, dispersion analysis in urban areas, hemodynamics of vascular diseases, design and analysis of subway stations and stadiums, as well as the large pilgrimage sites. He is the author of more than 750 articles covering the fields enumerated above as well as a textbook on applied CFD techniques.

Dinesh Manocha is Phi Delta Theta–Matthew Mason Distinguished Professor of Computer Science at the University of North Carolina at Chapel Hill. He earned a BTech in computer science and engineering at the Indian Institute of Technology, Delhi in 1987 and a PhD in computer science at the University of California, Berkeley in 1992. He has coauthored more than 420 papers in the leading conferences and journals on computer graphics, robotics, and scientific computing. He has earned awards including IBM Fellowship, Alfred P. Sloan Fellowship, NSF Career Award, Office of Naval Research Young Investigator Award, SIGMOD IndySort Winer, Honda Research Award, Hettleman Award at UNC Chapel Hill, and 14 best paper awards at leading conferences. He is a fellow of ACM, AAAS, and IEEE and received the Distinguished Alumni Award from Indian Institute of Technology, Delhi. He has served on the editorial board of 10 leading journals and program committees of 100+ conferences in computer graphics, robotics, high-performance computing, geometric computing, and symbolic computation. He has been the program chair and general chair of more than 13 conferences and workshops in these areas and served as director-at-large of ACM SIGGRAPH from 2011 to 2014. He has supervised 28 PhD dissertations. His research group has developed many well-known software packages for collision detection, triangulation, GPU-based algorithms, solid modeling, and solving algebraic systems. These packages have been downloaded by more than 150,000 users worldwide and licensed to more than 55.

Soraia Raupp Musse is an associate professor in the Department of Computer Science at the Pontifical Catholic University of Rio Grande do Sul, Brazil. She earned a PhD in computer science from EPFL-Switzerland in 2000, supervised by Professor Daniel Thalmann. Her research interests include crowd simulation and analysis, facial animation and integration between computer graphics, and pattern recognition and computer vision. She created and currently coordinates the Virtual Human Lab (VHLab) where projects supported by private companies and the Brazilian government are developed. She also supervises postdocs, PhD, master's, and undergraduate students. She has been a reviewer of journals such as *IEEE TVCG* and *CG&A* and conferences such as SIGGRAPH and Eurographics. She is a coauthor with Professor Daniel Thalmann of a crowd simulation book (2007, second edition, 2013). She was a visiting faculty at the University of Pennsylvania from 2015 to 2016 in a research group supervised by Professor Norman Badler.

Julien Pettré is a research scientist at INRIA, the French National Institute for Research in Computer Science and Control (www.inria.fr). He earned an MS in 2000. He prepared his thesis under the supervision of Jean-Paul Laumond and earned a PhD in 2003 at the University of Toulouse III in France. He then spent 18 months in postdoc work at VRlab, EPFL, Switzerland, headed by Daniel Thalmann. At INRIA in Rennes, in 2016, he joined the Lagadic team headed by F. Chaumette. His research interests include crowd simulation, motion planning, autonomous virtual humans, computer animation, and virtual reality.

Glenn Reinman is a professor in the Department of Computer Science at University of California, Los Angeles, where he has been a faculty member since 2001. He earned a BS in computer science and engineering at the Massachusetts Institute of Technology in 1996, and a PhD and an MS in computer science from University of California, San Diego, in 2001 and 1999, respectively. His primary research interests lie in microprocessor design, mobile augmented reality, computational genomics, graphics processing, and neuromorphic hardware.

Shawn Singh earned an MS in computer science at the University of Southern California (USC) in 2006 and a PhD in computer science at the University of California, Los Angeles (UCLA) in 2011. His research interests include real-time photorealistic rendering and novel techniques for agent navigation, such as footstep planning. Since 2011, he has been a software engineer at Google, working on Chrome's accelerated compositor as well as YouTube's video and audio transcoding infrastructure.

Section I

Navigation and Steering

1

Anticipatory Local Navigation

Stephen J. Guy, Ioannis Karamouzas, Ming C. Lin, and Dinesh Manocha

CONTENTS

Local navigation is one of the fundamental aspects of simulating crowds. Here, a crowd is viewed as any collection of many independent agents, each making its own navigation decisions. The task of a local navigation algorithm is to ensure that each agent in the crowd makes progress to its goals while smoothly and naturally avoiding collisions with others nearby. While agents are typically assumed to act in a decentralized fashion, there is generally an implicit goal that global human-like, high-level behavior patterns should emerge as the commutative result of the many local interactions between the agents.

This chapter overviews decentralized, local collision avoidance methods commonly used in crowd simulations. After providing a brief overview of the field, we will focus on two recent families of local navigation algorithms that highlight the role the anticipation of future collisions has on local avoidance. Finally, we will wrap up with a brief discussion of how these methods can be extended beyond simple collision avoidance to incorporate a wider range of behaviors.

1.1 What Is Local Navigation

While simulating (human) crowds is a broad, multifaceted topic, for the purposes of this chapter, let us consider a simplified view of crowd simulation as planning paths for humans represented as circular agents, each with some center of mass and radius. (More complete representations of humans, such as psychological modeling and character animation will be discussed in Chapters 6 and 7.) In contrast to what are known as macroscopic crowd simulation approaches (like modeling crowd flows), an agent-based approach allows us to represent each agent in the crowd uniquely with its own corresponding goals and characteristics. We are now poised to discuss some of the most important challenges to address in order to produce compelling, human-like motion for these simple, two-dimensional (2D) agents. Let us consider some common aspects for the motion of agents in a crowd:

- *Goal-directed.* Agents should move toward their goals, and be sure to reach their goals in a reasonable period of time.
- *Collision-free.* At no point should two different agents occupy the same portion of space (i.e., their extents should not overlap).
- *Efficient.* Unnecessary and unmotivated movement should be avoided for all agents as it detracts the eye and typically looks "unnatural."
- *Smooth.* Related to being efficient, trajectories should generally be smooth. Paths that are too jerky will be difficult to animate naturally.
- *Anticipatory.* Agents should plan paths that react not only to the current crowd state (i.e., not walking into their immediate neighbors), but they should also anticipate the likely future condition of the crowd and account for that in their planning (i.e., avoiding collisions imminent in the near future).

Taken together, path computations for the agents that consider all these factors can produce compelling crowd behaviors. However, it can be difficult to design algorithms that perform well on all of these criteria. In practice, crowd simulation algorithms are typically subjected to further practical constraints. For example, if the crowd simulation is to be used in a video game or virtual reality training environment, the simulation needs to run in real time at interactive rates. Additionally, the same approaches are expected to work well for small-scale interactions with just a few agents and to scale up to simulating thousands of people. In the next section, we will discuss some approaches that strive to meet all of these requirements.

The Importance of Anticipation

Of the five objectives for good crowd motion, anticipation is one of the most important issues in ensuring that the crowd's motion faithfully captures the key aspects of human motion. Watching people react to upcoming collisions before they even occur is indicative of *intelligent motion*, rather than simple physical interactions that occur between inanimate objects.

Global navigation. In many simple environments, local navigation methods alone are sufficient to steer the agents toward their goals. However, because agents act based only on local information, they can easily get trapped in complex, cluttered environments. For example, imagine an agent inside an office building trying to get to the adjacent room. Simply approaching the wall separating the room will not achieve the agent's goal (as the wall will never move) and no local variation on this path will work either. Instead, the agent should walk out of the door, down the hallway, and into the door of the next room. The process of finding these high-level guiding paths is known as *global navigation* or global path planning. This is a well-studied problem in the field of robotics with many solutions having been applied to crowd simulation (a popular approach is using heuristic A* search to find a path along a map of the free space of the environment). For the purposes of discussion below, we will assume that if an agent is in a complex scenario, its local goal is not the agent's intended final position, but rather just a point that is further down the agent's global guiding path.

1.2 Approaches

At a high level, most agent-based crowd simulation approaches share many common features. Typically, each person in the crowd is represented by one agent who has a position in space, along with a velocity, acceleration, radius, or other elements of state. Updating the simulation is done on a timestep basis, with each agent following a sense–plan–act simulation loop where the agent senses the state of its local neighborhood for the current timestep, updates its state accordingly based on its local navigation algorithm, and then updates its position (typically using Eulerian integration). Typically, all agent updates are assumed to be done in parallel.

Below, we overview both historical and recent styles of approaches that have been used for local navigation, all of which more or less conform to the above framework. After that, the following two sections dive into a deeper exploration of two of the more recent techniques.

1.2.1 Rule-Based

One of the key seminal works in the field of local navigation was the *boids* approach by Craig Reynolds [1], which showed how several agents, each following a small number of simple, local navigation rules, can produce global flocking behavior. The emergent nature of the global behavior served as powerful validation of this type of approach for multi-agent simulation (i.e., local rules guiding each agent). Following the success of this work, many approaches in the graphics and animation community have focused on modeling human crowds using rule-based techniques. Funge et al. [2], for example, combined rule-based behaviors with cognitive models to simulate sophisticated agents that are able to learn from the environment. Shao and Terzopoulos [3] extended this model and integrated motor, perceptual, behavioral, and cognitive components in order to generate an artificial life model of autonomous pedestrians. Musse and Thalmann [4] simulated the collective behavior of groups of virtual humans in a crowd using concepts from sociology, whereas the HiDAC approach of Pelechano et al. [5] combined psychological and geometrical rules with physical forces to control individual agents in dense crowds.

Rule-based methods have also been integrated into a number of commercially available systems for crowd simulation. The *Massive Software* [6], for example, which was used in *The Lord of the Rings* film trilogy, combines simple rules with fuzzy logic to allow an artist to author behavior for each individual agent within the crowd. In general, rule-based approaches are able to simulate complex, life-like behaviors and can be used to create visually compelling crowd motions. However, it is generally difficult to design rules that consistently generate desired crowd behaviors, across a wide variety of situations. This problem can become worse in complex and dynamic environments where careful parameter tuning is usually required to obtain a satisfactory simulation result.

Cellular automata (CA) methods are closely related to rule-based methods. The academic study of CA dates back to at least the 1950s, and it has been widely applied to many fields with important implications for physics, mathematics, biology, computer science, and economics (see the detailed survey of Wolfram [7] and his subsequent book [8] for an extensive overview). More recently, CA methods have also been applied in modeling the motions of multiple agents for crowd simulation [9,10] and evacuation planning [11–13]. In these approaches, the space is discretized into a regular grid of cells. The automaton evolves through timesteps, where, at each timestep, each agent occupies one cell and can only move to an adjacent cell that is not occupied by other agents or obstacles. The locations of the agents are updated sequentially based on a set of rules based on the state of the agent and its immediate neighbors. The main advantage of using CA for simulating virtual crowds is the inherent simplicity. The motions of the agents are governed using a small set of rules, which are typically fast to compute, and have been shown to reproduce important key features of real human crowds [11]. However, owing to the discrete nature of these methods, the spatial movements of the agents are limited to adjacent free cells. This assumption can lead to unrealistic simulations, especially when complex interagent interactions must be addressed, and are generally inappropriate when smooth, continuous animations need to be created from the simulated crowd motion.

1.2.2 Local Forces

Inspired by physical-based simulation techniques, many researchers have sought to model individuals in crowds as particles. Typically, these models do not simulate literal Newtonian physics, but rather follow a structure typical of physical simulation: each agent experiences (potentially nonphysical) forces that are a function of its local environment. These forces are generally computed in a pair-wise fashion (a separate force is computed for each neighbor), and the acceleration, velocity, and position of each agent are computed on a per-timestep basis using standard numerical integration techniques. This particle-based approach has been used broadly in pedestrian dynamics community, with one of the most influential examples being the *social force model* developed by Helbing and his colleagues [14,15].

In Helbing's approach, the force an agent feels is predominately determined by the distance between two agents, with nearby neighbors inducing a large repulsive force, and far-away neighbors induce little to no force. Despite their simplicity, these types of models have been shown to be able to reproduce a wide variety of empirically observed crowd phenomena. Examples include the formation of lanes when there are two opposing flows, the appearance of vortices when there are multiple intersecting flows, and arching and clogging behavior at narrow exits [14,16,17]. The simplicity of these models, combined with their success in reproducing important crowd phenomena, has led to their widespread adoption as the basis for various crowd simulation approaches in both transportation research (e.g., [5,18–22]) and computer graphics [23–25].

While the details of different local forces models vary considerably, we can analyze a representative distance-dependent social force model here. First, consider a collection of n independent agents. Each agent, a, may have several parameters such as a 2D position $\mathbf{x}_a$ and a 2D velocity $\mathbf{v}_a$. We can now propose an interaction energy that captures how much discomfort a pair of pedestrian will feel. In the case of the simplest models, this interaction depends only on the distance between the two agents, which we will call d (we will discuss more complex interaction energies in the following section). Given this interaction energy, the force an agent will feel is the spatial derivative of the energy, so in the case of an agent i with a neighboring agent j, the force agent j induces on agent i is

$$\mathbf{F}_{ij} = -\nabla_{\mathbf{x}_{ij}} E(d), \tag{1.1}$$

where $\nabla_{\mathbf{x}_{ij}}$ is the spatial gradient with respect to the relative displacement between i and j.

Because the interaction energy captures an agent's discomfort, the force is formulated to push agents away from states of high energy. In social force models, the primary role of forces is to prevent collisions between agents. We therefore need to define a force that quickly rises as the distance between two agents approaches zero. A common choice for this function is a power law relationship:

$$\mathbf{F}_{ij} = -\nabla_{\mathbf{x}_{ij}} \left(\frac{k}{d^n} \right), \tag{1.2}$$

where k and n are tuning parameters that control the overall magnitude of the force, and how quickly it falls off at large distances, respectively.

Agents in these systems can experience a wide variety of forces beyond collision avoidance. The most important of these is a force that encourages goal-directed motion, though other common forces may include forces from obstacles, grouping forces, or following forces. One simple, common way to encode goal-directed motion is to give each agent a a goal velocity $\mathbf{v}_a^{pref}$ indicating both the desired direction of the motion and the preferred speed for the agent. Agents will now feel a new force that draws them to their goal velocity

$$\mathbf{F}_{G_a} = \frac{\mathbf{v}_a^{pref} - \mathbf{v}_a}{\xi} \tag{1.3}$$

where ξ controls the amount of time that agents need to accelerate to their goal velocities.

Each agent will respond to the sum of all the various forces acting on it over a given timestep (e.g., both the per-agent goal forces and the pair-wise collision avoidance forces). The effect of the forces on an agent's position and velocity are applied via numerical integration:

$$\mathbf{v}_a \mathrel{+}= F_a * \Delta t, \tag{1.4}$$

$$\mathbf{x}_a \mathrel{+}= \mathbf{v}_a * \Delta t, \tag{1.5}$$

where $\mathbf{F}_a$ is the sum of all forces on agent a and Δt is the simulation timestep.

This simple force-based simulation approach has formed a very successful framework for crowd simulation, and simple, distance-based forces like those discussed here can often produce surprisingly compelling results. Nevertheless, all these simple (social) forces can fail to produce the correct microscopic behavior in many circumstances. Owing to lack of anticipation and prediction, the simulated pedestrians only interact when they get sufficiently close, which results in unrealistic motions and oscillatory behavior. Additionally, similar to rule-based techniques, approaches using distance-based forces often need to be hand-tuned on a per-scenario basis to get good behavior, especially when dealing with high-density crowds.

Several approaches have been proposed that make significant efforts to overcome the limitations of simpler force-based models. As mentioned above, the HiDAC approach [5] extended this model by augmenting these forces based on a combination of psychological and geometrical rules in order to better simulate high-density crowds. The predictive avoidance model (PAM) of Karamouzas et al. [26] replaces distance-dependent forces with a model that account for upcoming interactions, thereby accounting for the role of anticipation. More recent work has taken a data-analytical approach to show that human collision avoidance motion can be well modeled by anticipatory forces [27]. The simulation model arising from this paper will be discussed in more detail in Section 1.3.

1.2.3 Predictive Planning Approaches

Recently, methods have been proposed that exploit space–time planning to generate trajectories that react to the likely future trajectories of all of an agent's neighbors. Early progress toward this direction came from the work of Reynolds on *unaligned collision avoidance behaviors* [28], in which agents tried to steer away from upcoming collisions predicted by linearly extrapolating their current trajectories. The work of Paris et al. [29] provided a means of mathematically formalizing this notion of steering away from upcoming collisions, while the work of van den Berg et al. [30] introduced the notion of "reciprocity" in collision avoidance, thereby allowing formal guarantees of collision-free motion. Linear prediction models for collision avoidance have also been successfully combined with global planning such as the work of Singh et al. [31]. A different approach was taken by Kapadia et al. [32], which formulates the collision prediction problem using the psychology concept of affordances. Similarly, Ondřej et al. [33] adopted a formulation to collision prediction based on cognitive and biological principles of the human visual system and motor response laws. One of the most popular predictive planning methods is the *optimal reciprocal collision avoidance* (ORCA) framework [34]. The ORCA framework allows each agent in a simulation to select a collision-free, oscillation-free, and locally optimal velocity in an efficient manner by solving a simple, low-dimensional linear program for each agent. The ORCA approach will be discussed further in Section 1.4.

As an example of predictive planning, consider an agent a having a goal velocity $\mathbf{v}_a^{pref}$ that needs to navigate amidst other agents without collisions. At each simulation step, we can solve this problem by uniformly sampling N candidate velocities that respect the agent's kinematic constraints (e.g., its maximum allowed speed) and selecting an optimal one according to a specific cost function. Typically, we would like to choose a new velocity $\mathbf{v}_a$ that minimizes the distance to the goal velocity and the risk of collision with any of the other agents, that is,

$$\mathbf{v}_a = \underset{\mathbf{v}_i^{cand}, i\in[1,N]}{\arg\min} \left\{ \frac{\gamma}{tc_i} + \|\mathbf{v}_i^{cand} - \mathbf{v}_a^{pref}\| \right\}. \tag{1.6}$$

Here, tc_i denotes the minimum time that will take for agent a to collide with any of the other agents assuming that a selects a velocity $\mathbf{v}_i^{cand}$ (see Equation 1.7 for how to compute a time-to-collision value for a pair of agents). The constant γ controls the relative importance of the two cost terms and can vary among the agents to simulate different avoidance behaviors.

The reciprocal velocity obstacles approach of van den Berg et al. [30] uses the same objective function as above but assumes that the agents reciprocate when estimating their minimum predicted collision time tc, which results in oscillation-free motion between pairs of agents. In Reference 35, Karamouzas and Overmars extended Equation 1.6 for small groups of agents by sampling both velocities and formations and adding a cost term that promotes formations observed in real pedestrians. Finally, Moussaïd et al. [36] considers the minimum distance rather than time to a collision when sampling candidate velocities for each agent.

1.2.4 Other Approaches

Recently, authors have proposed many methods that do not easily fit into any of the above categorization. For example, many models have been proposed that break down the artificial barriers between local and global navigation, or which try to explicitly account for how characters will be animated when generating their motion [37]. Another recent trend is the strong use of data to drive local motion. For example, the work of Lerner et al. [38] uses a database of human trajectories gathered from video recordings of real pedestrian crowds to look up the trajectory humans took in the situation that most closely matches that of any given simulated agent. Similarly, Lee et al. [39] used a regression-based learning to synthesize realistic group behaviors from crowd videos, and Ju et al. [40] used spatiotemporal behavior interpolation to drive large crowds from video examples. More recently, Charalambous and Chrysanthou introduced the perception–action graph to accelerate the synthesis of virtual crowds from data [41]. In general, data-driven methods share the advantage of being able to reproduce complex, subtle aspects of behaviors not well captured by other techniques, at the expense of poor performance in scenarios unlike those captured in the source data.

1.3 Force-Based Methods

The simple force-based crowd simulation approach outlined in Section 1.2.2 captures many aspects of crowd simulations, but fails to account for the importance of anticipation in human interactions. When two people interact, they are responding not only based on their current state, but on their expected future trajectories. This anticipation is a key aspect that differentiates human motion from that of flocks or herds. One of the simplest ways to account for the effect of anticipation is to recast collision avoidance forces not in terms of current distances, but rather predicted future positions. The PAM approach of Karamouzas et al. [26] follows this approach. Here, the distance term in Equation 1.2 is replaced with a term that scales with the distance to the predicted collision between the two agents. PAM makes several additional modifications to increase the realism of the simulation model, including restricting agents to considering neighbors within a limited field of view, adding a personal space to each agent, and eliminating interactions between agents whose collisions are far off in distances or time.

An alternative way to formulate an anticipatory force is to base interactions on the time it would take for two agents to collide if they maintained their current trajectories (we will refer to this as time to collision or TTC). Then, agents who are not on a collision course will not react to each other, while those whose collisions are imminent, can make small adjustments early on in order to efficiently avoid the collision. In fact, recent research have suggested that time to collision plays a fundamental role in human collision avoidance, and is well suited for the basis of collision avoidance techniques [27]. As an illustrative example of the workings of a force-based, anticipatory collision avoidance method, we will walk through the details of the time-to-collision simulation method of Karamouzas et al. [27].

The first step in this approach is to define the condition that determines if two agents are heading to an imminent collision. As above, an agent a will be represented by a 2D disk, with position x_a, velocity v_a, and fixed radius of r_a. Two agents i and j are said to be in collision if their representative disks are overlapping. We are interested not only in current collisions, but also in potential future ones. However, because we cannot know the actual future trajectory of any agent, we will use the simple approximation that agents will continue along their current velocity indefinitely. This means, given two agents i and j, we can define the condition of being on a collision course as follows:

$$\left\| (\mathbf{x}_j + \mathbf{v}_j \tau) - (\mathbf{x}_i + \mathbf{v}_i \tau) \right\| < r_i + r_j, \tag{1.7}$$

where τ is a free parameter representing the amount of time (in seconds) until the collision. Expanding this inequality leads to the following quadratic equation:

$$(\mathbf{v} \cdot \mathbf{v})\tau^2 + 2(\mathbf{w} \cdot \mathbf{v})\tau + \mathbf{w} \cdot \mathbf{w} - (r_i + r_j)^2 = 0, \tag{1.8}$$

where $\mathbf{w} = \mathbf{x}_j - \mathbf{x}_i$ and $\mathbf{v} = \mathbf{v}_j - \mathbf{v}_i$. This equation can be directly solved using the quadratic formula, resulting in the value for the time to collision τ. (Note that we are only interested in positive values of τ corresponding to upcoming collisions in the future.)

To incorporate the notion of time to collision into our simulations, we need to develop a collision avoidance force based on the value of τ. Intuitively, we imagine that the strength of the avoidance force should grow infinitely large as τ approaches zero (i.e., as collision becomes immediate), in order to prevent agents from ever colliding. Additionally, the force should quickly fall to zero for collisions more than a few seconds away. Studies on human trajectory data show that the discomfort people feel from collisions falls off with an inverse quadratic relationship with time to collision [27]. Interpreting this discomfort as a social "energy" function suggests that a collision avoidance force can be obtained by taking the negative of the spatial gradient of this energy. Overall, this leads to the following collision avoidance force:

$$\mathbf{F}_{ij} = -\nabla_{\mathbf{x}_{ij}} E(\tau) = -\nabla_{\mathbf{x}_{ij}} \left(k\tau^{-2} \right). \tag{1.9}$$

Note that this gradient can be evaluated numerically though it also has a closed-form analytical expression. This resulting force has a direction based on relative position of the two agents at the moment of impact and its magnitude exhibits an inverse cubic relationship with the time to collision. We refer the reader to Reference 27 for more details.

The above collision avoidance force should be combined with a goal force (such as Equation 1.3) to produce goal-directed, collision-free simulations. The value of k in Equation 1.9

serves to balance the strength of the avoidance forces with the strength of the goal-directed force.

1.3.1 Simulation Results

Despite their simplicity, force-based models can capture the emergence of visually interesting and empirically confirmed phenomena that have been observed in real pedestrian crowds, such as the dynamic formation of lanes, clogging, slowing down and stopping behavior, etc. We refer the reader to Figure 1.1 for three simulation results obtained using the anticipatory force introduced in Equation 1.9. These include

- *Head-on collision*: Two agents have to avoid a head-on collision while swapping positions. The agents exhibit anticipatory behavior by performing lateral avoidance maneuvers.
- *Circle*: Eight agents are evenly distributed along the circumference of a circle and have to move toward their diametrically opposite positions. By adapting their speed and directions, the agents are able to quickly reach their goals without getting stuck in time-consuming situations
- *Evacuation*: 150 agents exit an office through a narrow doorway. Owing to the restrictions imposed on the agents' movements, arch-like blockings are formed near the exit leading to clogging phenomena similar to the ones observed in granular media.

1.3.2 Scalability

Besides being easy to implement, force-based approaches are extremely fast to compute, allowing simulations of thousands of agents at real-time rates. In case a time-to-collision approach needs to be employed, the main bottleneck is to compute for each agent its nearest neighbors that induce collision avoidance forces on it. A naive implementation would be to iterate over all the other agents in the scene and check whether a collision will take place, which results in a quadratic runtime complexity. A more efficient implementation is to prune the search of nearest neighbors and only consider a fixed number of at most k

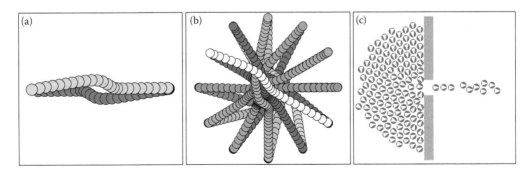

FIGURE 1.1
Stills from simulations of agents following the time-to-collision force-based model proposed in Reference 27. (a) Two agents exchange positions. (b) Twelve agents walk to antipodal points on a circle. (c) Agents exit a room through a narrow doorway. In all cases, the agents anticipate and avoid upcoming collisions.

nearby agents within a certain sensing radius. Then, by using a spatial data structure for nearest-neighbor queries, such as a kd-tree or a uniform grid, the runtime per simulation cycle is nearly linear in the number of agents.

1.3.3 Limitations

Force-based methods are not exempt from failure. As the behavior of each agent is described by a collection of forces, there may be cases that no final force can lead to a collision-free velocity. Furthermore, the forces can assume large values and vary quickly giving rise to numerical stability issues that may lead to unrealistic simulations (oscillatory behavior, backward movement, overlapping, etc). To avoid stiffness and retain stability, typically, a very small simulation timestep should be chosen, especially if a simple forward Euler integration scheme is employed. In general, as in any second-order model, the method of integration and the size of the timestep is very important in force-based models [42]. This explains the recent popularity that velocity-based (first-order) models for local navigation have gained.

1.4 Optimization-Based Methods

The ORCA collision avoidance framework provides a popular alternative to force-based local avoidance methods. In contrast to force-based methods, ORCA removes the ideas of forces and accelerations, instead allowing agents to directly choose a new velocity at each timestep by solving a constrained optimization problem. Here, the constraints are that the velocity must trace out a trajectory that is collision-free with respect to all other agents, for at least T seconds into the future. The optimization aspect is that the agent should choose collision-free velocities that are as close as possible to their goal velocity.

The first step in the ORCA algorithm is to construct the constraints on an agent's velocity. This is best understood by thinking in terms of velocity space. Imagine a 2D Cartesian plane, but with the X and Y axes replaced by the X and Y components of an agent's velocity. In this space, (0,0) corresponds to an agent standing still, where (1,1) corresponds to an agent moving up and to the right. Given an agent A with a neighbor B, A can compute the set of velocities that may collide with B. This set of forbidden velocities is know as a velocity obstacle or VO [43]. If B is standing still, the VO will be a cone starting from the origin, and encompassing a circle centered around agent B with a radius the size of $r_A + r_B$. That is to say, A must either go fully left or fully right of B to avoid collisions. If B is moving, the center of this VO cone is shifted to lie at B's current velocity (i.e., A must either speed up pass B or slow down to let B pass).

Anytime that A's current velocity $\mathbf{v}_A$ is inside the VO it forms with agent B, we know A is on a collision course with B. In order to resolve this collision, A must move its velocity to lie outside of this cone. Let us call the vector $\mathbf{u}$ the minimum such change in velocity A must take to resolve this collision (i.e., to move the current velocity outside of the VO cone). This vector $\mathbf{u}$ can be found quickly by projecting the current velocity to the closest side of the VO cone. Were A to take this vector $\mathbf{u}$, and *nothing else here to change by the next timestep*, the new velocity of $\mathbf{v}_A + \mathbf{u}$ is *guaranteed* to be collision-free as it, by definition, lies outside the VO cone.

In practice, we know the assumption that nothing changes is flawed. In fact, we can prove by symmetry that agent B is in the exact same condition as agent A. B sees that it is on a collision course with A and will adjust its velocity by $-\mathbf{u}$ following the same reasoning as A above. This duplication of effort has two negative consequences for the agent behavior. First, agents are wasting effort by both accounting entirely for the collision that the other is already resolving completely. Second, because in the next timestep the two agents will no longer be on a collision course, both agents will simultaneously think it is safe to return to their goal velocities, and both will find themselves again in collision. This process leads to unnatural oscillations in agent motions, especially with larger timesteps.

The oscillation problem is addressed in ORCA by exploiting the notion of reciprocity. That is, each agent in the collision assumes the other agent will "carry its own weight" by also working to resolve the collision. In practice, it means that an agent does not have to adjust its velocity by $\mathbf{u}$, but rather only by $\frac{1}{2}\mathbf{u}$, safe in the knowledge the other agent will take care of the rest. This carries the additional advantage that two agents will maintain a path where their borders will exactly touch. This prevents agents from oscillating in and out of collision.

We can now define the ORCA constraint cast on agent A by B as the set of all velocities that move A by at least $1/2\,\|\mathbf{u}\|$ in the direction of $\mathbf{u}$, that is, velocities that get at least halfway out of the VO between A and B. Formally,

$$ORCA_{A|B} = \left\{ \mathbf{v} \mid \left(\mathbf{v} - \left(\mathbf{v}_A + \frac{1}{2}\mathbf{u} \right) \right) \cdot \mathbf{u} \geq 0 \right\}, \qquad (1.10)$$

where $\mathbf{u}$ is the smallest change in relative velocity needed to resolve the collision between A and B (Figure 1.2). If two agents are not on a collision course, $\mathbf{u}$ is the smallest change needed to get onto a colliding path with B. These agents likewise must ensure not to change their relative velocity by more than $\mathbf{u}$ in order to remain collision-free.

It is important to note that the constraint defined by Equation 1.10 is a linear constraint on an agent's velocity. This means very fast methods exist for solving the constrained optimization problem presented by the ORCA framework. For example, take the case of agent A with a single neighbor B. Testing if the goal velocity of A is allowed by the ORCA constraints is a simple point-in-half-plane test. If the goal velocity is forbidden by the ORCA test, we must now find the closest velocity that is allowed. While the term "closest" is somewhat subjective, we note that choosing a new collision-free velocity that minimizes

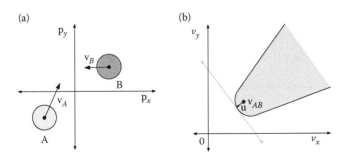

FIGURE 1.2
ORCA collision avoidance. (a) Two agents (in world space) on a collision course. (b) The velocity space of agent A. The shaded region shows which relative velocities will lead to collisions within the given time horizon. The relative velocity $\mathbf{v}_{AB}$ is inside the shaded region, indicating that A must choose a new velocity outside this region. The gray line shows a linear approximation of the shaded forbidden region.

the Euclidean distance to the goal velocities (in velocity space) is the same as minimizing the acceleration needed to return to the goal velocity. Following this intuition, we define the "best" velocity as that which is closest (L2 distance) to the goal, while respecting the ORCA constraints. Again, we can easily find this point with geometric operations. This time, it is a simple vector projection of A's goal velocity onto the ORCA constraint.

The notion of ORCA constraints can easily be extended to cases where an agent has multiple neighboring agents to avoid. In this case, the agent must choose a velocity that is collision-free with respect to all the ORCA constraints from all the neighboring agents simultaneously. Formally, we define $ORCA_A$ as the union of all constraints on agent A from all neighbors B:

$$ORCA_A = \bigcap_{A \neq B} ORCA_{A|B}. \qquad (1.11)$$

$ORCA_A$ should be viewed as a set of n linear constraints on agent A's velocity, one for each neighbor of A. Choosing a new velocity now involves finding the velocity that is as close as possible to A's goal velocity, while respecting all the linear constraints. Unlike the single-neighbor case described above, we cannot solve this problem using only vector projections (as that considers only one constraint at a time). However, optimizing the distance to a point subject to several linear constraints is the exact problem solved by linear programming. Conceptually, the linear programming process can be viewed as first intersecting all the linear constraints to build a convex hull representing the allowed space of velocities, and then projecting the goal velocity onto the closest line segment in this hull. While a naive implementation of this "hull-building" approach is $O(n^2)$ in the number of neighbors, faster methods exist, and the ORCA authors use a randomized method with an expected runtime of $O(n)$ [44]. The resulting velocity will respect all the VO-derived ORCA constraints, and is therefore *guaranteed* to be collision-free.

To recap the steps of the ORCA framework: First, the VO cone between agents A and B is built in velocity space. Then, the vector **u** is computed as the minimum distance between the relative velocity $\mathbf{v}_A - \mathbf{v}_B$ and the VO boundary. Next, a linear constraint is generated, which represents the set of all velocities that accelerate A by at least $1/2\,\|\mathbf{u}\|$ in the direction of **u**. Then the union of all of the linear constraints is taken over all of A's neighbors. Finally, the linear programming constrained optimization method is used to find a velocity that is as close as possible to A's goal velocity while respecting all the linear constraints. As in the force-based simulation approaches, the velocity that comes from the optimization step is used to update the agent's position and velocity at each timestep.

1.4.1 ORCA Practicalities

Many improvements can be made to the approach outlined above, which improves the quality of the agent motion. For example, new constraints can be added to the velocity space to further direct the motion. A simple example is adding a disk constraint centered at **0** with a radius of $\mathbf{v}_{max}$. This will prevent the velocity optimization step from choosing any velocity greater than the maximum speed $\mathbf{v}_{max}$.

In many cases, forbidding any velocity that lies at all inside a VO cone is too restrictive of an assumption. In particular, it does not typically make sense for an agent to plan now based on collisions that will not happen until many seconds or even minutes from now—especially in the case of simulating crowd motion. The concept of a VO cone can easily be modified to account for this, by defining a planning *time horizon* of T seconds. We can define a $VO^T_{A|B}$ as the set of velocities that will cause agent A to collide with B in the next T seconds. This space has the same conic shape as a regular VO, but with the sharp point of the cone, replaced with a rounded edge; the velocities closest to the apex of the cone correspond to collisions far in the future, which are now considered allowed velocities. This new time-horizon-truncated VO is used to compute the minimally avoiding acceleration **u**, after which ORCA proceeds exactly as before, following Equations 1.10 and 1.11 unmodified. Agents will now take velocities that are guaranteed collision-free for at least the next T seconds.

An important consideration when using an optimization-based method such as ORCA is that the optimization step (in this case, the linear programming step) may fail to find a velocity that satisfies the constraints; this can happen when there are conflicting ORCA constraints resulting in no velocities that satisfy the union of all constraints. In this case, we cannot fully trust any output from the optimizer as the velocity is no longer guaranteed to be collision-free. A simple approach in these scenarios is to run the optimization step again, but remove the constraint corresponding to the furthest-away agent. If this fails, continue removing agents until a satisfying velocity can be found. As long as we maintain the very closest agents when building the ORCA constraints, we are still likely to be collision-free for the next timestep. (To maintain guarantees, we must keep all agents within a distance of $\mathbf{v}_{max}\Delta t$). In practice, this approach can be quickly implemented by sorting agents based on their distance to A, and adding ORCA constraints one at a time until all agents are accounted for or the constraint optimization fails. Other options including reducing the time horizon or invoking a higher-dimensional linear programming step to find the "least-bad" velocity are described in Reference 30.

1.4.2 Simulation Results

ORCA is extremely fast, allowing simulations of thousands of agents in real time, providing at the same time some formal guarantees about the collision-free motion of the agents. In order to verify its performance, we selected a varying number of agents and placed them along a circle. Each agent had to walk toward its antipodal position (Figure 1.3). Such a scenario is very challenging since all the agents cross paths nearly at the same time and each one can potentially collide with any of the other agents. Typically, congestion conditions evolve in the center of the circle as the agents try to reach their destinations.

We performed experiments for up to 5000 agents and used OpenMP to efficiently parallelize the simulations by distributing the computations of the new agent's velocities across

FIGURE 1.3
Simulation of 1000 ORCA agents trying to move toward their antipodal positions on a circle. Agents move through the congestion without colliding.

eight Intel Xeon 2.66 GHz cores. The running time of ORCA increased nearly linearly with the number of agents. Even for 5000 agents, it took 8 ms per simulation step to solve the OCRA linear programming and update the velocities of the agents. Importantly though, each agent was able to safely navigate through the dense, packed crowd that forms in the center and reach its goal without any collision.

ORCA has also been applied to the computationally challenging scenario of simulating the very large, dense crowds that form at Mecca during the Hajj [45], as demonstrated in videos shown at

http://gamma.cs.unc.edu/LARGE/

1.5 Extending VOs beyond Collision Avoidance

As mentioned before, simply avoiding collisions is only one consideration that can affect an agent's local motion. One example, we have already discussed is expressing an agent's intent through a goal velocity, but there are many other important examples. For instance, agents who come into unexpected contact with each other may experience physical pushing from the collision that alters their trajectory. Likewise, agents who are stressed or afraid will take different local paths than those who are confident or aggressive. Ideally, all of these aspects should work with the local collision avoidance method to direct an agent's motion. In force-based approaches, there is often a very natural formulation for considering these features. Physical forces from pushing can be directly modeled with Newton's law, and added as an additional force acting on the agent [5]. Psychological forces can likewise be defined, which gently push or pull the agent's trajectory based on forces whose effects are derived from the psychological literature [46]. Some approaches following this style will be discussed in subsequent chapters.

The same types of effects can be achieved when using collision avoidance approaches based on geometric optimization, such as ORCA. However, the geometric nature of these approaches raises unique challenges in adding physical forces or accounting for psychological effects. New forces cannot be simply added to the system after the fact if we wish to still maintain the geometric guarantees that the approach is based on. For example, trying to make an ORCA agent act aggressive by giving it an extra force in the direction of its goal may cause it to adopt a velocity that is not outside a VO, violating the ORCA constraints and potentially leading to collisions. Below, we briefly describe several different algorithms for addressing high-level behavior while maintaining the general ORCA optimization framework.

1.5.1 Stress and Personality

In real life, the walking behavior of pedestrians is strongly influenced by their personality and mood. Nevertheless, such factors are often overlooked in crowd simulations. A simple, yet effective, approach to address this issue is by tuning, in a principled way, the simulation parameters of the agents (e.g., their preferred speeds, the distance that they prefer to maintain from other agents, and the number of nearest neighbors). In fact, based on a user perception study, Guy and colleagues proposed a linear mapping between the parameters of the ORCA optimization framework and six distinct types of agent behaviors (aggressive,

FIGURE 1.4
Agents evacuating a building using the approach proposed in Reference 47. Aggressive agents (wearing red shirts) tend to exit the room faster than the shy agents (brown shirts).

shy, assertive, tense, impulsive, active) [47]. A shy agent, for example, can be modeled by maintaining a high separation distance from other agents and a low preferred speed, whereas an active agent favors high time horizon values. Using these mappings from the experimental study, different types of agents can be generated that add heterogeneity and realism to the simulations (Figure 1.4). For instance, Kim et al. tuned the aggressive and impulsive parameters of the agents using concepts from psychology literature to model a wide variety of behavior changes in response to different stressors [48].

1.5.2 Physical Forces

The work in Reference 49 extends the ORCA approach to allow agents to interact in a physical manner exhibiting behaviors such as pushing, deceleration, resistance, etc. Similar to the force-based models introduced earlier in this chapter, the agents are subject to a number of physical forces during each cycle of the simulation. Let $\mathbf{f}$ denote the sum of all these forces acted on an agent A and let $\mathbf{v}^f$ be the velocity of the agent after applying $\mathbf{f}$. Then the net force $\mathbf{f}$ introduces an additional linear constraint to the ORCA optimization framework as follows:

$$FC_A = \{\mathbf{v} \mid (\mathbf{v} - \mathbf{v}^f) \cdot \mathbf{f} \geq 0\}. \tag{1.12}$$

Here, FC denotes all velocities that are inside the half plane defined by the line through $\mathbf{v}^f$ that is perpendicular to the force $\mathbf{f}$. The force constraint FC is combined with the existing ORCA constraints induced by the other agents as introduced in Equations 1.10 and 1.11. A new collision-free velocity is then computed using linear programming that generates physically plausible behavior.

1.5.3 Group Formations

Throughout this chapter, we assumed that agents can be well approximated as (isotropic) disks. Such a formulation, though, is not particularly appealing when agents have to navigate as a group through the world while maintaining a specific formation. Modeling a formation as a disk can lead to overly approximated VOs, and, hence, many collision-free velocities will be characterized as inadmissible and discarded by ORCA. In addition, many formations have a wide aspect ratio (e.g., a group of friends walking line abreast) or a single leader (e.g., soldiers marching together in a column formation). In these cases, it is important that the formation rotates as its members move through the environment.

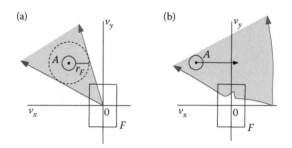

FIGURE 1.5

FVO collision avoidance for a formation F approximated by an oriented bounding box. (a) The FVO induced by a static agent A depends on the half-width r_F of the formation. (b) The FVO induced by a dynamic agent is more complex, having nonlinear boundaries. See Reference 50 for a derivation.

To address these issues, Karamouzas and Guy [50] introduced the concept of formation velocity obstacles (FVO) for guaranteed collision-free navigation of group formations. Their formulation conservatively approximates a formation F as an oriented bounding box. Then, for a given neighboring agent A, the FVO denotes the set of all velocities for the formation that will lead to a collision between F and A. In case the agent is standing still, the FVO is a (truncated) cone starting from the origin and encompassing a circle centered around agent A with radius $r_A + r_F$, where r_F is the half-width of the formation (Figure 1.5a). In case the agent is moving, the resulting FVO is more complex having nonlinear boundaries (Figure 1.5b). This is due to the fact that the actual velocity of F determines the orientation of the formation rather than the relative velocity between F and A. Hence, simply translating the apex of the VO to lie at the agent's velocity (as in a rotationally invariant VO) is not sufficient. Having computed the FVOs for each static and dynamic agent present in the environment, a new optimal collision-free velocity for the formation can be selected by approximating each FVO as a line and employing the linear programming constrained optimization method of the ORCA framework.

More recently, He et al. [51] have presented a novel algorithm to generate dynamic group behaviors in crowds. This formulation is general and makes no assumptions about the environment, shape, or size of the groups. The underlying formulation extends the reciprocal collision avoidance algorithm to perform agent–group and group–group collision avoidance and uses the least-effort principle to perform group navigation. The additional overhead of group computation and maintenance is relatively small and the algorithm can generate smooth trajectories in dense scenarios.

1.5.4 Bayesian Inference for Trajectory Prediction

The same kind of geometric analysis used to simulate agent motion in ORCA can be used to more robustly predict the paths of real humans. Having statistically robust predictions of human paths are important not only in crowd simulation but also in computer vision and robotics to help alleviate the uncertainty of sensing and interacting with the real world. Kim et al. [52] present a new motion model, called BRVO, that integrates agent-based velocity–space reasoning with Bayesian statistical inference. BRVO can be regarded as a dynamically changing or personalized motion model that takes into account environment changes and interactions with other agents. It uses the data from prior observations for each agent in the environment and predicts the agent motion for the next several timesteps using ensemble Kalman filtering. The overall method performs online per-agent learning and can generate more accurate predictions than prior methods. It has been extended to learn the pedestrian dynamics characteristics from tracked trajectories, which can be used for adaptive data-driven simulation [53], as well as crowd content generation and analysis [54].

1.6 Improving Behavioral Fidelity

While the work discussed in this chapter so far can produce interesting, high-quality, collision-free simulations, they are certainly not the end of the story. Given the dynamic nature of the field, the complexity of human motion and ongoing research in the fields of biomechanics, fire safety, and traffic engineering, the state of the art is frequently changing. Researchers continue to find important phenomena in human motion, which, in turn, inspires new methods for crowd simulation. Below, we briefly describe some recent projects that seek to enhance the accuracy of crowd simulations to match trends and phenomena known to occur in real human crowds.

1.6.1 Non-Circular Agents

Most prior work on multiagent and crowd simulation use disks to represent each agent. This simplified representation has many advantages in terms of collision avoidance algorithms based on social forces, velocity obstacles, or rule-based methods. However, these disks tend to overestimate the actual profile of the agent and the resulting algorithms tend to be overly conservative. Recently, Best et al. [55] have proposed an efficient multiagent navigation algorithm based on elliptical agents and velocity obstacles. This algorithm uses linear approximations of ellipses and precomputed Minkowski sums to efficiently perform conservative collision avoidance, which makes the overall performance comparable to that of circular agents. Furthermore, the approach explicitly computes the orientation of each agent in dense environments, which can be used to simulate local pedestrian interactions including side-stepping, back-pedaling, and shoulder-turning. The overall approach can reproduce the pedestrian interactions observed in real-world crossing flows and bidirectional flows.

Beyond improving flow accuracy, modeling the crowds with anisotropic agents opens up new types of animation opportunities, such as allowing agents to turn their hips and shoulders to avoid collisions. Related techniques such as footstep planning [37] also allow agents to turn and take natural strides as they walk through the environment, leading to more dynamic animations. Recent work in this area has focused on capturing oriented human motion in dense scenarios [56], and quickly computing if complex full-body animations lead to any collisions [57].

1.6.2 Fundamental Diagram Adherent Crowd Behaviors

Crowds of humans tend to exhibit a phenomenon called the *fundamental diagram* [58]— as density increases, speed decreases. Many widely used local collision avoidance and navigation algorithms are unable to reproduce these behaviors. Building on the elliptical agents, Best et al. [59] describe density-dependent filters that can reproduce those behaviors. These filters are designed based on a combination of physiological and psychological components. The physiological component takes into account the relationship between stride length and walking speed from biomechanics. The psychological component takes into account the sensitivity to density and can vary based on individual personalities and cultural factors. The resulting filters are used between global and local planners and can be used to generate fundamental diagram behaviors using reciprocal velocity obstacles and social forces. Furthermore, these behaviors have been validated by comparing the trajectories and densities with real-world crowd data.

1.6.3 Hybrid Long-Range Collision Avoidance for Anticipatory Behaviors

Existing collision avoidance methods ignore agents beyond a neighborhood of a certain size. This cutoff can result in sharp changes in trajectory when large groups of agents enter or exit these neighborhoods. Golas et al. [60] exploit the insight that exact collision avoidance is not necessary between agents at such large distances, and propose a novel algorithm for extending existing collision avoidance algorithms, such as VO-based techniques, to perform approximate, long-range collision avoidance. This formulation performs long-range collision avoidance for distant agent groups to efficiently compute trajectories that are smoother than those obtained with state-of-the-art techniques and at faster rates. Comparison to real-world crowds demonstrates that crowds simulated with this algorithm exhibit an improved speed sensitivity to density similar to human crowds.

In this work, Golas et al. further formulate a hybrid technique for crowd simulation that can accurately and efficiently simulate crowds at any density with seamless transitions between continuum and discrete representations. The resulting approach blends results from continuum and discrete algorithms, based on local density and velocity variance. In addition to being robust across a variety of group scenarios, it is also highly efficient, running at interactive rates for thousands of agents on portable systems.

1.6.4 Modeling of Crowd Turbulence

Based on the velocity-based formulation and the hybrid long-range collision avoidance, Golas et al. [61] further hypothesize that simulation of crowd turbulence requires modeling of both collision avoidance and frictional forces arising from pedestrian interactions. Accordingly, they present a model for turbulent crowd simulation that incorporates a model for interpersonal stress and acceleration constraints similar to real-world pedestrians. The simulated results demonstrate a close correspondence with observed metrics for crowd turbulence as measured in known crowd disasters.

References

1. C. W. Reynolds. Flocks, herds, and schools: A distributed behavioral model. *Computer Graphics*, 21(4):24–34, 1987.
2. J. Funge, X. Tu, and D. Terzopoulos. Cognitive modeling: Knowledge, reasoning and planning for intelligent characters. In *26th Annual Conference on Computer Graphics and Interactive Techniques*, pp. 29–38, 1999.
3. W. Shao and D. Terzopoulos. Autonomous pedestrians. *Graphical Models*, 69(5–6):246–274, 2007.
4. S.R. Musse and D. Thalmann. A model of human crowd behavior: Group inter-relationship and collision detection analysis. In *Computer Animation and Simulation*, Springer, pp. 39–51, 1997.

5. N. Pelechano, J.M. Allbeck, and N.I. Badler. Controlling individual agents in high-density crowd simulation. In *ACM SIGGRAPH/Eurographics Symposium on Computer Animation*, pp. 99–108, 2007.

6. Massive Software—Simulating Life. http://www.massivesoftware.com/.

7. S. Wolfram. Statistical mechanics of cellular automata. *Reviews of Modern Physics*, 55(3):601–644, 1983.

8. S. Wolfram. *Cellular Automata and Complexity. Collected Papers*. Addison-Wesley Publishing Company, Reading, MA, 1994.

9. C. Loscos, D. Marchal, and A. Meyer. Intuitive crowd behaviour in dense urban environments using local laws. *Theory and Practice of Computer Graphics*, pp. 122–129, 2003.

10. F. Tecchia, C. Loscos, R. Conroy, and Y. Chrysanthou. Agent behaviour simulator (ABS): A platform for urban behaviour development. In *ACM/EG Game Technology Conference*, pp. 17–21, 2001.

11. C. Burstedde, K. Klauck, A. Schadschneider, and J. Zittartz. Simulation of pedestrian dynamics using a two-dimensional cellular automaton. *Physica A: Statistical Mechanics and Its Applications*, 295(3–4):507–525, 2001.

12. H. Klüpfel, T. Meyer-König, J. Wahle, and M. Schreckenberg. Microscopic simulation of evacuation processes on passenger ships. In *4th International Conference on Cellular Automata for Research and Industry: Theoretical and Practical Issues on Cellular Automata*, pp. 63–71. Springer-Verlag, 2000.

13. G. Still. *Crowd Dynamics*. PhD thesis, University of Warwick, August 2000.

14. D. Helbing, L. Buzna, A. Johansson, and T. Werner. Self-organized pedestrian crowd dynamics: Experiments, simulations, and design solutions. *Transportation Science*, 39(1):1–24, 2005.

15. D. Helbing and P. Molnár. Social force model for pedestrian dynamics. *Physical Review E*, 51:4282–4286, 1995.

16. D. Helbing, P. Molnár, I.J. Farkas, and K. Bolay. Self-organizing pedestrian movement. *Environment and Planning B*, 28:361–384, 2001.

17. S. Hoogendoorn and W. Daamen. Self-organization in pedestrian flow. In S.P. Hoogendoorn, S. Luding, P.H.L. Bovy, M. Schreckenberg, and D.E. Wolf (Eds.), *Traffic and Granular Flow '03*, pp. 373–382. Springer-Verlag, 2005.

18. A. Braun, S.R. Musse, L.P.L. de Oliveira, and B.E.J. Bodmann. Modeling individual behaviors in crowd simulation. In *Computer Animation and Social Agents*, pp. 143–148, IEEE, 2003.

19. O. Cordeiro, A. Braun, C. Silveira, S. Musse, and G. Cavalheiro. Concurrency on social forces simulation model. In *First International Workshop on Crowd Simulation*, 2005.

20. D. Helbing, I. Farkas, and T. Vicsek. Simulating dynamical features of escape panic. *Nature*, 407(6803):487–490, 2000.

21. M. Moussaïd, D. Helbing, S. Garnier, A. Johansson, M. Combe, and G. Theraulaz. Experimental study of the behavioural mechanisms underlying self-organization in human crowds. *Proceedings of the Royal Society B: Biological Sciences*, 276(1668):2755–2762, 2009.

22. K. Teknomo. Application of microscopic pedestrian simulation model. *Transportation Research Part F: Traffic Psychology and Behaviour*, 9(1):15–27, 2006.

23. E. Bouvier and P. Guilloteau. Crowd simulation in immersive space management. In *Eurographics Workshop on Virtual Environments and Scientific Visualization*, pp. 104–110, 1996.

24. D.C. Brogan and J.K. Hodgins. Group behaviors for systems with significant dynamics. *Autonomous Robots*, 4:137–153, 1997.

25. L. Heigeas, A. Luciani, J. Thollot, and N. Castagné. A physically-based particle model of emergent crowd behaviors. In *Graphicon*, pp. 5–10, 2003.

26. I. Karamouzas, P. Heil, P. van Beek, and M.H. Overmars. A predictive collision avoidance model for pedestrian simulation. In *Motion in Games*, Vol. 5884. *Lecture Notes in Computer Science*, pp. 41–52. Springer, Berlin, Heidelberg, 2009.

27. I. Karamouzas, B. Skinner, and S.J. Guy. Universal power law governing pedestrian interactions. *Physical Review Letters*, 113:238701, 2014.

28. C.W. Reynolds. Steering behaviors for autonomous characters. In *Game Developers Conference*, pp. 763–782, 1999.

29. S. Paris, J. Pettré, and S. Donikian. Pedestrian reactive navigation for crowd simulation: A predictive approach. *Computer Graphics Forum*, 26(3):665–674, 2007.

30. J. van den Berg, M. Lin, and D. Manocha. Reciprocal velocity obstacles for real-time multi-agent navigation. In *IEEE International Conference on Robotics and Automation*, pp. 1928–1935, 2008.

31. S. Singh, M. Kapadia, B. Hewlett, G. Reinman, and P. Faloutsos. A modular framework for adaptive agent-based steering. In *ACM Symposium on Interactive 3D Graphics and Games*, pp. 141–150, 2011.

32. M. Kapadia, S. Singh, W. Hewlett, and P. Faloutsos. Egocentric affordance fields in pedestrian steering. In *ACM SIGGRAPH Symposium on Interactive 3D Graphics and Games*, pp. 215–223, 2009.

33. J. Ondřej, J. Pettré, A.-H. Olivier, and S. Donikian. A synthetic-vision based steering approach for crowd simulation. *ACM Transactions on Graphics*, 29(4):1–9, 2010.

34. J. van den Berg, S.J. Guy, M.C. Lin, and D. Manocha. Reciprocal n-body collision avoidance. In *International Symposium of Robotics Research*, pp. 3–19, 2011.

35. I. Karamouzas and M. Overmars. Simulating and evaluating the local behavior of small pedestrian groups. *IEEE Transactions on Visualization and Computer Graphics*, 18(3):394–406, 2012.

36. M. Moussaïd, D. Helbing, and G. Theraulaz. How simple rules determine pedestrian behavior and crowd disasters. *Proceedings of the National Academy of Sciences*, 108(17):6884–6888, 2011.

37. S. Singh, M. Kapadia, G. Reinman, and P. Faloutsos. Footstep navigation for dynamic crowds. *Computer Animation and Virtual Worlds*, 22(2–3):151–158, 2011.

38. A. Lerner, Y. Chrysanthou, and D. Lischinski. Crowds by example. *Computer Graphics Forum*, 26:655–664, 2007.

39. K.H. Lee, M.G. Choi, Q. Hong, and J. Lee. Group behavior from video: A data-driven approach to crowd simulation. In *ACM SIGGRAPH/Eurographics Symposium on Computer Animation*, pp. 109–118, 2007.

40. E. Ju, M.G. Choi, M. Park, J. Lee, K.H. Lee, and S. Takahashi. Morphable crowds. *ACM Transactions on Graphics*, 29:140:1–140:10, 2010.

41. P. Charalambous, I. Karamouzas, S.J. Guy, and Y. Chrysanthou. A data-driven framework for visual crowd analysis. *Computer Graphics Forum*, 33(7):41–50, 2014.

42. E. Hairer and G. Wanner. *Solving Ordinary Differential Equations. II. Stiff and Differential-Algebraic Problems*. Springer Series in Computational Mathematics. Springer, Heidelberg, New York, 2010.

43. P. Fiorini and Z. Shiller. Motion planning in dynamic environments using velocity obstacles. *International Journal of Robotics Research*, 17:760–772, 1998.

44. M. de Berg, O. Cheong, M. van Kreveld, and M.H. Overmars. *Computational Geometry: Algorithms and Applications*. Springer-Verlag, Berlin, Germany, vol. 3, pp. 1217–1220. IFAAMAS, 2008.

45. S. Curtis, S. Guy, B. Zafar, and D. Manocha. Virtual tawaf: A case study in simulating the behavior of dense, heterogeneous crowds. In *Proceedings of IEEE Workshop on Modeling, Simulation and Analysis of Large Crowds*, 2011.

46. F. Durupinar, J. Allbeck, N. Pelechano, and N. Badler. Creating crowd variation with the ocean personality model. In *Autonomous Agents and Multiagent Systems*, 2008.

47. S.J. Guy, S. Kim, M.C. Lin, and D. Manocha. Simulating heterogeneous crowd behaviors using personality trait theory. In *ACM SIGGRAPH/Eurographics Symposium on Computer Animation*, pp. 43–52, 2011.

48. S. Kim, S.J. Guy, D. Manocha, and M.C. Lin. Interactive simulation of dynamic crowd behaviors using general adaptation syndrome theory. In *ACM SIGGRAPH Symposium on Interactive 3D Graphics and Games*, pp. 55–62, 2012.

49. S. Kim, S.J. Guy, and D. Manocha. Velocity-based modeling of physical interactions in multi-agent simulations. In *ACM SIGGRAPH/Eurographics Symposium on Computer Animation*, pp. 125–133, 2013.

50. I. Karamouzas and S.J. Guy. Prioritized group navigation with formation velocity obstacles. In *IEEE International Conference on Robotics and Automation*, pp. 5983–5989, 2015.
51. L. He, J. Pan, S. Narain, and D. Manocha. Dynamic group behaviors for interactive crowd simulation. Technical Report, Department of Computer Science, University of North Carolina at Chapel Hill, 2015.
52. S. Kim, S.J. Guy, W. Liu, R.W.H. Lau, M.C. Lin, and D. Manocha. Predicting pedestrian trajectories using velocity-space reasoning. In *The Tenth International Workshop on the Algorithmic Foundations of Robotics (WAFR)*, 2012.
53. S. Kim, A. Bera, A. Best, R. Chabra, and D. Manocha. Interactive and adaptive data-driven crowd simulation. In *Proceedings of IEEE VR*, 2016.
54. S. Kim, A. Bera, and D. Manocha. Interactive crowd content generation and analysis using trajectory-level behavior learning. In *Proceedings of IEEE Symposium on Multimedia*, 2015.
55. A. Best, S. Narang, and D. Manocha. Real-time reciprocal collision avoidance with elliptical agents. Technical Report, Department of Computer Science, University of North Carolina at Chapel Hill, 2015.
56. S.A. Stüvel, T.F. de Goeij, A.F. van der Stappen, and J. Egges. An analysis of manoeuvring in dense crowds. In *Proceedings of the Eighth International Conference on Motion in Games*, pp. 85–90, 2015.
57. S.A. Stüvel, N. Magnenat-Thalmann, D. Thalmann, A. Egges, and A. Frank Stappen. Hierarchical structures for collision checking between virtual characters. *Computer Animation and Virtual Worlds*, 25(3–4):331–340, 2014.
58. U. Weidmann. Transporttechnik der fussgaenger. Technical Report, 90, 1993.
59. A. Best, S. Narang, S. Curtis, and D. Manocha. Densesense: Interactive crowd simulation using density-dependent filters. In *Symposium on Computer Animation*, pp. 97–102, 2014.
60. A. Golas, R. Narain, S. Curtis, and M.C. Lin. Hybrid long-range collision avoidance for crowd simulation. *IEEE Transactions on Visualization and Computer Graphics*, 20(7):1022–1034, 2014, Preliminary version appeared in the *Proc. ACM* I3DG 2013.
61. A. Golas, R. Narain, and M.C. Lin. Continuum modeling of crowd turbulence. *Physical Review E*, 90:042816, 2014.

2

Efficient and Flexible Navigation Meshes for Virtual Worlds

Marcelo Kallmann

CONTENTS

The design and implementation of new techniques for navigation meshes can play a significant role in the navigation capabilities of agents populating modern virtual worlds. This chapter reviews the main approaches used to compute flexible and efficient navigation meshes for three-dimensional (3D) virtual worlds, and discusses the use of *local clearance triangulations* (LCTs) as the underlying cell decomposition representing the navigable surfaces in a virtual environment.

2.1 Introduction

Modern virtual worlds tend to be large and rich in details designed to maximize user engagement during interactive experiences. An important part of modeling interactive virtual worlds is the inclusion of its semantic information, which informs multiple modules of the simulation engine controlling the virtual environment. One of the most basic type of semantic information is the definition and representation of the accessible and navigable regions of the environment. This is exactly the purpose of a navigation mesh.

The term *navigation mesh* [1,2] has been coined by the computer games community and in general refers to any polygonal mesh that describes navigable surfaces for path planning and other navigation queries. While the term is commonly employed to refer to a structure without any specific underlying construction or property, recent research in the area has greatly contributed to the definition of key approaches for different types of navigation meshes [3].

Choosing a suitable representation for a navigation mesh is important because it will directly influence the types of navigation queries that can be computed, and how efficiently they are computed. A useful navigation mesh has to be flexible to support a number of needed operations, without compromising the ability to compute free paths efficiently. Recent advances have proposed innovative solutions for supporting collision-free paths with arbitrary clearance, real-time dynamic updates, robustness in geometric operations, etc. To address these problems, classical methods from computational geometry and discrete search have been revisited with new solutions suitable for addressing the real-time constraints of virtual worlds.

The recently introduced LCT [4] proposes to refine a constrained Delaunay triangulation (CDT) until all narrow passages of the environment can correctly encode clearance information per triangle traversal. The refinements are bounded so that the triangulation remains with $\mathcal{O}(n)$ number of triangles, where n is the number of vertices needed to describe all obstacles in the environment. In this way, an LCT can efficiently answer path queries of arbitrary clearance, allowing the representation to be shared by agents of multiple sizes without the need to compute and maintain the medial axis of the environment (see Figure 2.1). Being a simplicial decomposition, triangulations are flexible to support a number of operations and are often chosen as the starting point for several geometric algorithms relevant to navigation and environment processing.

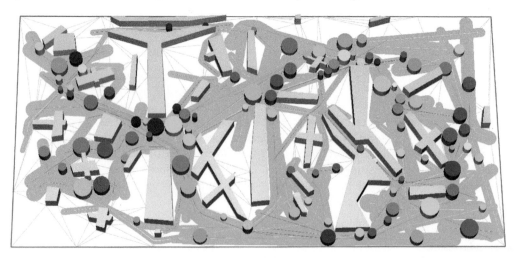

FIGURE 2.1

Local clearance triangulation being shared by agents of different clearance requirements. Agents are represented as cylinders. Paths are shown in gray as thick paths delimiting the respective path clearance required by each agent.

This chapter presents an overview of the stages involved in the process of building navigation meshes for virtual worlds, and discusses the use of LCTs as the underlying cell decomposition scheme.

2.2 Computing Navigation Meshes

The main function of a navigation mesh is to represent the navigable regions of a virtual world and to efficiently support the computation of navigation queries. By delimiting the free navigable regions, the navigation mesh also provides important spatial limits that agents can use during collision avoidance and behavior execution. This is a key advantage that navigation meshes offer over graph-based representations such as waypoint graphs or roadmaps.

The process of constructing a navigation mesh can be subdivided in two main phases: detection and extraction of the navigable surfaces in a given 3D virtual world, and cell decomposition and representation of the navigable surfaces. An analysis of these two phases is given in the next subsections. The presented analysis extends an equivalent analysis available in previous work [5].

2.2.1 Detection and Extraction

A number of steps have to be taken into account in order to extract navigable surfaces from a given environment. First of all, the navigation capabilities of the agents to be simulated have to be clearly specified. Based on these capabilities, surfaces that are acceptable for navigation can be then detected and finally connected to each other according to the chosen representations.

2.2.1.1 Specifying Navigation Capabilities

The most common case involves the specification of limits related to usual human-like locomotion behaviors: the maximum step height that agents can accommodate when climbing stairs or when walking over small obstacles, the maximum terrain slope that agents can accept when navigating on a surface, the minimum height that agents require for being able to pass under obstacles, the maximum jumping distance that agents can overcome with a jumping behavior (when available), etc.

Clearly, depending on the scenario and application at hand, a number of additional parameters can be considered. Different sets of parameters may also be needed in order to specify specific limits for distinct locomotion modes. For example, agents in walking and climbing modes will likely choose different acceptable limits when considering a terrain slope. Agents driving cars or riding bicycles may also be associated with different sets of parameters.

An added complexity appears when a single representation is sought for different types of agents or locomotion modes. For example, if agents can have different sizes, the free regions represented in the navigation mesh have to include narrow passages that only the smallest agents can traverse. Later at run-time, additional tests will have to be performed for determining if larger agents can pass or not at a given passage. The advantage is that the navigation mesh can be shared by agents of different sizes. This is the case of LCTs [4] and of representations based on the medial axis [6].

In some particular cases, the navigation mesh can be optimized for a certain parameter value. For example, if all agents being simulated have the same clearance requirement, the navigation mesh can be already built with boundaries respecting the needed clearance from obstacles. The recast navigation mesh toolkit [7] offers this capability. In case of agents of different sizes, the minimum clearance requirement can still be taken into account in the navigation mesh construction.

When agents can navigate different types of terrains, for example, water, grass, or pavement, such information should be annotated in the virtual world so that the boundaries between the different types of terrain can be automatically detected and represented. These regions will generally lead to varied traversal costs to be taken into account during path planning, and to locomotion behavior transition points annotated in the navigation mesh. The work of Ninomiya et al. [8] illustrates a number of navigation constraints that can be taken into account, such as avoiding the line of sight of other agents and defining attracting and repelling constraints.

Given the collection of parameters specifying navigation capabilities, the environment can then be processed automatically. Although it is a preprocessing step, fast processing times are important for allowing designers to interactively edit the environment until achieving their design goals. In certain virtual worlds, the navigation characteristics of the environment are key to the application. For instance, in strategy and exploration games, several regions of the environment are carefully designed with critical navigation goals designed for achieving specific game play experiences. Depending on the goals of the application, multiple levels of representation can also be designed in order to account for different types of locomotion behaviors [9].

2.2.1.2 Processing 3D Worlds

The typical approach is to analyze the virtual world globally with the use of a volumetric decomposition of the whole space occupied by the scene. A volumetric analysis is the most generic approach for handling an environment described without any guarantees on the connectivity or correctness of its polygons. Because it is desirable to not impose any restrictions on the work of designers, the processing has to be robust with respect to degeneracies in the models such as interpenetrating geometry, gaps, etc. The process can also adjust the vertex density describing the boundaries of the navigable surfaces in the scene.

Oliva and Pelechano [10] use Graphics Processing Unit (GPU) techniques to quickly voxelize and process an input scene. The approach first identifies voxels containing scene polygons that respect the navigation capabilities of the agents, and then progressively joins voxels that should make part of the same navigable surface. The result generates multiple navigable layers that are connected to compose the final navigation mesh. The method used by recast [7] also relies on a voxelization of the scene. It then partitions the scene with a cell and portal identification method [11] based on the distance field of the voxelized scene.

When the input scene does not require generic volumetric processing, specialized methods operating directly on the input geometry can be developed. For example, Lamarche [12] projects polygons from different layers in the lowest layer to then compute a subdivision that encodes the heights of the layers above it. The information allows to determine navigable regions with respect to height constraints. Later, Jorgensen and Lamarche [13] further subdivide the surfaces according to spatial reasoning metrics able to detect and annotate information relative to rooms and doors.

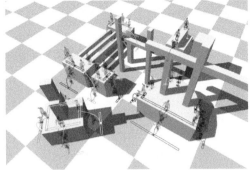

FIGURE 2.2
Example of off–mesh links representing feasible jumps between disconnected surfaces. (From M. Kapadia et al. PRECISION: Precomputed environment semantics for contact-rich character animation. In *Proceedings of the 2016 ACM SIGGRAPH Symposium on Interactive 3D Graphics and Games, I3D'16*, New York, USA, 2016. ACM.)

2.2.1.3 Building a Unified Representation

Additional steps are required to convert navigable surfaces into a unified navigation mesh representation. At this point, semantic information relative to special navigation or access features are considered. For example, doors and elevators will create connections between surfaces, and the connections can be turned on or off at run-time.

An example of a typical special navigation capability that may connect disconnected layers are jumps. A jump can be specified as a simple behavior able to overcome small obstacles, or as a complex behavior that can connect relatively distant layers in varied relative positions. Given a jump specification, layers that can be connected by the jump are typically augmented with special links specifying the connection. These links are usually called off-mesh links, as illustrated in Figure 2.2.

The final step in the construction of a navigation mesh often involves merging adjacent navigable surfaces, resulting in a multilayer representation with each layer represented in a chosen polygonal cell decomposition scheme. Most of the approaches are developed as planar decompositions, which are extended to connect different layers [10,15].

2.2.2 Cell Decomposition

The chosen polygonal cell decomposition scheme will play a key role on the properties, efficiency, and types of navigation and path planning queries that can be handled. The analysis that follows is based on selected properties that are important to be observed.

2.2.2.1 Linear Number of Cells

A navigation mesh layer should represent the environment with $\mathcal{O}(n)$ number of cells in order to allow search algorithms to operate on the structure at optimal running times. Here, n denotes the total number of vertices used to describe the planar polygonal obstacles in the layer.

A linear number of cells will allow the popular Dijkstra [16] and A* [17] graph search algorithms to run on a cell adjacency graph that depends linearly on the number of vertices in the obstacles. Graph search algorithms will then typically run in $\mathcal{O}(n \log n)$ time. This approach is followed by most of the navigation meshes used in practice. Although the search time can be reduced to $\mathcal{O}(n)$ with specialized planar graph search algorithms [18], implementation attempts have not yet been reported in a navigation mesh.

Optimizations are also possible to reduce the number of cells to a minimum. For example, it is possible to build a higher-level adjacency graph connecting only the degree-3 cells, which are the junction cells that connect three or more corridors. Such a higher-level graph can be encoded in the structure with additional links allowing search algorithms to visit a reduced number of cells. Another optimization is to reduce the number of cells by relying on larger cells. For example, the Neogen approach is based on large almost-convex cells [19]. The drawback is that there is less resolution to encode information or to ensure properties in the mesh.

An important observation is that, while several graph search algorithms will find a globally shortest path in the adjacency graph of a subdivision, a shortest path in the graph will most often not be a globally shortest path in the plane, as discussed next.

2.2.2.2 Optimality of Computed Paths

Computing globally shortest paths in the plane, or Euclidean shortest paths (ESPs), from a generic cell decomposition is not a simple task. Perhaps the most well-known approach for computing ESPs among polygonal obstacles is to build and search the *visibility graph* [20–22] of the environment. This can be achieved in $\mathcal{O}(n^2)$ time [23,24], and although several optimized algorithms exist, this time cannot be reduced for the generic case because the number of edges in the graph is $\mathcal{O}(n^2)$. in the obstacles.

Visibility graphs are also difficult to be efficiently maintained in dynamic scenarios. The difficulty comes from the possibly high number of edges and also because visibility is independent of vertex proximity. This leads to local changes often having global effects. Despite these difficulties, visibility graphs still represent the most direct approach for computing shortest paths in the plane.

The ESP problem can however be solved in sub-quadratic time [25] and an algorithm running in $\mathcal{O}(n \log n)$ time is available [26]. The approach is based on the *continuous Dijkstra* paradigm, which simulates the propagation of a wavefront maintaining equal length to the source point, until the goal point is reached. After the environment is preprocessed in $\mathcal{O}(n \log n)$ time for a given source point, paths to any destination can be retrieved in $\mathcal{O}(\log n)$ time. The preprocessing generates the *shortest path map* (SPM) of the environment, a subdivision of the plane with boundaries being straight line segments or hyperbolic arcs. The approach involves complex geometric computations but GPU techniques recently developed [27] may lead to a practical alternative for achieving optimal paths in applications, in particular when several paths for the same source point are required. See Figure 2.3 for examples. In this case, because the SPM is computed in the frame buffer, a query point can be located in the SPM in constant time and its shortest path to the source will take time proportional to the number of vertices in the path.

While optimal algorithms for computing ESPs will require specific subdivision structures (like the SPM), triangulations offer a natural approach for cell decomposition and have been explored as the base decomposition for several ESP algorithms. For instance, Kapoor et al. [28] have explored the reduction of a triangulated environment in corridors and junctions in order to compute the relevant subgraph of the visibility graph for a given path query. The method computes globally optimal paths in $O(n + h^2 \log n)$, where h is the number of holes in the planar description of the environment. While other algorithms for computing ESPs from a triangulation have been explored, the quadratic running time remains a difficult barrier to break.

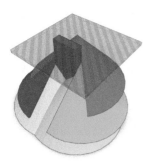  

FIGURE 2.3
The shown SPM was computed with GPU rendering. Clipped cones are placed at generator vertices and at heights according to their distances to the source point (left image). Cones are then rendered from an orthographic vertical camera placed above the obstacle plane (center image). The result in the frame buffer will encode the SPM with respect to the source point, which is denoted as a yellow cross (right image). The SPM encodes globally shortest paths to all points in the plane. Given a query point, it is connected to the generator point of the region containing it, then progressively connected to the parent generators until reaching the source node. The traversed sequence of points is the shortest path. (From C. Camporesi and M. Kallmann. Computing shortest path maps with GPU shaders. In *Proceedings of Motion in Games (MIG)*, 2014.)

Although several alternatives exist for computing ESPs, most navigation applications in virtual worlds do not impose the computation of globally shortest paths as a requirement. Fast, simple, and robust approaches are often preferred, and the $\mathcal{O}(n \log n)$ path computation time with standard graph search algorithms has been the approach of choice.

A navigation mesh should however facilitate the computation of quality paths. If ESPs cannot always be found, other guarantees on the type of paths that are computed should be provided. A reasonable expectation is that locally shortest paths should be efficiently computed, and additional characterizations related to quality may be adopted. Triangulations, including LCTs, are suitable for computing locally shortest paths efficiently. After a graph search determines a corridor containing a solution path, the shortest path in the corridor can be computed with a linear pass in the triangles of the corridor by using the *funnel algorithm* [29–31].

2.2.2.3 Paths with Arbitrary Clearance

Clearance is an important aspect of navigation and a navigation mesh should provide an efficient mechanism for computing paths with arbitrary clearance from obstacles. This means that the structure should not need to know in advance the clearance values that will be used. A weaker and less desirable way to address clearance is to precompute information specifically for each clearance value in advance.

The most complete approach for addressing clearance is to explicitly represent the medial axis of the environment [6,32]. The medial axis can be computed from the Voronoi diagram of the environment, and methods based on hardware acceleration have been developed to improve computation times [33]. One benefit of explicitly representing the medial axis is that locally shortest paths can be easily interpolated toward the medial axis in order to reach maximum clearance when needed. Interpolation toward the maximum clearance path may however not be the most appropriate way of adjusting path clearance and several other approaches are possible. Section 2.4 further discusses this point and presents one alternative approach.

LCTs do not encode the medial axis and instead offer a triangular mesh decomposition that carries just enough clearance information to be able to compute paths of arbitrary clearance, without the need to represent the intricate shapes the medial axis can have. If a path of maximum clearance is required, the medial axis of a triangulated path corridor can still be computed in linear time with available algorithms [34].

Simple techniques for handling clearance directly from a standard CDT have also been explored; however, no simple method has been found to always produce correct results with only local $\mathcal{O}(1)$ time tests. One approach to capture the width of a corridor is to refine constrained edges that have orthogonal projections of vertices from the opposite side of the corridor, adding new free CDT edges with length equal to the width of the corridor [35]. However, such a refinement can only address simple corridors and the total number of vertices added to the CDT can be significant. The LCT decomposition provides a solution that correctly and efficiently determines clearance in a triangulation with straight edges. The approach is based on a novel type of refinement operation, and clearance values can be precomputed and stored in the free edges so that online clearance tests are reduced to a simple value comparison per traversed edge. Details are presented in Section 2.3.

Specific precomputation per clearance value is usually needed when clearance is addressed by structures not specifically designed to capture clearance in all narrow passages of the environment. For example, in the Neogen approach, the larger cells require specific computations at the portals for each clearance value to be considered [36].

2.2.2.4 Representation Robustness

A navigation mesh should be robust to degeneracies in the description of the environment. This aspect is first handled during the volumetric extraction of the navigable surfaces in the virtual world (Section 2.2.1.2), but robustness issues may still arise at the planar level both during construction time and during run-time operation.

It is well known that the limited precision of floating point operations is often not sufficient for achieving robustness in geometric computations. One approach is to rely on arbitrary precision representation, however imposing a significant performance penalty on the final system. Certain specific operations can be implemented robustly with the use of exact geometric predicates [37,38].

Robustness becomes particularly difficult when obstacles are allowed to be removed and inserted in the navigation mesh at run-time. When obstacles are inserted, undesired self-intersections and overlaps may occur, and intersection points computed with floating point operations may not exactly lie on the intersecting lines. Such imprecision eventually leads to vertices placed at illegal locations. Being robust is crucial for allowing dynamic updates to occur, in particular when users are allowed to make arbitrary updates at run-time.

An approach for handling robust dynamic updates that can be extended to any type of triangulation has been proposed as part of the LCT approach [4]. The solution is based on fast floating point arithmetic and relies on a carefully designed combination of robustness tests, one exact geometric predicate, and adjustment of illegal vertex coordinates. Robustness is achieved for any set of input polygons, including self-intersecting or overlapping polygons, which are robustly handled online in any configuration.

2.2.2.5 Dynamic Updates

A navigation mesh should be able to efficiently update itself in order to accommodate dynamic changes in the environment. Dynamic updates are crucial for supporting many common events that happen in virtual worlds. Updates can reflect large changes in the environment or small ones, such as doors opening and closing. An interesting example of small updates is when agents decide to stop for a while and can thus become obstacles for other agents, a situation encountered in specific multiagent simulations such as in the computer game *The Sims 4* [4].

In general, all approaches for navigation meshes can be extended to accommodate dynamic operations. The general trade-off is: the more complex the structure, the more complex and expensive it is to maintain it dynamically. For instance, there are several hierarchical representations that are possible to be implemented for speeding up path search; however, if a navigation mesh is associated with a hierarchical structure, the hierarchy also has to be updated for every change in the navigation mesh.

The overall chosen approach to address dynamic updates should take into account how often path queries and dynamic updates are executed, and the correct representations and methods should be determined accordingly.

2.3 Local Clearance Triangulations

The properties discussed in the previous section summarize basic needs that navigation meshes should observe in typical virtual-world simulations. This section defines LCTs and later in Section 2.4 the use of LCTs as a flexible and efficient underlying representation for navigation meshes is discussed. A full exposition of LCTs is available in a previous work [4].

2.3.1 Definition

Let $S = \{s_1, s_2, \ldots, s_m\}$ be a set of m input segments describing polygonal obstacles. Segments in S may be isolated or may share endpoints forming closed or open polygons. The number of distinct endpoints is n^* and the set of all endpoints is denoted as $\mathcal{P}$. When inserted in a triangulation, the input segments are also called constraints.

Let T be a triangulation of $\mathcal{P}$, and consider two arbitrary vertices of T to be visible to each other if the segment connecting them does not intercept the interior of any constraint. Triangulation T will be a CDT of S if (1) it enforces the constraints, that is, all segments of S are also edges in T, and (2) it respects the *Delaunay criterion* for visible points to each triangle, that is, the circumcircle of every triangle t of T contains no vertex in its interior, which is visible from all three vertices of t.

Although $CDT(S)$ is already able to well represent a given environment, an additional property, the *local clearance property*, is needed in order to achieve correct and efficient clearance determination per triangle during path search.

Let $T = CDT(S)$ and π be a free path in T between points p and q. Path π is considered free if it does not cross any constrained edge of T. A free path may cross several triangles sharing unconstrained edges and the union of all traversed triangles is called a *channel*. Let t be a triangle in the channel of π such that t is not the first or last triangle in the channel. In this case, π will always traverse t by crossing two edges of t. Let a, b, c be the vertices of t and consider that π crosses t by first crossing edge ab and then bc. This particular

---

* Here, the term *distinct endpoints* is used to clarify that shared endpoints, when existent, should only be considered once when counting the total number of points *n*.

traversal of t is denoted by τ_{abc}, where ab is the entrance edge and bc is the exit edge. The shared vertex b is called the traversal corner, and the traversal sector is defined as the circle sector between the entrance and exit edges, and of radius $min\{dist(a,b), dist(b,c)\}$, where $dist$ denotes the Euclidean distance. Edge ac is called the interior edge of the traversal. The local clearance of a traversal is now defined.

Definition 2.1: Traversal Clearance

Given a traversal τ_{abc}, its clearance $cl(a,b,c)$ is the distance between the traversal corner b and the closest vertex or constrained edge intersecting its traversal sector.

Because of the Delaunay criterion, a and c are the only vertices in the sector, and thus $cl(a,b,c) \leq min\{dist(a,b), dist(b,c)\}$. In case $cl(a,b,c)$ is determined by a constrained edge s crossing the traversal sector, as illustrated in Figure 2.4, then $cl(a,b,c) = dist(b,s)$ and s is the closest constraint to the traversal. If edge ac is constrained, then ac is the closest constraint and $cl(a,b,c) = dist(b,ac)$. If the traversal sector is not crossed by a constrained edge, then $cl(a,b,c) = min\{dist(a,b), dist(b,c)\}$.

The closest constraint to a traversal is now formalized in order to take into account relevant constraints that may not cross the traversal sector of τ_{abc}.

Definition 2.2: Closest Constraint

Given a traversal τ_{abc}, its closest constraint is the constrained edge s that is closest to the traversal corner b, such that s is either ac or s lies on the opposite side of ac with respect to b.

In certain situations, the closest constraint of a traversal may generate narrow passages that are not captured by the clearance value of the traversal. The clearance value only accounts for the space occupied by the traversal sector. If a triangle happens to be too thin and long, other vertices not connected to the traversal may generate narrow passages that are not captured by any clearance value of the involved traversals.

The essence of the problem is that when a triangle is traversed, it is not possible to know how the next traversals will take place: if the path will continue in the direction of a possibly long edge (and possibly encounter a narrower space ahead) or if the path will *rotate around* the traversal corner. Each case would require a different clearance value to be considered. For example, Figure 2.7 (left) shows an example with long CDT triangles where their clearance values are not enough to capture the clearance along the direction of their longest edges. The LCT refinements will fix this problem by detecting these undesired narrow passages and breaking them down into sub-traversals until a single clearance value

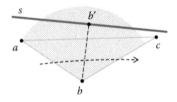

FIGURE 2.4

The triangle traversal with entrance edge ab and exit edge bc is denoted as τ_{abc}. Segment s is the closest constraint crossing the sector of τ_{abc}, thus $cl(a,b,c) = dist(b,s) = dist(b,b')$, where b' is the orthogonal projection of b on s.

per traversal can handle all possible narrow passages. The vertices that cause undesired narrow passages are called disturbances, and they are defined below.

Definition 2.3: Disturbance

Let τ_{abc} be a traversal in T such that its adjacent traversal τ_{bcd} is possible, that is, edge cd is not constrained. Let s be the closest constraint to τ_{abc} and let v be a vertex on the opposite side of bc with respect to a. Among the vertices connected to v, let d and e be the ones forming $\triangle dve \in T$ crossed by segment vv', where v' is the orthogonal projection of v on s. In this situation, vertex v is a disturbance to traversal τ_{abc} if

1. v is not shared by two collinear constraints
2. v can be orthogonally projected on ac
3. Segment vv' crosses ac and bc
4. $dist(v,s) < cl(a,b,c)$
5. $dist(v,s) < dist(v,e)$

Figure 2.5 illustrates the definition. A disturbance will always be paired with a constraint disturbing the traversal. A disturbed traversal may contain an arbitrary number of edges between bc and v; however, disturbed traversals will in most cases appear in simpler forms.

Disturbances can occur on any side of a triangle but only need to be defined with respect to the exit edge of a traversal. In this way, the set of exit edges for all the possible traversals of a given triangle will address the disturbances that may occur on any traversable side of a triangle. For example, with respect to Figure 2.5, disturbances on the left side of $\triangle abc$ will be detected with respect to τ_{cba}, but not τ_{abc}.

The LCT can be now defined with the following definitions:

Definition 2.4: Local Clearance

A traversal τ_{abc} in T has local clearance if it does not have disturbances.

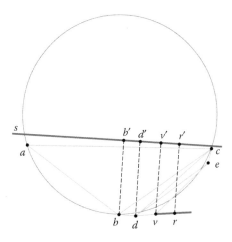

FIGURE 2.5
The shown traversal τ_{abc} is disturbed by vertex v because $dist(v,v') < dist(b,b') = cl(a,b,c)$ and $dist(v,v') < dist(v,e)$. The dashed lines show the orthogonal projections of several vertices on s. Vertices d, e, and r are not disturbances since $dist(d,d') > cl(a,b,c)$, $dist(e,s) > dist(e,c)$, and r is shared by two collinear constraints.

Definition 2.5: LCT

An LCT is a CDT with all traversals having local clearance.

2.3.2 Computation

A first approach for computing $LCT(S)$ is based on iterative refinements of disturbed traversals. The algorithm starts with the computation of triangulation $T_0 = CDT(S)$. A linear pass over all traversals of T_0 is then performed, and traversals detected to have a disturbance are refined with one subdivision point p_{ref} added to the current CDT. Every time a constraint $s \in S$ is refined, s is replaced by two new subsegments. After all disturbed traversals are processed, a new (refined) set of constraints S_1 is obtained. Triangulation $T_1 = CDT(S_1)$ is the result of the first global refinement pass. T_1 however may not be free of disturbances and the process has to be repeated until $T_k = CDT(S_k)$ is free of disturbances, in which case T_k is the desired $LCT(S)$. The number of iterations k mainly depends on the existence of multiple disturbances with respect to the same constraint. The process basically subdivides long edges in order to achieve the local clearance property. Alternatively, the LCT can be built incrementally, maintaining the needed refinements for each segment inserted. In general, incremental operations are more suitable for dynamic updates while global processing of an input CDT is more efficient when computing the LCT for the first time [4].

Let v' be the orthogonal projection of disturbance v on constraint s. A suitable refinement point p_{ref} for solving disturbance v with respect to τ_{abc} and s can be obtained with the midpoint of the intersections of s with the circle passing by vertices d, v, and e, where dve is the triangle crossed by segment vv'. See Figure 2.6 (left). Most often, v will be directly connected to b and c, and in such case, the circle passing by b, v, and c is taken. In case of multiple disturbances, v is selected such that no other disturbance on the left side of vv' is closer to s.

Given a desired clearance radius r, the achieved local clearance property guarantees that a simple local clearance test per triangle traversal is enough for determining if a path π can safely traverse a channel with clearance r from constraints. Path π will have enough clearance if $2r < cl(a, b, c)$ for all traversals τ_{abc} of its channel. Figure 2.7 presents an example where local clearance tests are not enough to produce correct results in a CDT, while correct results are obtained in the corresponding LCT.

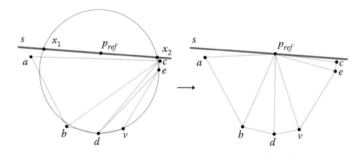

FIGURE 2.6

Vertex v is a disturbance to traversal τ_{abc} and therefore constraint s is subdivided. Points x_1 and x_2 are the intersection points of s and the circle passing by d, v, and e. The subdivision point p_{ref} is defined as the midpoint between x_1 and x_2. After refinement, all vertices between b and v will connect to p_{ref}.

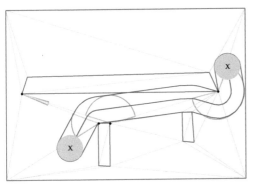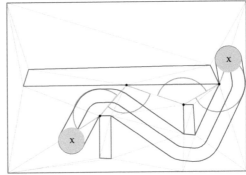

FIGURE 2.7
The left triangulation is a CDT showing an illegal path that however satisfies all its local clearance tests per traversed triangle. The traversal sectors are highlighted and they all have enough clearance. This example shows that local clearance tests per traversal are not enough in CDTs. However, once the existing disturbances are solved and the corresponding LCT is computed (triangulation on the right), local clearance tests become sufficient.

2.3.2.1 Lazy Clearance Computation

A lazy approach is used to compute clearance values stored in the edges of the LCT. There are eight possible traversals passing by an edge, and among them four traversals may have distinct values. Each traversal passes by two edges (the entrance and exit edges) and thus only two of the four values have to be stored per edge.

Clearance values stored in the edges are initialized with a flag (or a negative value) indicating that they have not yet been computed. The values are then computed and stored as needed during path search queries. Every time a path search is launched, each clearance value that is not yet available will be computed and stored in its corresponding edge in order to become readily available for subsequent queries. With this approach, clearance values are only computed in regions reachable by the path queries, avoiding computations in parts of the environment that are not used. The strategy is also valuable during LCT construction and during dynamic updates. Clearance values associated with modified traversals are simply marked as invalid, and later recomputed only when needed by a path query.

2.3.2.2 Bounded Clearance

One important optimization is to consider the local clearance property only up to a given maximum value M representing the maximum clearance allowed to be used in path queries. In most cases, M will be the clearance required by the largest agent that needs a path. The triangulation can be then optimized accordingly. Let traversal τ_{abc} be disturbed with respect to disturbance v and constraint s. In order to perform the bounded clearance optimization, refinement operations are adapted to only refine τ_{abc} if $dist(v, s) < min\{cl(a, b, c), M\}$, instead of the original $dist(v, s) < cl(a, b, c)$ condition in Definition 2.3. This optimization can greatly reduce the number of required refinements, leading to faster computation of the corresponding LCT^M and to less cells processed during path search.

2.3.3 Path Search

Once an LCT of the environment is available, a graph search can be performed over the adjacency graph of the triangulation in order to obtain a channel of arbitrary clearance r

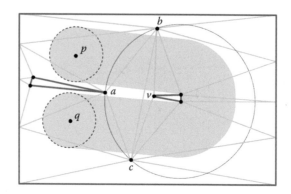

FIGURE 2.8

The shown path is the only solution with clearance r, and in the given cell decomposition, it traverses $\triangle abc$ and $\triangle bcv$ twice. Clearly, the given triangulation is not an LCT and not a CDT since the circumcircle of $\triangle abc$ has visible vertices in its interior.

connecting two input points p and q. During channel search, a search expansion is only accepted if the clearance of the traversal being expanded (which is precomputed in the free LCT edges) is greater or equal to $2r$.

In addition, LCTs can be safely searched assuming that every cell will be traversed by a given path only once, allowing search algorithms to mark visited triangles and to correctly terminate after visiting each triangle no more than once. Figure 2.8 shows that this is not always the case for all types of cell decompositions.

The example of Figure 2.8 illustrates a situation that is often overlooked by cell decompositions which are not carefully designed, and that nevertheless has to be addressed in order to guarantee that the employed path search algorithm will correctly execute. A simple proof showing that the situation illustrated in Figure 2.8 cannot happen in CDTs (and in LCTs) is available in a previous work [4].

2.4 Discussion and Extensions

LCTs address all the expected properties analyzed in Section 2.2.2. Most importantly, although it adds refinements to the underlying CDT, the decomposition remains of linear size. As established in a previous work [4], the total number of refinements is limited by the upper bound of $3n$, what translates into a cell decomposition of no more than $6n$ triangles since, using the Euler formula, $t = 2n - 2 - k \Rightarrow t < 2n$, where t is the number of triangles in a triangulation and k is the number of edges in the boundary, that is, the floor map border ($k = 4$ in all presented examples). In practice, the number of added vertices has shown to be much lower than the bound of $3n$, and the number of triangles remains close to $2n$ [4].

Because the underlying structure is a triangulation, LCTs provide a straightforward solution for computing locally shortest paths. Solution channels are already triangulated and can be quickly processed by the funnel algorithm in order to produce a path that is locally optimal and respecting the desired clearance without the need of any additional data structures or representation conversions. If needed, there are algorithms available for extracting globally shortest paths directly from a triangulation [28,39], however, with either not so simple implementations or with running times worse than $\mathcal{O}(n^2)$.

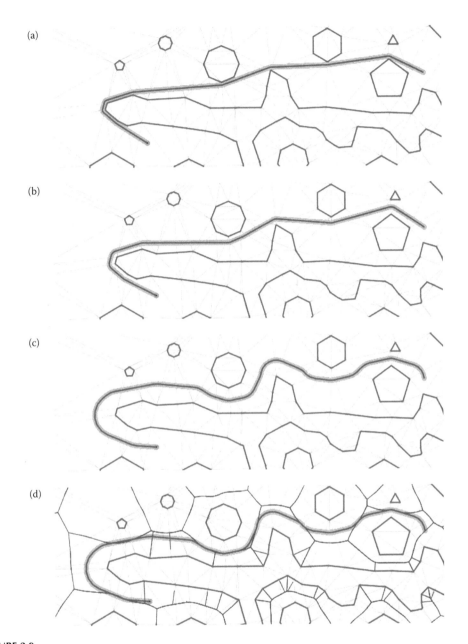

FIGURE 2.9

(a) Locally shortest path respecting its minimum clearance requirement. (b) Path with small extra clearance added at each path corner. (c) Large extra clearance added, reaching maximum in narrowest passages. (d) Same path as in the previous case but shown together with the medial axis. Only in the narrowest passages the path converges to the medial axis. Different approaches are possible for customizing path clearance. In this example, additional clearance is added to an LCT path in order to make it converge toward the medial axis only in the narrowest passages. This is typically an appropriate clearance criterion for paths in virtual worlds.

Clearance information is compactly encoded in LCTs and paths of arbitrary clearance can be efficiently extracted. While LCTs require the maintenance of refinements in the underlying triangulation, it achieves a structure that maintains less nodes than the medial axis [4]. LCTs basically compute refinements just as much as needed in order to determine the maximum clearance (bounded or not) of all its passages. A triangulation is also a simpler structure than the medial axis and algorithms for dynamic updates robust to intersections are available [4].

Although the medial axis is not represented, it can be computed in linear time from a channel by using available algorithms [34]. In practice, however, there is little need for computing exact paths of maximum clearance. A typical path for agents in virtual worlds will be more likely to be one that has a minimum clearance requirement and a desired additional clearance, to be kept when possible, in order to avoid passing too close to obstacles when there is extra space available. Since LCTs encode acceptable clearances for all triangle traversals, path clearance can be adjusted at each traversal as needed. Figure 2.9 exemplifies such a path with customized extra clearance, computed during the funnel algorithm pass by taking into account different clearance values at traversal corners. Additional criteria for further customizing paths can certainly be devised.

Another aspect that is important to be addressed in several virtual world applications is to take into account regions of different types of terrain. In the LCT formulation, obstacles are only described by constrained edges, and edges of non-obstacle regions can be equally inserted in the LCT and have their interiors triangulated in the same way as in the free regions of the environment. The insertion algorithms will guarantee that regions defined as closed polygons will remain watertight after insertion, and so flood fill algorithms can be applied to annotate the region type in the interior triangles. In this way, path search can take into account different traversal weights when traversing triangles of different terrain types. Clearance checks during path search have however to be updated to only take into account clearance to obstacle boundaries, since in this case not all constrained edges will be representing obstacles.

2.5 Conclusion

LCTs introduce a new approach for modeling and computing navigation queries with clearance constraints, and at the same time being able to address key requirements: fast computations, robustness, and dynamic updates. Being a recently developed approach, future work is still needed in order to achieve complete solutions integrating LCTs in multi-layered environments and taking into account nonplanar surfaces, boundaries of weighted regions, different agent capabilities, etc. Nevertheless, the presented results and possibilities for extensions demonstrate that LCTs achieve a flexible and efficient approach for representing navigation meshes.

References

1. G. Snook. Simplified 3D movement and pathfinding using navigation meshes. In M. DeLoura, editor, *Game Programming Gems*, pp. 288–304. Charles River Media, 2000.

2. P. Tozour. Building a near-optimal navigation mesh. In S. Rabin, editor, *AI Game Programming Wisdom*, pp. 171–185. Charles River Media, 2002.

3. M. Kallmann and M. Kapadia. Navigation meshes and real-time dynamic planning for virtual worlds. In *ACM SIGGRAPH 2014 Courses, SIGGRAPH '14*, pp. 3:1–3:81, New York, USA, 2014. ACM.

4. M. Kallmann. Dynamic and robust local clearance triangulations. *ACM Transactions on Graphics*, 33(5):161:1–161:17, 2014.

5. M. Kallmann and M. Kapadia. *Geometric and Discrete Path Planning for Interactive Virtual Worlds*. Morgan & Claypool, 2016.

6. R. Geraerts. Planning short paths with clearance using explicit corridors. In *ICRA'10: Proceedings of the IEEE International Conference on Robotics and Automation*, pp. 1997–2004, Alaska, 2010.

7. M. Mononen. Recast navigation mesh toolset, 2015. https://github.com/memononen/recast-navigation.

8. K. Ninomiya, M. Kapadia, A. Shoulson, F. Garcia, and N. Badler. Planning approaches to constraint-aware navigation in dynamic environments. *Computer Animation and Virtual Worlds*, 26(2):119–139, 2014.

9. M. Kapadia, A. Beacco, F. Garcia, V. Reddy, N. Pelechano, and N. I. Badler. Multi-domain real-time planning in dynamic environments. In *Proceedings of the 12th ACM SIG-GRAPH/Eurographics Symposium on Computer Animation, SCA '13*, pp. 115–124, New York, USA, 2013. ACM.

10. R. Oliva and N. Pelechano. Neogen: Near optimal generator of navigation meshes for 3D multi-layered environments. *Computer and Graphics*, 37(5):403–412, 2013.

11. D. Haumont, O. Debeir, and F. Sillion. Volumetric cell-and-portal generation. In *EUROGRAPH-ICS Conference Proceedings*, pp. 303–312, Grenade, Spain, 2003.

12. F. Lamarche. Topoplan: A topological path planner for real time human navigation under floor and ceiling constraints. *Computer Graphics Forum*, 28(2):649–658, 2009.

13. C.-J. Jorgensen and F. Lamarche. From geometry to spatial reasoning: Automatic structuring of 3D virtual environments. In *Proceedings of the 4th International Conference on Motion in Games (MIG)*, pp. 353–364, Berlin, Heidelberg, 2011. Springer-Verlag.

14. M. Kapadia, X. Xianghao, M. Kallmann, M. Nitti, S. Coros, R. W. Sumner, and M. Gross. PRECI-SION: Precomputed environment semantics for contact-rich character animation. In *Proceedings of the 2016 ACM SIGGRAPH Symposium on Interactive 3D Graphics and Games, I3D'16*, pp. 29–37, New York, USA, 2016. ACM.

15. W. G. van Toll, A. F. Cook IV, and R. Geraerts. Navigation meshes for realistic multi-layered environments. In *Proceedings of the IEEE/RSJ International Conference on Intelligent Robots and Systems (IROS)*, pp. 3526–3532, San Francisco, USA, 2011.

16. E. Wybe Dijkstra. A note on two problems in connexion with graphs. *Numerische Mathematik*, 1:269–271, 1959.

17. P. E. Hart, N. J. Nilsson, and B. Raphael. A formal basis for the heuristic determination of minimum cost paths. *IEEE Transactions on Systems Science and Cybernetics*, 4(2):100–107, 1968.

18. P. Klein, S. Rao, M. Rauch, and S. Subramanian. Faster shortest-path algorithms for planar graphs. *Journal of Computer and System Sciences*, 55:27–37, 1994.

19. R. Oliva and N. Pelechano. Automatic generation of suboptimal navmeshes. In *Proceedings of the Fourth International Conference on Motion in Games (MIG)*, pp. 328–339, Berlin, Heidelberg, 2011. Springer-Verlag.

20. M. de Berg, O. Cheong, M. van Kreveld, and M. Overmars. *Computational Geometry: Algorithms and Applications*. Springer, Berlin, Heidelberg, 2008.

21. T. Lozano-Pérez and M. A. Wesley. An algorithm for planning collision-free paths among polyhedral obstacles. *Communications of ACM*, 22(10):560–570, Washington, 1979.

22. N. Nilsson. A mobile automaton: An application of artificial intelligence techniques. In *Proceedings of the 1969 International Joint Conference on Artificial Intelligence (IJCAI)*, pp. 509–520, Washington, 1969.

23. M. H. Overmars and E. Welzl. New methods for computing visibility graphs. In *Proceedings of the Fourth Annual Symposium on Computational Geometry (SoCG)*, pp. 164–171, Illinois, USA, 1988. ACM.

24. J. A. Storer and J. H. Reif. Shortest paths in the plane with polygonal obstacles. *Journal of ACM*, 41(5):982–1012, 1994.

25. J. S. B. Mitchell. Shortest paths among obstacles in the plane. In *Proceedings of the Ninth Annual Symposium on Computational Geometry (SoCG)*, pp. 308–317, New York, USA, 1993. ACM.

26. J. Hershberger and S. Suri. An optimal algorithm for euclidean shortest paths in the plane. *SIAM Journal on Computing*, 28:2215–2256, 1997.

27. C. Camporesi and M. Kallmann. Computing shortest path maps with GPU shaders. In *Proceedings of Motion in Games (MIG)*, pp. 97–102, Playa Vista, California, 2014.

28. S. Kapoor, S. N. Maheshwari, and J. S. B. Mitchell. An efficient algorithm for Euclidean shortest paths among polygonal obstacles in the plane. In *Discrete and Computational Geometry*, 18:377–383, 1997.

29. B. Chazelle. A theorem on polygon cutting with applications. In *SFCS '82: Proceedings of the 23rd Annual Symposium on Foundations of Computer Science*, pp. 339–349, Chicago, Illinois, 1982. IEEE Computer Society.

30. J. Hershberger and J. Snoeyink. Computing minimum length paths of a given homotopy class. *Computational Geometry Theory and Application*, 4(2):63–97, 1994.

31. D. T. Lee and F. P. Preparata. Euclidean shortest paths in the presence of rectilinear barriers. *Networks*, 3(14):393–410, 1984.

32. P. Bhattacharya and M. L. Gavrilova. Roadmap-based path planning—Using the Voronoi diagram for a clearance-based shortest path. *Robotics Automation Magazine, IEEE*, 15(2):58–66, 2008.

33. K. E. Hoff III, T. Culver, J. Keyser, M. Lin, and D. Manocha. Fast computation of generalized Voronoi diagrams using graphics hardware. In *ACM Symposium on Computational Geometry*, 2000. http://dl.acm.org/citation.cfm?id=311567.

34. F. Chin, J. Snoeyink, and C. A. Wang. Finding the medial axis of a simple polygon in linear time. Discrete and computational geometry, *ISAAC: 6th International Symposium on Algorithms and Computation*, 21(3):405–420, 1999. http://dl.acm.org/citation.cfm?id=688576.

35. F. Lamarche and S. Donikian. Crowd of virtual humans: A new approach for real time navigation in complex and structured environments. *Computer Graphics Forum*, 23(3):509–518, 2004.

36. R. Oliva and N. Pelechano. A generalized exact arbitrary clearance technique for navigation meshes. In *Proceedings of Motion on Games (MIG)*, pp. 81:103–81:110, New York, 2013. ACM.

37. O. Devillers and S. Pion. Efficient exact geometric predicates for Delaunay triangulations. In *Proceedings of the 5th Workshop Algorithm Engineering and Experiments*, pp. 37–44, Baltimore, Maryland, 2003.

38. J. R. Shewchuk. Adaptive precision floating-point arithmetic and fast robust geometric predicates. *Discrete and Computational Geometry*, 18(3):305–363, 1997.

39. J. S. B. Mitchell, D. M. Mount, and C. H. Papadimitriou. The discrete geodesic problem. *SIAM Journal on Computing*, 16(4):647–668, 1987.

3

Learning Heterogeneous Crowd Behavior from the Real World

Panayiotis Charalambous and Yiorgos L. Chrysanthou

CONTENTS

3.1 Introduction

Crowds are an important part of our daily lives. We are constantly surrounded by and are part of crowds, in streets, workplaces, shopping malls, football stadiums, concerts, etc. The presence and the dynamics of crowds greatly affect the ambiance of any given scene. Computer-generated crowds have become an important feature of modern applications and simulations of virtual worlds such as computer games, movies, training, and architectural visualizations. As these applications continue to strive toward higher levels of realism and scene complexity, there is an increasing need for more believable crowd simulations.

Most of the existing techniques make simplifying assumptions regarding the behavior of simulated individuals, while striving to convey the complexity of a real human crowd. While such approaches might capture the broad, overall behavior of the crowd, they often miss the subtle details displayed by the individuals—details that typically give variety to the crowd. The range of individual behaviors that may be observed in a real crowd is typically too complex to simulate using a simple behavioral model; people have varying interpersonal distances and different velocities, and react differently in similar situations. One way of conveying complex behaviors is by employing information extracted from real crowds (such as videos); that is, instead of manually defining a crowd behavior model, learn it from the data. Data from real crowds can be used to either (a) learn values for parameters of an existing simulation system (such as a velocity- or force-based approach) to achieve behavior similar to the real world or (b) produce an example-based system where behaviors are extracted directly from the data.

The focus of this chapter is on the latter: designing and building new data-driven crowd simulation systems. We start with a brief overview of some data-driven techniques (Section 3.2), then the general architecture of an agent (Section 3.3), followed by a general data-driven system pipeline and methods for each component (Sections 3.4 through 3.8). We conclude with some discussion on possible future directions (Section 3.9).

3.2 Related Work

Recently, data-driven crowd simulation methods have emerged as an attractive alternative to manually defining the crowd simulation model. The promise in these approaches is that agents will "learn" how to behave from real-world examples, keeping the natural crowd ambiance with a wide range of complex individual behaviors without the effort of defining an explicit behavioral model. One of the earliest data-driven techniques for groups of characters employed a motion graph approach for synthesizing group behavior [1]. In order to be able to build a tractable motion graph, this method makes the assumption that the input follows a well-defined behavior model, such as a flocking system with a restricted configuration space. Graph-based simulation was also employed by Kwon et al. [2] for guiding a single group of agents navigating together. These methods though are impractical for general human pedestrian crowds due to the high degree of behavior variation.

In recent works, trajectories learned from videos of crowds are stored in a database alongside some representation of the stimuli that affected them [3,4]. During simulation, agents match their stimuli to the ones stored in the database and navigate accordingly. Following from these, Lerner et al. [5] used a database approach to add secondary actions to simulated characters such as talking or looking at their watches. Charalambous and Chrysanthou [6] introduced a temporal representation for agent state and a graph-based approach to enhance the performance of data-driven crowd simulation. Ju et al. [7] take a different approach; input data that represent different styles of crowds are blend together to generate new crowd animations. Metoyer and Hodgins [8] allow the user to define specific examples of behaviors, while Musse et al. [9] extract paths from a video for a specific environment.

As an alternative to employing databases of example situations, some techniques use observations of real people to extract simulation parameters. Several works [10–12] estimate collision avoidance and anticipation parameters by examining motion capture data in a controlled environment and propose prediction-based approaches for crowd steering. Moussaïd et al. [13] used data from videos of real crowds to modify Helbing's social forces model [14] to handle group formations in a more realistic way. In the work of Courty and Corpetti [15], a macroscopic approach is followed; the crowd is seen as a continuous flow and the captured data are used to define the guiding vector field. Looking a bit further away, biology researchers proposed using input from stereoscopic videos of Starling birds to estimate a statistical model of their massive and complex flocking behavior [16]. In all of these techniques, examples are used to refine an underlying behavior model; therefore, they are still bound by the limitations of the underlying model.

3.3 Agent-Based Crowd Simulation

Typical crowd simulation systems consist of two main components: an environment where the simulation takes place and the characters. If one of the goals of simulation is diversity, characters are represented as autonomous agents instead of being simulated as a whole (microscopic vs. macroscopic view)*. A typical architecture for agent-based crowd simulations can be seen in Figure 3.1. An agent decides on actions to perform based on information it receives through sensors from the environment and its own internal state; applying these actions (e.g., "turn left," "accelerate," etc.) can potentially affect both the agent state and the environment. The behavior of an agent is typically divided into multiple hierarchical layers (components); not all of them need to be implemented and not all of them are executed continuously and at each update step (typically, lower layers are executed more often than higher layers). Starting from the top to the bottom, we have the following behavior layers:

- *Action selection:* Here, agents select and prioritize high-level goals such as walk from house to bus station, get on bus, buy ticket, get off bus, walk toward the office, etc. This is typically executed after an action is completed or an event is raised (e.g., fire alarm).

- *Path finding:* It is where a path between two places in the virtual environment is found. A path typically consists of a set of control points that define lines or curves (e.g., sidewalks). Path planning is typically executed when goals from the upper layer or the environment change (e.g., a demonstration blocks a previously set path).

- *Navigation/steering:* It is the process by which agents follow a path (or move toward a goal) while interacting with other moving characters or obstacles. This is a continuous process and is responsible for collision avoidance without violating physical constraints of the agents; for example, a character has a maximum allowed velocity and acceleration.

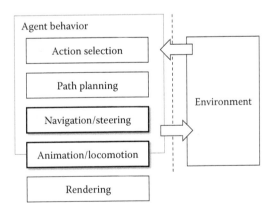

FIGURE 3.1
Typical agent architecture in a crowd simulation environment.

---

* Since we want heterogeneous crowds, macroscopic approaches are not presented.

- *Locomotion/secondary behaviors:* During navigation (even when standing still), some animations have to be played to demonstrate the actions implied by the higher-level layers; for example, proper walking cycles, running, chatting, and talking to the phone. Additionally, some animations can be added to enhance the believability of the agent behavior such as talking to another character that walks besides it.

Since the lower layers are executed more frequently, possibly multiple times per second on an interactive application, efficiency is an important factor.

3.4 Data-Driven Crowds Pipeline

In this section, we present the general pipeline for agent-based data-driven crowd simulation approaches: agent-based approaches allow for finer control of individual character simulation whereas by using data from real-life crowds, we hope to capture dynamics that would be difficult to capture in a manually defined rule-based system. Using the appropriate data, agents adapt and different behaviors can emerge as demonstrated in Figure 3.2.

It is important to note that people's behavior is affected by both intrinsic and extrinsic factors. *Intrinsic* factors include person-specific information such as intent, mood, athleticism, age, etc.—things that are most of the times difficult to capture or identify in the limited view of a video. *Extrinsic* factors or stimuli include other people in the vicinity of a person, walking companions, buildings, obstacles, points of interest, etc.—contrary to intrinsic factors, these are easier to identify even though there could be factors of this type not observed in the video. Assuming we start from a limited view of the subject crowd, we can infer behaviors that deal with more immediate reactive actions; steering and subtle actions (talking,

Chatting dataset　　　　　　　　　　Pedestrian dataset

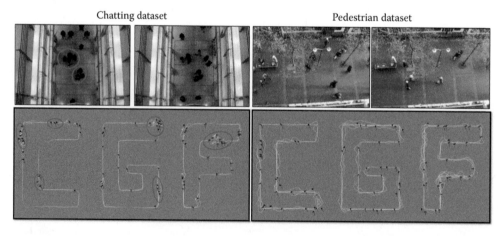

FIGURE 3.2
Using different data, different behaviors can emerge in the same scenario. Lines indicate the past 20 s for each agent. Results were generated using the PAG method [6]. By using a "chat" input [3], agents stop and generate chatting groups with minimal deviations from their high-level goals whereas by using a pedestrian "dataset" agents avoid each other.

FIGURE 3.3
Adding secondary behaviors to characters. (From A. Lerner et al. Fitting behaviors to pedestrian simula-tions. In *Proceedings of the 2009 ACM SIGGRAPH/Eurographics Symposium on Computer Animation*, pp. 199–208, New Orleans, USA. ACM, 2009.)

looking at a certain direction, etc.) and therefore, for the rest of this chapter, we will deal only with data-driven techniques for steering. Lerner et al. [17] address the problem of han-dling secondary behavior using data to enhance the believability of a crowd; this method allows for adding animations such as talking on the phone, look left or right, etc. based on the state of agents (Figure 3.3).

Data-driven approaches could also be used for action selection and path planning given that data at these level can be found; such data could come from sources such as cellular tracking, GPS [18], and drones [19]. To our knowledge, this kind of data have not been used for crowd simulation applications and could be an interesting area to explore.

Pipeline: Roughly speaking, a data-driven crowd simulation system consists of two main phases: preprocessing and simulation (Figure 3.4). During the preprocessing phase, videos of crowds are tracked (Section 3.6), then analyzed to extract (*state, action*) pairs. These (*state, action*) pairs are then used to find some model of the crowd behavior; this model can be considered as a function $f : S \rightarrow A$ that takes as input a state $\mathbf{s} \in S$ and returns back an action $\mathbf{a} \in A$. These behavior models are then used to synthesize a new crowd exhibit-ing similar behavior in a new environment. Typically, most of the processing time is spent

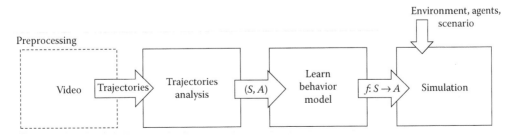

FIGURE 3.4
Data-driven crowd simulation pipeline.

on the preprocessing phase so that during simulation, performance is affected as little as possible.

We will first give the description of a general data-driven crowd simulation algorithm in Section 3.5. Then, we will cover all the steps of preprocessing, starting from collecting the data (Section 3.6), trajectory analysis to extract (*state, action*) examples (Section 3.7), and finally we give approaches to generate the crowd model (Section 3.8).

3.5 Data-Driven Simulation

Each agent in the environment is equipped with a set of characteristics (such as size, age, gender, etc.) and a set of goals (typically a priority queue), which are decomposed into simpler tasks (such as move from point A to point B).

On the most basic level, a simple crowd simulator (Algorithm 3.1) loops over all agents and lets each agent query the environment to get its current state (Line 4), select appropriate actions (Line 5), and performs them (Line 7). Querying the environment is usually performed through some spatial data structures such as grids or Kd-trees that hold the positions of other agents and static objects. Action selection can be performed using a model of the agent's behavior as we discuss in Section 3.8. Typical actions in a crowd simulation system include velocity vectors, accelerations (or forces) for smoother transitions, or even entire trajectories to follow. Performing an action involves moving the agent to its new position based on current position and velocity; additionally, in a 3D simulation environment, proper animations for locomotion and secondary actions are played. Applying the actions influences both the agent and the environment and therefore the previously mentioned spatial data structures are informed for changes (depending on the degree of changes, it could be easier and faster to rebuild them). This process typically continues until all agents accomplish their goals.

Algorithm 3.1: Basic Update Step of a Crowd Simulator

> **input** : $\mathbb{A} = \{A_1, A_2, \ldots\}$ the set of simulated agents.
> **input** : **E** a representation of the environment.
> **input** : **M** the crowd model that returns an action given a state.
>
> **forall the** *agents* $A_i \in \mathbb{A}$ **do**
> > **if** $A_i.hasGoals()$ **then**
> > > **if** $A_i.mustUpdate()$ **then**
> > > > $A_i.state \leftarrow \mathbf{E}.getAgentState(A_i)$;
> > > > $A_i.currentAction \leftarrow \mathbf{M}.getAction(A_i.state)$;
> > > >
> > > **end**
> > > $A_i.applyAction(A_i.currentAction)$;
> > > **if** $A_i.currentGoal().achieved()$ **then**
> > > > $A_i.proceedToNextGoal()$;
> > > >
> > > **end**
> > **end**
> **end**

Updating each individual at every simulation frame is usually not recommended since (a) typically human beings take actions that last more than a percentage of a second and do not change so often and (b) it is computationally expensive. Typically, agents are split into N_b subsets of agents; at each simulation step, either only one subset is updated in a sequential manner or all are updated but each one on a different thread. If the environment is highly dynamic, updating at longer periods (i.e., N_b is large) might introduce artifacts in the simulation such as collisions, so a more careful approach in scheduling agents for updates should be applied.

3.6 Collecting Crowd Data

We collect data from videos of crowds (see Figure 3.5). Tracking of people and obstacles in a video can be done manually or automatically; automatic computer vision techniques typically introduce noise in the data and therefore the data should be filtered and smoothed out before analysis. Manual approaches are sometimes tedious, but careful selection of key positions of characters can be used to interpolate and find the remaining positions saving time spent on filtering the data from automatic methods.

In any case, to be able to simulate the steering behavior of people, only spatiotemporal positions of people and rough approximations of obstacles need to be tracked; state description for any person at any given time can then be extracted (see Section 3.7). If a person gets out of the view of the video, then the trajectory is split into sub-trajectories and each one is considered separately. To additionally simulate secondary behavior, we can track features that might influence these behaviors; typical features include if the person belongs to a group and the group id, gender, age (child, adult, or senior), and some subtle

FIGURE 3.5
Tracking crowd data. Letters indicate secondary behaviors.

action performed such as talk left, point right, no action, etc. Typically, these are recorded by adding tags on the trajectories [17].

3.7 Extracting States and Actions

The most important factor of the quality of crowd behavior is the quality of the actions that any individual takes; therefore, in a crowd simulation environment, we want agents to generate plausible and rational actions. Rational actions are, for example, steering to avoid nearby and not far away agents. Therefore, care should be taken on defining both a good state representation and a model that generates plausible rational actions and not necessarily designing an overcomplicated artificial intelligence system that "thinks" and "acts" like real people.*

State is defined as any factor that can influence an agent's decisions; extrinsic factors such as other agents (their actions, positions, velocity, etc.), buildings, inanimate obstacles, and intrinsic factors such as an agent's current action, velocity, target, mood, age, etc. Therefore, state needs only record agent-centric information (Figure 3.6) and not all of the information present in the scene. Additionally, state can also record temporal information such as agent velocities, past history, etc. Typically, state is a vector $s \in \mathbb{R}^n$, where n is the number of features. In the case of data-driven systems, state is indirectly extracted from tracked data: spatiotemporal trajectories and user annotations. Only some of these factors are apparent in a video; these are the static geometry (obstacles) in the scene, and the positions and velocities of the individuals in the crowd at different points in time. In some cases, it is

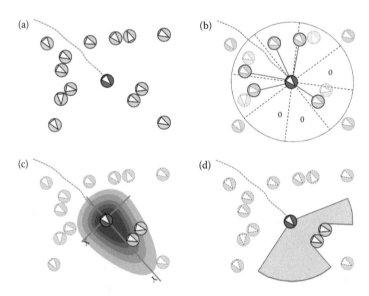

FIGURE 3.6
Different agent-centric states/perception patterns. (a) Original agent configuration, (b) Lee et al. [3], (c) Lerner et al. [4], and (d) Charalambous and Chrysanthou [6].

---

* The current trend in the artificial intelligence community is designing *rational agents* and not mimicking the brain as some older approaches tried to do [20].

possible to identify if people belong in groups, their gender, and some secondary behaviors (e.g., look left). Thus, the basic simplifying assumption underlying the described approaches is that those are the only influencing factors that will be accounted for. Finally, we note that if agents are goal oriented (e.g., moving toward a point or along a path), then state representation should at least include information about the goal achievement capabilities of agents; examples include distance and angle to goal and current and preferred velocity. To infer goals of real people, we can assume that goals are their final positions or a position after a few seconds, or we could analyze trajectories to find points with high curvature. In the following, we give some state representations from data-driven systems.

3.7.1 Group Behavior from Video

Lee et al. [3] divide a small oriented circular area[*] around an agent in eight sectors and find the distance to the closest agent for each sector (Figure 3.6b). They do this for two consecutive frames to record temporal information. They additionally record intended moving direction, current speed, and in case of a pivot point scenarios (such as passing through a door), relative position and orientation to the pivot point. This results in 21-dimensional state vectors that are then projected into a lower-dimensional space using principal component analysis (PCA) to handle the curse of dimensionality. Finally, actions are 2D vectors representing instantaneous velocities.

3.7.2 Crowds by Example

Lerner et al. [4] proposed an approach where the influence of each agent on another agent is stored in the state vector. Each agent in the vicinity of an agent is considered as an influencing factor; paths are stored for agents and endpoints and type for obstacles. In either case, an influence value is also stored for both. All paths are of a predefined length (set to 40 frames) and can be stored either in a compact form (splines) or as a triple of *position, direction, speed* per frame, which is more verbose but faster to use.

   Examples. Each (*state, action*) example is defined using a local coordinate system, with the subject person placed at the origin (0,0) and facing down the positive Y-axis (Figure 3.6c). All of the influencing factors (other agents and geometry) and their corresponding paths are expressed in this coordinate system. Consider an agent A_i at time step t, and let E denote the example that will be created from it. Each agent A_j in the environment potentially influences the trajectory of A_i. The influence function $Inf_E(j, t')$ denotes the *distance-based influence* of agent A_j on agent A_i at time t'. The function is a cross-product of two Gaussian falloff functions, one in the direction perpendicular to the walking direction and another (asymmetric) falloff function aligned with the walking direction. Specifically, let d be the (scaled) distance of A_j from A_i at time t' and v the walking speed of A_i at time t'. Then

$$Inf_E(j, t') = \exp\left(\frac{-0.5d^2}{2/v}\right) \begin{cases} \exp\left(\frac{-0.5d^2}{v}\right) & A_j \text{ in front of } A_i. \\ \exp\left(\frac{-0.5d^2}{1/2v}\right) & A_j \text{ is behind } A_i. \end{cases} \tag{3.1}$$

---

[*] They use a radius of 1 m around each agent.

In order to obtain the *influence function*, $Inf_E(j)$, over a finite time window, the maximal value attained by $Inf_E(j, t')$ in that time window, normalized by that of all the influencing factors, is selected:

$$Inf_E(j) = \frac{\max_{t'} Inf_E(j, t')}{\sum_k (\max_{t'} Inf_E(k, t'))}. \tag{3.2}$$

If the maximal influence value is below a predefined cutoff value, then it is assumed that the agent has negligible influence on A_i's trajectory. Intuitively, the above approach gives more weight to agents in front of the subject agent and to those moving toward the agent.

Actions. Finally, sub-trajectories of 40 frames of length are stored as actions; this allows for more complex behaviors compared to velocity vectors.

3.7.3 PAG Crowd

In the work by Charalambous and Chrysanthou [6], most of the agent states are encoded using a visibility-based approach; the assumption is that behavior is directly correlated to what people *observe* in their optical field, similar to the work by Ondřej et al. [21]. In contrast to the work done in Ondřej et al. [21], we do not use whole images to represent the visibility of agents and each agent is not represented as a cone; rather, we use a more simplified version in two dimensions, assuming that each person is a circle (which translates into a cylinder in three dimensions). It is important to emphasize here that the underlying method can be used with other pattern representations also (e.g., the ones in Figure 3.6).

Visibility encodes the free space in the field of view (FOV) of a pedestrian, that is, the space that is not occluded by other people or static objects at a given instance (Figure 3.6d). The FOV is defined by its spread angle ϕ and the maximum search radius R. It is additionally aligned to the moving direction of the pedestrian and is sampled at regular angular intervals. For each angular sample, the distance to the closest object (static and dynamic) is found. The sampling interval is dependent on the spread angle ϕ, the search radius R, and the radius of the agents; denser sampling gives better approximation of the visibility at the expense of computation time and memory storage. For most of the conducted experiments, angle ϕ was selected to be between 90° and 240° and was sampled using 20–40 rays.

Temporal perception pattern (TPP). A predefined number of consecutive visibility samples, with each sample consisting of a visibility pattern are grouped together and form a TPP (Figure 3.7). This representation encodes the perception of people over some time period; usually in the range of 0.5–2 s. It indirectly records relative movement of everything that is inside the vicinity of the agent in an abstract manner. Each of these states has a relatively large dimensionality: if, for example, a person's trajectory is sampled 5 times per second and for each sample the visibility is represented with 20 values, the state for a TPP of 1 s length is encoded with a total of 100 values. After recording all TPPs from the input data, they are split into two subsets; the interaction and interaction-free states. Interaction-free states are those states where nothing was present in the visibility of the agent. As it will be described later, these TPPs alongside the trajectories that resulted after them are processed into a graph that will be the driving force of the simulation algorithm.

TPP compression. To speed up calculations and reduce memory requirements, TPPs are compressed using the type-II Discrete Cosine Transform (DCT). First, the TPP is converted into the frequency domain and the first few frequencies are kept (typically 8–12 coefficients are enough to capture the local dynamics of the crowd movement). An additional benefit of removing high frequencies is that sensitivity on movement of the boundaries is reduced;

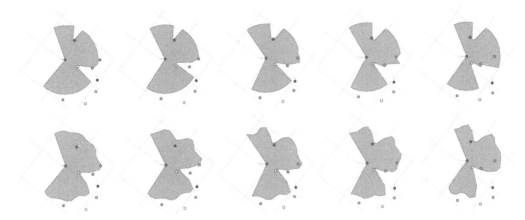

FIGURE 3.7
A temporal perception pattern (TPP) consists of a set of consecutive in-time visibility patterns. Top row: Five equally spaced in-time visibility patterns define a TPP. Bottom row: A DCT compressed version of the TPP.

this also allows to find more matches during simulation. In the bottom row of Figure 3.7, we see the compressed version of the TPP; on the top row, the state consists of 200 values, whereas the compressed version uses only 12 values (one value per dominant frequency).

Actions. Similar to the approach in Section 3.7.2, actions are partial trajectories stored as a sequence of relative vector displacements. These trajectories are always aligned to the moving direction of the character; therefore, applying the trajectory simply means adding the displacement vectors in order to the current position of an agent.

3.8 Creating the Behavior Model

A behavior model can be considered as a mapping $f : S \rightarrow A$, from a state $s \in S$ to a *rational* action $a \in A$. A data-driven model for crowds is learned from N observations of $E_i = (state, action)$ pairs collected as described in the previous sections; these observations are also called examples. In the current data-driven crowd simulation literature, the model consists of (a) a structured database $DB = \{E_i : i \in [1, N]\}$ of examples and (b) sets of methods for returning appropriate actions based on observed states. Any model learned from pairs of $(state, action)$ observations belongs to the general category of supervised learning approaches. It is important to note that most of the current approaches in the crowd simulation community use simplified approaches; more advanced machine learning methods such as reinforcement learning [22] are rarely used. Whatever methodology is used to learn the model, simulation-time query states are constructed similarly to the examples in the database; if feature positions for agents are required (e.g., like in Lerner et al. [4]), then these are extrapolated using the agents' current velocities.[*]

We will present two methods that use the example database directly [3,4] concluding with a graph-based method [6].

---

[*] For example, $\mathbf{p}_i(t + \Delta t) = \mathbf{p}_i(t) + \mathbf{v}_i(t)\Delta t$ for any agent A_i.

3.8.1 Database Approaches

The simplest approach to finding appropriate actions is searching the database DB to find the example with the closest matching state and then simply apply the retrieved action. The obvious advantage of this approach is simplicity; only one action is retrieved and no further processing is applied. This method though has its limitations; most of the times, the single action that is returned might not be appropriate even though more appropriate actions might be available in the database. One way of minimizing this problem, is retrieving a set of k-best matches and then selecting the best possible action; that is, the action that will navigate the characters with as few collisions as possible (ideally, this should be similar to the input data—even real people collide sometimes). Additionally, if actions are taken frequently and the state does not encode satisfying temporal information, artifacts will appear in the simulation since similar states could give drastically different actions; that is, agent movement will appear jerky. Finally, this approach does not generalize well; during simulation, characters will have a local state that is vastly different to the ones in the data.

One possible solution to this would be to find a set of close matches and then carefully combine all the retrieved actions to handle the situation. This is not as trivial as it sounds, especially if the best retrieved actions are contradicting. One simple, frequently encountered example is when someone walks directly toward some other person; some people turn to the left and some to the right. Naively taking an average of the retrieved velocities would force the agent to move forward! Therefore, care should be taken to avoid such situations.

Simple search: Lerner et al. [4] use one of the simplest approaches where they simply search the database for the single closest match that does not introduce collisions (Figure 3.8). To perform the search, a Gaussian-based matching function was defined. As described in Section 3.7.2, actions in this work are sub-trajectories of 40 frames length (1.5 s). Agents follow these trajectories until either the sub-trajectory has finished or the state changed considerably since the last action assignment. This method does not scale well with the number of agents since if the closest match does not give a collision-free trajectory, the database is searched sequentially to find a better action.

Regression for actions: An example of an approach that combines examples is the one proposed by Lee et al. [3]. Given a state, a search to find the 100 closest matches in the crowd database is performed; therefore, 100 different actions are collected. To find the best possible action, the retrieved actions are clustered and one cluster is selected probabilistically. Finally, the actions in the selected cluster are combined using weighted linear regression to return back a single velocity vector.

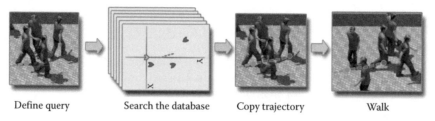

Define query   Search the database   Copy trajectory   Walk

FIGURE 3.8
Lerner et al. [4] model for simulation.

3.8.2 A Graph-Based Approach for Efficient Data-Driven Crowd Simulation

In typical data-driven crowd steering methods such as the ones described in Section 3.2, the (*state, action*) database is queried multiple times per simulation step, potentially once for each character, in order to retrieve the best matching examples and then the best possible action is selected or estimated. These queries are usually the bottleneck due to both the high dimensionality of the state representation and the number of results that are returned. High dimensionality searching can typically be addressed using approaches such as PCA that infer some penalty on accuracy [3]. Even though search performance is improved, selecting the best action is still costly since all of the returned results need to be processed. In addition, decisions are based on the current state of agents or at most the previous step's decision and not previously taken actions and states.

In order to improve both run-time speed and quality for data-driven crowd simulations, Charalambous and Chrysanthou [6] proposed a method that groups similar states and interconnects them in a graph-like structure, the *perception-action graph* (PAG) that is employed at simulation time (Figure 3.9). The proposed approach differs from the work by Ju et al. [7], where given a set of crowd data (simulated or real), new and potentially much larger crowds are generated by interpolation.

Constructing PAG nodes. The PAG uses TPPs as the state representation (Section 3.7.3). As a first step, the database is split into two: those examples having states where there was at least one interaction and those that there was none. The latter are not used in the PAG construction; rather their actions are stored in an interaction-free database (IFDB), which is used by agents when there are not interactions. The former are grouped together to form the PAG using an approach conceptually similar to that employed in single character animation [23]. The distance metric in this work measures similarities between TPPs: for each pair of agents (A, B) and each pair of TPPs $(P_{A,k}, P_{B,m})$ at frames k and m, respectively, their distance is found using a correlation metric and a normalized distance matrix is calculated for all sampled frames (Figure 3.10) (with 1 indicating maximum and 0 minimum similarity, respectively). For an input dataset of N pedestrians, $N^2/2$ distance matrices are generated due to symmetric properties of the data.

Unlike pose comparisons for single characters [23] where the number of joints is constant, the number of stimuli in an agent's TPP might vary from 0 to any number. To measure similarity between TPPs, a metric is required that has a constant number of features and

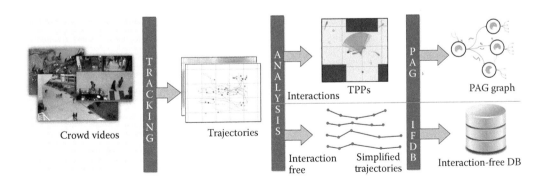

FIGURE 3.9
PAG preprocessing pipeline. People from videos of real-life crowds or expensive simulations are tracked, and trajectories are extracted and analyzed resulting in two auxiliary data structures to be used during simulation. The PAG graph used during interactions and the IFDB, a database of interaction-free trajectories.

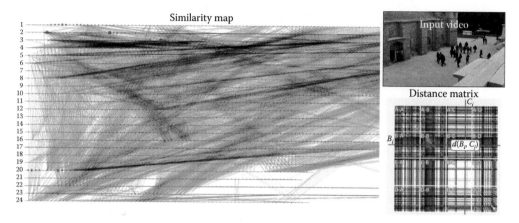

FIGURE 3.10
Similarity map for a video of a "flock" of 24 people in a tourist site. Each horizontal line indicates the trajectory of a tracked pedestrian over time whereas diagonal lines interconnect points where pedestrians had similar TPPs as these were found by distance matrices.

in addition compresses well and is insensitive to small changes, especially in the distant stimuli. The proposed metric is based on smoothed-out versions of the TPPs using the lower-frequency coefficients of their type-II DCT [24] (Figure 3.7). In effect, this approach smooths out the distance matrix (Figure 3.10). To compare two signals x and y, the root mean squared error (RMSE) between their lowest $M \in [8, 12]$ DCT frequency coefficients is found and normalized to $[0, 1]$.

One row of the distance matrix indicates the similarity of a specific TPP to all other TPPs in the input data and the local maxima of each row indicate the best matches of that TPP. This approach differs slightly from the one followed by Kovar et al. [23], where the best transition points are found in a local neighborhood since it generates relatively well-connected graphs. Out of these maxima, the best over a threshold are selected (typically > 0.9); increasing this threshold value results in increased quality but with fewer interconnections and therefore less choices during simulation.

Connecting PAG nodes. Once the best matches are found, a directed graph (the PAG) connecting transitions between TPPs is generated. A semantically similar graph to the PAG displaying the connections between similar TPPs can be seen in Figure 3.10. Each node V_i of the graph groups together similar TPPs and an edge $E_{i,j}$ between nodes V_i and V_j is created when a TPP in node V_j was a followup of a TPP belonging in V_i. These TPPs are temporally overlapped; that is, the starting section of the TPP in V_j is similar to the ending section of V_i. The edges of the PAG store trajectory segments that the pedestrian in the source data followed. The length of these segments is a multiple of the data sampling period and it is the period by which an agent must select a new action (edge); small values allow for finer control whereas larger ones allow for better performance. A node has as many edges as the number of TPPs clustered there. Potentially, node V_i can have multiple edges pointing to node V_j but each edge can store different actions (trajectories). After the nodes are interconnected, the PAG is post-processed to remove dead ends so that the graph can be used at simulation time without any special handling.

Interaction-free database. As mentioned before, states where there was no interaction are stored in a separate database. To query this database, we do not use the TPPs; rather we use a coarse version of the trajectory segment that was followed by an agent over the past few

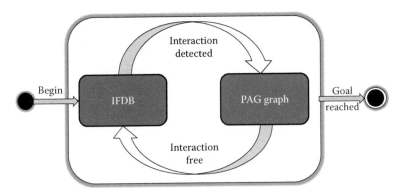

FIGURE 3.11
Agents' state diagram.

seconds (4–5 $2D$ displacement vectors). This trajectory is aligned to the moving direction of the character. Therefore, during simulation, an agent has two states: its TPP and the trajectory it moved on for the past few seconds. Depending on the TPP values, one of the two is used to get an action.

The PAG model. The PAG model consists of two structures: the PAG graph and the IFDB. Depending on if a simulated agent is having an interaction or not, one of these structures is used to decide on actions. If the agents sense no stimuli in their view, they simply move toward their goals by selecting appropriate trajectories from the IFDB. Whenever interactions are sensed (i.e., some external stimuli enters the sensing area of the agent), agents search the PAG to find the best-matching node as a starting point to handle the interactions (Figure 3.11). As long as there are interactions, the model traverses PAG returning as actions the trajectories stored on the edges. Graph traversal leads to behaviors such as collision avoidance, stopping to talk to each other, following someone, etc. (Figure 3.2). The best actions are selected at each simulation step by performing constrained walks of the PAG. Best actions are defined as the ones that minimize the error between actual agent states and those stored on the currently traversed nodes of the PAG.

Using this approach, we observe a significant gain in performance compared to database methods. In Figure 3.12, we demonstrate that this method can achieve up to an order of magnitude better performance compared to an approach similar to Lerner et al. [4] (marked as k-NN in the graph). These results are consistent for other scenes and datasets. We refer interested readers to Charalambous and Chrysanthou [6] and Charalambous [25] for more details and results. Additionally, animated results of simulations can be watched in the following online video: https://youtu.be/QaEQpXDspvo.

3.9 Discussion and Future Trends

Given enough data and a good model, data-driven techniques can prove beneficial over traditional rule-based methods; they can reproduce behaviors present in the input data without having to find parameters or needing to write complex rules. Most of the techniques used in the crowd simulation literature do not take advantage of more advanced machine learning techniques such as reinforcement learning. We believe that methods from

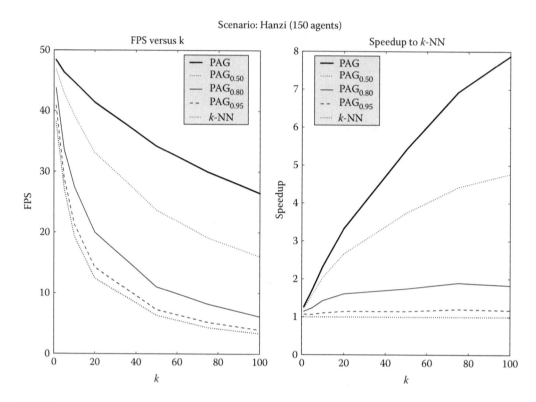

FIGURE 3.12
Performance of PAG using a medium-sized input dataset.

these areas can generalize better to new unseen states and could potentially give better simulation quality.

The methods we discussed in this chapter cover only steering or secondary behaviors in at most the street level. With the emergence of new technologies such as drones and the widespread use of mobile devices, large-scale crowd data covering entire neighborhoods and cities can be recorded and potentially used to learn high-level behaviors such as path selection and everyday actions. These data could also be used to learn environment-specific information for high-level control of the entire simulation, not just for individuals. Additionally, since most of the people in real crowds rarely move alone, more advanced data-driven methods that take into account different social interactions should be considered. Importantly, evaluating crowds using data can prove beneficial compared to traditional evaluation methods as we discuss in Chapter 10.

References

1. Y.-C. Lai, S. Chenney, and S. H. Fan. Group motion graphs. In *SCA '05: Proceedings of the 2005 ACM SIGGRAPH/Eurographics Symposium on Computer Animation*, pp. 281–290, Los Angeles, USA, 2005.
2. T. Kwon, K. H. Lee, J. Lee, and S. Takahashi. Group motion editing. *ACM Transactions on Graphics*, 27:80, 2008.

3. K. H. Lee, M. G. Choi, Q. Hong, and J. Lee. Group behavior from video: A data-driven approach to crowd simulation. In *Proceedings of the 2007 ACM SIGGRAPH/Eurographics Symposium on Computer Animation, SCA '07*, pp. 109–118, Aire-la-Ville, Switzerland, Switzerland, 2007. Eurographics Association.

4. A. Lerner, Y. Chrysanthou, and D. Lischinski. Crowds by example. *Computer Graphics Forum*, 26(3):655–664, 2007.

5. A. Lerner, Y. Chrysanthou, A. Shamir, and D. Cohen-Or. Context-dependent crowd evaluation. *Computer Graphics Forum*, 29(7):2197–2206, 2010.

6. P. Charalambous and Y. Chrysanthou. The PAG crowd: A graph based approach for efficient data-driven crowd simulation. *Computer Graphics Forum*, 33(8):95–108, 2014.

7. E. Ju, M. G. Choi, M. Park, J. Lee, K. H. Lee, and S. Takahashi. Morphable crowds. *ACM Transactions on Graphics*, 29(6):140:1–140:10, 2010.

8. R. A. Metoyer and J. K. Hodgins. Reactive pedestrian path following from examples. In *CASA '03: Proceedings of the 16th International Conference on Computer Animation and Social Agents*, p. 149, Washington, DC, USA, 2003. IEEE Computer Society.

9. S. R. Musse, C. R. Jung, A. Braun, and J. J. Junior. Simulating the motion of virtual agents based on examples. In *ACM/EG Symposium on Computer Animation, Short Papers*, pp. 83–93, Vienna, Austria, 2006.

10. S. Paris, J. Pettre, and S. Donikian. Pedestrian reactive navigation for crowd simulation: A predictive approach. *Computer Graphics Forum*, 26(3):665–674, 2007.

11. J. Pettré, J. Ondrej, A.-H. Olivier, A. Crétual, and S. Donikian. Experiment-based modeling, simulation and validation of interactions between virtual walkers. In *ACM SIGGRAPH/Eurographics Symposium on Computer Animation*, pp. 189–198, New Orleans, USA, 2009.

12. B. J. van Basten, S. E. Jansen, and I. Karamouzas. Exploiting motion capture to enhance avoidance behaviour in games. *Lecture Notes in Computer Science*, 5884:29–40, 2009.

13. M. Moussaïd, N. Perozo, S. Garnier, D. Helbing, and G. Theraulaz. The walking behaviour of pedestrian social groups and its impact on crowd dynamics. *PloS One*, 5(4):e10047, 2010.

14. D. Helbing and P. Molnár. Social force model for pedestrian dynamics. *Physical Review E*, 51(5):4282–4286, 1995.

15. N. Courty and T. Corpetti. Crowd motion capture. *Computer Animation and Virtual Worlds*, 18(4–5):361–370, 2007.

16. H. Hildenbrandt, C. Carere, and C. K. Hemelrijk. Self-organized aerial displays of thousands of starlings: A model. *Behavioral Ecology*, 21(6):1349, 2010.

17. A. Lerner, E. Fitusi, Y. Chrysanthou, and D. Cohen-Or. Fitting behaviors to pedestrian simulations. In *Proceedings of the 2009 ACM SIGGRAPH/Eurographics Symposium on Computer Animation*, pp. 199–208, New Orleans, USA. ACM, 2009.

18. E. Cho, S. A. Myers, and J. Leskovec. Friendship and mobility: User movement in location-based social networks. In *Proceedings of the 17th ACM SIGKDD International Conference on Knowledge Discovery and Data Mining*, pp. 1082–1090, San Diego, USA. ACM, 2011.

19. A. Robicquet, A. Alahi, A. Sadeghian, B. Anenberg, J. Doherty, E. Wu, and S. Savarese. Forecasting social navigation in crowded complex scenes. *ArXiv e-prints*, January 2016.

20. S. Russell and P. Norvig. *Artificial Intelligence: A Modern Approach*. Prentice Hall, New Jersey, USA, 1995.

21. J. Ondřej, J. Pettré, A.-H. Olivier, and S. Donikian. A synthetic-vision based steering approach for crowd simulation. *ACM Transactions on Graphics*, 29(4):123:1–123:9, 2010.

22. D. Vasquez, B. Okal, and K. O. Arras. Inverse reinforcement learning algorithms and features for robot navigation in crowds: An experimental comparison. In *2014 IEEE/RSJ International Conference on Intelligent Robots and Systems (IROS 2014)*, pp. 1341–1346, Chicago, USA. IEEE, 2014.

23. L. Kovar, M. Gleicher, and F. Pighin. Motion graphs. *ACM Transactions on Graphics*, 21(3):473–482, 2002.

24. N. Ahmed, T. Natarajan, and K. R. Rao. Discrete cosine transform. *IEEE Transactions on Computers*, January:90–93, 1974.

25. P. Charalambous. *Data-Driven Techniques for Virtual Crowds*. PhD thesis, University of Cyprus, 2014.

Section II

Editing and Realism

4

Animating Large Crowds in Huge Environments

Julien Pettré

CONTENTS

4.1 Introduction

It is today a common experience to navigate huge three-dimensional (3D) environments that reach up to the size of entire cities, whether this is by playing recent video games or by exploring online digital globes. In entertainment applications, the benefit of populating those environments with a population of virtual characters is undeniable. This creates lively game scenes, making them more realistic and attractive; it clearly improves the overall experience with the game. In other kinds of applications, such as the virtual globe, it is noticeable that those huge 3D environments still remain empty of population, even though this can be easily understood for technical reasons.

Figure 4.1 illustrates an example of a 3D city (a view of the Manhattan district in New York) populated with many virtual characters. A typical solution to create such a populated scene is to use a crowd engine that gathers technical solutions to simulate the global displacement of characters, to animate characters for them to follow the simulated motion, and to render them to the screen. Each of these three components (simulation, animation, and rendering) raises high computational needs. A critical one is simulation where interactions, such as collision avoidance between characters, is considered. As a

FIGURE 4.1
A view of a 3D model of Manhattan, New York, populated with many virtual characters.

character may have interactions with others in the scene, those simulation algorithms have a quadratic complexity by nature. Underlying models are kept voluntarily simplistic to avoid explosive computational costs. This simplicity unfortunately sometimes results in visual artifacts, such as deadlocks, residual collisions, spinning or oscillating motions, etc. Another kind of problem is motion uniformity because simplistic models capture the variety of human motions and behaviors badly. Also, in a simulation, the global motion of characters is not explicitly controlled but more indirectly generated from simulation and general directives (e.g., characters goals and properties): this can make the matching of some simulation results with a desired visual aspect of global motions difficult (such as local densities and the distribution of characters in the environment).

Crowd engines are certainly making rapid progress to address these issues, and always improve results one after the other. Still, given the required level of expertise to use them and set them correctly to populate one given environment, we explored alternative ways to animate many characters with the best possible trade-off between the visual quality of animation and the associated computational cost. Inspired by existing work on textures, we proposed the crowd patches approach to populate virtual environments.

What is the crowd patches approach? The key idea behind this approach is to precompute global trajectories for crowd characters so that the computational efforts normally dedicated to simulation is canceled. The precomputation of trajectories is however done in a specific manner and stored in patches. A patch is a delimited portion of space and time. Trajectories defined over this portion may concern traversing characters or characters always staying in the boundaries of patches. In any of these two cases, trajectories are periodic in time and may be replayed endlessly. Those for traversing characters have well-identified boundary conditions (entry–exit points on the boundaries of patches). In order to connect two adjacent patches, they must share compatible boundary conditions (i.e., one character exiting one patch must enter the other one at the right place and time). Figure 4.2 illustrates this principle. The left image displays one example of a patch, with visible trajectories for traversing characters. The right image shows two connected patches: the boundary conditions of trajectories are so that a continuous trajectory is ensured for traversing characters. Based on this principle, a large-scale animation is achieved by assembling a set of interconnected patches. Because all trajectories are periodic in time, this large-scale animation can be repeatedly played with no limit of time.

(a) (b)

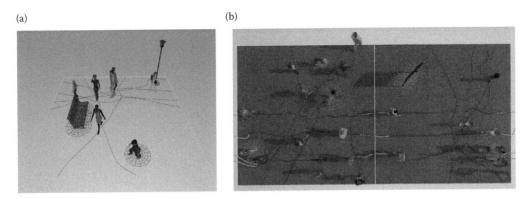

FIGURE 4.2
(a) One square patch with visible precomputed trajectories for characters. (b) Two assembled crowd patches with compatible boundary conditions.

In this chapter, we detail the principles of patches and define some important terms to describe this approach in Section 4.2. In Section 4.3, we describe how internal trajectories are computed: this is one of the most difficult problems to be solved in our approach because of the need for matching boundary conditions to connect patches. In Section 4.4, we describe intuitive crowd animation techniques made possible based on crowd patches, which, in addition to computational performances, appear to be one of the benefit of the crowd patches approach. The chapter concludes with some perspectives for the future development of this approach.

4.2 Principle

In this section, we present a more formal definition of patches and as well as the different elements composing them: endogenous and exogenous animated characters, and patterns and boundary conditions.

4.2.1 Patches

Patches are geometrical areas with convex polygonal shapes. They may contain static and dynamic objects. Static objects are simple obstacles whose geometry is fully contained inside the patch. Dynamic objects typically are animated characters: their position is moving in time according to a trajectory $\tau(t)$. Animated characters have π-periodic trajectories, so that $\tau(0) = \tau(\pi)$.

Two categories of characters are distinguished: *endogenous* and *exogenous* ones. The trajectory of *endogenous* characters always remains inside the geometrical boundaries of the patch for the whole period π. An example of endogenous trajectory is displayed in Figure 4.3a. If the animation is looped with a period π, the character appears to be moving endlessly inside the patch. Note that still characters can be considered as endogenous objects with no global motion. *Exogenous* characters have a trajectory $\tau(t)$ that goes out of the patch boundaries at some time, and thus cannot meet the periodicity condition. This condition can be satisfied by considering another instance of exogenous characters whose

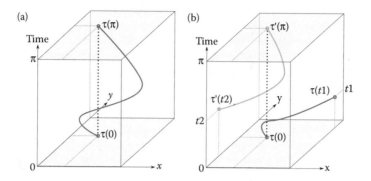

FIGURE 4.3

Example of square patches. The vertical axis represents time. (a) The patch contains an endogenous point that performs a periodic animation: its start and end positions $\tau(0)$ and $\tau(\pi)$ are the same. (b) The patch shows an exogenous point that performs a periodic motion, even if its trajectory leaves the patch at time t_1 to reappear at t_2 on the other side of the patch.

trajectory is $\tau'(t)$ (Figure 4.3b). Then, different cases are to be distinguished:

1. Trajectory $\tau(t)$ is defined for $t : 0 \to T$ with $0 < T < \pi$: we impose the patch to contain another instance of the exogenous object with a trajectory $\tau'(t)$ defined for $t : T' \to \pi$ with $0 < T' < \pi$, and with condition $\tau(0) = \tau'(\pi)$.

2. Trajectory $\tau(t)$ is defined for $t : T \to \pi$ with $0 < T < \pi$: we impose the patch to contain another instance of the exogenous object with a trajectory $\tau'(t)$ defined for $t : 0 \to T'$ with $0 < T' < \pi$, and with condition $\tau'(0) = \tau(\pi)$.

3. Trajectory $\tau(t)$ is defined for $t : T_1 \to T_2$ with $0 < T_1 < T_2 < \pi$. Then, the first condition is respected (because trajectory is not defined at $t = 0$ and π, the presence of another instance of the exogenous character is not required).

In the example of Figure 4.3a, $\tau(t)$ is defined inside the patch for $t : 0 \to t_1 < \pi$. This trajectory is associated with another instance of a moving point $\tau'(t)$ so that $\tau'(\pi) = \tau(0)$. Note that $t_1 \neq t_2$ and no order relationship is required: the two instances of the moving characters can be simultaneously outside or inside the patch.

4.2.2 Patterns

In the previous section, we defined exogenous characters: their trajectory exits the geometrical boundaries of a patch. The overall role of patterns is to register the trajectories of boundary conditions of exogenous characters in order to allow the connection of patches. A pattern is defined for each face of a polygonal patch. As a result, patterns fully delimit patches. They are two-dimensional: with a space dimension with length l and a time dimension with duration (period) π. Patterns identify limit conditions for exogenous object trajectories. These conditions are either an input point I or an output point O at a specific position on the patch face $p \in [0,l]$, and at given time $t \in [0, \pi]$. Thus, a pattern is fully defined from its dimension l, its duration π, and a set of inputs and outputs: $P = \{l, \pi, I_i[p_i, t_i], O_j[p_j, t_j]\}$.

We build a large-scale animation by assembling patches. Thus, two adjacent patches have at least one common face. They also share identical limit conditions for the trajectories of

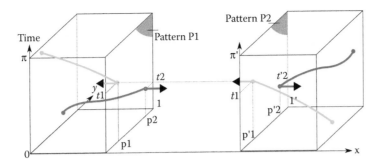

FIGURE 4.4
Example of two square patches sharing patterns with mirrored conditions and thus, connectible. Once connected, the point following the green trajectory passes from the right patch to the left one seamlessly, while the point with the red trajectory moves from left to right.

exogenous characters. Indeed, when an exogenous character goes from one patch to an adjacent one, it first follows the trajectory contained by the first patch, and then switches to the one described by the second patch. These two trajectories have to be at least continuous C^0 in order to ensure a continuous motion from the first patch to the second one. The patterns standing between the two adjacent patches allow sharing of these limit conditions. Let us consider the case of two adjacent patches with one common face as illustrated in Figure 4.4: the two patches each contain two exogenous characters going through their common face. The common face is delimited by pattern P_1 for the first patch on the left and by pattern P_2 for the second patch on the right. We have $P_1 = \{\pi, l, I[p_1, t_1], O[p_2, t_2]\}$ and $P_2 = \{\pi', l', I[p'_2, t'_2], O[p'_1, t'_1]\}$. In order to satisfy C^0 continuity for endogenous character trajectories, we must ensure

$$\pi = \pi', \quad l = l', \quad p_1 = p'_1, \quad t_1 = t'_1, \quad p_2 = p'_2, \quad t_2 = t'_2 \tag{4.1}$$

We then say that P_1 is the mirror pattern of P_2. As a summary, mirrored patterns have the same duration, length, and number of mirrored inputs and outputs.

4.3 Computing Internal Trajectories for Patches

One major difficulty in the crowd patches approach is to compute internal trajectories for exogenous characters. Indeed, trajectories need to strictly satisfy some boundary conditions at their two extremities in patches (could be at the boundary of patches or when time reaches the end of the period). Those boundary conditions are defined both in space and time; as a result, each character needs to start moving in a patch at a given location and at a given time, as well as to reach another given location at another given time. Enforcing boundary constraints with accuracy is required to enable continuous motion between patches or when animation is looped over time. In addition to those constraints, trajectories should be humanly feasible (not too fast, for example) and should not provoke collisions with other characters and obstacles inside patches.

We have developed a technique to solve this problem. The computation of trajectories starts from the definition of patterns (i.e., boundary conditions): a set of patterns is assembled to geometrically form a patch. Trajectories are then generated so as to strictly pass through a set of space–time waypoints.

4.3.1 Overview

In this first approach, internal trajectories are generated from a set of boundary conditions, that is, a set of input and output waypoints set on the boundary conditions as defined by patterns. The process consists of four steps, as illustrated in Figure 4.5:

1. At the beginning of the process, input and output waypoints are not connected to one another. All we are sure of is that we have the same number of inputs as outputs by definition of a patch. As a result, we first need to connect input and output points to form initial guess trajectories for characters. As explained in the next section, this should not be done randomly as certain combinations of input–output points are clearly more interesting than others.

2. We make sure that the initial guess trajectories are valid (not generating high or not connecting points in a bad order of passage time).

3. We finally solve collisions for those initial guess trajectories when required, because they can go through the obstacles contained into the patch, or pass at too close distance one another provoking a collision between the characters following them.

A more detailed look at all three steps follows in the remainder of this section.

4.3.2 Connecting Boundary Waypoints

In this first step, we try to match and connect with initial guess trajectories a set of entry and exit points in an optimal way. To do this, a measure of the match's quality has to be defined. Intuitively, there are some matches that are better than others; for example, judging by observation, trajectories passing near the center of the patch look better than the ones staying close to the borders. Some other aspects can also be considered, such as how close the speed needed by an agent to travel from an entry to an exit point is compared to

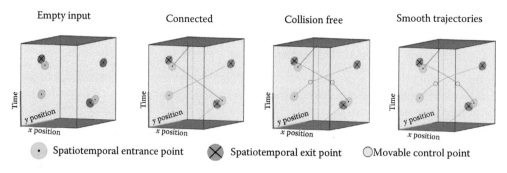

FIGURE 4.5

Input and output points are initially connected to form the initial guess traejctories (two left images). Trajectories are then subsequently modified using the proposed optimization approach to be collision free (middle right image). They can be additionally smoothed out in a final step (right image).

Algorithm 4.1: Gale–Shapley Stable Marriage Algorithm from Reference 3

Initialize all $i \in \mathbf{I}$ and $o \in \mathbf{O}$ to *free* ;
while ∃ *free entry point i who still has an exit point o to propose to* **do**
$\quad$ $o \leftarrow i$'s highest ranked exit point to whom it has not yet proposed ;
$\quad$ **if** *o is free* **then**
$\quad\quad$ (i, o) become paired ;
$\quad$ **else**
$\quad\quad$ some pair (i', o) already exists ;
$\quad\quad$ **if** *o prefers i to i'* **then**
$\quad\quad\quad$ (i, o) become paired ;
$\quad\quad\quad$ i' becomes *free* ;
$\quad\quad$ **else**
$\quad\quad\quad$ (i', o) remain paired;

typical walking comfort speeds of humans. A comfort speed of $u_{cft} = 1.33$ m/s, which is the normal walking speed of humans in an unconstrained environment is used in this work [1].

For a square patch, an order of preference between matching patterns is defined; matching points between opposing patterns are preferred, followed by neighboring ones and finally with points that lie on the same pattern. For any of these cases, if there exist multiple possible matching options on the same pattern, the point whose associated trajectory is closest to the u_{cft} is selected.

To solve this matching problem, the *Gale–Shapley algorithm* [2] (see Algorithm 4.1), commonly referred to as the algorithm to solve the *stable marriage problem*, is employed. This algorithm assures that at the end, if we have Alice engaged to Bob and Carol engaged to Dave, it is not possible for Alice to prefer Dave and Dave to prefer Alice—this is called a *stable match*. Algorithm 4.1 demonstrates the Gale–Shapley algorithm in relation to two equal lists of entry and exit points that are being matched for pairing.

In order to apply Algorithm 4.1, preference values for all pairs of entry and exit points should be defined. To do so, all entry and exit points keep a *proposal list* $\mathbf{L}_s$ indicating the order of preference for their matching. The following approach is employed to rank each possible match-up:

1. Find the speed it would take to travel from an entry point to all exit points. Assuming that $(\mathbf{p}_1, t_1)$ and $(\mathbf{p}_2, t_2)$ are the position and time of the entry and exit points, respectively, speed is defined as $u = s/\Delta t$, where $s = |\mathbf{p}_2 - \mathbf{p}_1|$ and $\Delta t = t_2 - t_1$ when $t_2 > t_1$, otherwise $\Delta t = \pi + t_2 - t_1$.[*]

2. Next, each pair of points is assigned a preference value:

$$pr_{score} = u_{match} + p \qquad (4.2)$$

where $u_{match} = arctan(|u_{cft} - u|) \in [0, \pi/2)$ indicates closeness to a desired speed, with 0 indicating maximum closeness. $p = \{0, 2, 4\}$ defines a *penalty* value that

---

[*] More details on why this last assumption is made will be presented later during the creation of the initial set of trajectories.

depends on where the two points lie relative to each other; for points on opposing patterns, there is no penalty; for neighboring patches, it is 2; and for points on the same pattern, it is 4.[*]

3. Sort $\mathbf{L}_s$ in ascending order; the first entry indicates the most desired exit point.

It should be emphasized here that all waypoints (both entry and exit) keep their own proposal lists. After each entry point has been assigned a proposal list, Algorithm 4.1 is used to define matches between the entry and exit points; every two points that remain engaged at the end of the algorithm become a pair.

4.3.3 Creating Initial Trajectories

The next step is creating the initial batch of trajectories. First, the paired points are connected via straight lines; if a line tries to connect two points backward in time (i.e., if $t_2 < t_1$), the initial trajectory is split into two parts—from t_1 to π and from 0 to t_2 as in Reference 4. The positions of these new control points are in the same straight line, taken in such a way that the speed is the same in both segments. The same approach is used if the trajectory enforces unrealistically high speed values.

Further adjustments to the initial trajectories are done for some special cases. For agents traveling only over an edge, a control point is added near the center of the patch. For agents moving slowly, a control point with the same position but on a different time is added, resulting in agents that stop suddenly (as if pausing to look around) but later on continue their journey at a better speed.

This step results in linear trajectories that are optimized for speed and coverage of space using an objective function (Equation 4.2). These trajectories though can be colliding with each other, since no special care has been taken up to this point to handle this. To address this issue, the iterative technique, described in the next paragraphs, has been proposed.

4.3.4 Removing Collisions

The set of linear trajectories generated by Algorithm 4.1 will most likely have collisions with the obstacles or other trajectories. As collisions rarely take place in real-life human crowds, a strategy to remove them from the initial trajectories should be defined. For this, we propose an algorithm that manipulates the linear trajectories by moving control points. Since patches are concatenated together to create larger crowds, care *must* be taken during trajectory modification so that the spatiotemporal boundary control points (i.e., entry and exit ones) are not modified; other control points can be added and manipulated.

Algorithm for collision handling. An iterative algorithm for handling collisions is proposed (Algorithm 4.2). The main idea is the following: given a matrix M that stores the current minimum distances in-between all trajectories, the algorithm iterates modifying the trajectories (and therefore their closest distance value) until $min(M) > \alpha$, where α represents a minimum allowed distance value. Given typical circular agents of radius r, $\alpha = 2r$ (therefore, $min(M) > \alpha \Leftrightarrow$ patch is collision free). To do so, new control points are added during iterations (i.e., trajectories are split into segments) that are moved under some constraints until the trajectories are collision free (see Figure 4.6 for an example).

---

[*] This can be generalized to any prism-like patch.

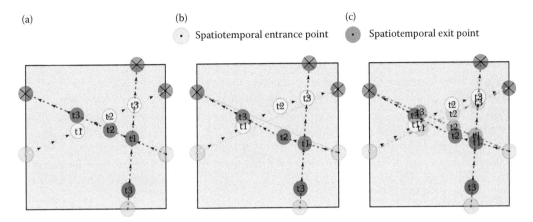

FIGURE 4.6
Illustration of our collision solving technique. (a) The "worst" collision is currently identified to be the one between the yellow and pink trajectories at timestep t_2. (b) The two trajectories are deformed to handle the collision. (c) Overlayed difference between the two trajectories.

First, the minimum distance matrix is calculated (see below). As long as collisions exist, trajectories τ_i and τ_j having the minimum value are found—that minimum value corresponds to a moment in time and two points $\mathbf{p}_i$ and $\mathbf{p}_j$. These two points are moved to handle the collision using correction forces $\mathbf{F}_i$ and $\mathbf{F}_j$:

$$\mathbf{F}_i = R(\phi) * \Delta\hat{\mathbf{p}}_{i,j} * \alpha * w_i \tag{4.3}$$

$\Delta\hat{\mathbf{p}}_{i,j}$ is the normalized vector connecting the two points ($\Delta\mathbf{p}_{i,j} = \mathbf{p}_i - \mathbf{p}_j$), $\alpha = r_i + r_j$ is the sum of the two agents' radii and defines a threshold value for minimum distance,[*] $R(\phi)$ is a small random noise rotation matrix to help prevent infinite loops ($\phi : -0.5 \leq \phi \leq 0.5$ *rad*), and finally w_i is a weight to reduce speed artifacts and prevent agents from leaving the bounds of the patch:

$$w_i = \begin{cases} u_j/(u_i + u_j) & \text{if point stays in patch} \\ 0 & \text{otherwise} \end{cases} \tag{4.4}$$

u_i and u_j are the speeds of trajectories τ_i and τ_j.

Algorithm 4.2: The Control Points Generation Algorithm

> Compute minimum distance matrix M;
> **while** *there exists at least one entry in M below the threshold* **do**
> > Find indices i and j for which $M(i, j)$ has the smallest value d;
> > Create temporary control points $\mathbf{cp}_i$ and $\mathbf{cp}_j$ in τ_i and τ_j that are at distance d ;
> > Apply repulsion forces to $\mathbf{cp}_i$ and $\mathbf{cp}_j$;
> > Update τ_i and τ_j;
> > Update M ;

---

[*] In our implementation, $r_1 = r_2 = r$, making the threshold constant.

Having the correction force $\mathbf{F}_i$, point $\mathbf{p}_i$ is displaced using the following equation:

$$\mathbf{p}_i^{new} = \mathbf{p}_i + \mathbf{F}_i \tag{4.5}$$

Once $\mathbf{p}_i^{new}$ is found, a check to find if there is an existing control point within a small time interval is performed; if successful, then that point is moved to $\mathbf{p}_i^{new}$; otherwise, a new control point is added at $\mathbf{p}_i^{new}$. Finally, columns i, j and rows i, j of the distance matrix M are updated with new distances. Calculations for force $\mathbf{F}_j$ and point $\mathbf{p}_j$ are symmetric.

We have found that in most situations this algorithm has fast convergence rate and produces collision-free trajectories. However, there are still situations where it converges slowly or even gets stuck in an infinite loop; and therefore a maximum number of iterations is set.

Distance matrix. The first step of the collision handling algorithm is generating a distance matrix $M \in \mathbb{R}^{n \times n}$ between all the n trajectories; that is, the value at $M(i, j)$ represents the minimum distance between trajectories τ_i and τ_j.

The following properties apply for all $i, j \in [1, n]$ and can be employed to reduce computation time:

- $M(i, i) = 0$
- $M(i, j) = M(j, i)$, that is, the matrix is symmetric
- $M(i, j) = \infty$, $\forall (\tau_i, \tau_j)$ that are never present at the same time

Minimum distance. The minimum distance between two trajectories is defined as their minimum spatiotemporal distance, that is, at the point in time where they are closest to each other. Recall that a trajectory can consist of one or more segments separated by control points and therefore the minimum has to be found in-between all the trajectories' segments.

Given any two linear trajectory segments $\mathbf{s}^{(1)}$ and $\mathbf{s}^{(2)}$, their minimum distance can be found with an analytic approach. First, their common time interval is found; that is, the period of time that the trajectories coexist in the patch. If the two segments do not have any common time interval, then their distance is set to infinity (practically a large value). If there exists a common interval $[t_s, t_e]$, then we set $\mathbf{p}_s^{(1)}$ and $\mathbf{p}_s^{(2)}$ as the two segments position at time t_s. Additionally, agents moving on these two segments have a velocity of $\mathbf{v}^{(1)}$ and $\mathbf{v}^{(2)}$, respectively. So, for any point in time $t : 0 \le t \le t_e - t_s$, their distance is

$$d(t) = ||(\mathbf{p}_s^{(1)} + \mathbf{v}^{(1)} * t) - (\mathbf{p}_s^{(2)} + \mathbf{v}^{(2)} * t)|| \tag{4.6}$$

Setting $\mathbf{w} = \mathbf{p}_s^{(1)} - \mathbf{p}_s^{(2)}$ and $\Delta \mathbf{v} = \mathbf{v}^{(1)} - \mathbf{v}^{(2)}$, Equation 4.6 becomes

$$d(t) = ||\mathbf{w} + \Delta \mathbf{v} * t|| \tag{4.7}$$

To find the minimum distance, we set the derivative $d'(t) = 0$ and solve for t to get the time of closest approach:

$$t_c = (-\mathbf{w} \cdot \mathbf{dv}) / ||\mathbf{dv}||^2 \tag{4.8}$$

If $0 \le t_c \le t_e - t_s$, then by setting $t = t_c$ in Equation 4.6, the minimum distance between segments $\mathbf{s}^{(1)}$ and $\mathbf{s}^{(2)}$ is found. If t_c is outside the bounds of the segment, we check the endpoints of the line segment for collision. By having the minimum distances between all the segments of the two trajectories, it is trivial to find the minimum distance.

4.4 Sculpting Crowd Animations Based on Patches

In this section, we describe a method for interactively sculpting crowd animations at large spatial and temporal scales, based on the principle of crowd patches. In our framework, users design populated environments through simple interaction gestures such as stretching, shrinking or bending pieces of crowds, cutting and connecting pieces of crowds together, and locally playing on motion variety over time. Meanwhile, local trajectory distortions are minimized and continuity of animations is ensured. Users immediately visualize the results as they interact with the crowds, enabling them to progressively populate and tune the crowd's behavior in the target environment. Technically, our solution consists of representing a crowd as an aggregation of spatially and temporally linked pieces of cycled animations, using the crowd patch principle. In order to sculpt and deform the crowd patches (through stretching, bending, and cutting tools) while maintaining the crowd structure, we extend the concept of mutable elastic models (MEMs) [5], introduced for static shapes, to spatiotemporal crowd structures, leading to the new concept of "mutable space–time models."

4.4.1 Overview

The principle of our approach is to represent an animated crowd as a graph-based structure in which nodes represent animated crowd patches [4] and edges represent the connected flows between the crowd patches. See Figure 4.7 for an overview: the top part represents the structure of the crowd as a graph, the middle part displays the non-deformed crowd patches corresponding to the graph nodes, and the bottom part represents the final deformed patches that shape the crowd animation and ensure continuity. From there, by proposing a novel extension of MEMs [5], user interactions applied to this representation can (i) impact the topology of the graph by inserting, removing, or connecting nodes together, thereby switching patches and changing the way patches are connected, (ii) impact the geometry of the patches (bending, stretching, and shrinking, thereby changing

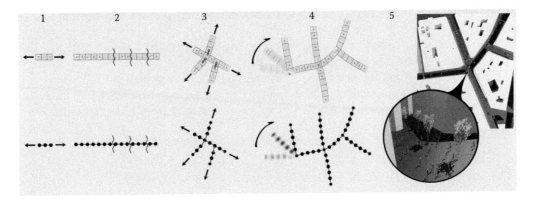

FIGURE 4.7
A simple example to illustrate the principle of our approach. Top: A geometrical graph $\mathcal{G}$ captures the structure of crowd patches. Middle: Each vertex of $\mathcal{G}$ corresponds to a crowd patch. Bottom: Crowd patches are locally deformed to enable seamless animation continuity between patches.

the way agents are moving inside a patch), or (iii) impact the temporal parameters inside the patches.

Let us first recall the principle and main properties of crowd patches in more detail. A crowd patch is a delimited portion of a precomputed crowd animation. Animations can be of any type: moving objects, pedestrians, vehicles, etc. A crowd patch is delimited both spatially (by a convex polygon) and temporally (by a period of time π). Animated objects smoothly move from patch to patch, thanks to continuity constraints enforced between adjacent patches: a pattern is defined on each edge of each patch to record the position and time at which objects traverse it; a mirror pattern (where an object going in becomes an object going out and vice versa) is given to the adjacent patch. All connected patches share the same period of time π, which allows smooth, endless animation to be produced by simply reusing the same trajectories over time.

In practice, crowd patches are organized into a bidirectional graph structure storing adjacency relationships. Up to now, no feature was proposed to deform the individual patches or to change the topology or geometry of this graph. In addition, since time continuity was just obtained by replaying the patches content over time, no temporal structure was added. Our insight is to extend MEMs [5] to the crowd patches framework: MEMS are a unique solution for enabling large deformations of a complex structure while limiting the distortion of individual elements (here, the geometry of crowd patches, and therefore of the trajectories). Whenever local deformation is too large, elements are either interactively swapped with more suitable ones, or some of them are inserted, removed, connected, or disconnected, as necessary, within the graph.

More precisely, MEMs were introduced for static shapes able to take a number of different *rest states*, all preserving a meaningful structure. Let us take the example of a castle wall. Rest states for each section of the wall can either be "straight" or "corner." When the designer bends a straight wall beyond a certain point, one of the sections will turn into a corner because this new rest position will best minimize the associated deformation energy. Interestingly, the structure of shapes is also captured in this work by a bidirectional graph representation $\mathcal{G}$, which deforms following the as-rigid-as-possible model [6]: deformation is computed so that the graph parts globally remain as close as possible to their rest states. The method therefore plays on the mapping between each graph node and rest states using a state space representation. Changes of the graph topology are also allowed, through node insertion and removals. Both changes of state and topology changes are based on a shape grammar, to ensure that only valid transformations are applied.

Although we are inspired by the original idea, MEMs cannot be directly applied to our crowd patches framework. First, Milliez et al. did not solve for spatial continuity between the geometric elements they manipulate. In contrast, local deformations maintaining C_0 continuity at least is required in our case, in order to ensure smooth trajectories for virtual agents. Second, the elements of animation we manipulate require specific treatments to ensure proper temporal connections.

In the following section, we therefore present new, *mutable space–time models*, based on crowd patches. They require defining

- A set of rest state configurations, each rest state representing a specific patch type and containing a patch instance (see Section 4.4.2.1)
- A state space that maps user interactions to changes in the topology of the graph structure (see Section 4.4.2.2)

- A technique to locally deform the geometry of crowd patches to follow the graph deformations (see Section 4.4.2.3)
- A visual way to manipulate animated content over the time line, in order to increase motion variety and control, making loops almost undetectable

4.4.2 A Mutable Space–Time Model for Sculpting Crowds

The first step is to define a number of rest states together with their corresponding patches and then the state space that describes the possibilities to swap rest states or change the topological structure of the graph.

4.4.2.1 Patches Rest States

A rest state is a predefined local configuration in the graph, that is, a specific spatial arrangement of nodes and edges. Figure 4.8 illustrates the different rest states available in our system, typically:

- A *dead end* (one edge only), $\chi^{(DE)}$
- A *flat node* (two aligned edges only), $\chi^{(F)}$
- An *L-corner* (two orthogonal edges), $\chi^{(L)}$
- A *T-junction* (three orthogonal edges), $\chi^{(T)}$
- or An *X-junction* (four orthogonal edges), $\chi^{(X)}$

Each rest state is first associated with a patch type. The patch type typically defines the side on which agents flow between patches, yet without precisely defining densities of

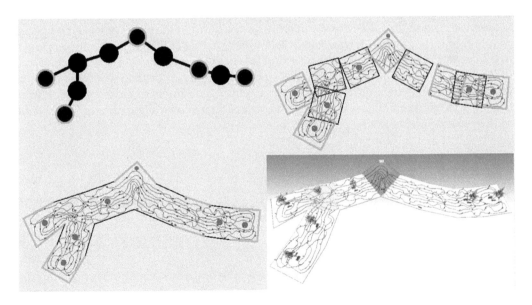

FIGURE 4.8
Table of possible rest states defined in our system (first column), corresponding types of patches (second column), patches layout (third column), and examples of patches instances (fourth column). The red dots represent obstacles in the patches.

agents or entry/exit patterns of agents. For the sake of simplicity, we restricted our patches to square-shaped regions. Each rest state can therefore be connected to a maximum of four other patches. Each patch type is then associated with a collection of *frame patches*, including only entry/exit patterns and obstacles, displayed in red in Figure 4.8. Each frame patch is then associated with different patch instances each of which contains different agent trajectories (all satisfying the entry/exit patterns and avoiding the obstacles), thereby providing a good degree of variability.

4.4.2.1.1 *Frame Patches and Patch Instances*

Frame patches are delimited by patterns, which capture space–time waypoints for characters traversing patch boundaries. Frame patches do not contain trajectories, but simply specify constraints. Patterns capture the flow going through each of the patch boundary. This means that we can easily deduce crowd patches instances from their type and frame patch. We set empty patterns $p_\emptyset$ (without any waypoint) where there is no flow allowed. We set a desired number of waypoints for other patterns depending on the density of the patch. Combinations in the densities and in the patterns enable a first level of variety in the possible patches.

However, we must guarantee that the set of patches we use easily interconnects. Our solution is to create patches instances from a very limited set of patterns $\{p_1, \ldots, p_n\}$ as well as their mirror patterns $\{p'_1, \ldots, p'_n\}$. Indeed, we recall that two patches can connect if the space–time waypoints on their boundary match: one input point should correspond to one output point in the adjacent patch. This condition is true for two mirrored patterns p_i and p'_i. By using a limited set of patterns, it is possible to precompute all the possible combinations of patterns to create different frame patches, and then different patch instances. For example, an instance of a patch of type dead-end is built with the following four patterns for each node: $\mathcal{P}_{dead\,end} \leftarrow \{p_i, p_\emptyset, p_\emptyset, p_\emptyset\}$. This patch can be connected, for example, to a flat-node-type patch built with these four patterns: $\mathcal{P}_{flat} \leftarrow \{p'_i, p_\emptyset, p_j, p_\emptyset\}$.

Once patterns and obstacles are set in a frame patch, different trajectories can be generated (the computation of such trajectories is not the purpose of this paper, see Reference 4). These combinations therefore enable a second level of variety in the possible patches.

Each time a new node N is inserted in the graph, all the patch instances of that node type for which all entry/exit patterns are compatible with its neighbors in the graph are selected in a pool of possible candidates. A random process then chooses one among the possible candidates, and associates this patch instance with the node.

4.4.2.2 Patches State Space

We now describe how the graph deforms and evolves under a set of possible user actions, as well as how patches switch between different rest states.

4.4.2.2.1 *State Space*

A state space is introduced to map each node in $\mathcal{G}$ with one rest state. There is no ambiguity in this mapping when nodes are dead ends or T- or X-junctions because the number of connected edges straightforwardly determines the corresponding rest state. We however have an indetermination in the case of two-edge nodes that can have either a flat or an L-corner node rest state. To solve this ambiguity, we define a state for nodes with two edges (rightmost green region in Figure 4.9). Our state space is two dimensional. The state

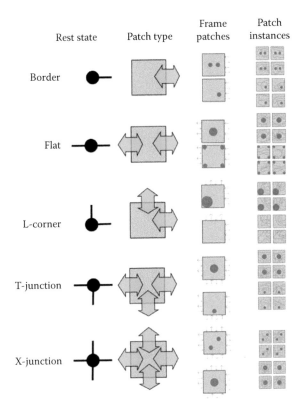

FIGURE 4.9
Presentation of the state space. A colored region represents a state and boundaries represent transitions. User deformations move nodes away from their rest state and inside this state space (the distance is measured using a specific metric integrating position and orientation information of edges). When reaching a boundary in the state space, the current rest state is either switched to another one (e.g., flat toward L-corner) or leads to a change in the graph structure (e.g., node insertion or removal).

s_i of the node i is defined in the 2D state space as

$$s_i = [l_i, \beta_i] \tag{4.9}$$

where β is the angle formed by the two edges connected to the node and l the length sum of the connected edges. We can now project the node into the state space. The state space is displayed in Figure 4.9. Depending on the position of the node in this space, we deduce its corresponding rest state (color-coded areas in the state space). The figure also illustrates that, as detailed later, the user's actions will change the state of nodes, depending on their distance to the rest states we defined. Distance and projection in the state space are computed according to the metric presented in Reference 6 and based on the deformation energy $E(f)$:

$$E(f) = \sum_{p_i \in \mathcal{G}} dist(R_i(A_i), f(\chi_i)) \tag{4.10}$$

where $E(f)$ is the energy to minimize, p_i the graph nodes, and $dist$ the distance between the configuration of the considered node $R_i(A_i)$ to its rest position $f(\chi_i)$. A_i is the set of

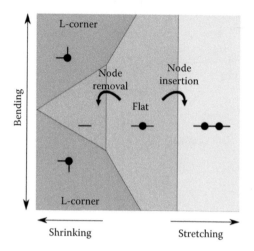

FIGURE 4.10
Illustration of the deformation energy $E(f)$. Each node is associated with a rest state (closest one its state space).
Here, three rest states are illustrated in red, each one associated with a state space in which the current configuration of the nodes (in black) are positioned. Distance between each node and its rest state is then evaluated (using
angles and edge lengths). Distances are then summed on all nodes to compute deformation energy.

possible rest states $A_i = \{\chi_i^{(DE)}, \chi_i^{(F)}, \chi_i^{(L)}, \chi_i^{(T)}, \chi_i^{(X)}\}$. An example of mapping between the
nodes of an example graph and the rest states is displayed in Figure 4.10.

4.4.2.2.2 Cutting and Merging
The user is able to cut or merge parts of the graph. These actions are direct and explicit
actions on the graph $\mathcal{G}$. The user determines an edge to delete from the graph (cutting) or
some new edges to add to the graph between two nodes (merging). In our application, the
user performs cutting by selecting two adjacent patches and selecting the "cut" action. To
merge two components of $\mathcal{G}$, the user moves one of the component (global translation/
rotation) close to the other one, selects two close patches and select the "merge" action. An
edge is created between the two corresponding nodes of $\mathcal{G}$.

Cutting and merging actions directly result in changes of rest states for the considered
nodes. When cutting, the edge removal will mutate the connected nodes:

- X-junction into a T-junction: $\chi^X \rightarrow \chi^T$
- T-junction into a flat node ("trunk" edge is cut): $\chi^T \rightarrow \chi^F$
- T-junction into a flat node ("branch" edge is cut): $\chi^T \rightarrow \chi^L$
- Flat or L-corner node into a dead end: $\chi^L, \chi^F \rightarrow \chi^{DE}$

Note that we did not consider isolated nodes because this case is useless. And conversely,
when merging, edge insertion will result in a change in rest state for the newly connected
nodes: $\chi^{DE} \rightarrow \chi^L, \chi^F, \chi^L \rightarrow \chi^T, \chi^F \rightarrow \chi^T$. We choose whether χ^{DE} should turn into χ^L
or χ^F by choosing the rest state at closest distance from the current state of the considered
node.

Node rest state changes also result in a change of patches type (and consequently patch
instances). The newly mutated node will connect to existing neighbors. Connection is made
through patterns. These existing constraints define the correct patch frame to be used.

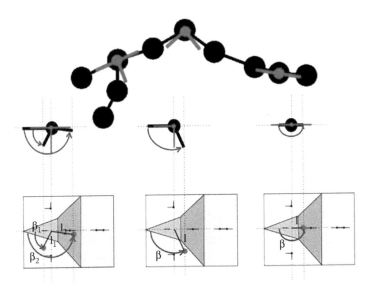

FIGURE 4.11
Five steps illustrating the creation and interactive manipulation of crowd patches to populate a virtual environment by introducing spatiotemporal mutable elastic models. Pictures on the top line illustrate the manipulation of the patches while pictures on the bottom line illustrate the changes in the graph representing the MEM.

We then randomly select any instance of a patch with the corresponding patch frame. Examples of cutting and merging operations are illustrated in Figure 4.11, steps 2 and 3. One can see flat nodes turning into dead-end nodes at step 2. In step 3, one flat node is successively merged with two other components: it turns into a T-junction node and then into an X-junction node.

4.4.2.2.3 Stretching, Shrinking, and Bending

Stretching, shrinking, or bending operations can be performed on the graph as illustrated in Figure 4.11, step 4. The part to be deformed is selected by defining control nodes (represented as pins in our examples). The in-between structure of nodes is deformed in as-rigid-as-possible way. As explained in Reference 6, this is done computing the node configuration that minimizes $E(f)$, Equation 4.10. This new configuration changes the two-edge node state.

Projection in the state space (Figures 4.9 and 4.10) determines whether a swap in state (or mutation) is required. For example, when a flat node is stretched, its state is moved to the left of the state space: indeed, this move in the state space corresponds to a shortening of edge length. At some point, the state will go beyond the limit (between the pink and violet areas) where node removal is triggered. In the same way, when bending a flat node, the angle formed by node edges will increase or decrease: mutation to an L-corner χ^L rest state is triggered (transition from the violet zone to the orange zone). A hysteresis at the frontier of different rest areas is implemented as suggested by Milliez to avoid disturbing oscillations between different rest states.

As for cutting and merging, when a node mutates to a new rest state or is added to $\mathcal{G}$, the matching patch frame is selected and any instance corresponding to this frame is added to the animation.

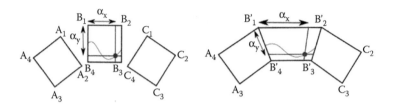

FIGURE 4.12
Local deformation of patches. Vertices of two adjacent patches are interpolated. A bilinear interpolation of the internal animation trajectories is performed to fit the new patch position and shape.

4.4.2.3 Geometric Deformations of Patches

The elastic deformations controlled by the user cause some changes of distance and alignment between patches. As crowd patches contain some animated characters that move from patch to patch, unalignment and distance change results in discontinuities in the animation that need to be addressed (an aspect not tackled by Reference 5).

To ensure animation continuity, we propose to locally deform the patches geometry together with the animation to connect them seamlessly. Such a local deformation is illustrated in Figure 4.12. The results of a complex deformation are illustrated in Figure 4.7. Patches adjacency is easily deduced from $\mathcal{G}$. It allows us to map patch vertices of adjacent patches two by two. In the example of Figure 4.12, A_2 and B_1 are mapped, as well as A_3 and B_4. This allows to compute the new coordinates of locally deformed patches: they stand at the center of mapped vertices. For example, B_1' is at the center of A_2 and B_1. Finally, all the internal trajectories as well as internal objects coordinates are deformed to follow the new shape of patches vertices. This local deformation is performed using a simple bilinear interpolation. Each trajectory control point τ_{xy} is located at the same coordinates (α_x, α_y) expressed relatively to the moving axis $(\overrightarrow{B_1' B_2'}, \overrightarrow{B_1' B_3'})$. Given that deformations on the patches are limited (due to changes in states that arise), the bilinear interpolation only leads to small deformations on the trajectories. The deformation process can lead to change in the character velocities. However, those deformations are of a limited quantity: large deformations will result in a mutation of the node (e.g., large stretching will trigger the insertion of new nodes).

4.5 Conclusion

In this chapter, we have described the crowd patches approach to populate large environments. The key idea of this approach is to precompute elements of crowd animations, and to store them in patches. Animations are computed to be time-periodic; thus, they can be replayed endlessly in time. As characters may go through patches and their trajectories cross the boundaries of patches, boundary conditions are carefully registered to enable assembling patches together to form large-scale animations.

In the introduction of this chapter, we pointed the importance of the animation quality versus computational performance trade-off in the design of crowd animation engines. This approach cannot do better: animations are precomputed and the level of animation quality can be checked beforehand, while the animation is performed by replaying animation.

This chapter also emphasizes that crowd patches can be used as a layer of abstraction of crowd animations, making them directly manipulable by users in a particularly intuitive way. Designers do not need expertise on crowd simulation systems to do so, or expertise in an animation system. They can focus on the artistic part of crowd animation.

However, we also showed that the the crowd patches raise a new kind of problem. The most difficult one certainly is to compute internal trajectories for patches. We proposed some technical solutions, but some issues still need addressing. For example, it would still be difficult reaching high levels of densities of moving characters using the proposed approach. Another issue which still need addressing is environment decomposition into set of patches.

But the perspectives for the crowd patches are numerous and opens promising directions to design new animation paradigms to populate virtual environments. We list some of them below:

- *Creating crowd patches libraries*: The key idea here is to create libraries of patches with different kinds of animation of behaviors (especially for endogenous characters) that would match typical kinds of environments, such as shopping streets, business districts, green parks, etc. Designers would then compose an animation by assembling patches of different types in a drag-and-drop fashion, with a pre-visualization of the animation content.

- *Making characters interactable*: When a character is animated by the crowd patches technique, he is moving according to a precomputed animation track. To enable interaction, we need to make those characters leave their animation track, providing them with interaction abilities as well as techniques to reintroduce the character (or new characters) on its animation track.

- *Dynamic changes of patches content*: A user focusing always on the same area of an environment populated with crowd patches may notice the animation periodicity. Also, the environment will always look the same in time, and, for example, day–night cycles cannot be reproduced. A solution would be to enable a dynamic change of patches content, but the difficulty is then to maintain coherent and continuous trajectories while performing this change.

Future developments will explore these directions, and cooperation with animation designers is also required to evaluate the usability and the advantages of the new crowd animation paradigms made possible by using the crowd patches approach.

References

1. M. W. Whittle. *Gait Analysis: An Introduction*. Butterworth-Heinemann, Oxford, UK, 2003.
2. D. Gale and L. S. Shapley. College admissions and the stability of marriage. *American Mathematical Monthly*, 69, 9–15, 1962.
3. D. Gusfield and R. W. Irving. *The Stable Marriage Problem: Structure and Algorithms*. MIT Press, Cambridge, MA, USA, 1989.

4. B. Yersin, J. Maïm, J. Pettré, and D. Thalmann. Crowd patches: Populating large-scale virtual environments for real-time applications. In *Proceedings of the 2009 Symposium on Interactive 3D Graphics and Games, I3D '09*, pp. 207–214, New York, USA, 2009. ACM.

5. A. Milliez, M. Wand, M.-P. Cani, and H.-P. Seidel. Mutable elastic models for sculpting structured shapes. *Computer Graphics Forum*, 32, 21–30, 2013.

6. O. Sorkine and M. Alexa. As-rigid-as-possible surface modeling. In *Symposium on Geometry Processing*, vol. 4, pp. 109–116, Barcelona, Spain, 2007.

5

Interactive Editing of Crowd Animation

Jongmin Kim and Jehee Lee

CONTENTS

Crowd simulation is the process of generating moving trajectories of many agents starting from initial conditions driven by rule-based models [1–4], flow models [5,6], logical formalisms [7,8], or prior observations [9–11]. The simulator usually has a number of parameters to tune and the quality of simulation often depends on the choice of parameter values. Even though many crowd simulation results are generally satisfactory, such visible artifacts as awkward behaviors and bottleneck situations may arise in a small portion of the simulation. An animator may need to tune the parameters carefully and rerun the simulator repeatedly until an overall satisfactory result is achieved. Sometimes, manual parameter tuning and repeated runs could be tedious and time consuming.

Alternatively, an animator can edit the simulation result interactively to make the desired changes [12–14]. Given a generally satisfactory simulation with small glitches, we can fix the glitches while the major portion of the simulation remains intact. In this way, animators can have immediate direct control over the simulation process and can manipulate multiple animated characters interactively by pinning and dragging the character motion as if they are tangible objects. The remainder of this chapter is organized as follows. We will begin with presenting the key requirements for interactive crowd editing. Next, we present a well-defined crowd model to take into account underlying crowd data structure, and then introduce two different but related types of crowd editing techniques: Laplacian crowd

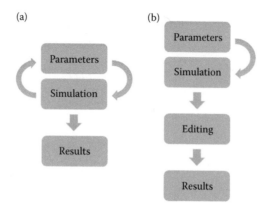

FIGURE 5.1
(a) Overall workflow of crowd simulation and (b) crowd simulation with crowd editing.

editing and cage-based crowd editing. We clarify some common concepts employed in the Laplacian crowd editing literature and describe the specific solutions of each approach. We conclude this chapter with a summary and introduction of further reading materials (Figure 5.1).

5.1 Requirements for Interactive Crowd Editing

Editing crowd animation is a cumbersome and challenging problem because crowd is not just a collection of agents but it has intrinsically complex properties. First, we can usually observe various types of interactions between agents in a crowd animation (e.g., carrying a box, holding hands). Handling such agents' various interactions during the animation production is not simple because the number of agents may be extremely large and agents should be carefully synchronized in both space and time. Second, a crowd animation usually includes hundreds of complex human actions; therefore, it is difficult for an animator to check carefully individual agents in the crowd scene. Finally, editing many character motions requires computational cost that grows significantly with the number of characters and their durations. To address these problems, the desired crowd editing technique should take into account the user with intuitive, easy-to-use user interfaces (UIs) and allow the user to directly manipulate crowd animations with computational efficiency.

5.1.1 UI Requirements

There are several UI requirements for interactive crowd editing. First, the crowd editing method should preserve the details and smoothness of the original crowd animation as much as possible since the user may want to manipulate crowd animation without visible artifacts, such as discontinuity of the agents' trajectories. Second, editing a group of characters coherently is highly required because manipulating individual characters independently is a laborious task. Third, the crowd editing algorithm provides not only for spatial domain but also for temporal domain to adjust the locations and speeds of the agents in the crowd animation. Finally, characters in crowd animation sometimes interact with each other so that the interaction should be maintained during the user manipulation.

5.1.2 Performance Requirements

The fast computation for editing crowd animation is a crucial requirement since the number of agents in the crowd animation may be extremely large. An animator may be faced with huge amounts of laborious tasks when adjusting the crowd animation as the number of agents, their durations, and interactions increase. The crowd editing system should provide a computational efficiency for handling hundreds of characters together, so that many agents in a crowd can promptly respond to the user's inputs while considering the given environment as well. Moreover, collision avoidance is a very important problem in the crowd animation community, especially in small local regions. The crowd editing method should have an advantage of easily detecting and resolving dense collisions between characters in a fast manner.

5.2 Crowd Modeling

Crowd animation is a set of motion segments. The motion path of a given motion fragment is a two-dimensional (2D) trajectory of the root positions, which are projected onto the flat ground. To be more precise, let $\mathbf{P}^\alpha, \mathbf{P}^\beta, \dots, \mathbf{P}^M$ be the motion paths of M characters. A motion path consists of a collection of linear curves, in which the points of a linear curve represents the time-varying location of a character $\mathbf{p}_i^\alpha \in \mathbb{R}^2$. Based on such a simple crowd representation, Kwon et al. [14] proposed 2D mesh graph structures as shown in Figure 5.2 for the group locomotion of characters, and defined the local coordinate for a motion path point $\mathbf{p}_i$ as an ordered triple of the points $(\mathbf{p}_i, \mathbf{p}_j, \mathbf{p}_k)$, where $\mathbf{p}_j$ and $\mathbf{p}_k$ are adjacent to $\mathbf{p}_i$.

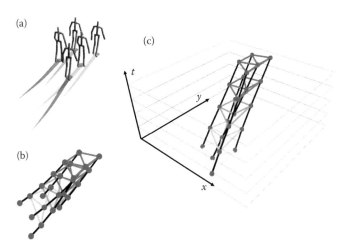

FIGURE 5.2
Graph representation of a group motion clip. (a) A short group motion clip. (b) A graph constructed from the clip. (c) Conceptual view of the graph. The graph encodes time-varying group formations. (From Kwon, T. et al., *ACM Trans. Graph.*, 27, 80, 2008. © 2008 ACM, Inc. Included here by permission.)

The tangent vector at the point $\mathbf{p}_i$ can be estimated by finite difference, $\mathbf{t}_i = \mathbf{p}_j - \mathbf{p}_k$, and the normal vector can be obtained as $\mathbf{n}_i = \mathbf{R}\mathbf{t}_i$, where $\mathbf{R}$ is a 2D rotation matrix of angle $90°$. The tangent vector $\mathbf{t}_i$ at point $\mathbf{p}_i$ is estimated by finite difference. Then, the coordinates of $\mathbf{p}_i$ can be represented with respect to its neighbors such that

$$\mathbf{p}_i = \mathbf{p}_j + c_x\mathbf{t}_i + c_y\mathbf{n}_i, \tag{5.1}$$

where (c_x, c_y) are the local coordinates of $\mathbf{p}_i$. Similar to the work by Kwon et al. [14], Kim et al. [13] defined the local coordinate with respect to each motion path point of a character by setting $j = i + 1$ and $k = i - 1$.

To handle interactive time warping, Kim et al. [13] first introduced the concept of the time track, which is a one-dimensional (1D) curve and uniformly sampled the time duration of a character. More precisely, a set of time tracks $\mathbf{T}^\alpha, \mathbf{T}^\beta, \ldots, \mathbf{T}^M$ of M characters are vertically aligned with their temporal relationships. Stretching and squeezing the time track of each motion in horizontal direction by simply clicking and dragging a time point achieve interactive time warping (Figure 5.3).

In addition, the interactions between characters are represented by both the spatial and temporal constraints, which are linear equations. If character α at frame i is interacting with character β at frame j, the relationship is written as

$$\mathbf{p}_i^\alpha = \mathbf{p}_j^\beta + d_x(\mathbf{p}_{j+1}^\beta - \mathbf{p}_{j-1}^\beta) + d_y\mathbf{R}(\mathbf{p}_{j+1}^\beta - \mathbf{p}_{j-1}^\beta), \tag{5.2}$$

where (d_x, d_y) is the spatial local coordinates between the character α and β. The temporal relationship of character α and β is written as follows:

$$t_i^\alpha = t_j^\beta + g. \tag{5.3}$$

Two characters are synchronized at frame i and j if g equals zero.

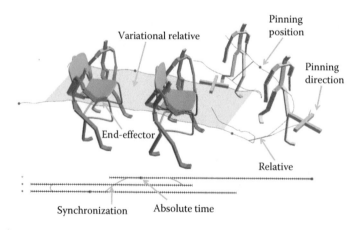

FIGURE 5.3
Interactive path editing with spatial and temporal constraints. (From Kim, M. et al., *ACM Trans. Graph.*, 28 (3), 79, 2009. © 2009 ACM, Inc. Included here by permission.)

5.3 Laplacian Crowd Editing

The basic idea of Laplacian crowd editing methods [13,14] is as follows: For a given set of motion clips, we combine them together, and then deform them to fit the requirements of a specific crowd animation scene. To achieve them successfully, the methods exploited and adapted as-rigid-as-possible (ARAP) mesh deformation algorithm [15], which accommodates both smoothly editing a 2D triangle mesh and preserving details of the original shape of the 2D mesh. First, Kwon et al. [14] provides a good set of editing operations that enable a user to edit a collection of trajectories of example character motions. The user can interactively deform the 2D mesh graph by pinning and dragging the 2D mesh vertices to the user's intended locations. The method then computes the new 2D mesh vertex positions in a way of preserving the initial 2D mesh configuration as much as possible while retaining the pinned or dragged vertex positions. Similarly, Kim et al. [13] tackled the problem of interactive editing of multiple character motions. They extended the scope of manipulation of crowd animation by handling an arbitrary type of character motions with a wider range of interpersonal interaction in the crowd animation scene. Moreover, they presented a technique for structural motion editing, which allows short motion fragments to be automatically inserted or deleted while interactively manipulating the character motions. Structural motion editing is a smart way of avoiding excessive deformation, if the crowd animation includes less than a dozen characters (Figure 5.4).

The Laplacian crowd editing [13,14] consists of two steps of optimizations: shape preserving deformation and scale compensation. In the first optimization step, it yields an intermediate result that often has large scaling artifacts. To address this issue, the second optimization step is performed to compensate scaling and maintain the original length of the character motion paths.

5.3.1 Shape Preservation

The first optimization step of Laplacian crowd editing tries to minimize the distortions in all local coordinates of the crowd animation while satisfying user-defined constraints. Concatenating all linear equations derived by Equation 5.1 leads to a linear system $\mathbf{A}_p\bar{\mathbf{p}} = \mathbf{0}$, where $\bar{\mathbf{p}} = (\bar{x}_0, \bar{y}_0, \bar{x}_1, \bar{y}_1, \bar{x}_2, \bar{y}_2, \ldots)^\top$ is a vector of deformed character motion

FIGURE 5.4
Laplacian crowd editing: The snapshot of the crowd animation in a downtown scene (left); 78 characters carry boxes in relay (right). (From Kim, M. et al., *ACM Trans. Graph.*, 28 (3), 79, 2009; Kwon, T. et al., *ACM Trans. Graph.*, 27, 80, 2008. © 2008, 2009 ACM, Inc. Included here by permission.)

path points. Combining it with user-defined spatial position constraints $\mathbf{B}_s \bar{\mathbf{p}} = \mathbf{b}_s$ forms an overdetermined linear system:

$$\mathbf{M}_p \bar{\mathbf{p}} = \begin{pmatrix} \mathbf{W}_p \mathbf{A}_p \\ \mathbf{B}_s \end{pmatrix} \bar{\mathbf{p}} = \begin{pmatrix} 0 \\ \mathbf{b}_s \end{pmatrix} = \mathbf{m}_p, \tag{5.4}$$

where $\mathbf{W}_p$ is a diagonal weighing matrix of how well the path deforms subject to the user-defined constraints.

5.3.2 Scale Compensation

The second optimization adjusts the intermediate result $\bar{\mathbf{p}}$ to remove scaling artifacts. Consider the k-th edge $\bar{\mathbf{e}}_k$ between two successive points $\bar{\mathbf{p}}_i$ and $\bar{\mathbf{p}}_j$ in the current character motion path of interest. Let $\bar{\mathbf{e}}_k = (\bar{\mathbf{p}}_i - \bar{\mathbf{p}}_j)\|\mathbf{p}_i - \mathbf{p}_j\|/\|\bar{\mathbf{p}}_i - \bar{\mathbf{p}}_j\|$ be a vector, which is scaled to its original length in the undeformed edge $\mathbf{e}_k$, and $\mathbf{l}_c$ is a vector of $\{\bar{\mathbf{e}}_k\}$. We can obtain the scale-adjusted motion paths by minimizing $E(\hat{\mathbf{p}}) = \sum_k \|\hat{\mathbf{e}}_k - \bar{\mathbf{e}}_k\|^2$, where $\hat{\mathbf{e}}_k = \hat{\mathbf{p}}_i - \hat{\mathbf{p}}_j$. Similarly, the second step optimization forms an overdetermined linear system:

$$\mathbf{M}_c \hat{\mathbf{p}} = \begin{pmatrix} \mathbf{W}_c \mathbf{A}_c \\ \mathbf{B}_s \end{pmatrix} \hat{\mathbf{p}} = \begin{pmatrix} \mathbf{W}_c \mathbf{l}_c \\ \mathbf{b}_s \end{pmatrix} = \mathbf{m}_c, \tag{5.5}$$

where $\hat{\mathbf{p}}$ is the final bended character motion paths and $\mathbf{W}_c$ is a diagonal weighing matrix how well character motion paths stretch. The two-step optimizations become the augmented linear systems because of taking hard spatial constraints $\mathbf{H}_s \bar{\mathbf{p}} = \mathbf{h}_s$ to enforce the user-defined constraints precisely:

$$\begin{pmatrix} \mathbf{M}_p^\top \mathbf{M}_p & \mathbf{H}_s^\top \\ \mathbf{H}_s & 0 \end{pmatrix} \begin{pmatrix} \bar{\mathbf{p}} \\ \lambda_p \end{pmatrix} = \begin{pmatrix} \mathbf{M}_p^\top \mathbf{m}_p \\ \mathbf{h}_s \end{pmatrix}, \tag{5.6}$$

$$\begin{pmatrix} \mathbf{M}_c^\top \mathbf{M}_c & \mathbf{H}_s^\top \\ \mathbf{H}_s & 0 \end{pmatrix} \begin{pmatrix} \hat{\mathbf{p}} \\ \lambda_c \end{pmatrix} = \begin{pmatrix} \mathbf{M}_c^\top \mathbf{m}_c \\ \mathbf{h}_s \end{pmatrix}, \tag{5.7}$$

where λ_p and λ_c are the Lagrange multiplier vectors. Solving two augmented systems sequentially completes the Laplacian crowd editing in the space domain. Furthermore, Kim et al. [13] achieved a better smoothness by reformulating the scale compensation energy in terms of the accelerations along the motion trajectory.

5.3.3 Interactive Time Warping

The crowd editing system proposed by Kim et al. [13] provides interactive time warping based on 1D Laplacian curve editing approach. A user can easily choose some arbitrary key-frames and modify the duration between key-frames. The time warping method interpolates between the given key-times as shown in Figure 5.5. Only the first optimization step of the Laplacian editing algorithm is done for interactive time warping because the scaling artifact do not occur in 1D time domain. Preserving the uniform distance between the i-th and j-th key-frames is formulated as $t_{i+1} - t_i = d_i$. Concatenating the linear equations of all key-frames leads to a linear system $\mathbf{T}_t \bar{\mathbf{t}} = \mathbf{d}_t$, where $\bar{\mathbf{t}} = (\bar{t}_0, \bar{t}_1, \cdots)^\top$ is a long

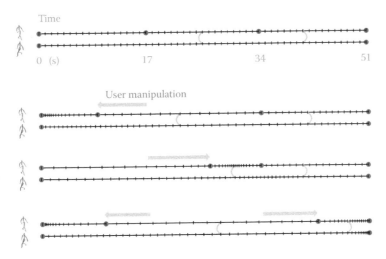

FIGURE 5.5
Interactive time warping of two synchronized time tracks. The original uniform time sequences at the top are interactively manipulated to generate smooth, synchronized time warps. The user manipulates only one track and the other track is warped accordingly. (From Kim, M. et al., *ACM Trans. Graph.*, 28 (3), 79, 2009. © 2009 ACM, Inc. Included here by permission.)

vector representing a warped time. Combining it with user-defined position constraints $\mathbf{B}_t \bar{\mathbf{t}} = \mathbf{b}_t$ forms an overdetermined linear system:

$$\mathbf{M}_t \bar{\mathbf{t}} = \begin{pmatrix} \mathbf{T}_t \\ \mathbf{B}_t \end{pmatrix} \bar{\mathbf{t}}_t = \begin{pmatrix} \mathbf{d} \\ \mathbf{b}_t \end{pmatrix} = \mathbf{m}_t. \tag{5.8}$$

Then, the augmented system considering hard temporal constraints $\mathbf{H}_t \bar{\mathbf{t}} = \mathbf{h}_t$ can be written as follows:

$$\begin{pmatrix} \mathbf{M}_t^\top \mathbf{M}_t & \mathbf{H}_t^\top \\ \mathbf{H}_t & \mathbf{0} \end{pmatrix} \begin{pmatrix} \bar{\mathbf{t}} \\ \boldsymbol{\lambda}_t \end{pmatrix} = \begin{pmatrix} \mathbf{M}_t^\top \mathbf{m}_t \\ \mathbf{h}_t \end{pmatrix}, \tag{5.9}$$

where $\boldsymbol{\lambda}_t$ is the Lagrange multiplier vector. For preventing time from going backward, the linear inequality constraints with predefined upper and lower boundaries, such as $d_{min} \le t_{i+1} - t_i \le d_{max}$, are necessary. Similar to the work by Kim et al. [12], we can easily solve the iterative time warping problem with the aforementioned inequality constraints by converting it into a quadratic programming (QP) optimization.

5.3.4 Structural Motion Editing

The structural (discrete) motion editing scheme, which was first proposed by Kim et al. [13], allows the user to change the structural shape of crowd animation automatically. The discrete editing strategy is also combined with continuous motion path editing and provides insertion, deletion, and replacement of the motion segments in response to interactive adjustments by the user (see Figure 5.6). If a user updates either spatial or temporal constraints, the Laplacian crowd editing system considers all possible discrete transformations and selects the most fitted transformation. Then, the given motion paths are deformed in order to meet user-defined constraints accurately using the continuous motion path editing (see Algorithm 5.1).

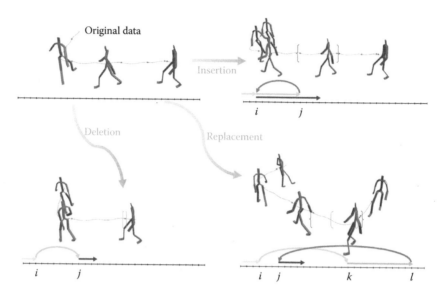

FIGURE 5.6
Three types of discrete transformations. (From Kim, M. et al., *ACM Trans. Graph.*, 28 (3), 79, 2009. © 2009 ACM, Inc. Included here by permission.)

Algorithm 5.1: Discrete Motion Path Editing

$\mathbb{P}$: A set of motion paths;
$\mathbb{P}'$: A set of deformed, time-warped paths;
$\mathbb{C}$: A set of spatial and temporal constraints;

1 **while** *user manipulation* **do**
2   **if** $\mathbb{C}$ *is updated* **then**
3          $\mathbb{P}_{new} \leftarrow \mathbb{P};$
4          $\mathbb{P}'_{new} \leftarrow \texttt{LaplacianEditing}\,(\,\mathbb{P}, \mathbb{C}\,);$
5          $E_{new} \leftarrow \texttt{DeformationEnergy}\,(\,\mathbb{P}_{new}, \mathbb{P}'_{new}, \mathbb{C}\,);$

6   **foreach** $\mathbb{P}_c \in \texttt{DiscreteTransform}\,(\,\mathbb{P}\,)$ **do**
7              $\mathbb{P}'_c \leftarrow \texttt{LaplacianEditing}\,(\,\mathbb{P}_c, \mathbb{C}\,);$
8              $E_c \leftarrow \texttt{DeformationEnergy}\,(\,\mathbb{P}_c, \mathbb{P}'_c, \mathbb{C}\,);$

9   **if** $E_c < E_{new}$ **then**
10                 $\mathbb{P}_{new} \leftarrow \mathbb{P}_c;$
11                 $\mathbb{P}'_{new} \leftarrow \mathbb{P}'_c;$
12                 $E_{new} \leftarrow E_c;$

13         $\mathbb{P} \leftarrow \mathbb{P}_{new};$
14         $\mathbb{P}' \leftarrow \mathbb{P}'_{new};$

5.4 Cage-Based Crowd Editing

While the Laplacian crowd editing is an effective method for the manipulation of the crowd animation with the original detail preservation, it leads to poor performance when editing large-scale crowd animations since the size of optimization gradually scales pertaining to the number of animated characters and the duration of the crowd animation. To achieve an interactive performance, Kim et al. [12] proposed a novel cage-based crowd editing method, based on the hybrid deformation that combines the surface-based deformation and the space-based deformation: a coarse controllable 2D mesh is embedded in a given crowd animation, and the 2D mesh is deformed using the ARAP mesh deformation [16] while satisfying a set of the user-defined constraints. The method then computes the desired crowd animation result using the precomputed barycentric coordinates in which the computations can be efficiently parallelized. As a result, the cage-based crowd editing method achieved almost two orders of magnitude faster performance than previous methods [13,14]. We would like to refer the readers to the survey by Cohen [17] for more overview of the hybrid deformation. In this section, we describe several convenient UI features of the cage-based crowd editing, and then explain the technical details of editing of the cage and the motion paths. Finally, we discuss how well cage-based editing method handles the dense collision problem between characters when compared to previous work [14].

5.4.1 UI Features

Aside from the performance gain that the cage-based crowd editing achieved, the cage-based interface provides many convenient UI features over previous systems presented in Kwon et al. [14] and Kim et al. [13]. The previous systems determine the deformable structure from input motion data, so the user manipulation is restricted by the underlying structure of the motion data. The key advantage of cage-based crowd editing system is that it allows animators to determine the control structure conveniently. Those UI features include globally and locally coordinated cages, efficient handling of arbitrary human motions in both space and time domains, convenient management of hundreds of time tracks, and cage conversion between spatial and temporal domains, and so on (Figure 5.7).

- *Global and local coordination.* A user often tries to manipulate a group of character motions in a globally coordinated manner in both space and time. The cage-based

FIGURE 5.7
Many pedestrians walk straight in the crowd animation (left). We interactively manipulate the crowd animation to follow an s-curve (right). (From Kim, J. et al., *ACM Trans. Graph.*, 33 (4), 83, 2014. © 2014 ACM, Inc. Included here by permission.)

interface provides the grouping operation to manipulate multiple characters coherently. The user often wants to edit only some portion of an animation while the other part remains intact. The UI for cage editing is similar to the lasso tool in image editing software and supports various types of locality in both space and time.

- *Versatility and flexibility.* The UI for cage editing is versatile and flexible to edit with arbitrary types of animations, including locomotions, static gestures, and even highly dynamic motions. The system automatically extracts space and time information from the original scene data regardless of motion types and the number of characters. Various types of animations are able to be included in a single or several spatial/temporal cages and edited simultaneously.

- *Time track management.* The crowd animation consists of a set of time tracks. The temporal cage encloses the entire (or some portions of) time tracks of many characters. Given hundreds of characters, the crowd editing system will have many time tracks to manage. To address this issue, the cage-based crowd editing system provides several convenient UI features to facilitate time track management. Basically, the user can reorder time tracks dynamically to exploit their coherence. Time tracks can be sorted along an arbitrary spatial direction. In addition, cage-based selection effectively clusters time tracks into groups. Time tracks can be selected and deselected in both spatial and temporal domains. The system can highlight a small subset of time tracks while leaving the others intact.

- *Cage conversion.* A temporal cage selects a portion of crowd animation in the time domain and a spatial cage can be constructed to enclose the corresponding portion of crowd animation in the spatial domain. Similarly, if the user produces a spatial cage, the system automatically converts it into the corresponding temporal cage. The cage conversion between spatial and temporal cages is necessary if the user wants to manipulate some specific portions from a cluttered crowd animation scene in which the character motion paths are tangled spatially; thus the spatial cage construction by freehand drawing is difficult for the user to precisely select the desired portions, which are untangled in the temporal domain. The cage conversion operation allows the user to automatically create a spatial cage, which are a compatible cage in time domain.

5.4.2 Cage Deformation

Because of the reduced degrees of freedom (DOFs) from the number of motion path points to the number of cage vertices, the cage-based crowd editing method has a crucial advantage of computational efficiency. The basic idea of cage-based crowd editing is as follows: The cage consists of a small number of vertices and encloses animated characters to be modified. The cage is a flexible deformable object, and the interior geometry of the cage is defined using Delaunay tessellation. A user is able to deform the cage by pinning and moving cage vertices to edit motion paths coherently (see Figure 5.8). The motion path and time track points inside the given 2D cage mesh are parameterized using the mean value coordinates (MVC) [18,19]. The MVC weights $\{\lambda_1, \lambda_2, \dots, \lambda_m\}$ of a motion path point $\mathbf{p}_k$ is computed from the cage boundary vertices $\mathbf{v} = \{\mathbf{v}_1, \mathbf{v}_2, \dots, \mathbf{v}_m\}$, and point $\mathbf{p}_k$ as follows:

$$\lambda_i = \frac{w_i}{\sum_{j=1}^{m} w_j}, \quad w_i = \frac{\tan(\phi_{i-1}/2) + \tan(\phi_i/2)}{\|\mathbf{p}_k - \mathbf{v}_i\|}, \tag{5.10}$$

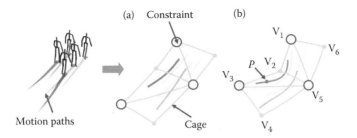

FIGURE 5.8
Editing motion paths with a cage. (a) The spatial cage shown in green encloses the motion paths. (b) The motion paths are edited according to the cage deformation.

where ϕ_i is angle $\angle \mathbf{v}_{i+1}, \mathbf{p}_k, \mathbf{v}_i$ in the polygon. The location of the motion path point is defined as the weighted linear combination of the cage vertices. When the user moves the cage vertex, the updated k-th motion path point $\hat{\mathbf{p}}_k$ is computed as

$$\hat{\mathbf{p}}_k = \sum_{i=1}^{m} \lambda_i^k \hat{\mathbf{v}}_i, \tag{5.11}$$

where $\hat{\mathbf{v}} = \{\hat{\mathbf{v}}_1, \hat{\mathbf{v}}_2, \ldots, \hat{\mathbf{v}}_m\}$ are the newly updated cage vertices. In a similar way, we can also define the MVC $\{\mu_1, \mu_2, \ldots, \mu_n\}$ of the time points t_k on the time track with the temporal cage vertices $\mathbf{u} = \{\mathbf{u}_1, \mathbf{u}_2, \ldots, \mathbf{u}_n\}$. In the temporal cage, the x-component of $\mathbf{u}_k$ represents the k-th reference time while its y-component is a constant value to list time tracks vertically. The time point $\hat{t}_k$ on a time track can be written as a weighted linear combination $\hat{t}_k = \sum_{i=1}^{n} \mu_i^k \hat{\mathbf{u}}_i$ with the temporal cage vertices.

The cage may not cover the entire motion paths and the cage-based crowd editing method has to ensure that motion paths are smooth across the cage boundary. The local cage allows an animator to edit a small portion of the animation enclosed by the local cage, while leaving the remaining portions of the crowd animation intact. The local cage has a user-specified padding area with smooth transitioning of the MVC weights along the motion paths. The motion path point $\mathbf{p}_k$ can be written as the linear interpolation between the weighted linear combination of the updated cage vertices and the original motion path point. Here, L is the user-defined padding length and L' is the arc-length from the inner motion point $\mathbf{p}_k$ to the intersection of the cage boundary and the corresponding motion path, respectively. The updated motion point $\hat{\mathbf{p}}_k$ in the padding area is computed by $\hat{\mathbf{p}}_k = \epsilon \sum_i \lambda_i \hat{\mathbf{v}}_i + (1 - \epsilon) \mathbf{p}_k$, where $0 \leq \epsilon \leq 1$. Here, ϵ is a smooth ease-in/ease-out function of arc-length ratio L'/L.

The interactive cage-based editing is based on the ARAP mesh deformation scheme [16] in order to reduce the DOFs for manipulation of the cage vertices and preserve the original shape of the cage mesh as much as possible. The ARAP mesh deformation tries to minimize the total deformation errors for all local regions:

$$E_s(\hat{\mathbf{v}}, \{\mathbf{R}_i\}) = \sum_i \sum_{j \in \mathcal{N}(i)} w_{ij} \|(\hat{\mathbf{v}}_i - \hat{\mathbf{v}}_j) - \mathbf{R}_i(\mathbf{v}_i - \mathbf{v}_j)\|^2, \tag{5.12}$$

where $\hat{\mathbf{v}}_i$ is the i-th vertex location in the deformed cage mesh, w_{ij} is the weight of the edge between the i-th and j-th vertex, and $\{\mathbf{R}_i\}$ is the estimated rotation matrices between the original and deformed triangles of the cage mesh. The user is able to impose position constraints on the cage vertices to manipulate it such as $\hat{v}_i = c_i$. Concatenating all position constraints forms a quadratic energy term $E_c = \|C\hat{v} - c\|^2$, where $c = \{c_i\}$. In addition, another quadratic energy term $E_d = \|D\hat{v}\|^2$ is obtained by considering all relative constraints from Equation 5.2. To obtain the resulting cage mesh, we have to minimize three energy terms E_s, E_c, and E_d with unknown variables $\hat{v}$ and $\{R_i\}$; however, it is a nonlinear optimization. Alternating least-squares optimization method [16] efficiently solves the nonlinear optimization. It starts from setting the initial configuration of $\{R_i\}$ as identity matrices, and all cage vertices $\hat{v}$ are computed. All rotation matrices $\{R_i\}$ are obtained using singular value decomposition (SVD). We then solve for cage vertices $\hat{v}$ while fixing $\{R_i\}$. These two steps iterate alternately several times until the solution converges.

5.4.3 Snapback

Excessive stretching of a crowd animation entails unrealistically longer strides. The cage-based crowd editing system includes the snapback algorithm, which automatically snaps motion paths back to allowable editing range when the user releases the mouse. The snapback method also has a role as an indicator informing whether or not the cages have enough freedom to support manipulation tasks. The key idea behind the snapback algorithm is to limit the length of the edges of the cage, and the snapback constraints are formulated as quadratic inequality constraints with both upper and lower bounds. Unfortunately, handling snapback constraints is intrinsically a non-convex problem since the constraints are non-convex. Therefore, it is not easy to solve the snapback problem when using a conventional QP solver. To address this issue, Kim et al. [12] relaxed the non-convexity using semi-definite programming (SDP) and solve it more efficiently. More details are provided in the studies [12,20].

5.4.4 Temporal Cage

The cage-based crowd editing system can also adjust the speeds of the characters coherently by editing the cage in temporal domain. Temporal cage manipulation is much simpler than spatial cage manipulation because temporal cage vertices are only allowed moving on the horizontal direction. The temporal cage encloses the time tracks, and is constructed by uniformly sampling the temporal cage's bottom and top boundaries only, such that $\hat{u}_{i+1}^x - \hat{u}_i^x = d_i$, where $\hat{u}_i^x$ is the x-component of the i-th temporal cage vertex. As we mentioned earlier in Section 5.3, merging all constraints yields a sparse linear system from Equation 5.8, and the desired temporal cage vertices are obtained by solving the QP-based optimization.

5.4.5 Collision Avoidance

Collision avoidance is an important problem in the field of the crowd animation. Cage-based collision resolution method efficiently addresses dense collisions between characters. When a collision is detected, the method creates the spatial cages, which enclose the related characters around the collision. The collision then is addressed via cage translation. Nevertheless, if other characters are moving around the collision areas, new collisions could occur. The method performs several iterations until all collisions are resolved. The cage-based collision avoidance approach includes three strategies to achieve interactive

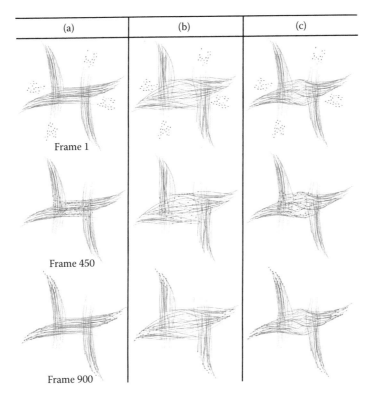

FIGURE 5.9
Comparison of collision handling: (a) 100 characters from four directions crossing in a narrow space. (b) Collision avoidance by Kwon et al. [14] (240 s). (c) Collision avoidance by our method (4 s). The cage-based collision avoidance is much faster and causes less deformation. (From Kim, J. et al., *ACM Trans. Graph.*, 33 (4), 83, 2014. © 2014 ACM, Inc. Included here by permission.)

performance. First, each spatial cage consists of only four vertices to reduce the computation cost of calculating the MVC. Second, the method uses the MVC only and one type of cage deformation, which is a rigid translation in opposite directions of the collision. Finally, the method gradually reduces the size of spatial cages over the iterations to achieve fast convergence. Figure 5.9 shows the collision handling results by Kwon et al. [14] and our cage-based method. Compared to the previous method, the cage-based collision avoidance scheme is about 60 times faster and also shows less deviation from the original animation. The navigation behaviors for collision avoidance depend on the size of spatial cages and thus are controllable. *Larger cages make smoother detouring behaviors, while smaller cages localize the effect of collision avoidance.*

5.5 Summary and Further Reading

We have presented an overview of the main paradigms of interactive crowd editing methods. The crowd editing methods [12–14] were inspired by well-known geometry editing methods [15,16,18,19]. However, geometry editing techniques cannot be applied directly to crowd editing because crowd editing requires different functionalities and features than geometry editing. Crowd animation has both spatial and temporal aspects, which are quite different in nature to each other. Handling the interactions between spatial and temporal aspects is important in crowd editing. The interpersonal relationship between individuals poses either dense, time-varying constraints or sparse, instantaneous constraints. Collision handling is very important for crowd animation, but often ignored in geometry editing.

The two major concepts of crowd simulation and crowd editing methods are not competing, but complementary to each other. Crowd simulation techniques can be effectively used when we create crowd animation from scratch. However, it is difficult and tedious to control character behaviors at specific local areas by simulation because it involves repeated parameter tuning and long simulation time. Using the crowd editing system, an animator can perform specific editing on top of the simulated results to achieve the desired animation.

For further readings, we recommend the recent work by Jordao et al. [21], which provides an efficient structure crowd editing method in a way of adding and deleting precomputed crowd patches using mutable elastic models proposed by Milliez et al. [22]. Lockwood and Singh [23] presented a motion path editing system with a set of biomechanically inspired constraints. Based on the Lapalcian motion editing method [13], Choi et al. [24] proposed an interactive path planning method for a character in cluttered environments. Finally, Kim et al. [25] created a dense crowd animation by packing continuously short motion clips while taking into account interactions between characters.

References

1. S. J. Guy, J. Chhugani, C. Kim, N. Satish, M. Lin, D. Manocha, and P. Dubey. Clearpath: Highly parallel collision avoidance for multi-agent simulation. In *Proceedings of the 2009 SIGGRAPH/Eurographics Symposium on Computer Animation*, pp. 177–187, New Orleans, USA, 2009.

2. S. R. Musse and D. Thalmann. A model of human crowd behavior: Group inter-relationship and collision detection analysis. In *Computer Animation and Simulation '97*, pp. 39–51, Budapest, Hungary, 1997.

3. N. Pelechano, J. M. Allbeck, and N. I. Badler. Controlling individual agents in high-density crowd simulation. In *Proceedings of the 2007 ACM SIGGRAPH/Eurographics Symposium on Computer Animation*, pp. 99–108, San Diego, USA, 2007.

4. C. W. Reynolds. Flocks, herds and schools: A distributed behavioral model. In *Proceedings of SIGGRAPH 87*, pp. 25–34, Anaheim, California, USA, 1987.

5. S. Chenney. Flow tiles. In *SIGGRAPH/Eurographics Symposium on Computer Animation '04: Proceedings of the 2004 ACM SIGGRAPH/Eurographics Symposium on Computer Animation*, pp. 233–242, Grenoble, France, 2004.

6. A. Treuille, S. Cooper, and Z. Popovic. Continuum crowds. *ACM Transactions on Graphics*, 25(3):1160–1168, 2006.

7. M. Kapadia, S. Singh, G. Reinman, and P. Faloutsos. A behavior-authoring framework for multiactor simulations. *IEEE Computer Graphics and Applications*, 31(6):45–55, 2011.

8. A. Shoulson, N. Marshak, M. Kapadia, N. Badler et al. Adapt: The agent development and prototyping test bed. *IEEE Transactions on Visualization and Computer Graphics*, 20(7):1035–1047, 2014.

9. E. Ju, M. G. Choi, M. Park, J. Lee, K. H. Lee, and S. Takahashi. Morphable crowds. *ACM Transactions on Graphics*, 29(6):140:1–140:10, 2010.

10. K. H. Lee, M. G. Choi, Q. Hong, and J. Lee. Group behavior from video: A data-driven approach to crowd simulation. In *Proceedings of the 2007 ACM SIGGRAPH/Eurographics Symposium on Computer Animation*, pp. 109–118, San Diego, USA, 2007.

11. A. Lerner, Y. Chrysanthou, and D. Lischinski. Crowds by example. *Computer Graphics Forum*, 26(3):655–664, 2007.

12. J. Kim, Y. Seol, T. Kwon, and J. Lee. Interactive manipulation of large-scale crowd animation. *ACM Transactions on Graphics*, 33(4):83, 2014.

13. M. Kim, K. Hyun, J. Kim, and J. Lee. Synchronized multi-character motion editing. *ACM Transactions on Graphics*, 28(3):79, 2009.

14. T. Kwon, K. H. Lee, J. Lee, and S. Takahashi. Group motion editing. *ACM Transactions on Graphics*, 27:80, 2008.

15. T. Igarashi, T. Moscovich, and J. F. Hughes. As-rigid-as-possible shape manipulation. *ACM Transactions on Graphics*, 24(3):1134–1141, 2005.

16. O. Sorkine and M. Alexa. As-rigid-as-possible surface modeling. In *Symposium on Geometry Processing*, vol. 4, pp. 109–116, 2007.

17. D. Cohen-Or. Space deformations, surface deformations and the opportunities in-between. *Journal of Computer Science and Technology*, 24(1):2–5, 2009.

18. M. S. Floater. Mean value coordinates. *Computer Aided Geometric Design*, 20(1):19–27, 2003.

19. K. Hormann and M. S. Floater. Mean value coordinates for arbitrary planar polygons. *ACM Transactions on Graphics*, 25(4):1424–1441, 2006.

20. A. d'Aspremont and S. Boyd. Relaxations and randomized methods for nonconvex qcqps. In *EE392o Class Notes*, Stanford University, 2003.

21. K. Jordao, J. Pettré, M. Christie, and M.-P. Cani. Crowd sculpting: A space-time sculpting method for populating virtual environments. *Computer Graphics Forum*, 33:351–360, 2014.

22. A. Milliez, M. Wand, M.-P. Cani, and H.-P. Seidel. Mutable elastic models for sculpting structured shapes. *Computer Graphics Forum*, 32:21–30, 2013.

23. N. Lockwood and K. Singh. Biomechanically-inspired motion path editing. In *Proceedings of the 2011 ACM SIGGRAPH/Eurographics Symposium on Computer Animation*, pp. 267–276, Vancouver, Canada. ACM, 2011.

24. M. G. Choi, M. Kim, K. L. Hyun, and J. Lee. Deformable motion: Squeezing into cluttered environments. *Computer Graphics Forum*, 30:445–453, 2011.

25. M. Kim, Y. Hwang, K. Hyun, and J. Lee. Tiling motion patches. In *Proceedings of the 11th ACM SIGGRAPH/Eurographics Conference on Computer Animation*, pp. 117–126, Lausanne, Switzerland. Eurographics Association, 2012.

6

Simulation of Collective Crowd Behavior with Psychological Parameters*

Funda Durupınar, Uğur Güdükbay, Aytek Aman, and Norman I. Badler

CONTENTS

6.1 Introduction

Simulating the behavior of human crowds requires an understanding of the interaction between individuals, which may be complex and unpredictable. Crowds sometimes display spontaneous collective behavior, the emergence of which is formulated by social scientists using different theories such as contagion models or predisposition hypotheses. Crowd simulation research as well as industrial applications have also gained a new direction of modeling and visualizing different categories of collective crowd behavior [1–5].

Crowds are categorized in terms of their dominant behavior according to a taxonomy defined by Brown [6]. The main categories of this taxonomy are audiences and mobs. Both audiences and mobs are composed of individuals with common purposes. However, audiences are passive crowds whereas mobs are active. Examples of audiences include students in a classroom and pedestrians who are polarized around a street player. Mobs are classified into four groups: aggressive, escaping, acquisitive, and expressive mobs. Aggressive

---

* This chapter is mostly based on our article describing the system that enables the specification of different crowd types ranging from audiences to mobs [2].

mobs are defined by anger, whereas escaping mobs are defined by fear. Acquisitive mobs are centripetal and they converge upon a desired object. For example, hunger riots and looting of shops and houses are performed by acquisitive mobs. Finally, expressive mobs congregate for expressing a purpose, such as in strikes, rallies, or parades. Mobs are discriminated from audiences by their emotionality, irrationality, and mental homogeneity. So, an expressive mob differs from an audience by its ease of bending social norms and proneness to violence. When mob behavior emerges, feelings preponderate reason. Thus, affective reasoning dominates the decision-making process [7].

We provide animators/designers with a tool to easily simulate the behavior of different crowd types, especially mobs, according to the described taxonomy [2]. Because the defining trait of mobs is their emotionality, we aim to build a system based on a psychological model that effectively represents emotions and emotional interactions between agents. There has been extensive research on incorporating psychological models into the simulation of autonomous agents. We follow the OCEAN (openness, conscientiousness, extroversion, agreeableness, neuroticism) personality mapping approach presented in Reference 8. Personality is valuable for designing heterogeneous crowd behavior. However, with its static nature, personality alone is not sufficient to represent an impulsive mob agent. Therefore, we introduce an emotion component that modulates agents' decision-making processes, superimposed on their personalities. Based on this strategy, agents' personalities and their appraisal of the environment and each other dynamically update their emotions, leading to different emergent behaviors. We employ the widely recognized OCC (Ortony, Clore, Collins) model [9] to simulate cognitive appraisal and emotions.

In addition to emotionality, mental homogeneity is attributed to collective behavior, where mental states of individuals are mirrored by others and these states are disseminated within the crowd. Gustav Le Bon explains mental homogeneity as a product of emotional contagion [10], which emphasizes a disease-like spreading of emotions. Serious implications of emotional contagion within crowds include panic, stampedes, lynchings—characteristic mob behaviors that result from widespread fear, anxiety, and anger. In light of these, in order to activate irrational behavior due to mental homogeneity, we formulate an emotion contagion model.

We suggest that using a parametric psychology component with emotion contagion facilitates the simulation of mob behavior as it requires minimal user expertise and provides scalability. Instead of defining probability functions over state transitions, we consult the affective state of the agent to determine which action to take in a specific situation; thus, different behaviors can be combined easily. The internal mechanisms of the psychology module are abstracted: the only information that a user needs to provide is the personality distribution of the crowd. With a simple adjustment of personality parameters, a regular calm crowd can transform into an emotional mob. The benefit of using a personality model as input lies in its ability to provide the animator with an intuitive and principled way to produce a range of different behaviors. Because our mapping is deep (a small input set fans out to control many more internal parameters), identifying input with personality parameters maintains interface simplicity over larger, cumbersome, interacting, parametric control sets.

In order to control the mapping from personality distribution to emotional crowd behaviors, we use a decision-making strategy also based on psychology literature. We utilize the pleasure–arousal–dominance (PAD) model [11] to determine the current emotional state and thus select relevant behaviors. Because the PAD model is associated with consistent mappings to the OCC emotions as well as the OCEAN personality traits, it provides a convenient medium between these two models.

Our system enables the authoring of various scenarios, where the animator can initialize agent groups with different roles and personality traits. Agents then act according to the scenario, exhibiting various behaviors based on their affective states triggered by interactions with each other and the environment. Personality, environmental stimuli, and agent roles contribute to the heterogeneity of the simulated crowds. We use the Unity [12] artificial intelligence (AI) path-finding system for crowd simulation. We demonstrate the performance of our framework on two cases: a protest scenario with protesters and police and a sales scenario similar to a Black Friday event, where agents rush into a computer store selling items with low prices (cf. Figure 6.1).

(a)

(b)

FIGURE 6.1
Still frames from two crowd scenarios representing expressive and acquisitive mobs: (a) protest and (b) sales.

6.2 System

The mind of a virtual agent consists of several elements that determine cognitive, perceptual, and psychological characteristics. The agent behaves according to the interaction of these features with environmental stimuli. The conceptual elements that comprise an agent are shown in Figure 6.2.

Perceived stimuli are passed on to the cognitive component, where agents process incoming data to create appropriate responses. The cognitive unit of an agent's mind is the appraisal component. Appraisal determines how individuals assess events, other individuals, themselves, and objects. Their evaluation produces an emotional outcome and aids decision making. Emotions are short term and elicited from events, other agents, and objects [9]. They influence memory, decision-making, and other cognitive capabilities [13,14].

Intrinsic, long-term personality traits and short-term emotions explicitly or implicitly determine an agent's behavior. For instance, facial expressions and static body postures depend on emotional state, whereas local motion choices such as collision avoidance or response to forces depend on personality and cognitive decisions.

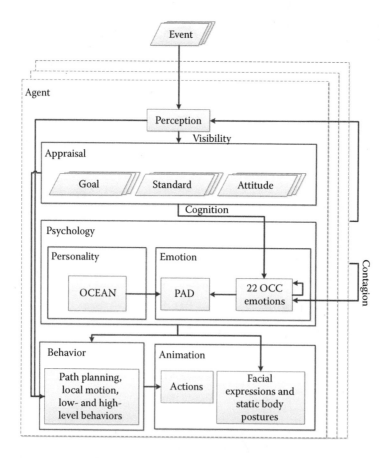

FIGURE 6.2

Framework of agent psychology. (F. Durupınar et al. Psychological parameters for crowd simulation: From audiences to mobs. *IEEE Transactions on Visualization and Computer Graphics*. In press. © 2015, IEEE.)

6.2.1 Personality

Personality is a pattern of behavioral, temperamental, emotional, and mental traits, which defines an individual. It defines a disposition to emotions. Initially, the animator creates groups with different personality traits. Distribution of traits within a group is not uniform; Gaussian distribution is applied to create distinctions within each group. Thus, during a simulation, variations in the emotions of virtual humans will emerge depending on the events they face and their roles in these events in addition to their intrinsic traits.

We represent personality using the five factor, also known as the OCEAN personality, model [15], which has gained recognition in computer graphics and virtual world research. The five factors—*openness, conscientiousness, extroversion, agreeableness,* and *neuroticism*—are orthogonal dimensions of the personality space. Personality is represented as a five-dimensional vector $\langle \psi^O, \psi^C, \psi^E, \psi^A, \psi^N \rangle$ where each dimension takes a value between -1 and 1. The only parameters that the animator needs to set are the mean and standard deviation of each personality dimension for a selected group of agents.

The orthogonality and continuity of these five factors allow a direct association with agent behaviors. We define local steering behaviors such as walking speed, pushing, or agent radius as functions of personality, and perform personality-to-behavior mapping following the approach given in Reference 8. The OCEAN model enables a one-to-one mapping between these low-level parameters and personality traits. Local steering parameters are defined as part of the Unity game engine's navigation feature. Aside from its function in determining the values of steering parameters, personality affects the tendency of the emotional state, for which we are going to give examples in the next section.

6.2.2 Emotion

We define an agent's emotional state as a combination of two components: the agent's cognitive appraisal of the environment and an instinctive, less conscious aspect—emotional contagion (cf. Figure 6.3).

Before explaining appraisal and contagion in detail, let us clarify how an emotion is updated in general. At each time step, t, we calculate the contribution of these two elements separately and clamp their sum between 0 and 1.

$$e_t = f(\text{goals, standards, attitudes}) + \lambda_t(\varepsilon), \tag{6.1}$$

where f is the appraisal contribution function and λ is the contagion contribution function. The experience of another's emotions through emotional contagion is the basis of empathy and it leads to imitation of behavior. Therefore, λ is a function of empathy, ε. Empathy is found to be positively correlated with all five factors of personality. Jolliffe and Farrington measured the correlation values between a basic empathy scale (BES) and personality factors [16]. We use these correlation values as coefficients of personality dimensions to define an empathy value ε between -1 and 1 for an agent j as follows:

$$\varepsilon_j = 0.354\ \psi_j^O + 0.177\ \psi_j^C + 0.135\ \psi_j^E + 0.312\ \psi_j^A + 0.021\ \psi_j^N \tag{6.2}$$

Emotions decay over time toward a neutral state. At each time step, t, the value of an emotion is decreased as

$$e_t = e_{t-1} - \beta e_{t-1} dt \tag{6.3}$$

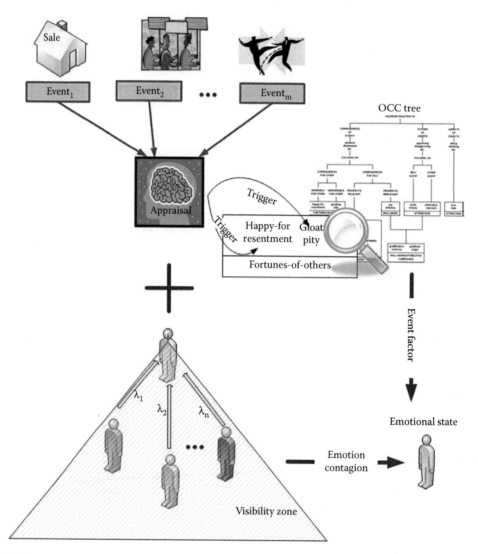

FIGURE 6.3
The emotional state update of an agent. (F. Durupınar et al. Psychological parameters for crowd simulation: From audiences to mobs. *IEEE Transactions on Visualization and Computer Graphics*. In press. © 2015, IEEE.)

The variable β determines the speed of emotional decay and it is proportional to neuroticism—the opposite of emotional stability.

6.2.2.1 Appraisal

As a widely acknowledged model of emotion synthesis, we employ the OCC model. The OCC model is based on the appraisal concept [9], which attributes emotion elicitation to the subjective interpretation of a person's environment. The OCC model suggests that emotions are positive or negative reactions to an individual's goals regarding consequences of events, standards regarding actions of other individuals, and attitudes toward aspects of objects. Using these three stimuli as the main branches, the OCC model describes a hierarchy that classifies 22 emotions. Figure 6.4 shows details of this hierarchy. For instance, pity is elicited when an individual is displeased about an undesirable event for other people and joy is elicited when a person is pleased about a desirable event for himself/herself; admiration is the approving of another person's praiseworthy action and shame is the disapproving of one's own action; love is the liking of an appealing object and hate is the disliking of an unappealing object. *Desirability* of goals, *praiseworthiness* of actions, and *appealingness* of objects determine the strength of emotions.

The OCC model has been widely used in AI applications because of its structural, rule-based form and the fact that it links emotions to a cognitive basis. It formulates the steps that activate each emotion and offers a sufficient level of detail to capture the emotional differences between virtual characters. The complexity of the OCC model ensures that most situations that an agent may encounter are covered, except internal events such as physiological responses. Because the OCC model enables us to formally define the rules that determine an agent's evaluation of its surrounding events and relationships with other agents, it provides a suitable basis for crowd simulation applications.

The comprehensive structure of the OCC model is useful in implementing a wide range of scenarios. However, such precision may prove unnecessary to develop a believable

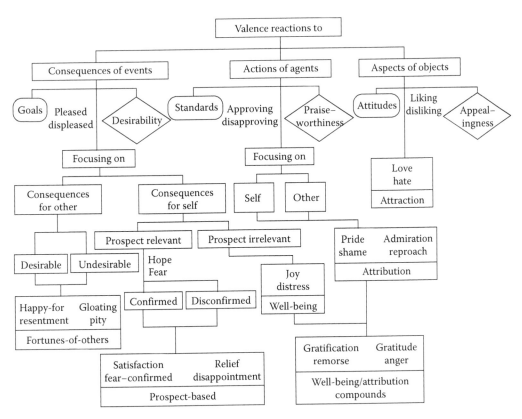

FIGURE 6.4
The OCC model of emotions. (F. Durupınar et al. Psychological parameters for crowd simulation: From audiences to mobs. *IEEE Transactions on Visualization and Computer Graphics*. In press. © 2015, IEEE.)

virtual character. In order to overcome the complexity of the OCC model, we use the following five phases that split the emotion process, as described by Bartneck [17]:

- *Classification*, where an event, action, or an object is evaluated by the agent and the emotional categories that will be triggered are determined. The OCC hierarchy determines which emotion is going to be triggered (cf. Figure 6.4). For example, if an agent has approving standards about another agent's actions, the triggered emotion will be admiration.
- *Quantification*, where the agent calculates the intensities of the emotional categories. For instance, the intensity of admiration will depend on the (un)praiseworthiness of the agent's standard. As an example, Algorithm 6.1 shows the computation of the contribution of an agent's standards on the emotion's appraisal factor. The contributions of goals and attributes are computed in the same manner.

Algorithm 6.1: Update Standard Contribution

```
for i ⟵ 0 to 22 do
    appraisalFactor[i] ⟵ 0;
foreach s ∈ Standards do
    if s.Approving then
        if s.Self then
            appraisalFactor[Pride]+ = s.praiseworthiness;
        else
            //Others appraisalFactor[Admiration]+ = s.praiseworthiness;
    else
        //Disapproving
        if s.Self then
            appraisalFactor[Shame]+ = s.praiseworthiness;
        else
            //Others
            appraisalFactor[Reproach]+ = s.praiseworthiness;
```

- *Interaction*, where the interaction of the current emotional category with existing emotional categories is calculated. Algorithm 6.2 shows the interaction of emotional categories.

Algorithm 6.2: Update Compound Emotions

```
if appraisalFactor[Admiration] > 0 ∧ appraisalFactor[Joy] > 0 then
    appraisalFactor[Gratification] ⟵ (appraisalFactor[Admiration] + appraisalFactor[Joy])/2;
if appraisalFactor[Pride] > 0 ∧ appraisalFactor[Joy] > 0 then
    appraisalFactor[Gratitude] ⟵ (appraisalFactor[Pride] + appraisalFactor[Joy])/2;
if appraisalFactor[Shame] > 0 ∧ appraisalFactor[Distress] > 0 then
    appraisalFactor[Remorse] ⟵ (appraisalFactor[Shame] + appraisalFactor[Distress])/2;
if appraisalFactor[Reproach] > 0 ∧ appraisalFactor[Distress] > 0 then
    appraisalFactor[Anger] ⟵ (appraisalFactor[Reproach] + appraisalFactor[Distress])/2;
```

- *Mapping*, where the 22 emotional categories are mapped to a lower number of different emotional expressions as the OCC model is too complex for the development of believable emotional characters. In order to tackle this and to incorporate the impact of personality on emotion, we exploit the PAD model, which will be explained in Section 6.3.1.

- *Expression*, where the emotional state is expressed through the facial expression, static body posture [18], and behavior of the agent. For instance, happy people tend to have a straight posture with high shoulders and look more confident, whereas sad people have collapsed upper bodies with low shoulders, and generally look downwards.

6.2.2.2 Emotion Contagion

In order to simulate the propagation of emotions, we adopt a generalized contagion model that unifies existing models of social and biological contagion, following the approach proposed by Dodds and Watts [19]. This is a threshold model, as opposed to an independent interaction model, where successive contacts may result in contagion with independent probability. Speaking in biological terms, threshold models suggest that the probability of contracting infection increases as individuals become exposed to a greater number of infected individuals. Because threshold models imply the presence of memory, which is relevant to the adoption of social behaviors, the model by Dodds and Watts is able to explain not only epidemiological contagion but also social contagion—an essential element of collective behavior. Threshold and memory effects characterize individual differences in a social group. We introduce several augmentations to the model by Dodds and Watts to account for emotion contagion in a crowd.

The model states that in a population, individuals can be in one of the two states: susceptible or infected. These terms are derived from biological contagion; however, they are also meaningful in a social or emotional context. Throughout this chapter, we will use the epidemiological terminology to refer to emotionally susceptible and emotion-contracted individuals. However, different from the epidemiological model, an emotionally infected individual is not necessarily capable of transmitting the contracted emotion. At this point, we introduce another condition: "expressiveness," which refers to the ability to spread an emotion. An agent is "expressive" of an emotion if the emotion's value exceeds a certain threshold, which is negatively correlated with extroversion [20]. The expressiveness threshold value $expT_j$ for an agent j is drawn from a normal distribution with mean $0.5 - 0.5\psi_j^E$ and a standard deviation $(0.5 - 0.5\psi_j^E)/10$.

When the amount of an emotion around a person exceeds a certain threshold, that person becomes infected. Here, infection means the individual is now affected directly by the surrounding individuals' emotions of that specific type. The value of the contracted emotions are then added up to the infected individual's existing emotion value. If the emotion intensity surpasses the expressiveness threshold, then that individual is capable of spreading that emotion to other people.

The formal definition is as follows: when a susceptible individual j sees an expressive individual i, j gets exposed by receiving a random dose d_j from a specified probability distribution multiplied by the emotion intensity of i. j sees i if i is within a certain proximity and the visibility cone of j. We take proximity as 4 m and viewing angle as $120°$.

All individuals keep a memory of their previous k doses as

$$D_j(t) = \sum_{t'=t-k+1}^{t} \sum_{\forall i \mid i \in Visibility(j) \,\wedge\, i \text{ is expressive}} d_j(t')e_i(t') \tag{6.4}$$

The dose values are normally distributed with a mean value of 0.1 and a standard deviation of 0.01 so as to ensure variation. We take k as 10. These parameter values are adjusted empirically to ensure optimal results in our simulations.

If the cumulative dose $D_j(t)$ exceeds a specified susceptibility threshold $susT_j$ at any time of the simulation, then the individual j becomes infected. There is no complete recovery from emotion contagion. Therefore, we have not integrated the "recovered" state as found in several epidemiological models. However, once an individual's cumulative dose falls below the infection threshold, the individual becomes susceptible again with a higher threshold.

The $\lambda(\varepsilon)$ function, which determines how emotions are contracted among humans, is computed as

$$\lambda_j(t, \varepsilon) = \begin{cases} D_j dt, & \text{if } D_j(t) > susT_j(t) \\ 0, & \text{otherwise} \end{cases} \tag{6.5}$$

The susceptibility threshold value $susT_j$ for an agent j is drawn from a normal distribution with mean $0.5 - 0.5\varepsilon_j$ and a standard deviation $(0.5 - 0.5\varepsilon_j)/10$. The susceptibility threshold is negatively correlated with ε_j because the more empathetic a person is, the more susceptible s/he becomes to the emotions of other people.

6.3 Decision-Making Based on the Psychological State

6.3.1 PAD Model Mapping

Agents experience a range of different emotions; they may even feel opposite emotions simultaneously. A strategy to determine which emotions affect the current behavior to what extent is therefore crucial. Because emotion intensities are prone to fluctuation, mapping the emotions directly to behaviors may cause erratic behaviors. For instance, consider the simple decision of determining the facial expression of an agent having similar levels of joy and distress. One option would be to reflect the emotion with the highest value in the expression. However, this strategy could cause oscillating facial expressions. Another solution would be to add up these emotions considering joy positive and distress negative in the same dimension. However, this cannot be generalized to all the OCC emotions. Fortunately, the literature gives us a solution: the PAD model, which determines the average emotional state across a representative sample of life situations [11]. OCC emotions are consistently associated with the PAD state [21,22]. The PAD space enables such a mapping with its three orthogonal scales used to assess emotional predispositions [11]. Pleasure defines the relative predominance of positive versus negative affective states. Arousal is a measure of how easily a person can be aroused by complex, changing, or unexpected information. Finally, dominance assesses whether a person feels in control of and is able to influence factors in his/her own life versus feelings of being controlled by others.

TABLE 6.1

Correlation between OCC Emotions and PAD Space

Emotion	P	A	D	Emotion	P	A	D
Admiration	0.50	0.30	−0.20	Hope	0.20	0.20	−0.10
Anger	−0.51	0.59	0.25	Joy	0.40	0.20	0.10
Disappointment	−0.30	0.10	−0.40	Love	0.30	0.10	0.20
Distress	−0.40	−0.20	−0.50	Pity	−0.40	−0.20	−0.50
Fear	−0.64	0.60	−0.43	Pride	0.40	0.30	0.30
Fears-confirmed	−0.50	−0.30	−0.70	Relief	0.20	−0.30	0.40
Gloating	0.30	−0.30	−0.10	Remorse	−0.30	0.10	−0.60
Gratification	0.60	0.50	0.40	Reproach	−0.30	−0.10	0.40
Gratitude	0.40	0.20	−0.30	Resentment	−0.20	−0.30	−0.20
Happy-for	0.40	0.20	0.20	Satisfaction	0.30	−0.20	0.40
Hate	−0.60	0.60	0.30	Shame	−0.30	0.10	−0.60

In addition to finding the dominant emotional state, we need to consider the impact of personality on behavior selection. Another advantage of the PAD model is that it constitutes a suitable link between the OCEAN personality factors and the OCC emotions. A direct mapping between the PAD space and the big five personality traits has been defined as [23]

$$PAD_0(P) = \qquad 0.21\psi^E + 0.59\psi^A − 0.19\psi^N$$

$$PAD_0(A) = \qquad 0.15\psi^O + 0.30\psi^A + 0.57\psi^N \qquad (6.6)$$

$$PAD_0(D) = \quad 0.25\psi^O + 0.17\psi^C + 0.60\psi^E − 0.32\psi^A$$

PAD_0 denotes a three-dimensional vector at time 0, where the three dimensions refer to P, A, and D, respectively. This vector determines the default PAD value of an agent, PAD_0, where all emotions are 0.

Table 6.1 shows the correlation between OCC emotions and PAD space. These parameters have been defined in the ALMA system [21]. We follow a similar approach to compute PAD values. However, unlike Gebhard, who uses the PAD model to denote mood, we utilize these values to determine the psychological tendency that regulates behaviors. According to the table, C_{ij} for $i = 1, \ldots, 22$ and $j = 1, 2, 3$ give the emotion constants for the 22 OCC emotions with respect to P ($j = 1$), A ($j = 2$), and D ($j = 3$) values, respectively. In the table, "admiration" refers to $i = 1$, "anger" to $i = 2$, "disappointment" to $i = 3$, etc.

Incorporating the emotions, the PAD vector at time t is computed as follows:

$$PAD_t = PAD_0 + \mathbf{C}\, e_t \qquad (6.7)$$

The octants of the PAD space are individually named (cf. Table 6.2). These octants, along with their intensities, determine agents' behaviors in a specific context.

6.3.2 Emotion Expression

A recent study reports that humans express four different facial expressions related to emotion: happiness, sadness, anger, and fear [24]. We define a correspondence between the PAD octants and emotional expressions in Table 6.3.

TABLE 6.2

PAD Space Octants

Octant	P	A	D	Octant	P	A	D
Relaxed	+	−	+	Anxious	−	+	−
Dependent	+	+	−	Disdainful	−	−	+
Exuberant	+	+	+	Bored	−	−	−
Docile	+	−	−	Hostile	−	+	+

TABLE 6.3

Expressions Related to PAD Space

Expression	Octants	P	A	D
Happy	Relaxed, dependent, exuberant, docile	+	+/−	+/−
Sad	Disdainful, bored	−	−	+/−
Angry	Hostile	−	+	+
Fearful	Anxious	−	+	−

We store offline static postures for the emotional extremes (e.g., when anger is maximum and all other emotions are 0) as joint rotation angles for all happiness, sadness, anger, fear, and neutral postures. At each time step t during the simulation, we perform spherical linear interpolation from the joint rotations of neutral posture to the posture of the predominant emotion using the emotion value at time t as the interpolation parameter. Similarly, we store the facial animations of emotional extremes and perform animation blending between neutral and emotional expressions for the faces of virtual characters.

6.3.3 Behavior Update

An agent is controlled by different high-level behaviors running synchronously, each represented as a separate component attached to it. These components are both reusable and flexible; they can be easily added and removed when they are no longer required by the agent. The component-based agent architecture borrows from the component structure in Unity game engine, where components are the essentials of the objects and behaviors in a game. With this technique, authoring a new scenario simply consists of introducing new behavior components or modifying the existing ones without the need to be aware of the underlying mechanisms of the psychological model.

An existing scenario can be modified to observe different behaviors by changing the physical distribution, roles, and personalities of agents in the crowd, and presenting external stimuli such as explosions. Physical distribution determines the location of different agent groups. Roles include "protester," "police," "shopper," "audience," etc. Roles are represented as behavior components so that an agent can adopt multiple roles or change its current one. Personality is edited through sliders in the user interface, selecting a group of agents, and adjusting the corresponding mean and standard deviation of each personality trait. We use behavior trees for depicting the operation of different components. Behavior trees are efficient representation structures for controlling the goals and actions of agents. We follow a similar convention for the design and style of behavior trees given in Reference 25.

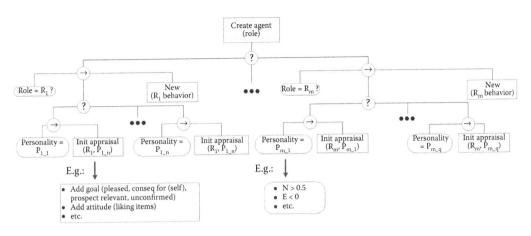

FIGURE 6.5
Behavior tree for initializing an agent in a crowd. (F. Durupınar et al. Psychological parameters for crowd simulation: From audiences to mobs. *IEEE Transactions on Visualization and Computer Graphics*. In press. © 2015, IEEE.)

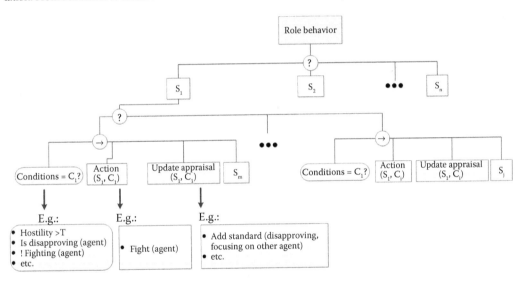

FIGURE 6.6
Behavior tree for roles. (F. Durupınar et al. Psychological parameters for crowd simulation: From audiences to mobs. *IEEE Transactions on Visualization and Computer Graphics*. In press. © 2015, IEEE.)

Figure 6.5 shows the behavior tree template for the initialization process of agents with different roles. Roles and personality determine the initial goals, standards, and attitudes of agents. Figure 6.6 displays the behavior tree template for state update of agents with different roles in different scenarios. Depending on local/global conditions and/or PAD values, agents perform actions and update their appraisal states.

6.4 Experimental Results

We demonstrate our working system on two scenarios depicting a protest scene and a sales event, which correspond to expressive and acquisitive mobs, respectively. Different simulations are run by altering the personalities of the agents in the crowds. Varying the personalities changes the overall behavior of the crowds, sometimes leading to mob behavior.

6.4.1 Scenarios

Protest scenario: The scene consists of 200 protesters and 40 police officers. The protesters' initial appraisal states include general unpleasant goals causing "distress" and approving standards about themselves and their group, leading to "pride" and "admiration" consequently. If they are not very conscientious (as opposed to yielding to authority), they have disapproving standards about the police. At the initialization, a *ProtesterBehavior* component is attached to a protester agent and a *PoliceBehavior* component is attached to a police agent. Protesters follow their leader if they have been assigned one, or they march directly to a predetermined destination. Meanwhile, if they are confronted by the police, they may get beaten, causing some damage. In case a policeman becomes highly hostile and overwhelmed, he uses tear gas to scare the protesters. Then, an *ExplosionBehavior* component is attached to the agents, causing protesters to become afraid and run away. The *ExplosionBehavior* component is removed once the gas diminishes. If a protester is hostile and disapproving the police, s/he may start a fight with a nearby police officer. In that case, a *FightBehavior* component is attached to the protester and the policeman. The outcome of the fight determines the appraisal status of the agents. For instance, if wounded, unconfirmed, pleasant, prospect-relevant goals about self become disconfirmed, diminishing "hope" and eliciting "disappointment." In addition to the agents involving in the fight, agents witnessing the fight also update their appraisal states depending on whom they approve or disapprove of. When the fight is over, the *FightBehavior* component is destroyed.

Sales scenario: Acquisitive mobs are simulated in a scenario that includes a sales event with 100 agents where customers rush into a store to get the items they desire. At the store's door, agents have pleasant goals regarding the sales event. Non-neurotic agents experience "hope." In addition, they have positive attitudes toward the discounted items leading to "love." On the other hand, neurotic agents are "distressed" and they experience "fear." Inside the store, agents disperse and rush to the closest item that they want. Sometimes, more than one agent wants to get the same item. In that case, they develop disapproving standards toward each other. Depending on their anger level, they might start a fight with each other. Based on their neuroticism and disagreeableness levels, agents tend to experience negative feelings toward others such as "resentment," "reproach," and "gloating." "Satisfaction" and "confirmation of fears" emerge toward the end of the simulation as they depend on whether agents achieve the desired items or not. Similarly, agents become "relieved" or "disappointed" at the end. After customers are finished in the store, they may either pay for the items they took or leave the store without paying depending on their conscientiousness.

6.4.2 Evaluation of the Scenarios

For each scenario, we display the results of four simulations for crowds in which (a) personality is randomly distributed with a Gaussian distribution of mean 0 and standard deviation 0.25, spanning the whole personality range, (b) personality is set to 0 for all

OCEAN dimensions (std = 0), (c) personality is set to −1 for agreeableness and conscientiousness with other dimensions set to 0 to simulate a crowd with aggressive tendencies (std = 0), and (d) personality is set to 1 for agreeableness and conscientiousness with other dimensions set to 0 to simulate a crowd with peaceful tendencies (std = 0). Figures 6.7 and 6.8 show the ratios of agents in different PAD octants at each time step.

A quick look at the graphs shows us that emotions of crowds change based on the personality distributions of their members as well as the specific situation the crowds are placed into. For instance, in the protest case, despite different PAD octants being observed in the beginning, the most dominant emotion turns out to be anxiety in the end. This is due to clashes with the police.

On the other hand, emotions are more varied in the sales scenario, and they are more affected by the personalities of agents. A sales crowd with random personalities displays all the emotions in the PAD space, whereas a crowd with disagreeable and unconscientious agents shows hostile and disdainful tendencies, turning into a mob. In contrast, crowds with neutral and peaceful personalities (agreeable and conscientious) exhibit mostly positive emotions. Personalities have impact on the emotions of the crowds in the protest scenario albeit with less effect. For example, aggressive and peaceful crowds display different emotion sets. However, the dominating emotion is always anxiety in the protest scenarios.

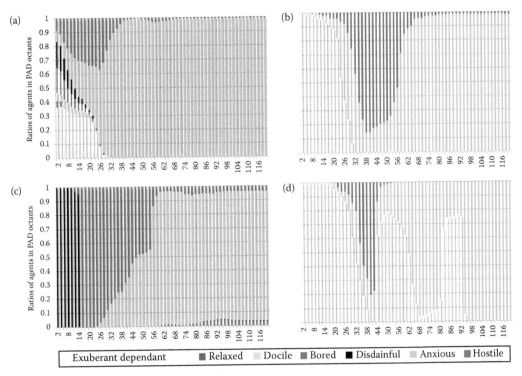

FIGURE 6.7
Ratios of agents in different PAD octants at each time step in the protest scenario: (a) random personalities, (b) all personalities equal to 0, (c) aggressive crowd with $\psi = \{0, -1, 0, -1, 0\}$, (d) peaceful crowd with $\psi = \{0, 1, 0, 1, 0\}$. (F. Durupınar et al. Psychological parameters for crowd simulation: From audiences to mobs. *IEEE Transactions on Visualization and Computer Graphics*. In press. © 2015, IEEE.)

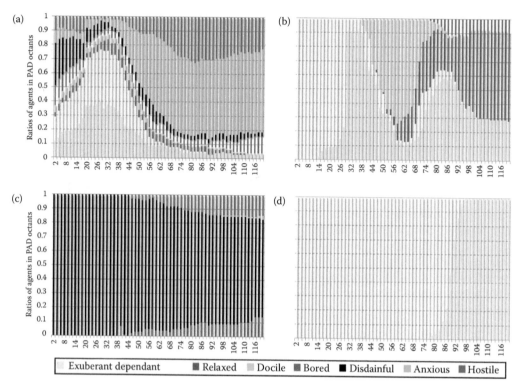

FIGURE 6.8
Ratios of agents in different PAD octants at each time step in the sales scenario: (a) random personalities, (b) all personalities equal to 0, (c) aggressive crowd with $\psi = \{0, -1, 0, -1, 0\}$, (d) peaceful crowd with $\psi = \{0, 1, 0, 1, 0\}$. (F. Durupınar et al. Psychological parameters for crowd simulation: From audiences to mobs. *IEEE Transactions on Visualization and Computer Graphics*. In press. © 2015, IEEE.)

6.4.3 Evaluation of the Contagion Model

We performed simulations to compare the influence of personality and threshold parameters on the outcome of emotion contagion. Figure 6.9 displays snapshots from these simulations, where the spread and decay of emotions are depicted in time. Individuals are shown as spheres, and time increases from the top to the bottom. Emotions are color-coded, where zero emotion is white, maximum emotion is red, and in-between values are interpolated between white and red. All the simulations start with 20% of the individuals initialized with "anger." Depending on the personality distribution of the crowd, expressiveness and empathy of agents are varied. This causes the difference in the emotion intensities captured at different times of the simulation. The images on the left show agents with all personality factors set to -1. Minimal empathy and expressiveness prevent the emotion from spreading before it disappears as a result of emotional decay. The middle images demonstrate the opposite case, where empathy and expressiveness take maximal values. In this case, anger spreads to the whole crowd before getting any chance to decay below the expression threshold. The images on the right show agents having personalities distributed with standard normal distribution. Anger spreads to part of the crowd and disappears after a certain time.

Figure 6.10 shows the graphics of average emotion when expressiveness and susceptibility thresholds are varied. The simulations are run in a crowd of 200 individuals where 20%

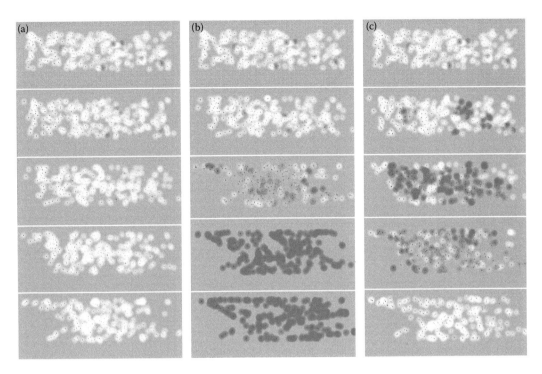

FIGURE 6.9
Snapshots of emotion distribution taken at $t = \{40, 360, 1060, 1860, 3840\}$ milliseconds of the simulations (from top to bottom), where (a) $\psi = \{-1, -1, -1, -1, -1\}$, expressiveness and empathy are 0; (b) $\psi = \{1, 1, 1, 1, 1\}$, expressiveness and empathy are 1; (c) personality is normally distributed with a mean value of 0 and standard deviation 1, expressiveness and empathy are 0.5. Intensity of emotion increases from white to red. (F. Durupınar et al. Psychological parameters for crowd simulation: From audiences to mobs. *IEEE Transactions on Visualization and Computer Graphics*. In press. © 2015, IEEE.)

are assigned *anger* $= 0.9$ and 80% are assigned *anger* $= 0.1$. Agents randomly walk around and they perceive the emotions of other agents within 4 m and 120° around the viewing direction.

A susceptibility threshold of 0 implies that all agents can get infected at any time, whereas a susceptibility threshold of 1 rules out contagion. Figure 6.10a indicates that expressiveness threshold does not have much effect on the slope of the average anger curve except when it is 0 or 1. Similar to susceptibility, an expressiveness threshold of 1 also prevents contagion because no individual is able to spread emotions. However, an expressiveness threshold of 0 where everyone is always expressive yields a different outcome of average emotion decrease over time. This is a result of calming down due to observing low anger. In Figure 6.10b, we can see that as susceptibility threshold decreases, population's average anger increase has a steeper slope.

Figure 6.11 shows how average emotion value of the crowd changes when dose mean (μ) and dose memory (k) values are varied. The initial setting is the same as before: a population where 20% of the individuals are assigned *anger* $= 0.9$ and 80% are assigned *anger* $= 0.1$. Agents randomly walk around and they perceive the emotions of other agents within 4 m and 120° around the viewing direction. Their personalities are all set to 0 in order to have both susceptibility and expressiveness thresholds equal to 0.5. A k value of 1 means that only the current dose is recorded as opposed to 10 and 100 previous doses

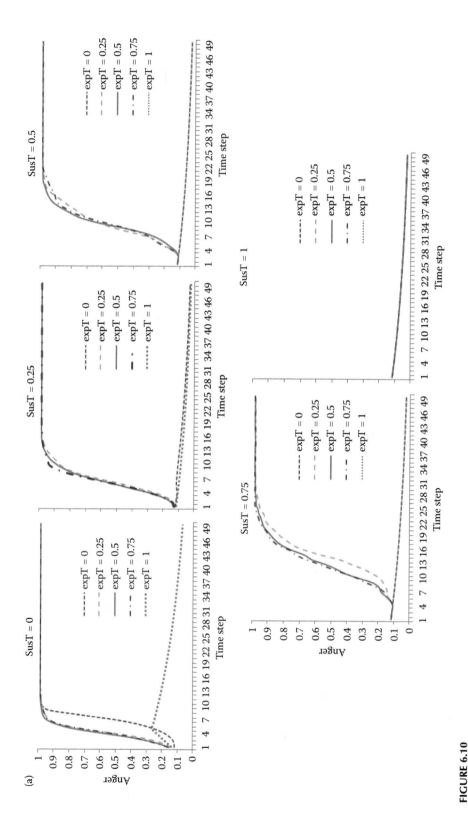

FIGURE 6.10

Average anger at each time step where (a) expressiveness thresholds are varied whereas susceptibility thresholds are kept constant. (F. Durupınar et al. Psychological parameters for crowd simulation: From audiences to mobs. *IEEE Transactions on Visualization and Computer Graphics*. In press. © 2015, IEEE.) (*Continued*)

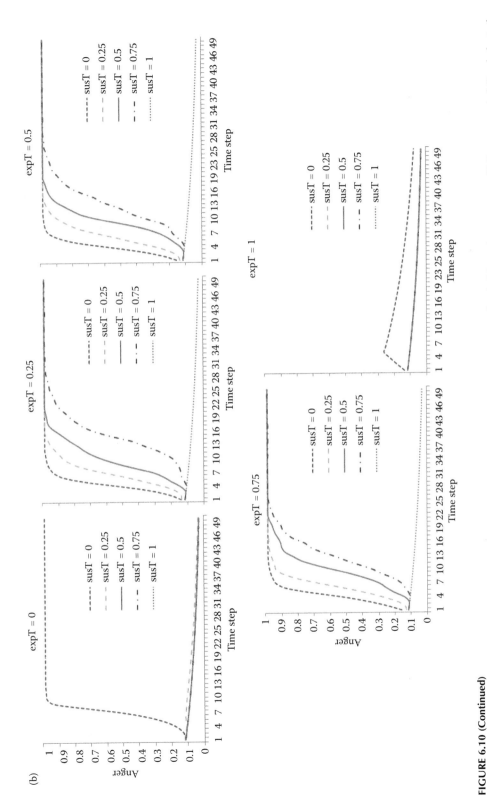

FIGURE 6.10 (Continued)
Average anger at each time step where (b) susceptibility thresholds are varied whereas expressiveness thresholds are kept constant. (F. Durupinar et al. Psychological parameters for crowd simulation: From audiences to mobs. *IEEE Transactions on Visualization and Computer Graphics*. In press. © 2015, IEEE.)

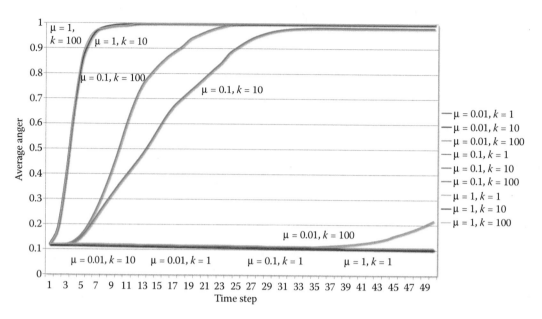

FIGURE 6.11

Average anger with respect to various dose mean (μ) and dose memory (k) values. (F. Durupınar et al. Psychological parameters for crowd simulation: From audiences to mobs. *IEEE Transactions on Visualization and Computer Graphics*. In press. © 2015, IEEE.)

for $k = 10$ and $k = 100$, respectively. The results indicate that anger is not diffused through the population with a small value of μ (0.01) unless k is big enough. On the other hand, a k value of 1 is not enough to trigger emotion contagion even if μ = 1.

We see that the difference between μ = 0.1 and μ = 1 is not as big as the difference between μ = 0.01 and μ = 0.1. Also, the difference between $k = 10$ and $k = 100$ is smaller than the difference between $k = 1$ and $k = 10$. Thus, we take μ = 0.1 and $k = 10$ as baseline values. The model is sensitive to changes only at the extremes. It is robust as long as the values are kept within a certain threshold (cf. Figure 6.12). We get similar results with different population sizes.

Glossary

Behavior tree: A well-defined visual representation tool for plan execution and decision making, which has become popular in game artificial intelligence development.

Emotion contagion: Synchronization of emotions within a group.

Five factor (OCEAN) personality model: A widely recognized personality model that categorizes personality into five orthogonal factors of (O)penness, (C)onscientiousness, (E)xtroversion, (A)greeableness, and (N)euroticism.

Ortony, Clore, Collins (OCC) model: An emotion model that suggests that emotions are triggered according to an individual's reactions to the consequences of events, actions of agents, and aspects of objects.

Pleasure–arousal–dominance (PAD): A three-dimensional emotion model that describes the average emotional state across a representative sample of life situations.

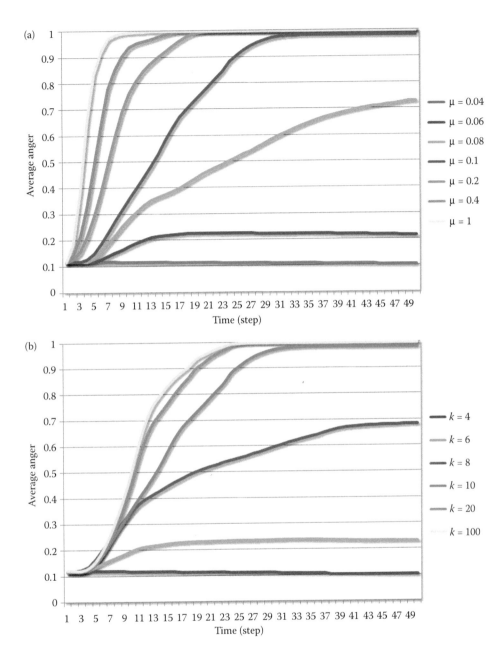

FIGURE 6.12
Average anger at each time step, where (a) $k = 10$ and dose mean μ is varied, (b) $\mu = 0.1$ and k is varied. (F. Durupınar et al. Psychological parameters for crowd simulation: From audiences to mobs. *IEEE Transactions on Visualization and Computer Graphics*. In press. © 2015, IEEE.)

References

1. T. Bosse, M. Hoogendoorn, M. C. A. Klein, and J. Treur. Modelling collective decision making in groups and crowds: Integrating social contagion and interacting emotions, beliefs and intentions. *Autonomous Agents and Multi-Agent Systems*, 27(1):52–84, 2012.

2. F. Durupınar, U. Güdükbay, A. Aman, and N. Badler. Psychological parameters for crowd simulation: From audiences to mobs. *IEEE Transactions on Visualization and Computer Graphics*. In press.

3. S. Kim, S. J. Guy, D. Manocha, and M. C. Lin. Interactive simulation of dynamic crowd behaviors using general adaptation syndrome theory. In *Proceedings of the ACM SIGGRAPH Symposium on Interactive 3D Graphics and Games (I3D'12)*, pp. 55–62, Costa Mesa, California, 2012.

4. Massive Software, Inc. Massive. http://www.massivesoftware.com, 2015. Accessed February 2016.

5. J. Tsai, N. Fridman, E. Bowring, M. Brown, S. Epstein, G. Kaminka, S. Marsella et al. Escapes: Evacuation simulation with children, authorities, parents, emotions, and social comparison. In *Proceedings of the 10th International Conference on Autonomous Agents and Multi-Agent Systems (AAMAS'11)*, vol 2, pp. 457–464. IFAAMAS, Taipei, Taiwan, 2011.

6. R. W. Brown. Mass phenomena. In *The Handbook of Social Psychology*, G. Lindzey (ed.), pp. 833–876. Addison-Wesley, Cambridge, MA, 1954.

7. E. S. Bogardus. *Fundamentals of Social Psychology*, chapter 3, pp. 26–33. The Century Company, New York, 1924.

8. F. Durupınar, J. Allbeck, N. Pelechano, U. Güdükbay, and N. Badler. How the Ocean personality model affects the perception of crowds. *IEEE Computer Graphics and Applications*, 31(3):22–31, 2011.

9. A. Ortony, G. L. Clore, and A. Collins. *The Cognitive Structure of Emotions*. Cambridge University Press, Cambridge, UK, 1988.

10. G. Le Bon. *The Crowd: A Study of the Popular Mind*. Dover Publications, Inc., New York, 1895.

11. A. Mehrabian. Pleasure-arousal-dominance: A general framework for describing and measuring individual differences in temperament. *Current Psychology*, 14(4):261–292, 1996.

12. Unity Technologies. Unity Game Engine. http://unity3d.com, 2000. Accessed February 2016.

13. G. H. Bower and P. R. Cohen. Emotional influences in memory and thinking: Data and theory. In *Affect and Cognition*, M. S. Clark and S. T. Fiske (eds.), chapter 13, pp. 291–331. Lawrence Erlbaum, Hillsdale, NJ, 1982.

14. C. E. Izard. *Human Emotions*. Plenum, New York and London, 1977.

15. J. S. Wiggins. *The Five-Factor Model of Personality: Theoretical Perspectives*. The Guilford Press, New York, 1996.

16. D. Jolliffe and D. P. Farrington. Development and validation of the basic empathy scale. *Journal of Adolescence*, 29(4):589–611, 2006.

17. C. Bartneck. Integrating the OCC model of emotions in embodied characters. In *Proceedings of the Workshop on Virtual Conversational Characters: Applications, Methods, and Research Challenges*, Melbourne, Australia, 2002.

18. M. Coulson. Attributing emotion to static body postures: Recognition accuracy, confusions, and viewpoint dependence. *Journal of Nonverbal Behavior*, 26(2):117–139, 2004.

19. P. S. Dodds and D. J. Watts. A generalized model of social and biological contagion. *Journal of Theoretical Biology*, 232(4):587–604, 2005.

20. H. R. Riggio and R. E. Riggio. Emotional expressiveness, extraversion, and neuroticism: A meta-analysis. *Journal of Nonverbal Behavior*, 26(4):195–218, 2002.

21. P. Gebhard. ALMA—A layered model of affect. In *Proceedings of the Fourth International Joint Conference on Autonomous Agents and Multiagent Systems (AAMAS'05)*, pp. 29–36, New York, 2005. ACM.

22. A. Mehrabian. Framework for a comprehensive description and measurement of emotional states. *Genetic, Social and General Psychology Monographs*, 121:339–361, 1995.

23. A. Mehrabian. Analysis of the big-five personality factors in terms of the PAD temperament model. *Australian Journal of Psychology*, 48:86–92, 1996.

24. R. E. Jack, O. G. B. Garrod, and P. G. Schyns. Dynamic facial expressions of emotion transmit an evolving hierarchy of signals over time. *Current Biology*, 24(2):187–192, 2014.

25. I. Millington and J. Funge. *Artificial Intelligence for Games*. Morgan Kaufmann, Burlington, MA, 2nd edition, 2009.

7

Impostor-Based Crowd Rendering

Alejandro Beacco, Nuria Pelechano, and Carlos Andújar

CONTENTS

Real-time rendering of detailed animated characters in crowd simulations is still a challenging problem in computer graphics. State-of-the-art approaches can render up to several thousand agents by consuming most of the graphics processing unit (GPU) resources, leaving little room for other GPU uses such as driving the crowd simulation. Polygonal meshes deformed through skinning in real time are suitable for simulations involving a relatively small number of agents, since the rendering cost of each animated character is proportional to the complexity of its polygonal representation.

A number of techniques have been proposed to accelerate the rendering of animated characters. Besides view frustum and occlusion culling techniques, related work has focused mainly on providing level-of-detail (LoD) representations. Unfortunately, most surface simplification methods do not work well with dynamic articulated meshes. As a consequence, the simplified versions of each character are often created manually and they still suffer from a substantial loss of detail. Image-based precomputed impostors for the whole character provide substantial speed improvements by rendering distant characters as a textured polygon, but suffer from two major limitations: all animation cycles have to be known in advance (and thus animation blending is not supported) and resulting textures are huge (as for each view angle and animation frame, an image has to be stored). In this chapter, we overview different approaches to crowd rendering, focusing on impostor-based techniques. We summarize and compare two recent approaches [1,2] based on rigidly animated impostors per body limb (Figure 7.1). Compared to having impostors representing an entire character, having animated per-joint impostors provides a more memory-efficient approach.

FIGURE 7.1
Different views of a heterogeneous crowd, using LoD for geometry and per-joint impostors.

7.1 Introduction

Crowd simulations [3,4] are becoming increasingly important in a many computer graphics applications. Although the most prominent use of crowd simulations is found in video games, crowd rendering is also crucial in a variety of applications, including evacuation planning (like Thunderhead's *Pathfinder* software), crowd management training, phobia treatments, and psychological studies. These applications often need to render in real time hundreds or thousands of moving agents with a certain level of visual quality.

A close look at the video game industry reveals that each new console generation gives rise to a new predominant genre that fully exploits the hardware improvements. In order to allow the player to feel immersed inside game environments such as virtual stadiums, villages, and cities, the scenes need to be populated with crowds of people that make the environment both alive and believable. In sandbox games, this is almost a requirement, and recent games from bestselling series such as Ubisoft's *Assassin's Creed* or RockStar's *Grand Theft Auto* have pushed the limits on the amount of agents shown on screen in real time. The recent *Assassin's Creed Unity* claims to show up to 12,000 agents in real time, although just 120 of them are rendered using high-resolution models.

Moving to strategy games, we can find massive armies of up to 100,000 soldiers animated in real time, as in Creative Assembly's *Total War: Rome 2*. Distant soldiers are not required to have individual appearance, animation, and behavior, which makes it easier to reach such a high performance. In sport games such as Electronic Arts' *FIFA 15*, stadiums can also be filled with up to 120,000 animated virtual spectators, although they remain seated in the same place with no navigation or collision avoidance.

Real-time realistic crowds thus have a massive impact in the current game industry. Despite substantial advances in the field, virtual crowds still suffer from a number of easy-to-spot artifacts, including popping effects when switching between LoD representations, limb self-intersections, prominent clones (sharing visual appearance and/or animation), and poorly simulated behaviors. It is therefore necessary to devise new techniques to simulate, animate, and render large numbers of autonomous agents in real time, minimizing visual artifacts and optimizing the use of central processing unit (CPU), GPU, and bandwidth resources, which have an obvious impact in performance, energy consumption, and, in mobile devices, battery life.

For a given graphics hardware, there is an obvious trade-off between the number of animated characters that can be simulated in real time, and the different factors affecting their visual quality, including geometric detail, materials, motion (path within the scenario), and animation (e.g., walking or running cycles).

Although there is a large variety of crowd rendering acceleration techniques, LoD rendering is the most effective and frequently used approach. LoD rendering refers to the possibility of drawing objects using different representations with varying complexity and accuracy [5,6]. In the context of character animation, each character type can be represented with different LoDs; at runtime, the most suitable representation for each character instance is chosen according to an estimation of its contribution to the image, which mostly depends on the distance to the camera. Current LoD representations for characters can be roughly classified into polygon-based techniques, point-based techniques, and image-based techniques.

Polygon-based techniques provide various LoD representations of the character geometry in the form of a polygonal mesh (faces are often limited to triangles and quads). These techniques are the *de facto* standard in character rendering, despite the difficulties in generating high-quality simplified meshes for animated characters automatically. *Point-based techniques* represent characters through point clouds with no explicit connectivity [7,8], which can be rendered using a surface splat primitive [9]. *Image-based techniques* replace three-dimensional (3D) characters by simple textured-mapped primitives called impostors [1,10–13].

LoD techniques are generally lossy and thus the primary goal is to maximize performance while minimizing visible artifacts. Besides LoD techniques, a variety of (mostly) loss-less techniques can be applied to accelerate crowd rendering with no impact on image quality. *Culling techniques* aim to avoid processing invisible geometry [14], either because it falls outside the viewing frustum (frustum culling [5,15,16]) or because it is hidden by occluding geometry (occlusion or visibility culling [17,18]). Although individual characters have little chances to occlude relevant geometry, the aggregation of many characters, as well as the environment they inhabit, offer great opportunities to optimize rendering performance in a conservative way. Current hardware features offer new possibilities for optimizing the rendering of large crowds. These techniques include primitive instancing, palette skinning, and key-pose caching [19–21].

In this chapter, we describe two impostor-based techniques that can be animated in real time, allowing us to have heterogeneity in behaviors while keeping a low memory footprint. In Figure 7.2, we show a sample character rendered with geometry and the two per-joint impostor techniques described in this chapter. Note that each joint is in charge of the transformations that applies to a segment of the skeleton. For the sake of simplicity, in this chapter, we use the term "joint" to represent both the articulation and the body segment that moves with it.

7.2 Per-Joint Impostors

The goal of per-joint impostors is to have a character representation that can be animated in real time. This representation maximizes performance by using a collection of precomputed impostors sampled from a discrete set of view directions. Characters are

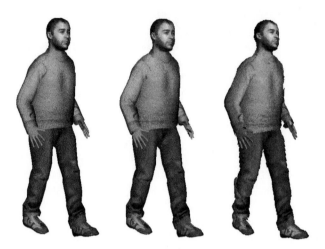

FIGURE 7.2
Comparison of rendering characters with geometry (left), relief impostors (middle), and flat per-joint impostors (right).

animated by applying the joint rotations directly to the impostors, instead of choosing a single impostor for the whole character from a set of predefined poses. This representation supports any arbitrary pose and thus the agent behavior is not constrained to a small collection of predefined clips. Two per-joint representations have been proposed for crowd rendering.

Relief impostors consist of having each character encoded through a small collection of textured boxes storing color and depth values (Figure 7.3). At runtime, each box is animated according to the rigid transformation of its associated bone and a fragment shader is used to recover the original geometry using a dual-depth version of relief mapping [22]. This compact representation is able to recover high-frequency surface details and reproduces view-motion parallax and self-occlusions effectively. It drastically reduces both the number of primitives being drawn and the number of bones influencing each primitive, at the expense of a slight per-fragment overhead. Beyond a certain distance threshold, this compact representation is much faster to render than traditional LoD triangle meshes [2].

Instead of using six orthogonal relief maps for each joint, which requires multiple dependent texture accesses per fragment, we can also use *flat impostors* created by sampling each joint from multiple view directions [1]. A spherical Voronoi map projected onto a cube map allows a quick retrieval of the impostor better aligned with the current view direction. At fragment level, a single texture lookup is enough to retrieve the fragment color, which is one order of magnitude faster than relief mapping. Since these impostors are intended to be valid for any pose, it becomes critical to decide which part of the geometry influenced by each joint must be represented by the impostor (see Figure 7.4). Rendering heterogeneous crowds with this approach outperforms competing animation-independent approaches for crowd rendering, being over five times faster than per-joint relief impostors.

A common advantage of per-joint impostors is the capacity of handling LoD by merging parts of the body within the same bounding box. The resulting impostors will obviously undergo the rigid transformation applied to the parent node. For instance, if we group the hand, forearm, and upper arm into a single joint, the hand will not move other than following the upper-arm rotations. Figure 7.5 shows several bone hierarchies with 21, 7,

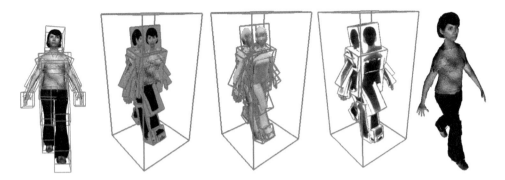

FIGURE 7.3
During preprocess, color, normal, and depth information is projected onto the six box faces. During real time, each character is rendered through relief mapping.

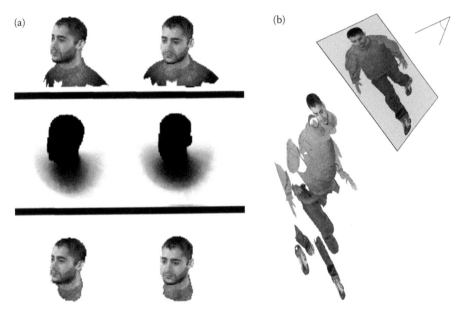

FIGURE 7.4
Preprocess to obtain each per-joint per-view impostor for the head of the character after applying the corresponding mask (a). Real-time rendering composing the per-joint textures for a given view point (b).

and 1 joint. The 1-bone LoD supports no deformations and thus cannot be animated, which makes it appropriate only for characters very far away from the camera.

7.3 Relief Per-Joint Impostors

Assuming that we have a 3D character with skeletal animation and rigging, the generation of relief per-joint impostors consists of finding an adequate relief map for each limb

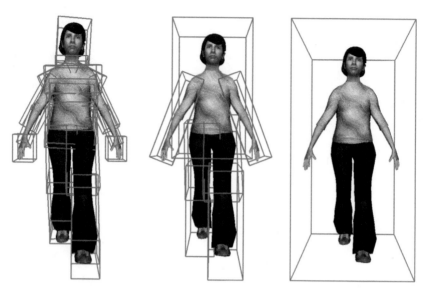

FIGURE 7.5
Relief impostors consisting of 21, 7, and 1 boxes.

of the skeleton that can be rigidly animated before rendering its relief map. The representation consists of a collection of oriented bounding boxes (OBB), one for each bone in the skeleton, along with a collection of textures projected into the OBB faces, encoding color, normal, and depth values. The OBB will be transformed in the same way as the bones of the skeleton, giving the impression that our impostor character is animated. Note how this representation requires much less memory than competing image-based approaches, which require pre-rendering the character for every possible animation frame for a large set of view angles.

7.3.1 Preprocessing

For a given 3D character, each per-joint relief impostor is created with the following steps:

1. Associate mesh triangles to impostors.
2. Select a suitable pose for capturing the impostors.
3. Compute the bounding boxes of every joint with the chosen pose.
4. Capture (render to texture) the color, normal, and depth data of each bounding box.

Since there will be an impostor per joint of the articulated character, the first step is to assign part of the triangle mesh to the corresponding impostor. Assuming that each input vertex v_i is attached to joints $J_1, \ldots J_n$ with weights $w = (w_1, \ldots w_n)$, and given a triangle with vertices v_1, v_2, v_3, the problem consists of deciding to which impostors the triangle will be assigned to (i.e., which triangles will be captured by the impostor). There are several ways to do this. One option is to distribute mesh triangles into joints, attaching each triangle to the joint with the highest influence over the triangle (e.g., measured as the sum

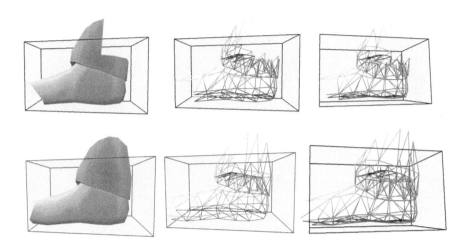

FIGURE 7.6
The top image shows the case when a triangle is drawn if the maximum weight of its three vertices is assigned to the current bone. The bottom image shows the case when a triangle is drawn if at least one of its three vertices is assigned to the current bone.

of the vertex weights). However, this simple partition tends to produce visible gaps in the joint boundaries during animation (see Figure 7.6, top).

Another option would be to assign a triangle to a bone if at least one of its vertices is influenced by the bone, regardless of the corresponding weight. Therefore, some triangles (those around joints) will be assigned to a variable number of impostors (see Figure 7.6, bottom). This second approach does not have as many gaps during animation, but it introduces another undesirable effect during animation as overlapping geometry appears with some movements.

The optimal solution consists of setting a threshold that determines which vertices are assigned to each bone based on the weight (rigging weights). Figure 7.7 shows how this choice is relevant when later animating the impostor. We can observe gaps in the second figure, protruding geometry on the third, and smoother visual appearance with the right threshold on the fourth figure.

The second step is to choose a suitable pose for capturing the impostors. Triangles are captured according to the chosen pose, that is, after mesh vertices have been blended according to the pose. This choice of pose affects the captured geometry.

Since impostors will undergo only a rigid transformation, choosing a pose corresponding to a walking animation keyframe tends to minimize artifacts around joints. Note that the above choice only affects triangles influenced by multiple joints; triangles influenced by a single joint will be reconstructed in their exact position regardless of the selected pose.

Once a suitable pose has been chosen, the mesh is deformed accordingly by applying linear blend skinning to the mesh vertices. The bounding box of each impostor is then computed as the OBB of the (transformed) triangles attached to the impostor.

The last step is to render the deformed mesh to capture the relief maps corresponding to each one of the six faces of its bounding box. For each bounding box face, an orthographic camera is set up with its viewing direction aligned with the face's normal vector,

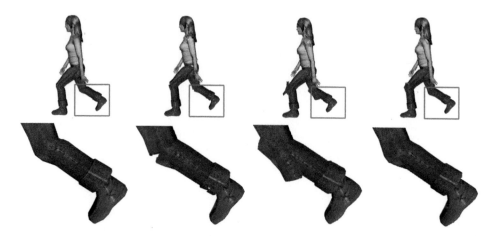

FIGURE 7.7
Artifacts due to lack of geometric skinning. From left to right: Original mesh, impostors created by assigning each triangle to a single joint, impostors created by assigning to each joint all the triangles influenced by the joint, and impostors created with a threshold-based strategy.

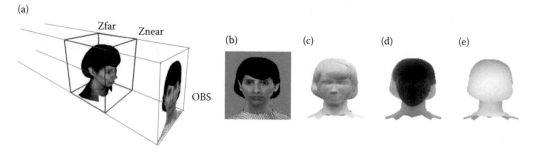

FIGURE 7.8
Projection of the model onto each face of the bounding box using an orthonormal camera (a). Color (b), normal (c), front depth (d), and back depth (e) values are encoded as two RGBA textures.

and finally the triangles attached to the corresponding impostor are rendered. The information captured consisted of color map (rgb), normal map (n_x, n_y, n_z), and front (z_f) and back (z_b) depth values. These eight values are stored in two RGBA textures, keeping both depth values stored in the same texture for performance purposes (see Figure 7.8).

This technique requires only about 4 MB of storage per character (considering 21 bones, 6 faces per OBB, 2 textures per face, texture resolution of 64×64, and 4 bytes per pixel), whereas traditional per-character impostors that need to be captured per viewing angle and pose require minimum of 22 MB per character.

7.3.2 Real-Time Rendering

Each character is rendered through an adapted version of relief mapping [22] over the fragments produced by the rasterization of the transformed bounding boxes. The CPU-based part of the rendering algorithm proceeds through the following steps:

1. Bind the corresponding texture arrays (color and normal maps) into different texture units, and also bind the vertex buffer object (VBO) with the geometry of the bounding boxes in the pose used to capture the impostors. These steps are performed only once per character type, not per instance.

2. For each instance, draw the bounding box associated with each bone, to ensure that a fragment will be created for any viewing ray intersecting the underlying geometry.

The vertex shader multiplies the incoming OBB vertices by the corresponding rigid transformation matrix so that they follow the original skeleton animation.

The most relevant part of the rendering relies on the fragment shader, which uses the depth values stored in the color and normal maps to find the intersection P of the fragment's viewing ray with the underlying geometry. For this particular task, any ray–heightfield intersection algorithm can be adopted. Pyramidal displacement mapping [23] is particularly suitable as it guarantees finding the correct intersection on any heightfield and viewing condition. Our timings though are based on the simpler relief mapping algorithm described in Reference 24.

Let E be the world space eye coordinates and let C be the world space fragment coordinates (see Figure 7.9a). The fragment shader computes the intersection of the fragment's viewing ray $r = (C - E)$ with the heightfield encoded by the displacement values stored in the relief map (see Figure 7.9). If no intersection is found, the fragment is discarded. As in Reference 24, we first use a linear search by sampling the ray r at regular intervals to find a ray sample inside the object, and then a binary search to refine the intersection point. This allows us to retrieve the diffuse color of the fragment being processed, along with a normal vector to compute per-fragment lighting. Unlike classic relief mapping, we use two

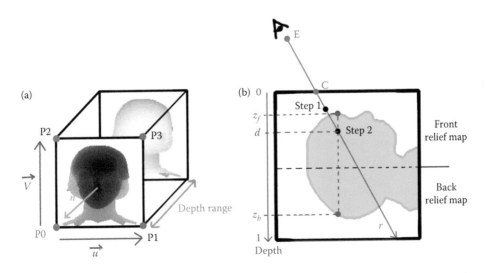

FIGURE 7.9
(a) Impostor parameters stored in the VBO, transformed by the vertex shader, and used by the fragment shader.
(b) Ray–heightfield intersection search. At each search step, the current depth d is compared with the front depth z_f and the back depth z_b to check whether we are inside the geometry or not.

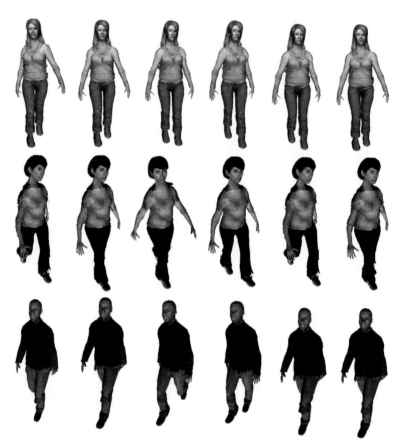

FIGURE 7.10
Some relief impostors examples.

depth values z_f and z_b per texel. During the search process, a sample along the ray with depth z is classified as interior to the object iff $z_f \leq z \leq z_b$.

Figure 7.10 shows some example frames of relief impostors while animated from a close-up view.

7.3.3 Improvements

Several improvements can be included to enhance the quality of the impostors while keeping a low memory footprint and having a negligible effect over performance. The first improvement consists of having adaptive texture resolution for different body parts. The overall representation is split into two VBOs, one for the head and another one for the rest of the body. Using a resolution of 64×64 for the body and 128×128 for the head, we obtain higher visual quality with just $1.3\times$ more memory, as opposed to the $4\times$ increment that would imply using higher resolution for the whole body.

To reduce the per-fragment cost, we can include an adaptive number of linear and binary steps into the relief mapping algorithm. As the agents move further away from the camera, the number of steps is reduced. Figure 7.11 shows the quality observed for different resolutions. We achieved a speed up of $3.7\times$ on average with linear search steps ranging from 16 to 128, and binary from 4 to 10. Another possible improvement consists of replacing the

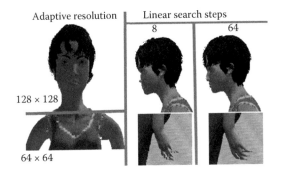

Adaptive resolution | Linear search steps

FIGURE 7.11
Improvements over relief impostors.

binary search with the secant method, which iteratively bounds the intersection with the view ray and the geometry using a segment-to-segment test. This reduces the number of steps compared to binary search (order of 1.5 times faster).

7.4 Flat Per-Joint Impostors

Flat per-joint impostors avoid the high per-fragment cost of relief mapping by using pre-generated renders of each joint from multiple view directions. This obviously increases the memory requirements of the technique, but rendering each body part now simply implies rendering two textured triangles. As in the previous technique, impostors are animated rigidly following the movement of the skeleton. Therefore, the challenge lies in finding the right impostors that can be animated rigidly without introducing noticeable artifacts.

In this technique, the input bone hierarchy can also be simplified by grouping joints, letting some parent nodes absorb small child nodes (see Figure 7.5).

7.4.1 Preprocessing

The construction of per-joint impostors from a given 3D character proceeds through the following steps (see Figure 7.12):

1. Choose a suitable set of samples from S^2 (view directions), compute the spherical Voronoi map of these samples, and build a cube map by projecting the Voronoi cells onto the cube faces.

2. For each joint and for each view, compute a proper mask and capture the impostor.

3. Pack all textures in a texture array of texture atlases.

The first step is to generate a small set of view directions from the unit sphere S^2. This can be carried out as both uniform and nonuniform (i.e., adaptive) sampling schemes. The main advantage of the latter, in the context of crowd rendering, is that we can sample S^2 more densely around views more likely to occur when animating the character, and around views capturing the more salient parts of the character. For the sake of simplicity, an icosahedron can be subdivided and its face normals taken as the view samples. The

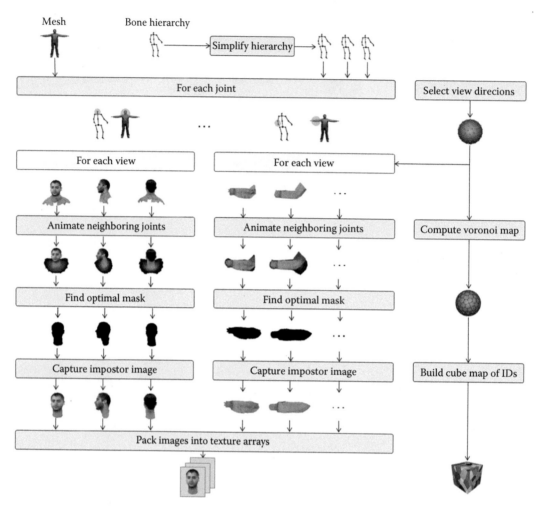

FIGURE 7.12
Overview of the algorithm for generating per-joint impostors.

subdivided triangles are taken as the Voronoi regions defined by these samples. To speed up the problem of finding the best-aligned impostor at runtime, a cube map is built by projecting the color-coded subdivided triangles onto the faces of a unit cube. Since the texel of the cube map representing a direction ω stores the ID of its nearest discrete sample, the nearest-neighbor problem is solved using a single texture lookup.

To generate the impostors, each joint is treated independently. Let B be a given joint from the bone hierarchy, and let $N_1, \ldots N_j$ be its neighboring joints. Each joint is controlled by a rotation matrix that changes during animation according to the character's pose. Suppose that we need to generate an impostor for the part of the mesh influenced by joint B. Since rotations are invertible, we can fix joint B (as if it were the root node) and represent the rotation matrices of its neighboring joints as relative to B.

Let T be the set of triangles influenced by B, that is, triangles with at least one vertex being influenced by B (see Figure 7.13a). Since mesh triangles can be influenced by

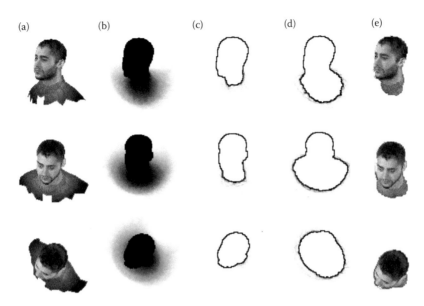

FIGURE 7.13
Defining impostor extents for multiple view directions: (a) triangles T influenced by the head bone, shown in a reference pose; (b) area swept by T when neighboring joints are rotated; the gray level indicates the number of realizations projecting onto each pixel; (c) and (d) two possible mask boundaries defining the extents of the impostors; (e) impostor captured using our optimized mask.

multiple joints, the final geometry of the triangles in T is determined by the rotation matrices attached to its neighboring joints (along with the procedure for implementing mesh skinning). Given a joint B and a collection of rotation matrices, the result of deforming the triangles in T according to these matrices is called a *realization* of B, and it will be denoted as R.

Let ω be some view sample from S^2. All the possible realizations of B can be orthogonally projected onto an image plane Π perpendicular to ω. The portion of the image plane Π filled by these projections will be referred to as the *swept area* S (see Figure 7.13b). Now the key problem is to decide which portion of S must be captured by the impostor representing B from ω.

In order to better illustrate the effect of the criterion for generating the mask boundary, let us consider first two extreme cases. The *undercoverage* criterion would define the mask as the region containing just the triangles uniquely influenced by B (i.e., triangles with vertices having unit weight for this joint, and null weight for the rest of joints). It turns out that this criterion would tend to produce visible gaps during animation, in particular around joint boundaries, as the corresponding blending triangles would not be represented in any impostor.

The opposite *overcoverage* criterion would define the mask as the swept area S. This obviously would result in overly large, overlapping impostors, causing protruding geometry artifacts around joint boundaries. We aim at choosing the mask boundaries minimizing the image error across all possible views and animations frames.

Mask Generation and Impostor Capture   For each joint B and view v, we need to generate a mask defining the portion of the swept area S that must be captured by the corresponding impostor. Mask boundaries can be restricted within the swept area S (which can be seen as the *union* of the orthogonally projected realizations).

The resulting masks exhibit rounded boundaries near joints due to the blending effect of neighboring joint rotations on the deformed geometry. These shapes are somewhat similar to the rounded joints used in traditional art mannequins and articulated figures (see Figure 7.13e). In order to obtain rounded endings for each mask, we obtain the realization of a joint by rotating each joint based on the real degrees of freedom (DoF) and limits existing on each joint of a human.

Each realization is rendered onto a frame buffer object (FBO), which plays the role of an accumulation buffer (Figure 7.13b). For a given joint B and view ω, the realizations are generated by applying linear blend skinning to the set of triangles influenced by B.

7.4.2 Real-Time Rendering

In order to render flat per-joint impostors, we proceed with the following CPU steps:

1. Bind the corresponding texture arrays (color and optionally normal maps) and the cube map texture that maps directions in S^2 to precomputed view samples. This step is performed only once per character type, not per instance.

2. Draw a VBO encoding each character type (all instances of a character type share the same VBO). The VBO contains one vertex for each per-joint impostor, corresponding to the center of its bounding cube. The rest of the impostor information is encoded as vertex attributes. In our OpenGL implementation, the VBO is rendered as GL_POINTS primitives that will be later converted into a pair of triangles. The rationale of this approach is to avoid duplicating per-joint computations.

Then the GPU needs to perform the following computations. The *vertex shader* transforms the vertex itself and its local orthonormal basis according to the character's pose, so that the joint follows the original skeleton animation, and computes the discrete view that best matches the joint duplicating these computations.

The *geometry shader* is executed for each GL_POINT primitive encoding a (transformed) per-joint impostor. It simply creates a couple of triangles defining the impostor quad. It also computes the (s,t,p) texture coordinates for accessing the texture array.

The *fragment shader* performs traditional texture mapping (and per-fragment lighting, if normal maps are available) to compute the final fragment color.

7.4.3 Improvements

Adaptive texture resolution can be used to have higher resolution for the head than for the rest of the body. This solution achieves higher visual quality with just $1.15\times$ more memory, as opposed to the the the $4\times$ increment that would imply using higher resolution for the whole body. Performing adaptive number of views can help to further sample the most noticeable part of the body, lessening the popping artifact that appears when changing views. Figure 7.14 shows the effects of these improvements. When creating the masks, instead of using three DoFs and all possible rotation angles, results can be more accurate if only real joint rotations obtained from biomedical studies [25] are used. This can further reduce artifacts due to gaps or overlapping parts around joints.

Num views: 16   16   128

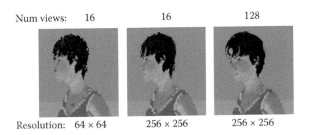

Resolution: 64 × 64   256 × 256   256 × 256

FIGURE 7.14
Flat per-joint impostors with adaptive resolution and views.

7.5 Performance Comparison

We measured the performance of both per-joint impostors techniques against some of the most representative techniques for crowd rendering: mesh-based LoD, and pre-generated impostors [13]. We used two test views, an aerial view with little overdraw and a street view with a significant amount of overdraw (Figure 7.15). In both views, the crowd was placed at a fixed distance from the 60-degree camera, with close-up characters at approximately 10 meters and the farthest ones at 100 meters. When testing different crowd sizes, we kept the area covered by the characters fixed, and only increased the density. The test hardware was a desktop PC equipped with an Intel Core i7-2600K @3.40 GHz and one NVidia GeForce GTX 560 Ti. All renders were performed at a rather high-quality profile: 1920 × 1080 resolution, with a single static light casting soft shadows on the ground, and each character being animated by blending two different animation clips. The pose of each character was updated at every application frame. Agents were animated in place to evaluate exclusively rendering and animation performance, without considering collision detection and simulation, which would affect all techniques. Several hardware optimizations were implemented for all techniques, including deferred rendering (soft shadows), instancing and palette skinning. Occlusion and frustum culling though were disabled.

For the sake of fairness, we used identical or similar parameters whenever possible across impostor representations. The original mesh had 25 K polygons, 2048 × 2048 textures, and a 67-bone skeleton. All impostor textures were 128 × 128 texels. Relief and flat per-joint

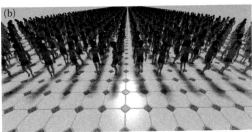

FIGURE 7.15
Aerial (a) and street (b) view used in our performance tests. Further characters are at 100 meters from the camera.

TABLE 7.1

Performance Comparison of Different Crowd Rendering Techniques in Frames per Second (fps)

	Number of Agents	2500		5000		10000	
	View	Aerial	Street	Aerial	Street	Aerial	Street
	Original mesh (25 K triangles)	1.4	1.4	0.7	0.7	0.3	0.3
	Simplified mesh (5 K triangles)	2.9	2.9	1.5	1.5	0.8	0.7
Approach	Simplified mesh (2.5 K triangles)	6.0	6.0	3.1	3.1	1.6	1.6
	Relief Per-Joint Impostors	20	17	11	9	5	4
	Flat Per-Joint Impostors	45	41	26	22	15	12
	Pre-generated Impostors	90	81	51	48	26	25

impostors used a 21-bone skeleton. For view-dependent impostors, 72 view directions were used for sampling. Relief mapping was configured to execute up to eight linear search steps, and up to two bilinear search steps. Animation clips of pre-generated impostors [13] were sampled at 30 fps.

Table 7.1 reports the results of our benchmark with different crowd sizes. As expected, image-based techniques clearly outperformed mesh-based approaches, even after significant simplification of the mesh. Pre-generated impostors offered the highest performance in our setup, but due to their visual-quality and animation limitations, this representation should be reserved to very distant characters. From the point of view of performance, flat per-joint impostors are good for not-so-distant characters. Relief per-joint impostors provided the highest-quality among image-based representations, but their output-sensitive nature and their high per-fragment cost makes them suitable for characters with small- to medium-size screen projection.

7.6 Conclusions

Per-joint impostors have been successfully used to replace geometry and speed up rendering with negligible visual artifacts. Relief impostors are good at recovering surface details and reproducing view-motion parallax effectively, at the expense of some per-fragment overhead. Beyond a certain distance threshold, this compact representation is much faster to render than traditional LoD triangle meshes. Encoding per-joint geometry and appearance with relief maps provides the highest image quality at the expense of a higher per-fragment overhead, which in practice limits their applicability to distant characters.

View-dependent flat impostors are more demanding in terms of texture memory and construction time, but provide the highest runtime performance even for close-up characters. With properly chosen switch distances, both representations outperform polygonal meshes with negligible visual artifacts. Regardless of the particular encoding, per-joint impostors support arbitrary animation cycles and animation blending, a missing feature in competing per-character impostors.

References

1. A. Beacco, C. Andújar, N. Pelechano, and B. Spanlang. Efficient rendering of animated characters through optimized per-joint impostors. *Journal of Computer Animation and Virtual Worlds*, 23(2):33–47, 2012.
2. A. Beacco, B. Spanlang, C. Andujar, and N. Pelechano. A flexible approach for output-sensitive rendering of animated characters. *Computer Graphics Forum*, 30(8):2328–2340, 2011.
3. N. Pelechano, J. Allbeck, and N. Badler. *Virtual Crowds: Methods, Simulation, and Control*. Morgan & Claypool, USA, 2008.
4. D. Thalmann and S. R. Musse. *Crowd Simulation*, Second Edition. Springer, USA, 2013.
5. J. H. Clark. Hierarchical geometric models for visible surface algorithms. *Communications of the ACM*, 19(10):547–554, 1976.
6. D. Luebke, B. Watson, J. D. Cohen, M. Reddy, and A. Varshney. *Level of Detail for 3D Graphics*. Elsevier Science Inc., New York, USA, 2002.
7. J. A. Bærentzen. Hardware-accelerated point generation and rendering of point-based impostors. *Journal of Graphics Tools*, 10(2):1–12, 2005.
8. M. Levoy and T. Whitted. *The Use of Points as a Display Primitive*. UNC Report. Department of Computer Science, University of North Carolina, 1985.
9. M. Zwicker, H. Pfister, J. van Baar, and M. Gross. Surface splatting. In *Proceedings of the 28th Annual Conference on Computer Graphics and Interactive Techniques, SIGGRAPH '01*, pp. 371–378, New York, USA, 2001. ACM.
10. A. Aubel, R. Boulic, and D. Thalmann. Animated impostors for real-time display of numerous virtual humans. In *VW '98: Proceedings of the First International Conference on Virtual Worlds*, pp. 14–28, London, UK, 1998. Springer-Verlag.
11. S. Dobbyn, J. Hamill, K. O'Conor, and C. O'Sullivan. Geopostors: A real-time geometry/impostor crowd rendering system. In *I3D '05: Proceedings of the 2005 Symposium on Interactive 3D Graphics and Games*, pp. 95–102, New York, USA, 2005. ACM.
12. L. Kavan, S. Dobbyn, S. Collins, J. Žára, and C. O'Sullivan. Polypostors: 2D polygonal impostors for 3D crowds. In *I3D '08: Proceedings of the 2008 Symposium on Interactive 3D Graphics and Games*, pp. 149–155, New York, USA, 2008. ACM.
13. F. Tecchia and Y. Chrysanthou. Real-time rendering of densely populated urban environments. In *Proceedings of the Eurographics Workshop on Rendering Techniques 2000*, pp. 83–88, London, UK, Springer-Verlag, 2000.
14. D. Cohen-Or, Y. L. Chrysanthou, C. T. Silva, and F. Durand. A survey of visibility for walkthrough applications. *IEEE Transactions on Visualization and Computer Graphics*, 9(3):412–431, 2003.
15. U. Assarsson and T. Möller. Optimized view frustum culling algorithms for bounding boxes. *Journal of Graphics Tools*, 5(1):9–22, 2000.
16. L. Bishop, D. Eberly, T. Whitted, M. Finch, and M. Shantz. Designing a PC game engine. *IEEE Computer Graphics and Applications*, 18(1):46–53, 1998.
17. J. T. Klosowski and C. T. Silva. Efficient conservative visibility culling using the prioritized-layered projection algorithm. *IEEE Transactions on Visualization and Computer Graphics*, 7(4):365–379, 2001.
18. M. Wimmer and J. Bittner. Hardware occlusion queries made useful. In M. Pharr and R. Fernando, editors, *GPU Gems 2: Programming Techniques for High-Performance Graphics and General-Purpose Computation*. pp. 91–108. Addison-Wesley, USA, March 2005.
19. B. Dudash. Skinned instancing. In *NVIDIA SDK 10*, 2007.
20. W. Lister, R. G. Laycock, and A. M. Day. A key-pose caching system for rendering an animated crowd in real-time. *Computer Graphics Forum*, 29(8):2304–2312, 2010.
21. E. Millan and I. Rudomin. Impostors and pseudo-instancing for GPU crowd rendering. In *GRAPHITE '06: Proceedings of the 4th International Conference on Computer Graphics and Interactive Techniques in Australasia and Southeast Asia*, pp. 49–55, New York, USA, 2006. ACM.

22. M. Oliveira, G. Bishop, and D. McAllister. Relief texture mapping. In *SIGGRAPH '00: Proceedings of the 27th Annual Conference on Computer Graphics and Interactive Techniques*, pp. 359–368, New York, USA, 2000. ACM Press/Addison-Wesley Publishing Co.

23. K. Oh, H. Ki, and C. Lee. Pyramidal displacement mapping: A GPU based artifacts-free ray tracing through an image pyramid. In *Virtual Reality Software and Technology (VRST)*, pp. 75–82, Limassol, Cyprus, 2006. ACM.

24. F. Policarpo, M. M. Oliveira, and J. Comba. Real-time relief mapping on arbitrary polygonal surfaces. *ACM Transactions on Graphics*, 24(3):935–935, 2005.

25. I. P. Herman. *Physics of the Human Body*. Springer, USA, 2007.

Section III

Evaluation

8

A Quantitative Approach to Comparing Real and Synthetic Crowds

Soraia Raupp Musse, Cláudio Rosito Jung, and Vinicius J. Cassol

CONTENTS

Despite advanced developments in crowd simulation, little attention has been given to the questions of evaluation and comparison among crowds. A big challenge when comparing crowds is the definition of which metric(s) should be used to compare and characterize crowds. Since seminal papers pioneered by Reynolds back in 1987 [1], who simulated flocks of birds and schools of fishes, the evaluation of crowd simulation results is mostly based on visual inspection. This chapter presents some real case studies that have been compared with simulation data. In addition, a quantitative method to compare crowds is also presented.

Examples of first methods proposed in the literature to control human crowds, Helbing et al. [2,3] introduced abstract attraction and repulsion forces to simulate groups of people in panic situations, while Musse and Thalmann [4] proposed a hierarchical crowd organization with groups of different levels of autonomy. Again, the evaluation of those models was only based on visual effects when compared with real and virtual crowds, and no quantitative comparisons with other approaches were provided. Since then, sophisticated techniques have been proposed concerning realistic behaviors, evolution in intelligent environments, and relevant collision avoidance methods, but still, very few have been made to characterize, evaluate, and compare crowds. Examples of applications are security, entertainment, and simulation. For instance, let us assume that a crowd in a mall can be filmed and data can be extracted. If crowds can be compared, an automatic system should be able to evaluate real-time crowds against the expected behavior for such period of the day, triggering alarms in the case of unusual behaviors.

Concerning the main challenges involved in the process of comparison/validation, the characterization of crowds is certainly one of them. To compare the two entities, it should be clear which are the relevant characteristics that can impact the comparison and evaluation. There are many possible parameters that can be used to characterize crowds, such as velocities (average, standard deviation, global, and local velocities), the density of people (average, standard deviation, global, and local densities), environment restrictions (that certainly impact velocities and densities), and spatial occupancy, among others. A big challenge to use these or other motion parameters is the way to detect/capture/store the required information. A simulation algorithm produces a set of trajectories, from which one can extract the position/velocity/orientation of agents as a function of time, but the extraction of such characteristics from real crowds is still an open problem (although tracking algorithms have rapidly evolved in the past year, dense environments are still challenging). Aside from the problem of extracting the trajectories in an environment (real or virtual), which parameters are suitable for summarizing the flow of people within an observation time window? And, given such parameters, which metrics are adequate for comparing two crowd flows? These questions are discussed in this chapter, where we present some real cases of crowd comparisons and describe a method to quantitatively compare the global flow of two crowds.

8.1 Related Work

This section presents some important works in two distinct contexts. First, we discuss methods for quantitatively comparing and evaluating crowds. Second, we discuss some methods that evaluate crowds focused on evacuation scenarios, which present specific characteristics.

8.1.1 Quantitative Evaluation of Crowds

Almost all methods proposed in the literature for human crowds simulation propose visual inspection as "the" way to compare their results with real life. One nice example is shown by Guy et al. [5], who describe a model for crowd simulation based on the least-effort principle. In their work, the authors describe a comparison based on visual inspection of Shibuya crossings. Although for the nice example and visually acceptable results, no quantitative data are presented to validate the visual inspection. In the same way, other works in the literature have also proposed ways to evaluate crowd simulation based on visual inspection. That is the case of known methods, from pioneering works to recent ones, such as References 3,4,6 through 8. Very few have proposed or performed a quantitative way to compare the crowds, and they are discussed in this section.

In 2005, Braun et al. [9] presented a model for crowd simulation and compared their results with a real-filmed scenario. The virtual environment was modeled based on the real physical environment and also populated according to the distribution of people in the real-life environment. A simulated scenario for evacuation happened in real life and parameters such as velocities and the density of people were manually captured based on a footage of the experiment. In the same way, the authors performed the crowd simulation in the virtual environment and compared results, which were mainly coherent according to the average density of people and mean speeds. Such evaluation was useful to validate the author's model, but restrictions concerning the environment must be declared explicitly in the geometric model, since the spatial occupancy was not evaluated. Although the evaluation was performed, no systematic method was proposed to compare two crowds in any environment.

In the past few years, some researchers have focused on using computer vision to feed crowd simulators with enough data to simulate crowds based on real life [10–13]. In these cases, computer vision algorithms are useful to improve the realism of simulations by using input data from real life, but none of these approaches proposes a quantitative way to compare crowds. The survey paper [14] tackles several issues concerning the possibilities of using crowd simulation to deal with crowd analysis problems (e.g., detection of unusual behavior), but no reference to quantitative comparison of crowds is provided.

Recently, substantial work has been developed for statistical analysis and evaluation of steering algorithms [15–17]. In their work, the authors propose metrics to compute traces and characterize the behavior of the simulation at specific points of time, over a window, or aggregated across the entire simulation. Steerbench [17] provides a benchmark framework for objectively evaluating steering behaviors for virtual agents. They proposed a diverse set of test cases and validated them with two different steering algorithms. Their model originated a framework that could be used to evaluate steering algorithms [15]. However, it is important to point out one of the main differences from our model: we do not define any test case or assumption concerning the possible crowd behavior. Our goal is not to define (neither evaluate) what is expected or what is good in a crowd simulation result, but to extract quantitative information for comparing the behavior of two crowds. In Reference 16, the authors mention some of their assumptions, for example, that steering algorithms should provide collision-free motion and solvable paths. Such assumptions are important in their work, since they are used to reduce the number of possible scenarios one agent can encounter while steering in the environment. In our case, no definition about real or virtual crowds has to be made. Crowds can collide, or be unstructured in the sense that people can change their minds and never reach an expected goal. In our point of view, the main difference between our method and the approaches described in References 15 through 17 is that we do not aim to evaluate algorithms. Instead, our main goal is to provide objective metrics that can be used to measure the similarity between the flow of two crowds, regardless of their "quality." However, if a given simulation can be considered a golden standard (for instance, based on a real-life crowd), the proposed approach could be used to measure the similarity of crowd simulation algorithms with such a golden standard.

Banerjee and Kraemer [18] present an automated technique for crowds evaluation and comparison. They compare the simulation run in the virtual environment and the actual scenario with real people navigating the corresponding real environment, with identical initial conditions. This comparison is accomplished by calculating the distance between the distribution of agents over the regions in the simulation and the distribution in the actual scenario over the same regions. A limitation of their method is that they should have similar initial conditions in both virtual and real scenarios, and the environment should be geometrically defined through polygons associated with regions in the real environment.

8.1.2 Evaluating Crowd Evacuation

The work of Fu et al. [19] was developed with a simple and punctual goal: simulate the usual process of evacuation. The motivation of the authors was to reproduce the pedestrian behavior to represent the exit selection taking into account a least-effort cellular automaton algorithm. It is represented by a set of two-dimensional (2D) cells where we can find pedestrians or obstacles. The motions and goals used to guide the movements are defined considering a probabilistic approach. The use of automaton cellular algorithms are also present in the work of Ji et al. [20] to simulate pedestrian dynamics as well as by Aik and Choon [21] with the main goal to reproduce a simple evacuation process. Chu et al. [22] developed the SAFEgress (Social Agent For Egress) platform, in which building occupants are modeled as agents able to make their actions according to their knowledge of the environment and their interactions with the social groups and the neighboring crowd. According to the authors, results show that both agents familiarity with the building and social influence can significantly impact evacuation performance.

More specifically, Huang et al. [23] have focused the work on the crowd simulation, but considering some distinct points to considering smoke into the simulation. The authors developed MIMOSA: Mine Interior Model of Smoke and Action, which integrates an underground coal mine virtual environment, a fire and smoke propagation model, and a human physiology and behavior model. Each individual agent has a set of physiological parameters as variables of time and the environment, simulating a miner's physiological condition during normal operations as well as during emergencies due to fire and smoke.

One of the main points considered when simulating crowds is concerned with results validation. The proper way should be to compare data from simulation with real-life experience. Current data-driven studies indicate this as a challenging point. Nowadays, there are just a few data-driven models developed to validate information from simulation and real life. Murphy et al. [24] present EvacSim, a multiagent building evacuation simulation. In the model, they detail pedestrian model elements that govern microscopic agent movement such as personal space preservation, obstacle avoidance, and moving together as a crowd. To validate the EvacSim pedestrian model against real-world pedestrian data, the authors made a comparison of flow rates, density, and velocity for corridor entry and for merging groups, considering data from simulation and real world in a controlled environment.

8.2 Simulated Case Studies and Comparison with Reality

To simulate coherent behaviors in an evacuation process, *CrowdSim* [25] was developed. Its main goal is to reproduce computationally crowd motion and behaviors during evacuation scenarios and also to present some data that are used to estimate people comfort and safety in a specific environment. The tool is organized in two distinct modules: *configuration* and *simulation*.

The configuration requests, as input, a three-dimensional (3D) representation of the environment that will be simulated. *CrowdSim* allows users to define information specifying the walkable regions considering the environment structure as well as physical restrictions. Also, in this module, the user is requested to define another set of parameters: number of agents to be simulated, regions of interest to be considered during agents motion (goals), and regions where agents will be created during simulation. Afterward, the user is able to specify behaviors that agents should perform during simulation. Such behaviors are

- *Goal seeking*: The agents should seek their goals immediately or vague, performing random motion.
- *Keep waiting*: The agents, when achieving some specific region of the environment, can spend some time on it before looking for another goal.
- *Perform random motion*: The agents can choose random destinations during a specific time, before trying to identify the best path to achieve the main goal.

When environment, parameters, and walkable regions are defined as well as desired behaviors, the user is able to run the second module of *CrowdSim*: simulation. This module considers as input the scenario previously defined in the configuration module to simulate it. Considering such information, this module is able to compute the routes to each agent to achieve a specific goal. Routes can be computed based on user specification (i.e., a graph determined by the user) or by using the best paths only considering the distance criterion. In addition, during the motion simulation, *CrowdSim* is able to avoid collisions among agents and/or obstacles (using a simple local geometry method). Each set of routes defined by the user or automatically computed by *CrowdSim* is called an evacuation plan. Indeed, *CrowdSim* uses A* [26] to compute the shortest paths.

The output of each simulation plan contains the following information: (i) agents trajectories during the simulation; (ii) speed variation for each agent; (iii) agents simulation time; (iv) local density along the time, that is, considering an agent in the center of a $1\,m^2$ region, we computed the local density; and (v) global time of simulation. The next few sections describe two scenarios that have been simulated and compared with real-life evacuation case studies.

8.2.1 College Building Simulation

In this case study, we applied *CrowdSim* to reproduce pedestrian behaviors when leaving the Faculty of Informatics (FACIN) building at PUCRS.[*] The building is composed of eight floors, where it is possible to identify classrooms (floors 2, 3, 4, and 5), professors offices, research labs (floors 6 and 7), and administration offices (floors 1, 7, and 8). Furthermore, there are two emergency exits that are accessed by stairs from all floors. The population of the building is around 800 people every day. This scenario is illustrated in Figure 8.1 where we can observe a real external picture of the building (a) as well as the respective 3D model (b) and the building environment represented in *CrowdSim* (c).

The 3D virtual environment was modeled by a 3D artist using Google Sketch Up according to the building's floorplans. Each floor of the building is coherent with the real environment dimensions. The illustration of the first floor is presented in Figure 8.2 where the two emergency exits previously described (one in the front and the other in the back of the building) are highlighted in red. For this case study, the furniture inside the building was not considered in the simulation.

For the simulation, the full environment is mapped to specify walkable regions for the agents. This process is performed by *CrowdSim* configuration module (see Figure 8.1c). The green areas represent the *starting* areas, regions where the agents can be created, while the

---

[*] www.pucrs.br/facin

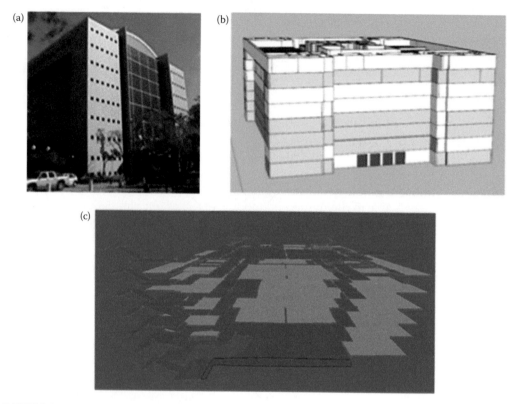

FIGURE 8.1
Three representations of the building simulated in this case study: The real picture (a), 3D environment (b), and simulation environment defined in *CrowdSim* (c).

external areas of the building (*goal* areas) are presented in red and are located near emergency exits. Connecting *start* and *goal* areas, we can observe the *walkable* areas (corridors and stairs) illustrated in blue.

To set up the simulation scenario, we take into account the average number of people at each floor of the building, during a normal day of work. Table 8.1 summarizes the numbers of simulated people. It is important to mention that this population distribution was similar when performing the real-evacuation exercise.

The high concentration of people in the first four floors is mainly because most of the classrooms and practical laboratories are located in this area. In the other floors are located research labs, professors, and business offices. In the performed simulation, all the agents are configured to leave the building using emergency exits except the agents from the first floor. The same orientation was considered when performing the real-evacuation exercise.

Table 8.2 summarizes the obtained information from real and simulated evacuation process. The evacuation times are presented in seconds.

In the real-egress exercise, we had the collaboration of volunteers who timed their walk time until they reach the goal areas. Indeed, since in real time we obtained the time that the first person (teacher in each room) exits the environment, we included such data also coming from the simulation. A quick analysis of the extracted data from real and simulation scenarios allows us to observe that the differences are small and coherent. We believe that

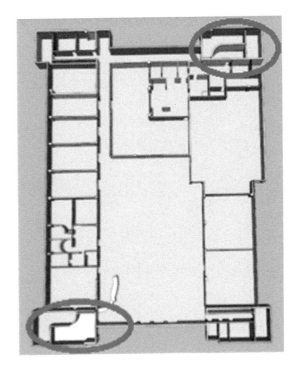

FIGURE 8.2
Illustration of the first floor of the building. Two emergency exits are highlighted in red.

TABLE 8.1

Population Simulated in Each Floor of the College
Building

Floor	1	2	3	4	5	6	7	8	Total
Agents	100	190	200	130	85	55	50	20	**830**

TABLE 8.2

Summarized Data from College Building Evacuation: Real and Simulated Process

	Real Process	Simulation
Place	Time to the First Person Leaving the Building (seconds)	Time to the First Agent Leaving the Building (seconds)
Classroom 205	32	56
Classroom 214	100	64
Classroom 301	180	68
Lab 309	163	76
Lab 310	120	64
Classroom 312	154	116
Classroom 412	312	132
Classroom 415	300	118
Professors room (fifth floor)	274	159

(a)   (b)

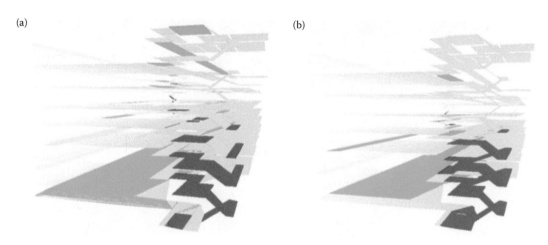

FIGURE 8.3
Density map of the college building. In (a) at second 40 and (b) at second 80.

the difference between the simulation and the real-exercise time is because all the simulation agents were created and started to move at the exact same time, in a different way from real life, where people have different response time to events. Another point to be considered regards the agents velocity. According to literature [27], we specify the velocity of the agents in 0.8 m/s adding a positive and negative variation of 20%. In addition, analyzing, for example, the classroom 309, we can observe a divergence between the simulation time (76 seconds) and real process time (163 seconds). Indeed, it can be explained because real people do not feel the panic voluntarily, since they know it is not a real fact.

After the simulation finished, we observed that the time taken for all the agents to leave the building was 250 seconds (4 minutes and 10 seconds) while the last person left the building during the real-egress process 410 seconds after the starting of the process.

The analysis of the simulation results provided by *CrowdSim* allows us to compute the density of the place during the simulated evacuation process. The density analysis makes it possible to identify attention points in the environment including bottlenecks. In Figure 8.3 we present a density map where we illustrate the environment density, specifically on the stairs located on the frontal emergency exit in two distinct moments of simulation (after 40 (a) and 80 (b) seconds of simulation). The regions in red mean attention areas (more than two people per m^2) while the yellow and green areas mean regions with medium (two people per m^2) and low (one person per m^2) concentration of people.

As expected, the greater concentration points are located in the first and the fourth floors. The high concentration in this region starts after 40 seconds of simulation when agents from the highest floors achieve half of the distance to reach the goal areas outside the building.

8.2.2 A Night Club Case Study

This section describes an experiment conducted in a night club in Porto Alegre, Brazil. The environment's area is 1100 m^2 and it has four floors. It was a shared experience developed in partnership with the night club owners and a safety company. The goal was to study

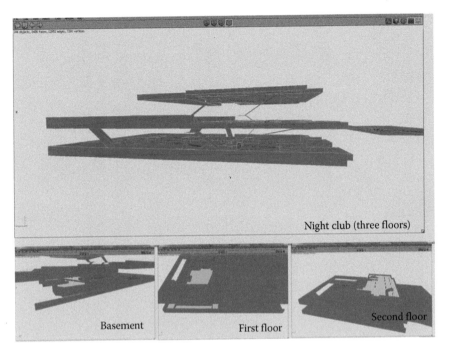

FIGURE 8.4
3D model of the simulated night club. Different point of views of three floors. Yellow and green areas as related with regions where people are at the beginning of the simulation.

how people perform an evacuation process in real life. The first step was the 3D modeling of the environment as illustrated in Figure 8.4.

It is important to mention that to compare results of real and virtual simulations, data from real life should be extracted, such as local and global times, local and global densities, and velocities. The real experience was performed in a night club where the audience accorded to leave the club exactly at 2 a.m. The experience was performed together with a security company that participates in generating evacuation plans using *CrowdSim*. Since one plan was selected using *CrowdSim*, the company starts to train individuals who work in the night club. The real evacuation was performed with 240 people who accepted to participate in the experience. During the real-escape exercise, we were able to collect different data to evaluate results of this experience. The collected data were composed of videos (from security cameras) and the number of people in different parts of the club (obtained from infra-red technology). This information was very important to evaluate this work. Figure 8.5 illustrates two frames of the simulation.

Table 8.3 summarizes the comparison between real and virtual evacuation scenarios. Figure 8.6 illustrates an image captured during the evacuation that shows the people in stairs (second floor) in time 40 seconds after the simulation started. Also, an image in the same time simulation illustrates the stairs in the virtual simulation.

The analysis in Table 8.3 reveals a noticeable difference in evacuation time between 119 and 175 seconds. It can be explained by the fact that real people do not behave voluntarily as in an emergency situation. This is justified by the fact that real people, not in panic, respect the space of others, not achieving so higher densities if compared to the simulation data, for instance.

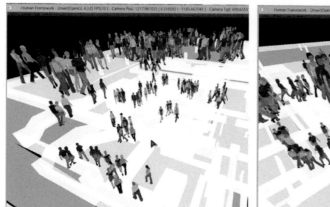

FIGURE 8.5
Images illustrating the simulation in the night club. Agents are leaving the environment.

TABLE 8.3

Quantitative Data Comparing Real and Simulated Worlds Considering Exactly the Same Evacuation Plan

	Simulation	Real-World Data
Total time for evacuation (seconds)	119	175
Highest density (people/m^2)	5.4	4.5
Place of the highest density	Stairs (second floor)	Stairs (second floor)
Time when the highest density was observed	Second 40	Second 50
Highest speed (m/s)	1.3	1.5
Smallest speed (m/s)	0.1	0.2

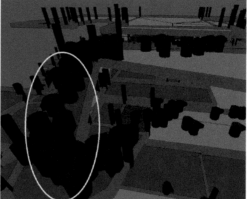

FIGURE 8.6
Images illustrating the stairs on the second floor 40 seconds after the beginning of the simulation in the real and virtual environment.

In this section, we presented two case studies where simulation and real scenarios have been compared. Data used in the comparison is mainly global and based on velocities and densities. The next section describes an automatic method to provide a quantitative similarity measure between the flows of two crowds.

8.3 A Quantitative Approach for Comparing Crowds

In this section, we propose a new model to compare quantitatively global flow characteristics of two crowds. The proposed approach explores a four-dimensional (4D) histogram that contains information on the local velocity (speed and orientation) for each spatial position, and the comparison is made using histogram distances. The 4D histogram also allows the comparison of specific characteristics, such as distribution of orientations only, speed only, relative spatial occupancy only, and combinations of such features.

First, we describe how the 4D histogram is built, based on Reference 28. Let us consider a discrete-time trajectory $(x(t), y(t))$, for $t = 1, \ldots, N$, where N is the number of points in the trajectory. Those trajectories can be either related to a crowd simulation algorithm or a tracked trajectory in a real-life scenario. For each time t, the 4D vector $(x(t), y(t), \dot{x}(t), \dot{y}(t))^T$ relates to the phase-space representation, which encodes valuable information on the dynamics of the particle at a given time. Similarly, a representation using polar coordinates of the velocity vector encodes the same information, allowing the analysis of the speed $s(t)$ and orientation $\theta(t)$ at each time t, which are useful for comparing the flow of two crowds. In fact, considering the whole trajectory of all agents in a given scenario, the distribution of such 4D vectors provides a global representation of the dynamics of the crowd.

One issue related to a higher-dimensional histogram is the exponential growth of memory requirements, so that the number of bins in the histogram should be large enough to describe the distribution, and at the same time small enough to cope with memory requirements (and to avoid generating a very sparse histogram). Let us assume that all trajectories were captured in a $W \times H$ region, so that $0 \leq x(t) \leq H$ and $0 \leq y(t) \leq W$. The spatial coordinates are discretized into N_x and N_y bins in the horizontal and vertical directions, respectively, and each position $(x, y)^*$ of the trajectory is mapped into a discretized bin value (x^d, y^d), where

$$\phi \gamma \eta \gamma \sum^{\beta x} \sum x^d \in \{0, 1, \ldots, N_x - 1\}, \quad y^d \in \{0, 1, \ldots, N_y - 1\} \tag{8.1}$$

Clearly, selecting larger values for N_x and N_y leads to a more precise discretization of spatial coordinates, at the cost of increasing the size of the 4D array.

The orientation θ of the local velocity vector is quantized into N_θ levels (we used $N_\theta = 8$ in this work), each one comprising a circular sector with an internal angle $2\pi/N_\theta$, and the angle θ is discretized into the center of the circular sector θ^d where it belongs. Similarly, the speed s is quantized into N_s levels. As in Reference 28, we select $N_s = 3$ to quantize the speed in only three levels: low, medium, and high. Our quantization scheme for the speed

---

* Time parameter t will be dropped from now on, and used only when necessary.

is given by

$$
v^d = \begin{cases} 0 \text{ (low speed)}, & \text{if } 0 \leq v < v_l \\ 1 \text{ (medium speed)}, & \text{if } v_l \leq v < v_h \text{ ,} \\ 2 \text{ (high speed)}, & \text{if } v_h \leq v \end{cases} \qquad (8.2)
$$

where v_l and v_h are thresholds that define limits for low and high speeds, respectively. Such values may be selected from pedestrian motion studies such as Reference 29, or computed adaptively based on the distribution of speeds found in the crowds to be analyzed. For instance, given a reference simulation result (containing a series of trajectories), we can compute the mean speed μ_s and standard deviation σ_s, and select the thresholds as

$$
v_l = \mu_s - k\sigma_s \quad \text{and} \quad v_h = \mu_s + k\sigma_s, \qquad (8.3)
$$

where k controls the spread of medium-speed trajectories (we used $k = 2$ in this work).

Another important consequence of the number of quantization bins is the effect when comparing two histograms. When building the histogram, similar space-phase vectors may be quantized into adjacent bins, which affects most histogram-based distance metrics. To alleviate this issue, we explore an approach similar to kernel density estimation to build the histogram, so that the original 4D values that lie close to the boundary of two bins will account for both of them, instead of being assigned to just one.

More precisely, given the observation point $(x_i(t), y_i(t), \theta_i(t), s_i(t))^T$ and its discretized counterpart $\left(x_i^d(t), y_i^d(t), \theta_i^d(t), s_i^d(t)\right)^T$, the 4D histogram H is built by spreading the information according to a kernel g

$$
H(x^d, y^d, \theta^d, s^d) = \sum_{i=1}^{N_T} \sum_{t=1}^{N_p(i)} g(x^d - x_i^d(t), y^d - y_i^d(t), \theta^d - \theta_i(t), s^d - s_i^d(t)), \qquad (8.4)
$$

where N_T is the number of trajectories, $N_p(i)$ is the length (number of points) of the ith trajectory, and $g(x, y, \theta, s)$ is the spreading kernel, defined as a separable product of individual kernels in the spatial dimensions (x and y), the orientation dimension θ, and the speed dimension s, that is, $g(x, y, \theta, v) = g_x(x, y)g_\theta(\theta)g_s(s)$.

The spatial kernel $g_x(x, y)$ is a truncated discrete Gaussian function

$$
g_x(x, y) = \begin{cases} \dfrac{1}{c} e^{-(-x^2/2\sigma_x^2)-(-y^2/2\sigma_y^2)}, & \text{if } -2\sigma_x \leq x \leq 2\sigma_x, -2\sigma_y \leq y \leq 2\sigma_y \\ 0 & \text{otherwise} \end{cases}, \qquad (8.5)
$$

where c is a normalization factor (so that the kernel values add up to 1). Parameters σ_x and σ_x control the spread of the kernel in the vertical and horizontal directions, and they are selected based on the size of each spatial bin and the influence around each position (related to the average diameter D of a person). In our experiments, we select $\sigma_x = DN_x/H$ and $\sigma_y = DN_y/W$, where $D = 0.5\,\text{m}$, for simulated results (for trajectories tracked from real-life video sequences, D is a quantity given in pixels related to the distance of $\sim 0.5\,\text{m}$).

The kernels $g_\theta(\theta)$ and $g_s(s)$ are selected using the method described in Reference 28. In a few words, $g_\theta(\theta)$ spreads the influence of a given angle into the two closest angular bins, based on the distances between the bin centers. As for the speed, the kernel function is a Dirac delta (unit impulse) function, since only three bins are used for s.

8.3.1 Finding Coherent Motion Flows

The 4D histogram described above provides information on the global flow of a given scenario. However, it may also be desirable to detect "sub-flows" within the crowd, that is, clusters of trajectories that are similar according to some criteria. As in Reference 28, in this work, we subdivide the trajectories based on global displacement vectors, using an unsupervised clustering algorithm.

For each trajectory i, the main displacement vector is given by $d_i = (x_i(N_p(i)) - x_i(1), y_i(N_p(i)) - y_i(1))^T$, that is, the vector connecting the start and end points of the trajectory. Similar trajectories according to such displacement vector form a cluster in a 2D feature space, and the distribution of each cluster is modeled as a bivariate Gaussian distribution. Hence, the overall distribution of d_i is a mixture of Gaussians (MoGs), and its parameters (number of components in the mixture, *a priori* probabilities, mean vectors, and covariance matrices) can be obtained automatically using the approach described in Reference 30.

In Reference 28, an outlier detection process was included to discard unusual trajectories. In this work, however, we just need the main subflows, so that we do not treat possible outliers. On the other hand, we merge components that present significant overlap, since the algorithm described in Reference 30 is sensitive to a random initialization (particularly when the number of samples is small), and may present oversegmented and highly over-lappling clusters. For that purpose, we compute the Bhattacharyya distance [31] between every pair of Gaussian components, given by

$$B(i, j) = \frac{1}{8} (\mu_i - \mu_j)^T \left[\frac{C_i + C_j}{2} \right]^{-1} (\mu_i - \mu_j) + \frac{1}{2} \ln \left(\frac{|(C_i + C_j)/2|}{\sqrt{|C_i||C_j|}} \right),$$

where μ_i, μ_j are the means of the distributions, and C_i, C_j are the corresponding covariance matrices.

Then, we find the pair of components that presents the smallest distance (highest overlap), and merge the components into a single bivariate distribution if the distance is smaller than a threshold T_B (defined experimentally as 5). Such merging comprises of summing the priors, and recomputing the mean vector and covariance matrix with the samples of both components. The distances between all classes are recomputed, and the merging process is repeated iteratively.

An example of the clustering approach is shown in Figure 8.7. Figure 8.7a shows a simple crowd simulation result, where agents move from left to right. As expected, a single cluster of trajectories is created, shown in Figure 8.7b. Figure 8.7c illustrates a simulation result with two groups of trajectories in a cross shape, and the two detected clusters are shown in Figure 8.7d.

The computation of the 4D histogram is done independently for each cluster, so that a given simulation is characterized by a set of 4D histograms $H_k(x^d, y^d, \theta^d, s^d), k = 1, \ldots, M$, where M is the number of clusters. The overall histogram for that simulation is given by

$$H(x^d, y^d, \theta^d, s^d) = \sum_{k=1}^{M} p_k H_k(x^d, y^d, \theta^d, s^d), \tag{8.6}$$

where p_k are the *a priori* probabilities related to each cluster, so that $\sum_{k=1}^{M} p_k = 1$.

The comparison between two crowd flows can be performed based on the overall distributions, or between individual clusters of each simulation (so that partial matches may

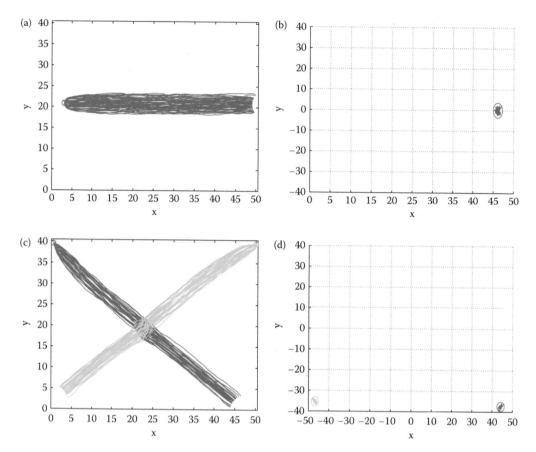

FIGURE 8.7
Examples of trajectories and the obtained clusters.

be found). Also, several individual aspects of the simulation results may be compared, as described next. It should be noticed that the clustering technique used in our approach is focused on structured environments, where the main flows are expected. The overall distribution given by Equation 8.6, however, does not depend on the clustering (any clustering leads to the same overall histogram), so that it might be used to compare arbitrary crowd flows.

8.3.2 Comparing Crowds

Let us consider two normalized histograms H and H', so that the summation over all bins equals 1. There are several ways to compare the similarity between histograms (an empirical comparison in the context of color–texture similarity was presented in Reference 32), but not all of them obey all metric distance axioms. In particular, the triangular inequality

$$d(H, H'') \leq d(H, H') + d(H', H'')$$ (8.7)

is important for comparing crowd flows, since it states that if the pairs of histograms (H, H') and (H', H'') are similar, so is the pair (H, H'').

In a different context (object tracking), Comaniciu et al. [33] showed that the following function satisfies all metric distance axioms

$$d(H, H') = \sqrt{1 - \rho(H, H')},$$
(8.8)

where

$$\rho(H, H') = \sum_{i=1}^{N_b} H(i) H'(i)$$
(8.9)

is the Bhattacharyya coefficient, and N_b is the number of bins in both histograms. The distance defined in Equation 8.8 lies in the range $[0, 1]$, and its minimum value (0) is achieved when the histograms are identical, while the maximum value (1) is reached when there is no overlap at all between nonzero bins of both histograms.

To compare the global flow of two crowds, we propose the use of Equation 8.8 applied to variations of the 4D normalized histograms of two crowd simulation results. More precisely, based on the 4D histograms, we are able to compare several aspects related to global behaviors of the crowds, as explained next.

8.3.2.1 Global Flow

We consider that two simulations are similar w.r.t. their "global flows" if the agents in both simulations move approximately through the same positions with similar velocities (orientation and speed). Such behavior can be detected by directly comparing the (normalized) 4D histograms of both crowds using Equation 8.8.

8.3.2.2 Spatial Occupancy

By spatial occupancy, we mean the preferred positions occupied by agents in the simulation. Given the original 4D histogram $H(x^d, y^d, \theta^d, s^d)$, the spatial occupancy can be easily obtained by disregarding information related to velocity, that is, by summing over the third and fourth dimensions of the histogram

$$H_{so}(x^d, y^d) = \sum_{\theta^d} \sum_{s^d} H(x^d, y^d, \theta^d, s^d),$$
(8.10)

so that the spatial occupancy of two simulations can be compared by measuring the distance between the corresponding collapsed (and normalized) 2D histograms H_{so} and H'_{so}. In fact, since the histograms are normalized, we cannot get an absolute value of the density of agents at each spatial position. Hence, histograms H_{so} measure in fact the relative spatial occupancy of the simulation, and the concept of density of agents can be obtained by including the number of agents in each crowd.

8.3.2.3 Main Orientations

Two crowds are considered similar w.r.t. their main orientations if the distributions of their local orientations are similar. As for the spatial occupancy, the distribution of orientations can also be extracted from the 4D histogram

$$H_{or}(\theta^d) = \sum_{x^d} \sum_{y^d} \sum_{s^d} H(x^d, y^d, \theta^d, s^d).$$
(8.11)

8.3.2.4 Main Speeds

The concept of main speeds is similar to main orientations, but considering only information regarding the speed of agents in both crowds:

$$H_{sp}(s^d) = \sum_{x^d} \sum_{y^d} \sum_{\theta^d} H(x^d, y^d, \theta^d, s^d). \tag{8.12}$$

If the crowd flows to be compared present more than one cluster, the distances defined above may be applied to individual clusters of each flow, aiming to detect matches of subflows within both crowds. Some experimental results are presented next.

8.3.3 Experimental Results

To evaluate the proposed quantitative metric to compare crowds, we have created some controlled simulations varying different aspects in the simulations. We have also compared flows related to real-life data.

Simulated trajectories were created using Reference 34, and they were generated in a rectangular room with 40×50 m. Although such simulations depict simple flows, they are useful to show that the distances provided by the proposed approach are in consonance with visual inspection. In the simulated flows, we varied specific parameters such as main orientations and average speed of the agents, and the main characteristics of simulated data are presented in Table 8.4.

In particular, simulations 2–6 are variations of simulation 1, changing specific aspects such as orientation of the main flows, variations in the spatial occupancy, and different average speed of agents. Table 8.5 summarizes the distances between simulation 1 and simulations 2–6, according to different criteria. As it can be observed, simulation 4 is very close to simulation 1 in all aspects, coherently with visual inspection (and the main crowd characteristics indicated in Table 8.4). It can also be observed that simulations 2–5 are similar to 1 w.r.t. spatial occupancy, whereas simulation 6 presents larger discrepancy (since

TABLE 8.4

Description of the Main Characteristics of the Simulated Flows Used for Comparison

Simulation	1	2	3	4	5
No. of agents	30	30	60	60	60
Average speed (m/s)	1.2	1.2	1.2	1.2	0.7
Trajectories					

Simulation	6	7	8	9	10
No. of agents	60	60	120	60	120
Average speed (m/s)	1.2	1.2	1.2	0.7	1.2
Trajectories					

Note: In the plots of the trajectories, circles indicate start points.

TABLE 8.5

Distance Values between Simulation 1 and Simulations 2–6, with Respect to Different Matching Criteria

Simulation	2	3	4	5	6
Global	1.00	0.53	0.11	0.74	0.46
Spat. Occ.	0.27	0.15	0.08	0.07	0.46
Orient.	0.99	0.47	0.01	0.01	0.01
Speed	0.02	0.07	0.01	0.70	0.01

the trajectories occupy a wider portion of the environment). Regarding the main orientations, simulations 4–6 are very similar to 1, since all of them present a unidirectional flow from left to right at all points. Simulation 3 presents partial coherence with simulation 1, while crowd 2 is not similar at all to the reference simulation (its main flow is from right to left). In particular, if we compare each cluster of simulation 2 with the single cluster of simulation 1, we can see that the blue cluster is similar to simulation 1 regarding all criteria (distances 0.19, 0.13, 0.07, 0.06, and 0.002, respectively); the red cluster, on the other hand, is very distant from simulation 1 according to the global flow and orientation (distances 0.99 and 0.94, respectively), but similar w.r.t. spatial occupancy and distribution of speeds (distances 0.19 and 0.02, respectively). Finally, Table 8.5 indicates that results 2,3,4, and 6 are coherent with the reference simulation concerning main speeds (in fact, all those simulations were performed aiming an average speed of 1.2 m/s), and simulation 5 presented a large discrepancy (since the average speed was 0.7 m/s).

It is also interesting to compare the flows shown in simulations 7–9. Using simulation 7 as the reference, our quantitative results show that simulation 8 is similar w.r.t. all criteria (distances 0.28, 0.17, 0.13, and 0.16, respectively). Simulation 9 is similar w.r.t. the main orientations (distance 0.02) and spatial occupancy (distance 0.09), but the global flows and speed distributions were considered different (distances 0.68 and 0.62, respectively).

Finally, we compared the flows generated in simulations 3 and 10. Both simulations present two main "sub-flows," detected as two clusters in each simulation. The orientation and speed distances yield 0.07 and 0.08, respectively, indicating that both simulations are very similar w.r.t. these two criteria. On the other hand, the global flow and spatial occupancy values are close to one, indicating that agents simulated in both scenarios move in very distinct portions of the space.

We have also tested the proposed approach using real-life trajectories, captured manually during different periods of the day (such trajectories were smoothed using a Chebyshev low-pass filter to reduce the noise when estimating the local orientation). These three sets of trajectories are shown in Figure 8.8, and different colors relate to different clusters obtained with the proposed approach.

Table 8.6 shows the proposed distance using different matching criteria for all three real-life scenarios, namely global flow (Global), spatial occupancy (Spat. Occ.), orientation (Orient.), and speed (Speed). As it can be observed, flows 1 and 2 are similar w.r.t. spatial occupancy (since trajectories populate approximately the same regions), but very distinct global flows (since the main orientations are mostly different). Also, it can be noted that flows 2 and 3 present a relatively low distance value w.r.t. global flow, since a group of trajectories in both flows coincide in terms of spatial occupancy, orientation, and speed. In fact, if we compare only the blue cluster of flow 2 with flow 3, the global distance is 0.142, indicating a high-coherence value.

 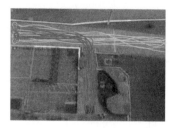 

FIGURE 8.8
Manually captured trajectories in a real scenario, at different periods of the day (illustrating different flow patterns).

TABLE 8.6

Distance Values Comparing the Three Flows of the Real-Life Scenario, with Respect to Different Matching Criteria

	Global			Spat. Occ.			Orient.			Speed		
Flow	1	2	3	1	2	3	1	2	3	1	2	3
1	–	0.89	0.83	–	0.20	0.48	–	0.74	0.72	–	0.34	0.35
2	0.88	–	0.43	0.20	–	0.36	0.74	–	0.36	0.21	–	0.04
3	0.83	0.44	–	0.48	0.36	–	0.72	0.36	–	0.28	0.04	–

8.4 Conclusions

This chapter first presents two case studies where crowd simulation and real-evacuation scenarios have been compared. In both cases, some information from real life could be extracted. In the first case, volunteers measured their time to evacuate the building. In this case, only times could be evaluated. In the second scenario, films and images have registered the real-evacuation exercise. In this case, the images were not good enough to track individuals and trajectories; so, we proceed with a manual process to count people to have densities and velocities. In both cases, we presented a way to compare the real and virtual simulation when few information is available.

In the second part of the chapter, we present a method for quantitatively comparing crowd flows based on the distribution of phase-space variables (position and velocity), stored in 4D histograms. In fact, a clustering approach is also applied, so that partial matches of "sub-flows" may also be detected. In this case, more information about the two crowds is considered and a more-refined comparison could be done. The experimental results were performed using synthetic data (results from crowd simulation algorithms) as well as real-life data (trajectories manually extracted from real footages). The synthetic dataset was created with controlled situations, aiming to detect variations of specific crowd flow parameters (such as global flow, main orientations, main speed, and spatial occupancy). Quantitative results obtained using the proposed approach matched a qualitative evaluation by visual inspection, suggesting its use as a crowd comparison metric. Unfortunately, this methodology could not be used to provide comparison in two cases presented in the first part of the chapter, since it was not possible to track the individual trajectories.

An underlying problem is that even in a real crowd, there is no guarantee that the same "results" will obtain if the real situation is simply replayed again. In other words, there is a space of "natural" variations and just having one single instance does not mean that a crowd simulation that results is a differing local or global behavior that is "wrong." The sensitivity of real crowds to initial conditions and multiple independent parameters (such as personal choices) make the space of plausible real situations immense—hence determining what is or is not a "good" simulation result extremely sensitive to multiple unknowns and conditions.

References

1. C. W. Reynolds. Flocks, herds and schools: A distributed behavioral model. In *Proceedings of the Annual Conference on Computer Graphics and Interactive Techniques (SIGGRAPH '87)*, pp. 25–34, New York, USA, 1987. ACM Press.

2. D. Helbing, I. Farkas, and T. Vicsek. Simulating dynamical features of escape panic. *Nature*, 407(6803):487–490, 2000.

3. D. Helbing and P. Molnar. Self-organization phenomena in pedestrian crowds. In *Self-Organization of Complex Structures: From Individual to Collective Dynamics*, pp. 569–577, London, UK, 1997. Gordon and Breach.

4. S. R. Musse and D. Thalmann. Hierarchical model for real time simulation of virtual human crowds. *IEEE Transactions on Visualization and Computer Graphics*, 7(2):152–164, 2001.

5. S. J. Guy, J. Chhugani, S. Curtis, P. Dubey, M. Lin, and D. Manocha. Pledestrians: A least-effort approach to crowd simulation. In *Proceedings of the 2010 ACM SIGGRAPH/Eurographics Symposium on Computer Animation*, SCA '10, pp. 119–128, Aire-la-Ville, Switzerland, Switzerland, 2010. Eurographics Association.

6. E. Bouvier, E. Cohen, and L. Najman. From crowd simulation to airbag deployment: Particle systems, a new paradigm of simulation. *Journal of Electronic Imaging (Special Issue on Random Model in Imaging)*, 6(1):94–107, 1997.

7. N. Pelechano, J. M. Allbeck, and N. I. Badler. Controlling individual agents in high-density crowd simulation. In *Proceedings of ACM SIGGRAPH/Eurographics Symposium on Computer Animation (SCA '07)*, pp. 99–108, Aire-la-Ville, Switzerland, Switzerland, 2007. Eurographics Association.

8. A. Treuille, S. Cooper, and Z. Popović. Continuum crowds. *ACM Transactions on Graphics*, 25(3):1160–1168, 2006.

9. A. Braun, B. E. J. Bodmann, and S. R. Musse. Simulating virtual crowds in emergency situations. In *Proceedings of ACM Virtual Reality and Software Technology 2005*, pp. 244–252, Monterey, California, USA, 2005. ACM.

10. N. Courty and T. Corpetti. Crowd motion capture. *Computer Animation Virtual Worlds*, 18(2):361–370, 2007.

11. K. H. Lee, M. G. Choi, Q. Hong, and J. Lee. Group behavior from video: A data-driven approach to crowd simulation. In *Proceedings of ACM SIGGRAPH/Eurographics Symposium on Computer Animation (SCA '07)*, pp. 109–118, Aire-la-Ville, Switzerland, Switzerland, 2007. Eurographics Association.

12. A. Lerner, Y. Chrysanthou, and D. Lischinski. Crowds by example. *Computer Graphics Forum*, 26(3):655–664, 2007.

13. S. R. Musse, C. R. Jung, J. C. S. Jacques Jr., and A. Braun. Using computer vision to simulate the motion of virtual agents. *Computer Animation Virtual Worlds*, 18(2):83–93, 2007.

14. J. C. S. Jacques Jr., S. R. Musse, and C. R. Jung. A survey of crowd analysis using computer vision. *IEEE Signal Processing Magazine*, 27(5):66–77, 2010.

15. B. Allen, G. Reinman, M. Kapadia, S. Singh, and P. Faloutsos. Steerbug: An interactive framework for specifying and detecting steering behaviors. In *Proceedings of ACM*

SIGGRAPH/Eurographics Symposium on Computer Animation (SCA '09), pp. 209–216, New York, USA, 2009. Eurographics Association.

16. S. Singh, G. Reinman, M. Kapadia, M. Wang, and P. Faloutsos. Scenario space: Characterizing coverage, quality, and failure of steering algorithms. In *Proceedings of ACM SIGGRAPH/Eurographics Symposium on Computer Animation (SCA '11)*, Vancouver, Canada, 2011. Eurographics Association.

17. P. Faloutsos, S. Singh, M. Kapadia, and G. Reinman. Steerbench: A benchmark suite for evaluating steering behaviors. *Computer Animation Virtual Worlds*, 20(5):533–548, 2009.

18. B. Banerjee and L. Kraemer. Evaluation and comparison of multi-agent based crowd simulation systems. *Lecture Notes in Computer Science—Agents for Games and Simulations II*, 6525/2011:53–66, 2011.

19. L. Fu, W. Song, W. Lv, and S. Lo. Simulation of exit selection behavior using least effort algorithm. *Transportation Research Procedia*, 2(0):533–540, 2014. *The Conference on Pedestrian and Evacuation Dynamics 2014* (PED 2014), October 22–24, 2014, Delft, The Netherlands.

20. L. Ji, Y. Qian, J. Zeng, M. Wang, D. Xu, Y. Yan, and S. Feng. Simulation of evacuation characteristics using a 2-dimensional cellular automata model for pedestrian dynamics. *Journal of Applied Mathematics*, 2013: 8 p., 2013. Article ID 284721.

21. L. Eng Aik and T. Wee Choon. Simulating evacuations with obstacles using a modified dynamic cellular automata mode. *Journal of Applied Mathematics*, 2012:17, 2012.

22. M. L. Chu, P. Parigi, K. Law, and J.-C. Latombe. Modeling social behaviors in an evacuation simulator. *Computer Animation and Virtual Worlds*, 25(3–4):373–382, 2014.

23. P. Huang, J. Kang, J. T. Kider, B. Sunshine-Hill, J. B. McCaffrey, D. V. Rios, and N. I. Badler. Real-time evacuation simulation in Mine Interior Model of Smoke and Action. Computer Animation and Social Agents, 2010.

24. S. Ó. Murphy, K. N. Brown, and C. Sreenan. The EvacSim pedestrian evacuation agent model: Development and validation. In *Proceedings of the 2013 Summer Computer Simulation Conference*, SCSC '13, pp. 38:1–38:8, Vista, CA, 2013. Society for Modeling and Simulation International.

25. V. Cassol, C. M. Bianco, A. Carvalho, J. Brasil, M. Monteiro, and S. R. Musse. An experience-based approach to simulate virtual crowd behaviors under the influence of alcohol. In *IVA'15: Proceedings of the 15th International Conference on Intelligent Virtual Agents*, pp. 124–127, Berlin, Heidelberg, 2015. Springer-Verlag.

26. P. E. Hart, N. J. Nilsson, and B. Raphael. A formal basis for the heuristic determination of minimum cost paths. *IEEE Transactions on Systems Science and Cybernetics*, 4(2):100–107, 1968.

27. J. Fruin. *Pedestrian Planning and Design*. Metropolitan Association of Urban Designers and Environmental Planners, New York, 1971.

28. C. R. Jung, L. Hennemann, and S. R. Musse. Event detection using trajectory clustering and 4-D histograms. *IEEE Transactions on Circuits and Systems for Video Technology*, 1:1565–1575, 2008.

29. R. Knoblauch, M. Pietrucha, and M. Nitzbur. Field studies of pedestrian walking speed and start-up time. *Transportation Research Record*, 1538(1):27–38, 1996.

30. M. A. T. Figueiredo and A. K. Jain. Unsupervised learning of finite mixture models. *IEEE Transactions on Pattern Analysis and Machine Intelligence*, 24(3):381–396, 2002.

31. K. Fukunaga. *Introduction to Statistical Pattern Recognition* (2nd ed.). Academic Press Professional, Inc., San Diego, CA, USA, 1990.

32. Y. Rubner, J. Puzicha, C. Tomasi, and J. M. Buhmann. Empirical evaluation of dissimilarity measures for color and texture. *Computer Vision and Image Understanding*, 84(1):25–43, 2001.

33. D. Comaniciu, V. Ramesh, and P. Meer. Kernel-based object tracking. *IEEE Transactions on Pattern Analysis and Machine Intelligence*, 25(5):564–575, 2003.

34. R. Rodrigues, M. Paravisi, A. de, L. Bicho, L. P. Magalhães, C. R. Jung, and S. R. Musse. An interactive model for steering behaviors of groups of characters. *Applied Artificial Intelligence*, 24:594–616, 2010.

9

Scenario Space: Characterizing Coverage, Quality, and Failure of Steering Algorithms

Mubbasir Kapadia, Glen Berseth, Shawn Singh, Glenn Reinman, and Petros Faloutsos

CONTENTS

Navigation and steering in complex dynamically changing environments is a challenging research problem, and a fundamental aspect of immersive virtual worlds. While there exist a wide variety of approaches for navigation and steering, there is no definitive solution for evaluating and analyzing steering algorithms. Evaluating a steering algorithm involves two major challenges: (a) characterizing and generating the space of possible scenarios that the algorithm must solve, and (b) defining evaluation criteria (metrics) and applying them to the solution. In this chapter, we address both of these challenges. First, we characterize and analyze the complete space of steering scenarios that an agent may encounter in dynamic situations. Then, we propose the representative scenario space and a sampling method that can generate subsets of the representative space with good statistical properties. We also propose a new set of metrics and a statistically robust approach to determining the coverage and the quality of a steering algorithm in this space. We demonstrate the effectiveness of our approach on three state-of-the art techniques. Our results show that these methods can only solve 60% of the scenarios in the representative scenario space.

9.1 Introduction

Immersive virtual worlds have quickly come to the forefront in both industry and academia with their applicability being realized in a wide variety of areas from education, collaboration, urban design, and entertainment. A key aspect of immersion in virtual environments is the use of autonomous agents to inject life into these worlds. Autonomous agents require efficient, robust algorithms for navigation and steering in large, complex environments where the space of all possible situations an agent is likely to encounter is intractable. The rich set of scenarios and corresponding steering choices have resulted in a large variety of techniques that are focused on tackling a subset of this problem. To our knowledge, there exists no definitive measure of the ability of a steering algorithm to successfully handle the space of all possible scenarios that it is likely to encounter in complex environments. This greatly limits future researchers and end users in objectively evaluating and analyzing the current state of the art before choosing their own direction of exploration.

There are two key requirements to doing a comprehensive evaluation of a steering technique. First, we must be able to sufficiently sample the representative set of challenging situations that an agent is likely to encounter. Next, we need a measure of scoring success for an algorithm for a particular scenario that has meaning on its own as well as in comparison with the scores for other approaches.

Previous approaches have addressed these issues with small sets of manually designed test cases, and ad hoc, scenario-dependent criteria. In this chapter, we address both of these challenges with rigorous, statistically based approaches.

We examine the complete space of possible scenarios that a steering algorithm may need to solve given a set of user-defined parameters, such as the size of the agents. After showing that an exhaustive sampling of this space is not practical, we propose the *representative scenario* and an associated sampling method. Both the representative scenario space and the sampling method are constrained to produce test sets that favor complexity, and avoid easy-to-solve cases. To evaluate a steering algorithm on a single scenario, we propose a set of metrics that can be normalized with respect to ideal values so as to become scenario independent. On the basis of these metrics, we then propose the concepts of *coverage*, *average quality*, and *failure set* and show how they can be computed over the representative scenario space. Computing these concepts over an entire scenario space provides a rigorous, statistical view of an algorithm, and can be used to evaluate a single approach or compare different approaches. In our opinion, our work is the first attempt to evaluate steering techniques in an automated and statistically sound fashion.

This chapter makes the following contributions:

- We propose three concepts to statistically evaluate steering algorithms over a scenario space: coverage, average quality, and failure set.
- We define the space of all possible scenarios that an agent could encounter while steering and navigating in dynamically changing environments. In addition, we present a method of sufficiently sampling the representative scenarios in this space in order to effectively compute the average quality and coverage for a particular steering algorithm.
- We provide a method of automatically determining a *failure set* for an algorithm— a subset of scenarios where the algorithm performs poorly based on some criteria.

This provides an invaluable tool for users and artificial intelligence (AI) developers in evaluating their own steering techniques.

- We demonstrate the effectiveness of our framework in analyzing four agent-based techniques: three state of the art [1–3], and one simple baseline algorithm that only reacts to the most immediate threat.

9.2 Related Work

There are three broad categories when it comes to the analysis and evaluation of crowd simulations: (1) comparing simulations to real-world data, (2) performing user studies to determine if the desired qualities of the simulation have been met and to manually detect the presence of anomalous behaviors, and (3) using statistical tools to analyze simulations. The real world and its real human characters are extremely complex, which makes it very difficult to compare a simulation to real events. There is a promising work to compare simulations to real events [4]; however, this requires the existence of data for a particular event. Manual inspection of simulations is prone to human error and personal inclinations. Surveys [5,6] show that automated evaluation, especially for autonomous characters, is yet to be fully realized in the games industry. Hence, the focus of this chapter is in the use of computational methods and statistical tools to analyze, evaluate, and test crowd simulations.

9.2.1 Benchmarks for Evaluation

Steering approaches, outlined in Section 9.2.3, are generally targeted at specific subsets of human steering behaviors and use their own custom test cases for evaluation and demonstration. The work in Reference 7 proposes a standard suite of test cases that represent a large variety of steering behaviors and is independent of the algorithm used. In addition, Singh et al. [8] provide a suite of tools and helper functions to allow AI developers to quickly get started with their own algorithms. However, even the 42 test cases described here still cannot capture the large space of possible situations an agent will encounter in dynamic environments of realistic complexity. Recent work in Reference 9 formulates a set of features that describe the predicted difficulty of a scenario.

9.2.2 Metrics for Evaluation

Prior work has proposed a rich set of application-specific metrics to evaluate and analyze crowd simulations. The work of Pelechano et al. [10] uses *presence* as a metric for crowd evaluation. The number of collisions and effort are often used as metrics to minimize when developing steering algorithms [11,12]. The work in Reference 13 uses "rate of people exiting a room" to analyze evacuation simulations. Lerner et al. [14] present a data-driven approach for evaluating the behaviors of individuals within a simulated crowd. Reitsma and Pollard [15] describe a set of task-based metrics to evaluate the capability of a motion graph across a range of tasks and environments. The work in References 7 and 16 proposes a rich set of derived metrics that provide an empirical measure of the performance of an algorithm. However, the values of these metrics (e.g., path length, total kinetic energy, total change in acceleration, etc.) are tightly coupled with the length and complexity of a scenario, which prevents users from interpreting these metrics in a scenario-independent fashion. Recent work [17] uses these metrics to automatically optimize the parameters of steering algorithms to meet different performance criteria.

9.2.3 Steering Approaches

Since the seminal work of Reynolds [18,19], there has been a growing interest in pedestrian simulation with a wide array of techniques being tested and implemented. A comprehensive overview of the related work in steering and navigation techniques can be found in References 20 and 21.

Centralized techniques [22–24] focus on the system as a whole, modeling the characteristics of the flow rather than individual pedestrians. Centralized approaches usually model a broader view of crowd behaviors as flows rather than focusing on individual specialized agent behaviors.

Decentralized approaches model the agent as an independent entity that performs collision avoidance with static obstacles, reacts to dynamic threats in the environment, and steers toward its target. Particle-based approaches [18,19] model agents as particles and simulate crowds using the basic particle dynamics. The social force model [25–27] solves equations of motion to simulate forces such as repulsion, attraction, friction, and dissipation for each agent to simulate pedestrians. Rule-based approaches [18,28–33] use various conditions and heuristics to identify the exact situation of an agent. Data-driven methods use the existing video data or motion capture to derive steering choices that are then used in virtual worlds (e.g., References 34 and 35). The works of Feurtey [36] and Paris et al. [37] use predictions in the space–time domain to perform steering in environments populated with dynamic threats. Predicting potential threats ahead of time results in more realistic steering behaviors. There is also a data-driven method that models the collision avoidance prediction of people [38].

We use three state-of-the-art steering techniques to serve as the basis for the analysis results shown in this chapter. In addition, we also evaluate a purely reactive approach to steering to demonstrate the efficacy of our framework over a variety of steering approaches.

- *Egocentric*: The work in Reference 1 proposes the use of egocentric affordance fields to model the local variable-resolution perception of agents in dynamic virtual environments. This method combines steering and local space–time planning to produce realistic steering behaviors in challenging local interactions as well as large-scale scenarios involving thousands of agents.
- *PPR*: The work in Reference 2 presents a hybrid framework that combines reaction, prediction, and planning into one single framework.
- *RVO*: The work in Reference 3 proposes the use of reciprocal velocity obstacles to serve as a linear model of prediction for collision avoidance in crowds.
- *Reactive*: This steering technique employs the use of a simple finite-state machine of rules to govern the behavior of an autonomous agent in a crowd. This technique is purely reactive in nature and does not employ the use of any form of predictive collision avoidance. A description of the implementation of this technique can be found in Reference 2.

9.2.4 Comparison to Related Work

Our work was inspired by SteerBench [7] and Reitsma and Pollard [15]. The work in Reference 15 presented a method of calculating the coverage of motion graphs for a set of animation and navigation benchmarks. SteerBench proposed an objective set of test cases and an ad hoc, automatic method of scoring the performance of steering algorithms. The approximately 42 test cases provide a fixed and very sparse sampling of the scenario space. In this chapter, we take a large step along this direction. First, we characterize the entire scenario space, and propose a sampling-based approach to estimate, for the first time, the coverage of a steering algorithm. We also propose a new set of performance metrics and a robust statistical method for automatically analyzing the effectiveness of steering algorithms.

9.3 Scenario Space

Like real people, virtual agents make their steering decisions by considering their surrounding environment and their goals. The environment usually consists of static obstacles and other agents. In this section, we describe how we represent all the elements of a steering problem, which we refer to as a *scenario*.

We define a *scenario* as one possible configuration of obstacles and agents in the environment. The configuration of an obstacle is its position in the environment along with the information of its bounding box (we assume rectangular obstacles). The configuration of an agent includes its initial position, target location, and the desired speed. The configuration of agents and obstacles can be extended or modified to meet the needs of any application. The *scenario space* is defined as the space of all possible scenarios that an agent can encounter while steering in dynamic environments. The ratio of the subspace of scenarios that a steering algorithm can successfully handle is defined as the *coverage* of the algorithm. An ideal steering algorithm would be able to successfully handle all the scenarios in this extremely high-dimensional space, thus having a coverage of 1. In order to be able to determine the coverage of a steering algorithm, we need the ability to sample the scenario space in a representative fashion and to objectively determine the performance of an algorithm for a particular scenario.

Section 9.3.1 describes a set of user-defined parameters used to define a space of scenarios. In Section 9.3.2, we describe the results of our experiment to determine the coverage of three steering algorithms in the complete space of scenarios. We observe that the value of coverage for each of these algorithms does not converge for even up to 10,000 sample points. Section 9.3.3 describes a set of constraints that are imposed on the complete scenario space to define the space of representative scenarios. We observe the rapid convergence of the coverage of steering algorithms in the representative scenario space.

9.3.1 Parameterization of Scenario Space

The space of all scenarios is determined by the number of obstacles and agents, the size of the environment, and the size of obstacles. A user may wish to test his steering algorithm on local interactions between agents in small environments with two or three agents. Alternatively, a user may wish to stress test his or her algorithm on large environments with a large distribution of agents and obstacles. We expose these parameters to the user to allow him to define the space of scenarios to meet the need of his application.

The set of parameters, P is defined as follows:

- *Environment size*: The size of the environment is defined as the radial distance, r, from the egocentric agent that is positioned at the center of the environment.
- *Obstacle discretization*: Obstacles are represented by a grid of rectangular blocks that are either on or off. The size of these blocks is determined by two parameters: the resolution in X, d_x and the resolution in Y, d_y. These values specify how many cells exist within the width and height of the environment as determined by the radial distance r defined above.
- *Number of agents*: The number of agents in a scenario is governed by two user-defined parameters: the minimum and maximum number of agents (n_{min}, n_{max}).
- *Target speed of agents*: Some steering algorithms can specify a target speed for an agent. The range of possible values is determined by a minimum and maximum speed parameter (s_{min}, s_{max}).

Given a specific set of parameter values P that define a space of scenarios, we can procedurally or randomly sample scenarios with initial configurations of obstacles and agents that lie in that scenario space.

9.3.2 The Complete Scenario Space

The complete scenario space, $\mathbb{S}(P)$ represents all the possible scenarios that can be generated for a particular set of user-defined parameters P. In order to prevent the sampling of *invalid* scenarios that have no solution, we place certain validity constraints on the scenario space.

- *Collision free*: The initial configurations of obstacles and agents must not be in a state of collision.
- *Solvable*: There must exist a valid path taking an agent from its initial position to its target location.

The space $\mathbb{S}(P)$ is infinite and cannot be sampled exhaustively. Instead, we aim to find a representative set of samples that describes this space sufficiently. To determine whether we can generate such a set, we first perform a random sampling experiment in $\mathbb{S}(P)$ where $P = \{r = 7, d_x = d_y = 10, n_{min} = 3, n_{max} = 6, s_{min} = 1, s_{max} = 2.7\}$.

A scenario is randomly generated as follows: First, we generate the obstacles by randomly turning on or turning off cells in our obstacle grid. Next, we select a number of agents to simulate by randomly sampling the range defined above. For each agent, we choose a random obstacle-free position and orientation. We also choose a random obstacle-free position for each agent's goal. All positions are chosen within the radius r and all orientations are sampled uniformly within $[0, 2\pi)$.

The performance of an algorithm for a scenario is evaluated as a boolean measure of whether or not it could complete the scenario. A scenario is said to be successfully completed if all agents reach the goal within a time threshold without any collisions. The coverage of an algorithm is the ratio of all scenarios that it could successfully complete.

In this experiment, we iteratively increase the number of sample points from $N = 100$ to $10,000$. The results are illustrated in Figure 9.1a. We observe that the coverage of an algorithm fluctuates between 0.9 and 0.95 and does not converge within reasonable bounds. Also, the minimum coverage of the three reference algorithms is quite high (>0.9). Similarly, even the baseline-reactive algorithm seems to perform well with a coverage of approximately 0.89. These observations suggest that the experiments contain many trivial or easy scenarios that greatly skew the computed measure of coverage, and affect its convergence. To get a better picture of the areas in the scenario space that algorithms may have trouble in succeeding, we propose the *representative scenario space*, and an egocentric evaluation method as illustrated Figure 9.2.

9.3.3 The Representative Scenario Space

We eliminate trivial scenarios by applying the following constraints on the complete scenario space and the associated sampling method:

- *Reference agent*: The first agent is always placed at the origin of the environment and is known as the reference agent. The scenario is evaluated with respect to the reference agent.
- *Goals and orientations*: The goal of an agent is restricted to one of the eight choices that are located at the boundary of the scenario, at regular intervals of $45°$. The agent's initial orientation is always pointing toward the agent's goal.
- *Agent spatial positions*: Instead of uniformly sampling the space for agent positions, we model the probability of a location in the environment $\vec{x}$ being sampled using a normal distribution $\mathbb{N}(\vec{x}, \vec{\mu} = \vec{O}, \sigma^2 = 0.4)$. This implies that agents are more likely to be placed closer to the origin, that is, closer to the reference agent, which increases the likelihood of interaction between agents.
- *Agent interactions*: We place a constraint on the configuration of an agent placed in the scenario to ensure that it interacts with the reference agent. We compute an optimal path (using A*) for the agent from its start position to its goal. If the planned path of the agent intersects with the planned path of the reference agent in space and time (we assume the constant speed of motion along the optimal path), then, the agent is considered relevant and is placed in the scenario.
- *Agent speeds*: Instead of varying the desired speed of agents, we keep it as constant ($1.7\,\text{m/s}$) as we observe that the desired speed variations do not have a large impact on the resulting behavior of most steering approaches.

The resulting space of scenarios that meet these constraints is the representative scenario space, denoted by $\mathbb{R}(P)$.

We change our evaluation method of a scenario to be with respect to the reference agent alone. Hence, an algorithm is successful on a scenario if the reference agent reaches its goal and there are no collisions with other agents.

We run the same sampling experiment described above in the representative scenario space (Figure 9.1b). We observe the convergence of coverage between $N = 5000$ and $10,000$. We also observe that the coverage of the algorithms is much lower. The three reference algorithms can only complete approximately half of the scenarios sampled. We also see a much larger difference in the coverage of the baseline-reactive algorithm in comparison to the

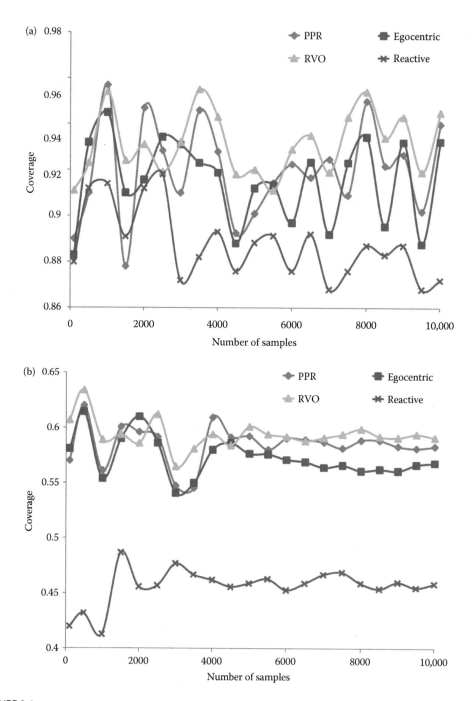

FIGURE 9.1
Success rate of the four algorithms in the complete (a) and representative (b) scenario space versus the number of samples (size) of the test set.

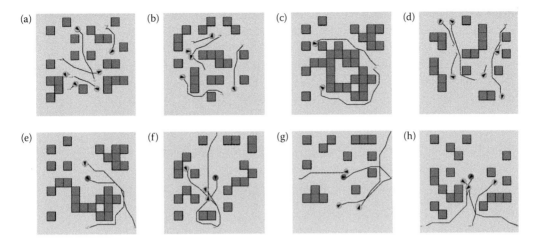

FIGURE 9.2
(a–d) Scenarios randomly generated in the complete scenario space. A black line indicates an agent's optimal path to the goal. (e–h) Scenarios randomly generated in the representative scenario space. Our sampling process ensures that all agents interact with the reference agent (in blue) that is always placed in the center of the environment.

Algorithm	$\mathbb{S}(P)$	$\mathbb{R}(P)$	SteerBench
PPR	0.919	0.583	0.86(36/42)
Egocentric	0.915	0.568	0.86(36/42)
RVO	0.931	0.591	0.86(36/42)
Reactive	0.887	0.459	0.83(35/42)

FIGURE 9.3
Estimated coverage of the steering algorithms in the complete space $\mathbb{S}(P)$, the representative space $\mathbb{R}(P)$, and the 42 cases of SteerBench [7].

three reference algorithms, as one would expect. Figure 9.3 compares the coverage of algorithms in $\mathbb{S}(P)$, $\mathbb{R}(P)$, and using the test cases provided in SteerBench [7]. The algorithms have very high coverage in both $\mathbb{S}(P)$ and SteerBench. The reactive algorithm fails in only one more scenario than the other three reference-steering techniques in the 42 test cases that SteerBench provides. In contrast, the scenarios generated are much more challenging in $\mathbb{R}(P)$ that is reflected in low-coverage values and a much larger difference between the baseline-reactive technique and the three more-sophisticated ones.

In conclusion, we can make two important observations. First, the representative space sampled with our constrained sampling technique can produce test sets that expose the difficulties of steering algorithms. Second, approximately 10,000 samples seem to be enough for analyzing an algorithm, as indicated by the convergence of the coverage of the four algorithms.

9.4 Evaluation Criteria

We evaluate a scenario by computing three primary metrics that quantify the success of the egocentric agent in completing the scenario. These metrics characterize whether or not the egocentric agent successfully reached its goal, the total time it took to reach its goal, and the total distance traveled in reaching the goal. By defining the metrics as a ratio to its optimal value, we can compare and evaluate these metrics on an absolute scale.

- *Scenario completion*: For an algorithm a and a scenario s, if the reference agent reaches its goal within the time limit without colliding with any agents or obstacles, the scenario is said to have successfully completed. In this case, $m_c(s, a) = 1$ else $m_c(s, a) = 0$.
- *Path length*: The path length $m_l(s, a)$ is the total distance traveled by the egocentric agent to reach its goal.
- *Total time*: The total time $m_t(s, a)$ is the time taken by the egocentric agent in reaching the goal.

In addition, we compute optimal values of the path length and the total time to serve as an absolute reference that can be used to normalize the values of $m_l(s, a)$ and $m_t(s, a)$. The optimal path length, $m_l^{opt}(s, a)$, and optimal time, $m_t^{opt}(s, a)$, are the path length and the time taken to travel along an optimal path to the goal by an algorithm a for a particular scenario s, ignoring neighboring agents. Using the optimal values, we can compute the ratio for a particular metric $m(s, a)$ as follows:

$$m^r(s, a) = \frac{m^{opt}(s, a)}{m(s, a)} \times m_c(s, a). \tag{9.1}$$

The value of $m^r(s, a)$ is equal to 1 when the value of the metric is equal to its optimal value and is close to 0 when the value is far away from its optimal value. Also, $m^r(s, a)$ is only computed when the scenario has successfully completed. Using Equation 9.1, we can compute $m_l^r(s, a)$ and $m_t^r(s, a)$ to effectively quantify the performance of a steering algorithm for a particular scenario that can be compared across algorithms and scenarios.

9.5 Coverage, Average Quality, and Failure Set

In this section, we show how we use our representative scenario space and evaluation criteria to derive a set of well-defined, statistical metrics that characterize the key aspects of a steering algorithm.

Scenario Set: The scenario set $S_m^a(T_1, T_1)$ for an algorithm a on a metric m is defined as the subset of all scenarios within the representative space of scenarios for which the value of m is in the range $[T_1, T_2)$.

$$S_m^a(T_1, T_2) = \{s \mid s \in \mathbb{R}(P) \wedge T_1 <= m < T_2\}. \tag{9.2}$$

Using only T_1, we can find the success set of an algorithm as the set of the scenarios for which the metric was greater than a threshold. Similarly, using only T_2 allows us to define a failure set of an algorithm.

The common failure set $S_m(0, T_{min})$ for all algorithms $a \in A$ is the intersection of the failure sets $S_m^a(0, T_{min})$ of all evaluated steering algorithms:

$$S_m(0, T_{min}) = \bigcap_{a \in A} S_m^a(0, T_{min}). \tag{9.3}$$

The common failure set can be used to identify particularly difficult scenarios.

Coverage: The coverage c_m^a of a steering algorithm a can be computed as the ratio of the subset of scenarios in the scenario space that a steering algorithm can successively handle with respect to a particular metric, m

$$c_m^a = \frac{|S_m^a(T_{max}, 1)|}{|\mathbb{R}(P)|}, \tag{9.4}$$

where $|S|$ denotes the cardinality of the set S.

Average Quality: The average quality of a steering algorithm for a particular method of evaluation can similarly be computed as the average value of $m(s, a)$ for all sampled scenarios.

$$q_m^a = \frac{\displaystyle\sum_{s \in S_m^a(T_{max}, 1)} m}{|\mathbb{R}(P)|}. \tag{9.5}$$

Using Equations 9.4 and 9.5, we can compute the coverage and average quality for ms, mlr, and mtr. Note that the coverage and average quality for ms will be the same since it is a boolean value.

The three concepts defined in this section provide a rigorous and objective statistical view of a steering algorithm. They can be intuitively used to evaluate the effectiveness of a single algorithm or to compare different approaches.

9.6 Results

Using the concepts and the evaluation method proposed in the previous sections, we can now analyze and compare our four steering algorithms. All algorithms are tested on the same set of 10,000 scenarios randomly selected from the representative scenario space, $\mathbb{R}(P)$, with user-defined parameters $P = \{r = 7, d_x = d_y = 10, n_{min} = 3, n_{max} = 6, s = 2.7\}$. In Section 9.3.3, we showed that the success rate of the four algorithms converges for test sets with 5000–10,000 samples in the representative scenario space. This is a good indication that a test set of size 10,000 should be sufficient for our analysis. It takes a few minutes for our system to run 10,000 samples (depending on the performance of the steering algorithm).

9.6.1 Coverage and Average Quality

The coverage and average quality for each algorithm for all three metrics are given in Figures 9.4 and 9.5. Note that the values of mlr and mtr are only considered when

Algorithm	mlr	mtr
PPR	0.789	0.683
Egocentric	0.723	0.63
RVO	0.743	0.731
Reactive	0.617	0.586

FIGURE 9.4

Average quality q_m^a of the steering algorithms for the ratio to an optimal path length, mlr, and the ratio to an optimal total time, mtr.

Algorithm	ms	mlr	mtr
PPR	0.583	0.748	0.608
Egocentric	0.568	0.681	0.515
RVO	0.591	0.762	0.662
Reactive	0.459	0.212	0.178

FIGURE 9.5

Coverage c_m^a of the steering algorithms for the three metrics.

the algorithm successfully completes the scenario, that is, $mc = 1$. To compute the coverage for mlr and mtr, we specify the thresholds equal to the mean of the average quality for each metric computed for the three algorithms (Reactive is not considered). Thus, the coverage gives us a measure of the ratio of the number of scenarios that are above the average-quality measure for that metric.

Observations: We observe that the average quality of the algorithms for the path length, mlr, is approximately 0.75. This implies that the three algorithms generally produce solutions with path lengths that are 75% of the optimal values. In contrast, the average quality of algorithms for the total time, mtr, is approximately 0.68 that is considerably lower. This is because steering algorithms generally prefer to slow down instead of deviating from their planned paths. When comparing PPR and RVO, we notice that PPR has a better quality measure for path length than time. This is because PPR has a greater proclivity for predictively avoiding dynamic threats by slowing down if it anticipates a collision. Owing to the variable-resolution nature of the perception fields modeled in Egocentric, the trajectories produced by this method are curved and produce less-optimal results. The performance of Reactive is reflected in its measure of coverage. We observe that Reactive can only solve 45% of the scenarios (compared to nearly 60% for the other three algorithms), and that only 20% of its solutions are above the average-quality measure.

9.6.2 Failure Set

The coverage and average quality provide a good aggregate measure of the performance of an algorithm over a large sample of scenarios and serve as a good basis of comparison. However, it is particularly useful to be able to automatically generate *scenarios of interest* where an algorithm performs poorly. Our framework automatically computes a failure set for an algorithm as the set of all scenarios where a particular metric falls below a threshold. Figure 9.6a and b measures the number of scenarios for which mlr and mtr fall within a specified region. The set $S_m^a(0, 0)$ clusters all scenarios for which the algorithm has failed to

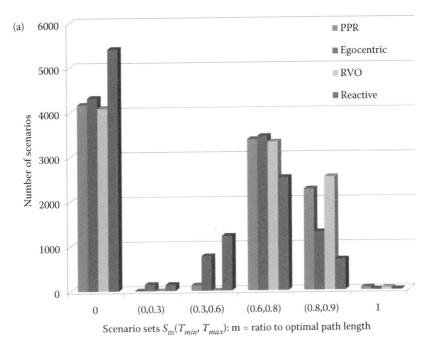

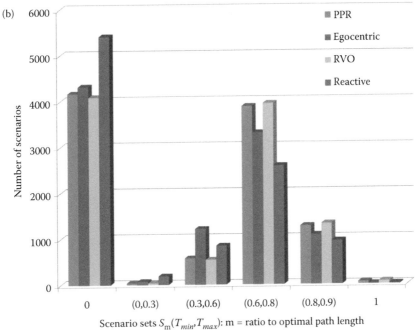

FIGURE 9.6
Failure sets of each algorithm for the ratio to an optimal path length mlr and the ratio to the optimal time mtr.

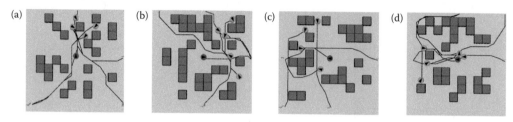

FIGURE 9.7
Examples scenarios from the failure set, for which the steering algorithms could not find a solution.

find a solution (ms = 0). The set $S_m^a(1,0)$ measures the number of scenarios for which the algorithms produced optimal solutions for mlr or mtr. A small number of samples in this cluster is indicative that scenarios produced in the representative space are challenging and require complex interactions between agents. The sets $S_m^a(0,0.3)$ and $S_m^a(0.3,0.6)$ represent scenarios for which a steering algorithm generated highly suboptimal solutions.

We also find the common failure set $S_m(0,0)$ of all four steering algorithms. This set represents the set of scenarios for which no steering algorithm could find a solution. In these cases, the agents either reach a deadlock situation and time out or reach their goals by colliding with other agents. Figure 9.7 highlights some particularly challenging scenarios that fall within the common failure set. Note that the narrow passageways in the figure are traversable. For 10,000 sample points, the cardinality of the failure set is $|S_m(0,0)| = 1710$. This means that 17% of the scenarios that were sampled could not be successfully handled by any steering approach. By visually inspecting these scenarios, we arrive at the following generalization for particularly challenging scenarios:

- *Series of sharp turns*: Narrow passageways where agents had to make a sequence of sharp turns often resulted in soft collisions.
- *Complex interactions*: Scenarios where the reference agent was forced to interact with multiple crossing and oncoming threats in the presence of obstacles often resulted in failure.
- *Deadlocks*: In certain situations, agents need communication and space–time planning to effectively cooperate on resolving a situation, such as one agent backing all the way up in a very narrow passage to allow another agent to pass first.

9.7 Conclusion and Future Work

In this chapter, we address the fundamental challenge of evaluating and analyzing steering techniques for multiagent simulations. We present a method of automatically generating and sampling the representative space of challenging scenarios that a steering agent is likely to encounter in dynamically changing environments with both static and dynamic threats. In addition, we propose a method of determining the *coverage* and *quality* of a steering algorithm in this space.

We observe that the three agent-based steering approaches we examined are capable of successfully handling 60% of the scenarios that are in the representative scenario space. After examining their failure sets, we see that particularly challenging scenarios include combinations of oncoming and crossing threats in environments with limited room to maneuver, and situations where agents find themselves in deadlocks that require complex coordination between multiple agents. Steering approaches usually time out in these cases or allow collisions so that agents can push through the deadlocks.

The work in References 11 and 39 optimizes metrics such as path length, time, and effort in order to generate collision-free trajectories in multiagent simulations. It would be particularly interesting to see if steering methods that are based on optimality considerations have better coverage and quality using our method of evaluation. Another factor contributing to the low coverage of the evaluated methods is the nonholonomic control of the agents. Many nuanced locomotion capabilities of humans such as sidestepping and careful foot placement are not modeled by these approaches, which greatly limits their ability to handle challenging scenarios. Recent work in navigation [40] has addressed these limitations in an effort to better model the locomotion of virtual humans. However, modeling agents as disks is still the common practice in interactive applications such as games. Our approach can be extended to handle different types of locomotion.

This chapter analyzes steering algorithms based on a particular parameterization of the scenario space that focuses on interactions between a small number of proximate agents. Further investigation is needed in order to determine the sensitivity of the evaluation based on these parameters. In addition, applications may require different scenario spaces, for example, situations involving large crowds in urban environments. It would be particularly beneficial to design a specification language, whereby users can specify and generate benchmarks that meet their requirements.

Our current approach performs random sampling in this space in order to calculate the coverage of an algorithm. In the future, we would like to investigate adaptive sampling methods that use our evaluation criteria to identify and sample more densely areas of interest. Further analysis is also required to automatically cluster and generalize scenarios that are challenging for steering algorithms. Defining subspaces in this extremely high-dimensional space that are of interest to the research community can prove valuable in the development of the next generation of steering techniques.

Acknowledgments

The work in this chapter was partially supported by Intel through a Visual Computing grant, and the donation of a 32-core Emerald Ridge system with Xeon processors X7560. In particular, we would like to thank Randi Rost and Scott Buck from Intel for their support.

References

1. M. Kapadia, S. Singh, W. Hewlett, G. Reinman, and P. Faloutsos. Parallelized egocentric fields for autonomous navigation. *The Visual Computer*, 28(12):1209–1227, 2012.
2. S. Singh, M. Kapadia, B. Hewlett, G. Reinman, and P. Faloutsos. A modular framework for adaptive agent-based steering. In *Symposium on Interactive 3D Graphics and Games*, I3D'11, pp. 141–150. New York, 2011. ACM.
3. J. van den Berg, M. C. Lin, and D. Manocha. Reciprocal velocity obstacles for real-time multi-agent navigation. In *Robotics and Automation, 2008. ICRA 2008*, pp. 1928–1935. IEEE, 2008.

4. S. J. Guy, J. van den Berg, W. Liu, R. Lau, M. C. Lin, and D. Manocha. A statistical similarity measure for aggregate crowd dynamics. *ACM Transactions on Graphics*, 31(6):190:1–190:11, 2012.

5. N. Llopis and B. Sharp. By the books: Solid software engineering for games, 2002. *Games Developers Conference*, San Francisco, California, Round Table.

6. C. McFadden. Improving the QA process, 2006. *Games Developers Conference*, San Francisco, California, Round Table.

7. S. Singh, M. Kapadia, M. Naik, G. Reinman, and P. Faloutsos. SteerBench: A steering framework for evaluating steering behaviors. *Computer Animation and Virtual Worlds*, 2009. http://dx.doi.org/10.1002/cav.277.

8. S. Singh, M. Kapadia, P. Faloutsos, and G. Reinman. An open framework for developing, evaluating, and sharing steering algorithms. In *Proceedings of the 2nd International Workshop on Motion in Games*, MIG '09, pp. 158–169, Berlin, Heidelberg, 2009. Springer-Verlag.

9. G. Berseth, M. Kapadia, and P. Faloutsos. Steerplex: Estimating scenario complexity for simulated crowds. In *Proceedings of Motion on Games*, MIG '13, pp. 45:67–45:76, New York, USA, 2013. ACM.

10. N. Pelechano, C. Stocker, J. Allbeck, and N. Badler. Being a part of the crowd: Towards validating VR crowds using presence. In *Proceedings of the 7th International Joint Conference on Autonomous Agents and Multiagent Systems—Volume 1*, AAMAS '08, pp. 136–142, Richland, SC, 2008. International Foundation for Autonomous Agents and Multiagent Systems.

11. S. J. Guy, J. Chhugani, S. Curtis, P. Dubey, M. Lin, and D. Manocha. Pledestrians: A least-effort approach to crowd simulation. In *Proceedings of the 2010 ACM SIGGRAPH/Eurographics Symposium on Computer Animation*, SCA '10, pp. 119–128, Aire-la-Ville, Switzerland, Switzerland, 2010. Eurographics Association.

12. W. Shao and D. Terzopoulos. Autonomous pedestrians. *Graph. Models*, 69(5–6):246–279, 2007.

13. D. Helbing, I. Farkas, and T. Vicsek. Simulating dynamical features of escape panic. *Nature*, 407:487, 2000.

14. A. Lerner, Y. Chrysanthou, A. Shamir, and D. Cohen-Or. Context-dependent crowd evaluation. *Computer Graphics Forum*, 29(7):2197–2206, 2010.

15. P. S. A. Reitsma and N. S. Pollard. Evaluating motion graphs for character animation. *ACM Transactions on Graphics*, 26:18, 2007.

16. M. Kapadia, S. Singh, B. Allen, G. Reinman, and P. Faloutsos. Steerbug: An interactive framework for specifying and detecting steering behaviors. In *SCA '09: Proceedings of the 2009 ACM SIGGRAPH/Eurographics Symposium on Computer Animation*, pp. 209–216. New York, USA, 2009, ACM.

17. G. Berseth, M. Kapadia, B. Haworth, and P. Faloutsos. SteerFit: Automated parameter fitting for steering algorithms. In *Proceedings of the ACM SIGGRAPH/Eurographics Symposium on Computer Animation*, SCA'14, pp. 113–122. Switzerland, 2014. Eurographics Association.

18. C. Reynolds. Steering behaviors for autonomous characters, *Games Developers Conference*, San Francisco, California, 1999.

19. C. W. Reynolds. Flocks, herds and schools: A distributed behavioral model. In *SIGGRAPH '87: Proceedings of the 14th Annual Conference on Computer Graphics and Interactive Techniques*, pp. 25–34, SIGGRAPH, Anaheim, CA, 1987. ACM.

20. N. Pelechano, J. M. Allbeck, and N. I. Badler. *Virtual Crowds: Methods, Simulation, and Control.* Synthesis Lectures on Computer Graphics and Animation. Morgan & Claypool Publishers, 2008.

21. D. Thalmann and P. Soraia Raupp Musse. *Crowd Simulation*, Second edition. Springer, 2013.

22. L. F. Henderson. The statistics of crowd fluids. *Nature*, 229(5284):381–383, 1971.

23. G. C. Løvås. Modeling and simulation of pedestrian traffic flow. *Transportation Research Part B: Methodological*, 28(6):429–443, 1994.

24. J. Milazzo, N. Rouphail, J. Hummer, and D. Allen. The effect of pedestrians on the capacity of signalized intersections. *Transportation Research Record*, 37–46, 1998.

25. A. Braun, S. R. Musse, L. P. L. de Oliveira, and B. E. J. Bodmann. Modeling individual behaviors in crowd simulation. In *CASA '03: Proceedings of the 16th International Conference on Computer Animation and Social Agents (CASA 2003)*, p. 143, Washington, DC, USA, 2003. IEEE Computer Society.

26. D. C. Brogan and J. K. Hodgins. Group behaviors for systems with significant dynamics. *Automaton Robots*, 4(1):137–153, 1997.

27. D. Helbing, L. Buzna, A. Johansson, and T. Werner. Self-organized pedestrian crowd dynamics: Experiments, simulations, and design solutions. *Transportation Science*, 39(1):1–24, 2005.

28. F. Lamarche and S. Donikian. Crowd of virtual humans: A new approach for real time navigation in complex and structured environments. In *Computer Graphics Forum*, 23, EURO-GRAPHICS 2004, Grenoble, France, 2004.

29. C. Loscos, D. Marchal, and A. Meyer. Intuitive crowd behaviour in dense urban environments using local laws. In *TPCG '03: Proceedings of the Theory and Practice of Computer Graphics 2003*, pp. 122, Washington, DC, USA, 2003. IEEE Computer Society.

30. N. Pelechano, J. M. Allbeck, and N. I. Badler. Controlling individual agents in high-density crowd simulation. In *SCA '07: Proceedings of the 2007 ACM SIGGRAPH/Eurographics Symposium on Computer Animation*, pp. 99–108, Aire-la-Ville, Switzerland, Switzerland, 2007. Eurographics Association.

31. I. Rudomín, E. Millán, and B. Hernández. Fragment shaders for agent animation using finite state machines. *Simulation Modelling Practice and Theory*, 13(8):741–751, 2005.

32. A. Sud, R. Gayle, E. Andersen, S. Guy, M. Lin, and D. Manocha. Real-time navigation of independent agents using adaptive roadmaps. In *VRST '07: Proceedings of the 2007 ACM Symposium on Virtual Reality Software and Technology*, pp. 99–106. New York, USA, 2007. ACM.

33. J. van den Berg, S. Patil, J. Sewall, D. Manocha, and M. Lin. Interactive navigation of multiple agents in crowded environments. In *SI3D '08: Proceedings of the 2008 Symposium on Interactive 3D Graphics and Games*, pp. 139–147. ACM, 2008.

34. K. H. Lee, M. G. Choi, Q. Hong, and J. Lee. Group behavior from video: A data-driven approach to crowd simulation. In *SCA '07: Proceedings of the 2007 ACM SIGGRAPH/Eurographics Symposium on Computer Animation*, pp. 109–118, Aire-la-Ville, Switzerland, Switzerland, 2007. Eurographics Association.

35. A. Lerner, Y. Chrysanthou, and D. Lischinski. Crowds by example. *Computer Graphics Forum*, 26(3):655–664, 2007.

36. F. Feurtey. Simulating the collision avoidance behavior of pedestrians. Master's thesis, The University of Tokyo, School of Engineering, 2000.

37. S. Paris, J. Pettré, and S. Donikian. Pedestrian reactive navigation for crowd simulation: A predictive approach. *Eurographics 2007*, 26:665–674, 2007.

38. I. Karamouzas, B. Skinner, and S. J. Guy. Universal power law governing pedestrian interactions. *Physics Review Letters*, 113:238701, 2014.

39. A. Treuille, S. Cooper, and Z. Popović. Continuum crowds. *ACM Transactions on Graphics*, 25(3):1160–1168, 2006.

40. S. Singh, M. Kapadia, G. Reinman, and P. Faloutsos. Footstep navigation for dynamic crowds. In *Symposium on Interactive 3D Graphics and Games*, I3D '11, pp. 203–203, New York, USA, 2011. ACM.

10

Data-Driven Crowd Evaluation

Panayiotis Charalambous and Yiorgos L. Chrysanthou

CONTENTS

Computer-generated crowds are nowadays commonly used in films, video games, online communities, and virtual environment applications. The realistic simulation of such crowds is an important factor in the level of user immersion and the value of the conclusions one can draw from these simulations. Over the past 20 years, the field of computer graphics has experienced a dramatic increase in the number of tools, approaches, and algorithms focusing on creating compelling crowd motions. As more approaches to generate virtual crowds are introduced, developing better methods to analyze, evaluate, and improve the quality of these simulations is becoming more important.

Evaluating the quality of crowd simulations though is not an easy task; crowd simulations involve interactions between multiple characters at potentially vastly different situations such as different crowd densities, with or without static obstacles and different types of characters. The complexity inherent in a simulation involving multiple interacting characters, makes evaluation a nontrivial, challenging problem. Some issues are easy to identify and measure such as characters colliding with each other or the environment, or characters moving too fast. Other issues are more subtle: for example, jamming at narrow passages or unnecessary backtracking. Some crowd simulation systems avoid these types of problems; however, the result might still not be satisfying to the eye. A crowd in a city, where each character walks directly to its target in the most efficient and "proper" way might end up looking robotic and spiritless; something that is completely different from what happens in real-life crowds where many phenomena appear such as people walking in groups, chatting, wandering from shop to shop, and so on.

Evaluating crowds is currently a difficult and often-neglected issue as far as simulation is concerned. Deciding on what is a correct simulation is most of the times a biased problem that depends on the point of view of the viewer. Additionally, evaluating crowds should take into account both local (micro) and/or global (macro) characteristics such as local collision avoidance behavior and implicitly generated lane formations, respectively. Finally, simulating a crowd typically involves a lot of components (as described in the other chapters of this book) and therefore care should be taken when evaluating them; that is, an algorithm for steering should be judged solely on that ability and not other aspects such as appearance or skeletal animation of characters. Despite the importance of evaluating the ability of a simulator in capturing required behaviors, there is still no generally accepted methodology in the crowd simulation literature for doing so. In this chapter, we present data-driven methods for evaluating crowd behavior; roughly speaking, these methods compare simulations to crowd data coming from the real world and acceptable simulations.

10.1 Related Work

Three approaches are typically followed when evaluating crowds: user studies, statistical measurements, and comparisons to reference crowd data.

User-based evaluation is a very common practice since human beings are accustomed to real-life crowds in their everyday lives and are going to be the final users/viewers of the system [1,2]. This approach poses some problems due to human bias to crowds; that is, if the task is evaluating steering behavior and simulated characters do not have human-like appearance with human-like animations, users might not rate the steering quality of the simulation correctly due to their real-life biases. This means that an approach where the appearance is abstracted (e.g., in the form of disks) could be selected to remove the bias; of course, this could introduce other issues such as being misleading in the character's ability to have a plausible walking animation to achieve a particular steering behavior.

Statistical approaches on the other hand, try to measure some characteristics of individual characters or the entire crowd such as speed behaviors, interpersonal distances, or distances to goals and then give scores in various scenarios [3–5]. These approaches can still be problematic since statistics are typically not linked to real-world experience and the ranking of a simulator could be subjective to the selection of statistics. Additionally, setting up a global ranking score typically involves manually setting up weights for the different criteria that is both subjective and difficult due to multiple, often-conflicting criteria.

Data-driven techniques aim in combining the benefits of both real-world experience and statistical measurements. In these methods, simulations are compared to real-world data such as videos of crowds or some user-defined sketches. Some measures are defined and estimated on the training data and simulation data are tested on their capability of replicating these behaviors/measures. Recently, Guy et al. [6] proposed an information-theoretic approach to measure the ability of a simulator in reproducing the collective behavior demonstrated in a real-world crowd. Lerner et al. [7] on the other hand measure both individualized and global characteristics of crowds. Wolinski et al. [8] propose an optimization approach to find the best parameters for sets of simulators so that comparisons between them are fairer. More recently, Charalambous et al. [9] introduced an outlier/novelty detection method for evaluating simulations against reference crowd data under multiple and often-conflicting criteria.

In the following section, we will demonstrate two different data-driven approaches for evaluating the steering behavior of crowds. First, one method that compares agents' states to reference states (Section 10.2) and second an approach that aims in automatically balancing the importance of different evaluation criteria (Section 10.3). Even though we are only considering steering behaviors, some of these approaches can be used for evaluating other behavior layers.

10.2 A Context-Sensitive Approach

Individual behavior in most crowd simulators can be described by the *state–action* paradigm. This view has been adapted for evaluation purposes by Lerner et al. [7]. According to the state–action paradigm, for each simulated individual (*subject person*) at a specific point in time and space, a *state S* is defined as a set of potentially influential attributes. These can include the position, speed, distance to the target, relative displacement vectors to nearby individuals or objects, temporal states, and so forth. On the basis of this state, an *action A* is chosen and assigned to the subject person. An action can be, for example, a velocity vector or a trajectory segment.

We define an evaluation measure using similar terms of state–action pairs, aside from two key differences. First, in an evaluation process, all the state attributes, such as the full trajectories (including future ones) of nearby individuals are known. This differs from a simulation where trajectories are synthesized and the future states require prediction. This difference allows for a more accurate definition of the action that should have been taken. Second, an evaluation requires a comparison measure between the "appropriate" action and the one that was actually performed in the simulation, thus assigning a value that describes how well the person performed. To allow for such a comparison, an evaluation measure defines a similarity function between state–action pairs.

In a preprocessing stage, one or more input videos are examined, and individuals in the observed crowd are tracked. Then, the trajectories are analyzed to create a database of examples of state–action pairs similar to data-driven crowd simulation approaches (Chapter 3). During evaluation, the simulated trajectories themselves are analyzed in a similar manner and state–action pairs are defined. The pairs extracted from the simulation are used as *queries* for searching the database.

For each query, a similarity function is used to search for the most similar examples in the database. This search is performed in two stages. First, a set of examples whose state best matches the query state are found. Second, their actions are compared using a normalized combination of both the state and action distances. The reason for a two-stage comparison is that sometimes the current state does not match any observed state and as a result, the comparison between the action can become meaningless. The two-stage process assures a context-dependent evaluation. The similarity to the closest example defines a local measure of quality for the query's action (Figure 10.1).

In the following sections, we define different measures for evaluating both short-term and long-term decisions (Sections 10.2.1 and 10.2.2, respectively). Since the measures evaluate the decisions of individuals within a crowd, one must account for the movement of both the subject person and the people surrounding him/her. This can be visualized best using animation. Therefore, we refer the reader to an online video (https://youtu.be/n6oa5XJg1G8) demonstrating the methodology shown here and visualizations for some evaluation results.

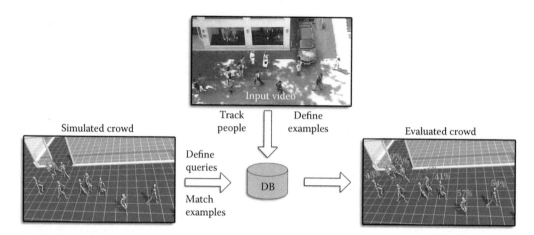

FIGURE 10.1

Overview of context-dependant evaluation: A specific context is defined by an input video. The video is analyzed and a database of examples is created. For a given simulation, each individual trajectory is analyzed and compared to the observed behaviors defined by the examples in the database. The results provide evaluation scores for all individuals at any given moment.

10.2.1 Short-Term Evaluation

A person constantly makes short-term steering decisions. These are the decisions that cause him to stop, turn, keep walking in the same speed, slow down, or speed up. These decisions are not influenced by some global objective, but rather by the local conditions surrounding the person. The impact of these short-term decisions is immediate and short lived. Their effects can be found in short segments of a person's trajectory.

We define two different measures to evaluate short-term individual behaviors that yield similar, but not identical, results (Figure 10.2). The *density measure* consists of samples of the local densities of the people surrounding the subject person. The *proximity measure* measures the proximity of the people surrounding the subject person. For both measures, the action is defined as a two-second-long trajectory segment (one second before and one second after the current position). The segment is aligned such that the position and orientation of the subject person in the middle of the segment is aligned with the origin of a global coordinate system.

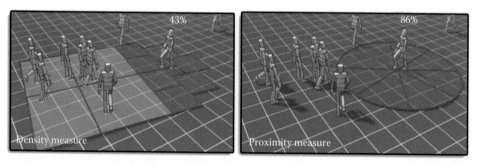

FIGURE 10.2
Short-term measures.

Density Measure The state of the *density measure* is composed of 65 attributes. The area surrounding the subject person is divided into 13 regions (Figure 10.2, left). For each region, the state stores the number of people that appear in it. These densities are taken at five time steps along the trajectory segment. This yields a compact representation of the local changes in densities in the vicinity of the subject person. The motivation for using this state definition stems from the common belief that people's reactions are influenced by the density of the people in their immediate vicinity. Depending on the person, one can either detach himself from the crowd and navigate toward an empty region or be attracted by it and navigate toward a populated region.

Proximity Measure In the *proximity measure*, the state is composed of 40 attributes. A circular region surrounding the subject person is divided into eight equal arcs (Figure 10.2, right). In each arc, five samples of the distance between the subject person and the person closest to him are stored. This is similar to the state representation used by Lee et al. [10]. This yields a compact representation of the local changes in proximity to the subject person. The motivation for using this state definition stems from a different common belief that our short-term decisions are influenced by the people closest to us.

Similarity Function For both measures, a similarity function, $D(Q, E)$, is used to evaluate the similarity between the query state–action pair Q and the example pair E:

$$D(Q, E) = (1 - D_S(S_Q, S_E)) * (1 - D_A(A_Q, A_E)) \tag{10.1}$$

The distance between actions A_Q and A_E is measured using the function $D_A(A_Q, A_E)$, as the sum of Euclidean distances between the positions along both trajectories, limited and normalized by some upper-bound distance. The distance between states S_Q and S_E is measured using the function $D_S(S_Q, S_E)$, as a normalized weighted Manhattan distance (L_1) between the state attributes.

10.2.2 Long-Term Evaluation

In the long run, a person's decisions reflect on his/her trajectory. The common consensus is that people try to maintain their walking speed and direction as much as possible; however, changes in speed and direction are allowed, as long as they are performed properly. Since we do not know each person's final objective, we can only consider evaluating segments of their trajectories. A key observation is that more often than not, a person's movement over a long period of time is influenced by the existence, or lack of, a companion. Hence, we distinguish the long-term behaviors of individuals from long-term behaviors of couples or groups. In this measure, the state is just a boolean value indicating the presence or absence of a walking companion. The action consists of 11 samples along a trajectory segment that is ten-seconds long, five before and five after the current position. The sample at the current position stores the person's speed and the rest of the samples store the relative changes in speed and direction at one-second intervals (Figure 10.3).

During evaluation, depending on the boolean state, either the solitary examples or the ones with companions are searched. A distance function $D_A(A_Q, A_E)$ is used to calculate the distance between the actions as the weighted sum of squared differences between the samples.

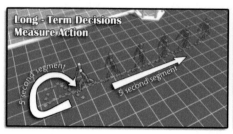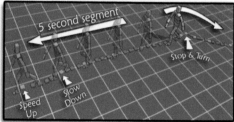

FIGURE 10.3
Long-term measures.

10.2.3 Experiments

Short-term evaluation: For the first experiment, a database created by videos of a sparse crowd was used as input [11]. This was used to evaluate several crowds using the two short-term measures.

Results of evaluating an example-based simulation using the density measure appear in the left of Figure 10.4, and results of evaluating a rule-based simulation using the proximity measure appears in the right. In both images, the percentages represent the quality of the matches that were found. Zero percent means no match whereas a hundred percent means that a perfect match was found. Low-quality matches are highlighted in red. A close inspection of the evaluation results shows that, for the most part, low-quality matches correspond to "curious" behaviors, traffic congestion, collisions, or near misses. In Figure 10.4 center for example, the agent that received a 20% similarity value stopped walking abruptly and the four others marked in red, either walked toward an imminent collision or performed "conspicuous" evasive maneuvers. In the rule-based simulation, the agents mostly keep walking in the same speed and direction, even at the cost of colliding with other agents. The agents marked in red in the right image either collided with each other, or came very close to it.

In several experiments, it was found that the two measures produce similar, however not identical evaluations. Figure 10.5 shows a comparison between the accumulated results of the two measures. The columns represent ranges of similarity values (or evaluation scores), and their height, the relative number of queries that received a value in the range. As it can be seen, the quantitative differences in the results are minor.

Long-term evaluation: A quantitative comparison between the long-term evaluation of various crowds appears in Figure 10.6. Two different example databases were used. The first was built using a video of a sparse crowd and the second using a video of a dense

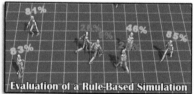

FIGURE 10.4
Evaluation results (left) of a crowd simulation using a sparse crowd video input and the density measure and (right) of a rule-based simulation using a sparse crowd input and the proximity measure.

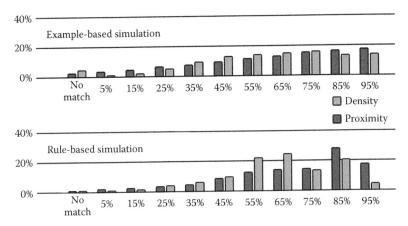

FIGURE 10.5

Comparison between the distribution of evaluation scores generated by the two measures when evaluating the example-based and rule-based simulations against the sparse crowd database. The horizontal axis represents the match values and the vertical axis the relative number of matched queries.

crowd. Some validation tests were conducted. First, a real crowd from a different video of a sparse crowd was evaluated. In this crowd, most of the people walk along smooth trajectories and the changes in speed and direction are usually not abrupt. Both databases found good matches for most queries using the long-term measure; however, the overall quality of the matches from the sparse database was higher.

Similarly, a real crowd from a different video of a dense crowd was evaluated. Again, both databases produced similar distributions; however, this time, the overall quality of the matches from the dense database was higher. Note also that in a dense crowd, people

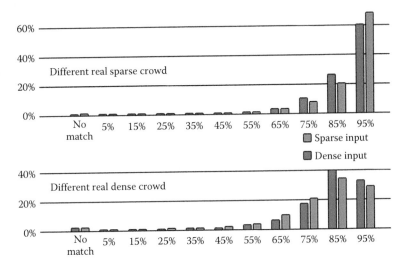

FIGURE 10.6

Comparison between the distribution of match values generated by the long-term measure for various crowds when evaluated against a sparse crowd and a dense crowd database. The horizontal axis represents the match value and the vertical axis the relative number of matched queries.

tend to change their walking direction and speed more frequently than people in a sparse crowd. Therefore, their trajectories are more complex and harder to match. This quality is reflected by the fact that the distribution of the matching values in the histogram is spread over a wider range and there are cases where an adequate match was not found at all. More results for both short and long-term metrics are discussed in Lerner et al. [7].

10.3 Pareto-Optimal Anomaly Detection for Crowd Evaluation

When people move, they balance their behavior based on multiple, often-conflicting criteria such as the number of people around them, distances to friends, nearest neighbors, flow of the crowd, etc. Additionally, different people give subconsciously different weights to each one of these criteria. A process to evaluate heterogeneous crowds therefore should be able to take these facts into account and be adaptable to different behaviors. To do so, we present a framework that automatically balances between different and often-conflicting criteria using the concept of Pareto optimality [9].

As in Section 10.2, we assume as input both a set of reference data (real or simulated) that captures typical, desired crowd motion and a set of user-selected evaluation criteria. We then use an outlier-detection algorithm that when trained can be used to evaluate any new set of trajectories. We note that the proposed system incorporates various other outlier-detection algorithms that are not described here but are described in Charalambous et al. [9] and Charalambous [12]. Both the data to be evaluated, and the reference-training data consist of trajectories that track the positions of agents in time. Paths (or segments of these paths) that are found to be anomalous are then highlighted for the user using a heatmap approach as important areas for further investigation. An overview of the framework is shown in Figure 10.7.

Modes of operation: There are two different modes of using our proposed approach: outlier detection and novelty detection (Figure 10.8). In pure *outlier detection*, the same data are used for both training and testing purposes. By using the same dataset, trajectories that are uncommon in the reference data will be detected. As we will show, this is useful for finding several types of erroneous behavior that arise from a simulation's poor handling of difficult crowd conditions or unusual local circumstances. Pure outlier detection is not sufficient for identifying all errors. For example, wide-spread and systematic problems in a simulation will not be labeled as erroneous using pure outlier detection (e.g., a simulation where all agents move too quickly).

To perform *novelty detection*, we use different sets of data for training and testing. By using the results from a simulation as testing data and data from humans in a similar environment as training data, we can detect instances where simulated agents act inconstantly with human motion. Importantly, we can perform novelty detection with simulated agents as the training data and real trajectories as testing data. By swapping training and testing data in this way, we are able to detect behaviors performed by the real humans that are *not captured* by the simulation method being examined.

The choice between outlier detection (the same reference and testing data) and novelty detection (different reference and testing data) presents an important trade-off. Outlier detection requires no special data and can be applied to any simulation; however, it will fail to capture systematic errors in a simulation. Novelty detection can find a wider range of erroneous behaviors, though it requires the user to find reference data with similar characteristics to the scenario being analyzed.

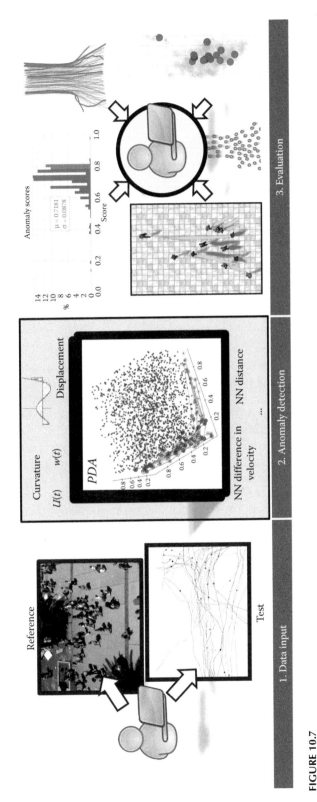

FIGURE 10.7
(1) Reference data from real crowds or relevant simulations are compared against testing data from simulations the user wishes to analyze. (2) Using a variety of metrics, anomaly detection techniques such as PDAs are used to find outliers. (3) The resulting analysis is then shown using a variety of visualizations; red indicates anomalous behaviors.

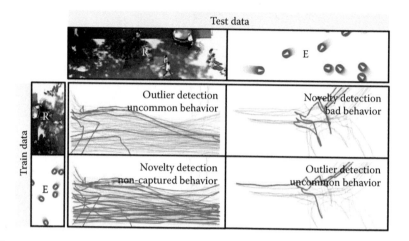

FIGURE 10.8
Different results can be produced in the proposed framework depending on which data are used as training and which as testing. In this table, R are reference data and E are the examined data.

10.3.1 Data and Notation

Our framework takes as input two sources of data: training and testing data. In general, we assume that the reference data provided by the user contain mostly nominal behavior. This assumption allows us to use unlabeled data, and avoids the need for a user annotating paths into good and bad. Each dataset is represented as a time-varying sequence of positions, velocities, and orientations for each agent in the scene, which, in the case of real crowds, we assume are already filtered out.

Trajectory Segmentation. In many graphics applications, it is common to find issues in an agent's motion that are localized to a small portion of its trajectory rather than its entire path. To account for this, rather than analyzing the entire trajectories at once, trajectories can be split into smaller segments of equal temporal length. This allows for a finer analysis of the simulations so that local abnormalities are detected and pinpointed. In order not to miss anomalies spanning a segmentation, we use overlapping segments (Figure 10.9).

Data Representation. Each segment is represented by a collection of measures that characterize the agent's state along that segment (e.g., speed, or distance to the nearest neighbor). As discussed below, the measures used to describe a trajectory will define the types of anomalous behavior being detected. Assuming a total of l difference measures

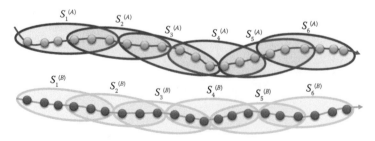

FIGURE 10.9
Overlapping trajectory segmentation.

(i.e., difference in speed, curvature, etc.) with each one denoted as m_j, $j \in [1, l]$, each of the n-possible segments in the training data is represented as a vector

$$\mathbf{s}_i = [m_1^{(i)}, m_2^{(i)}, \ldots, m_l^{(i)}]^T, \quad i \in [1, n] \tag{10.2}$$

where the superscript denotes the segment and the subscript indicates the difference measure. The set of segment representations $\mathbf{S}_T$ of the training data represents the space of nominal behaviors and can be considered as a training database:

$$\mathbf{S}_T = \{\mathbf{s}_1, \mathbf{s}_2, \ldots, \mathbf{s}_n\} \tag{10.3}$$

We can now formally specify anomaly detection as follows: Given a new testing segment $\mathbf{s}_t = \{m_1^{(t)}, m_2^{(t)}, \ldots, m_l^{(t)}\}$, $t \in [1, n_t]$ (n_t is the number of testing segments), we seek to measure how it compares to the space defined by the nominal data $\mathbf{S}_T$. Typically, normalization on both the training and testing data combined is applied for each of the dimensions of the data to account for differences in scale of different data measures.

10.3.2 Comparison Metrics

When training an anomaly detection method, a user must specify what metric(s) to use for the evaluation. Following the approach presented by Kapadia et al. [3], we split our metric into two parts: a *measure* and an *operator*. A measure seeks to characterize the state of an agent at a given timestep (examples include speed, acceleration, or number of neighbors). An operator (such as average, min, or max) then aggregates the effect of a measure over many time steps. Combining an operator with a measure will provide a complete metric, for example, two paths may be compared based on their average speed or maximum acceleration.

To assist users in choosing metrics, we broadly group our difference measures into three categories: individual, interpersonal, and group (Table 10.1). *Individual metrics* are based on properties of each agent in isolation. Examples include an agent's speed, acceleration, displacement, curvature, and other criteria that can be defined as a function of the agent's path over time. *Interpersonal metrics* seek to capture an agent's relationship to its neighboring agent. For example, the average distance to an agent's nearest neighbor may help reveal outliers in density. Finally, *group metrics* capture how agents behavior compares to their nearby neighbors. Examples include the difference between an agent's velocity and the velocity of all its nearby neighbors, which can capture the important aspects of social interactions between individuals.

Combining metrics. Often, multiple comparison metrics may be needed to capture a wider range of atypical behaviors. However, most anomaly detection approaches do not naturally handle multi criteria. As discussed above, the typical solution of taking a linear combination of multiple similarity measures (i.e., weighted average of the metrics) has important limitations. More importantly though, there exist outliers that *no linear combination of metrics can detect*! Consider, for example, the metrics of speed and neighbor distance. Assuming that training data come from an outdoor sidewalk, a simulated agent that moves with near-zero speed will not seem anomalous because real people frequently stop to talk to friends or slow down to avoid congestion. Likewise, a simulated agent who has no nearby neighbors is unlikely to be anomalous as people often walk alone. However, an agent who is simultaneously still and not near anyone is anomalous; outside of talking

TABLE 10.1

Set of Measures Used in the Proposed Analysis Framework

Difference Measures		
Individual	**Interpersonal**	**Group**
Speed	Nearest-neighbor speed	Neighborhood speed
Angular speed	Nearest-neighbor angular speed	Neighborhood angular speed
Acceleration	Nearest-neighbor direction	Neighborhood direction
Angular acceleration	Nearest-neighbor velocity	Neighborhood velocity
Curvature	Angle to the nearest neighbor	Number of neighbors
Displacement	Distance to the nearest neighbor	Collisions
Angular displacement		

Note: These measures are divided into three broad categories.

to someone or resolving a collision, it is unusual to stop walking in the middle of a sidewalk. Finding these types of outliers requires a method that captures the dependence of one metric on another.

The concept of *Pareto optimality* provides a principled way of accounting for multiple criteria simultaneously. In the following section, we briefly recap the state of the art in Pareto optimality analysis and discuss modifications necessary to allow the fast data analysis necessary to support a user-in-the-loop workflow.

10.3.3 Pareto Optimality and Dyads

Pareto optimality is the typical approach for defining optimality in a problem with multiple conflicting criteria. An item is considered Pareto optimal if there is no other item that is better or equal in all the defined criteria. The *Pareto depth analysis (PDA)* [13] method exploits the concept of Pareto optimality as follows:

Dyads. First, relationships between all the training segments are encoded using *dyads*, a vector representation of differences for each metric. More formally, a dyad $\mathbf{D}_{i,j} \in \mathbb{R}^l$ between segments $\mathbf{s}_i$ and $\mathbf{s}_j$ is defined as

$$\mathbf{D}_{i,j} = [d_1(i,j), d_2(i,j), \ldots, d_l(i,j)]^T \qquad (10.4)$$

where l is the number of metrics and $d_m(i,j)$, $m \in [1,l]$, indicates the difference between segments i and j for metric m. Typically $d_m(i,j)$ is the absolute difference between the segments for criteria m.

The set of all possible dyads between training segments are calculated and stored; if there are N segments in a dataset, a total of $\binom{N}{2}$ dyads are calculated—dyads between a segment and itself are not calculated. The set of all dyads $\mathbb{D}$ encodes the differences between each possible pair of training segments. For example, Figure 10.10b shows dyads plotted for the real-world pedestrian dataset in Figure 10.10a computed using two metrics; average distance to the nearest neighbor and average speed ($d_1(i,j) = |\Delta(E(nn_{dist}))|$ and $d_2(i,j) = |\Delta(E(speed))|$ respectively).

Pareto Fronts. After computing dyads, *Pareto fronts* are found. These are sets of dyads that are Pareto optimal (i.e., any dyad on the front which is better in one metric is worse in some other metric). These dyads are then removed and the next most Pareto-optimal dyads are taken to form the next Pareto front. This process continues iteratively until every

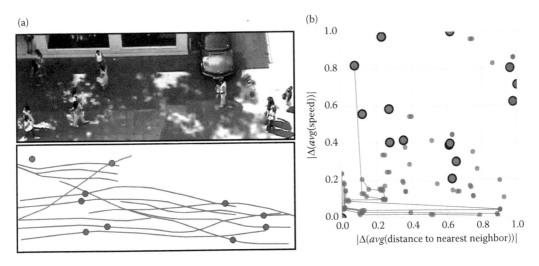

FIGURE 10.10
(a) *Zara* dataset (top) where two apparent outliers with usual behavior have been highlighted in red (bottom).
(b) The dyads from these pedestrians are shown based on the criteria of average speed and nearest-neighbor
distance. The first 10 Pareto fronts are shown as blue lines. All the dyads from the apparent outlying pedestrians
lie in deep Pareto fronts so that the agents would be identified as outliers.

dyad lies on a Pareto front. For each one of these fronts, a rank is given based on the order
they are found; that is, the first Pareto front has rank 1, the second 2, and so on. The lines in
Figure 10.10b indicate the first 10 Pareto fronts for the aforementioned example. Dyads on
low-rank fronts correspond to trajectory segments that are very similar to other segments,
and are considered nominal. Dyads on high-rank fronts indicate that the segments are very
different in one measure with respect to the other measure (e.g., an unusual path curvature
given the speed), and these paths are considered as outliers.

To illustrate the concept, in Figure 10.10a (bottom), we manually highlight in red two
agents with visually apparent anomalous behavior. As can be seen in the supplemental
video, these agents stand still or watch the building without talking to others or moving
for an unusually long time. The dyads corresponding to these apparent outliers are shown
in Figure 10.10b as large red circles. All these dyads have a high Pareto front depth, and
the trajectories are therefore considered as outliers by the PDA method.

Evaluating a Trajectory Segment. In general, to evaluate a new segment as a potential outlier, the *k*-closest matching training samples in each of the metrics separately are
selected (*k* can be different for each metric). Dyads between the test sample and these *k*-
neighboring samples are calculated and the first Pareto front that dominates every one of
these dyads is found. The average Pareto front depth of all the dyads (normalized from 0
to 1) serves as an evaluation of how anomalous the segment is, and can also be used for
coloring heatmaps or determining an anomaly threshold.

10.3.4 Interactive PDA

As described by Hsiao et al. [13], the PDA method is too slow to be used in interactive
analysis. The dyads and Pareto fronts must be recomputed each time a new set of metrics is chosen that can be a time-consuming process preventing quick user interactions.
We introduce two modifications to adapt the PDA computation for interactive analysis:

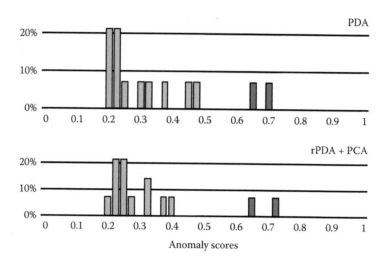

FIGURE 10.11

Using PCA to reduce the dimensionality from 10 to 4 criteria, finds similar outliers while speeding up computation. The red bars indicate the two idle agents in Figure 10.10a.

randomized PDA and criteria dimensionality reduction using PCA. We refer the reader to Charalambous et al. [9] for technical details of the method.

We can illustrate the effect of reducing dimensions in PDA analysis by comparing the outliers found in Figure 10.10 using 10 different individual and group metrics to those found using the top four PCA components. In this way, we can automatically derive new representative criteria without needing any prior knowledge of the scenario being tested. The results for this scenario are shown in Figure 10.11. The two individuals with anomalous trajectories previously identified are correctly labeled as outliers without any further manual intervention. Overall, randomization along with PCA-based dimensionality reduction leads to over-an-order-of-magnitude reduction in computation cost, while calculating similar scores and more importantly similar outliers.

Algorithm. The pseudocode for this PDA-based, multi-criteria outlier-detection technique, including our modifications, is given in Algorithm 10.1. The algorithm has two phases, training and testing, which can be performed separately. It takes as input the number of metrics l, the requested dimensionality $d \leq l$ (which can be given as a variance percentage), the percentage of dyads to keep $0 < p \leq 1$, and a threshold value σ for anomaly detection. **B** are the eigenvectors of the PCA space.

10.3.5 Experiments

We applied our tool to three different datasets to demonstrate the variety of different forms of analysis that can be performed in the proposed framework:

- *Bottleneck:* Group of automatically tracked participants navigating through a 2.5-m-wide bottleneck [14].
- *Zara:* Sparse crowd of manually tracked people interacting at a commercial street [11].
- *Ubisoft's Assassin's Creed:* Nonplayer characters (NPCs) were manually tracked from in game footage [15].

Algorithm 10.1: Randomized PDA

Training
$\mathbb{S}_{Tr} \leftarrow \text{TrainingSegments}()$;
$\mathbb{S}'_{Tr}, \mathbf{B} \leftarrow PCA(\mathbb{S}_{Tr}, d)$;
$\mathbb{D} \leftarrow \text{GenerateDyads}(\mathbb{S}'_{Tr})$;
$\mathbb{D}_r \leftarrow \text{RandomSelection}(\mathbb{D}, p)$;
$\mathbb{PF} \leftarrow \text{GenerateParetoFronts}(\mathbb{D}_r)$;

Testing
$\mathbb{S}_{Te} \leftarrow \text{TestingSegments}()$;
$\mathbb{S}'_{Te} \leftarrow \mathbf{B}^T \mathbb{S}_{Te}$;
forall the $s_t \in \mathbb{S}'_{Te}$ **do**
   $n_b \leftarrow []$;
   forall the $c \in [1, d]$ **do**
      $nb_c \leftarrow k_c$ nearest neighbors of $s_t \in \mathbb{S}'_{Tr}$;
   end
   Create new dyads $\mathbb{D}_n$ between s_t and samples in nb
   forall the $\mathbf{D_i} \in \mathbb{D}_n$ **do**
      $e_i \leftarrow Depth(\mathbb{D}_n)$;
   end
   $score(s_t) \leftarrow \frac{1}{s} \sum_{i=1}^{s} e_i$;
   if $score(s_t) \geq \sigma$ **then**
      s_t is anomalous;
   end
end

The interested reader can see animations of the evaluation results in an online video (http://goo.gl/BSUqqP).

Single-Criteria Analysis. We used the *Bottleneck* as reference data to analyze the quality of three crowd simulation algorithms: a social force model [16], a velocity-based model [17], and an anticipatory model tuned to closely match the input-training data following an approach similar to Wolinski et al. [8]. For each method, we created a 50-agent simulation closely matching the conditions of the reference data.

For each simulation, we computed the corresponding *entropy metric* scores [6]. As can be seen in the online video, the social force model has the lowest performance, as the agents do not match well the behavior of the real humans. However, both the velocity-based simulation and the tuned one have similar overall flows to the real data, and receive similar entropy scores. Our framework compliments the entropy score by allowing users to further investigate individual behaviors (rather than aggregate simulation results). Here, we can detect agents that exhibit various erroneous behaviors by some criteria even though the overall flow matches well. The tuned model, for example, has less nearest-neighbor outliers than the velocity-based model.

Multicriteria Novelty Detection. In this experiment, we used the ORCA framework [18] to simulate 60 agents wandering on a two-dimensional (2D) plane. To detect behaviors that are missing from the simulated agents, as compared to real pedestrians, we used the simulated trajectories as training data and the trajectories of the *Zara* dataset as testing. By performing anomaly detection on single criteria independently, a number of missing

(a)   (b)

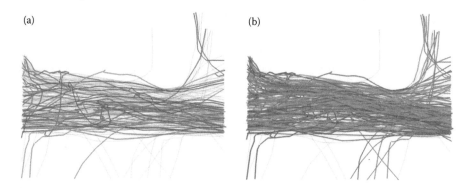

FIGURE 10.12

Missing Social Features. Simulations that account for small groups show different outliers than those without. The corresponding heatmaps were obtained by applying randomized PDA on speed and NN distance (threshold = 0.4). (a) Karamouzas and Overmars model [19]. (b) ORCA model.

behaviors can be detected. Using, for example, the average speed as an evaluation metric, both those that stand still to chat or run very fast are flagged as outliers. In addition, using the average distance to the nearest neighbor as an evaluation metric, all pedestrians that walk in groups are detected as outliers, since the ORCA model does not account for such groups. However, only the combination of both evaluation criteria using our proposed randomized PDA implementation allowed us to consistently capture both missing behaviors. To validate the accuracy of the randomized PDA, we replaced the ORCA simulation with a simulation that accounts for the local behavior of small pedestrian groups [19]. As expected, only pedestrians that have anomalous speed are detected as outliers (see Figure 10.12).

Multicriteria Outlier Detection. In this experiment, we used the *Assassin's Creed* dataset both for training and testing purposes in order to perform multicriteria outlier detection and analyze the quality of the manually tracked NPCs. The NPCs global motions are governed by waypoints along the medial axis of the environment, whereas a reactive technique is used to resolve local collisions between them. As such, the characters typically have to be very close to react to each other, which can result in undesired behaviors, such as backward motions and unwarranted oscillations (see outliers in Figure 10.13). Both the average and standard deviation of all individual measures were used in the analysis. Using PCA to reduce the 14-evaluation metrics down to two dimensions resulted in a 14× speedup without compromising the quality of the detected outliers.

10.4 Discussion/Future Trends

Evaluating crowd simulations is a very important subject, especially now that computer-generated crowds are common in various areas. We have presented some data-driven techniques to analyze and evaluate simulations since we believe that using data is very promising; peoples' knowledge of how crowds should behave is encapsulated in them. Even though these approaches are promising, there are a few things that could be added to enhance the quality of results and evaluation usefulness.

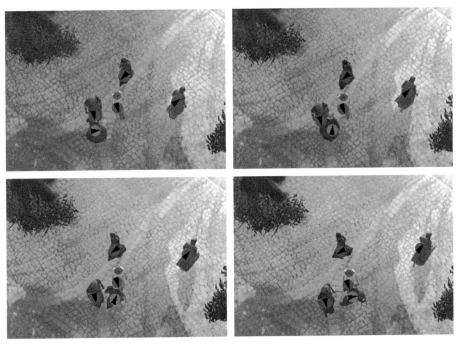

FIGURE 10.13
Assassin's Creed. Example outlier detected in a nonplaying character in the game Assassin's Creed (red circle). The outlying character can be seen to spin around quickly as it tries to avoid the upcoming collision too late. This outlier was found by applying PDA on path segments after performing principal component analysis on 14-evaluation criteria.

The proposed metrics capture either steering behaviors or limited long-term behaviors; some global metrics could be added to characterize the global behavior of the crowd such as lane formations, social gatherings, secondary behaviors, etc. Secondly, environment-sensitive metrics that measure the quality of agent behavior compared to them should be added (e.g., is there a shopping window nearby, stairs, certain attractors, etc.). Importantly, data-driven evaluation techniques could be added in the simulation loop so that during simulation, parameters of simulators are adapted to minimize "bad" behaviors (i.e., behaviors that do not match reference data). This could be done similarly to Wolinski et al. [8] for example.

References

1. R. McDonnell, M. Larkin, S. Dobbyn, S. Collins, and C. O'Sullivan. Clone attack! perception of crowd variety. *ACM Transactions on Graphics*, 27(3):26, 2008.
2. N. Pelechano, C. Stocker, J. Allbeck, and N. Badler. Being a part of the crowd: Towards validating VR crowds using presence. In *Proceedings of the 7th International Joint Conference on Autonomous Agents and Multiagent Systems—Volume 1*, AAMAS '08, pp. 136–142, Richland, SC, 2008. International Foundation for Autonomous Agents and Multiagent Systems.
3. M. Kapadia, S. Singh, B. Allen, G. Reinman, and P. Faloutsos. Steerbug: An interactive framework for specifying and detecting steering behaviors. In *Proceedings of the 2009 ACM*

SIGGRAPH/Eurographics Symposium on Computer Animation, SCA '09, pp. 209–216, New York, USA, 2009. ACM.

4. M. Kapadia, M. Wang, S. Singh, G. Reinman, and P. Faloutsos. Scenario space: Characterizing coverage, quality, and failure of steering algorithms. In *Proceedings of the 2011 ACM SIG-GRAPH/Eurographics Symposium on Computer Animation*, SCA '11, pp. 53–62, New York, USA, 2011. ACM.

5. S. Singh, M. Kapadia, P. Faloutsos, and G. Reinman. Steerbench: A benchmark suite for evaluating steering behaviors. *Computer Animation and Virtual Worlds*, 20(5–6):533–548, 2009.

6. S. J. Guy, J. van den Berg, W. Liu, R. Lau, M. C. Lin, and D. Manocha. A statistical similarity measure for aggregate crowd dynamics. *ACM Transactions on Graphics*, 31(6):190:1–190:11, 2012.

7. A. Lerner, Y. Chrysanthou, A. Shamir, and D. Cohen-Or. Context-dependent crowd evaluation. *Computer Graphics Forum*, 29(7):2197–2206, 2010.

8. D. Wolinski, S. J. Guy, A.-H. Olivier, M. Lin, D. Manocha, and J. Pettré. Parameter estimation and comparative evaluation of crowd simulations. *Computer Graphics Forum*, 33(2):303–312, 2014.

9. P. Charalambous, I. Karamouzas, S. J. Guy, and Y. Chrysanthou. A data-driven framework for visual crowd analysis. *Computer Graphics Forum*, 33(7):41–50, 2014.

10. K. H. Lee, M. G. Choi, Q. Hong, and J. Lee. Group behavior from video: A data-driven approach to crowd simulation. In *Proceedings of the 2007 ACM SIGGRAPH/Eurographics Symposium on Computer Animation*, SCA '07, pp. 109–118, Aire-la-Ville, Switzerland, Switzerland, 2007. Eurographics Association.

11. A. Lerner, Y. Chrysanthou, and D. Lischinski. Crowds by example. *Computer Graphics Forum*, 26(3):655–664, 2007.

12. P. Charalambous. *Data-Driven Techniques for Virtual Crowds*. PhD thesis, University of Cyprus, 2014.

13. K.-J. Hsiao, K. Xu, J. Calder, and A. Hero. Multi-criteria anomaly detection using Pareto depth analysis. In *Advances in Neural Information Processing Systems 25*, F. Pereira, C. J. C. Burges, L. Bottou, and K. Q. Weinberger (Eds.), pp. 854–862, Lake Tahoe, USA, Curran Associates, Inc. 2012.

14. A. Seyfried, O. Passon, B. Steffen, M. Boltes, T. Rupprecht, and W. Klingsch. New insights into pedestrian flow through bottlenecks. *Transportation Science*, 43(3):395–406, 2009.

15. Ubisoft Montreal. Assassin's Creed II, 2009.

16. D. Helbing, I. Farkas, and T. Vicsek. Simulating dynamical features of escape panic. *Nature*, 407(6803):487–490, 2000.

17. J. Pettré, J. Ondrej, A.-H. Olivier, A. Crétual, and S. Donikian. Experiment-based modeling, simulation and validation of interactions between virtual walkers. In *ACM SIGGRAPH/Eurographics Symposium on Computer Animation*, pp. 189–198, New Orleans, USA, 2009.

18. J. van den Berg, S. J. Guy, M. Lin, and D. Manocha. Reciprocal n-body collision avoidance. In *Robotics Research: The 14th International Symposium ISRR*, volume 70 of *Springer Tracts in Advanced Robotics*, pp. 3–19. Lucerne, Switzerland, Springer, 2011.

19. I. Karamouzas and M. Overmars. Simulating and evaluating the local behavior of small pedestrian groups. *IEEE Transactions on Visualization and Computer Graphics*, 18(3):394–406, 2012.

11

SteerFit: Automated Parameter Fitting for Steering Algorithms*

Glen Berseth, Mubbasir Kapadia, Brandon Haworth, and Petros Faloutsos

CONTENTS

In the context of crowd simulation, there is a diverse set of algorithms that model *steering*. The *performance* of steering models, both in terms of quality of results and computational efficiency, depends on internal parameters that are manually tuned to satisfy application-specific requirements. This chapter investigates the effect that these parameters have on an algorithm's performance. Using three representative steering algorithms and a set of established performance criteria, we perform a number of large-scale optimization experiments that optimize an algorithm's parameters for a range of objectives. For example, our method automatically finds optimal parameters to minimize turbulence at bottlenecks, reduce building evacuation times, produce emergent patterns, and increase the computational efficiency of an algorithm. We also propose using the Pareto optimal front as an efficient way of modeling optimal relationships between multiple objectives, and demonstrate its effectiveness by estimating optimal parameters for interactively defined combinations of the associated objectives. The proposed methodologies are general and can be applied to any steering algorithm using any set of performance criteria.

---

* The original version of this paper was published in the *Proceedings of the ACM SIGGRAPH/Eurographics Symposium on Computer Animation* 2014, pp. 113–122.

11.1 Introduction

Simulating groups of autonomous virtual humans (agents) in complex, dynamic environments is an important issue for many practical applications. A key aspect of autonomous agents is their ability to navigate (steer) from one location to another in their environment, while avoiding collisions with static as well as dynamic obstacles. The requirements of a steering approach differ significantly between applications and application domains. For example, computer games are generally concerned with minimizing computational overhead, and often trade-off quality for efficiency, while evacuation studies often aim to generate plausible crowd behavior that minimizes evacuation times while maintaining order.

There is no definitive solution to the steering problem. Most of the established methods are designed for specific classes of situations (scenarios), and make different trade-offs between quality and efficiency. The fine balance between these often competing performance criteria is governed by algorithm-specific parameters that are exposed to the user. Some of these parameters have intuitive direct effects. For example, the radius of a *comfort zone* affects how close agents may come to each other, while the *neighbor horizon* limits the distance from an agent within which other agents are considered during steering. This significantly influences both the predictive power and computational efficiency of the associated method. However, even when the parameters are fairly intuitive, their combined effect, or their effect on the macroscopic behavior of a large crowd, is not always easy to predict. For this reason, the inverse question is particularly interesting. Given a pattern of behavior, a performance criterion (metric), or a trade-off between performance metrics, can we automatically select the parameter values of a steering algorithm that will produce the desired effect? This is a timely and important question, and the main focus of our work.

We present a methodology for automatically fitting the parameters of a steering algorithm to minimize *any combination* of performance metrics across *any set* of environment benchmarks in a general, model-independent fashion. Using our approach, a steering algorithm can be optimized for the following: success; quality with respect to distance, time, or energy consumption of an agent; computational performance; similarity to ground truth; user-defined custom metrics; or a weighted combination of any of the above. Optimizing an algorithm's parameters across a representative set of challenging scenarios provides a parameter set that generalizes to many situations. A steering approach may also be fitted to a specific benchmark (e.g., a game level), or a benchmark category (e.g., evacuations) to hone its performance for a particular application. This may also allow context-dependent parameter swapping or individualization across agents.

We demonstrate our proposed methodology using three established agent-based algorithms: (1) ORCA: a predictive technique that uses reciprocal velocity obstacles for collision avoidance [1]; (2) PPR: a hybrid approach that uses rules to combine reactions, predictions, and planning [2]; and (3) SF: a variant of the social forces method for crowd simulation [3]. We thoroughly study these algorithms and compute their optimal parameter configurations for different metric combinations on a representative scenario set of local agent interactions and large-scale benchmarks. For example, our method automatically finds optimal parameters to minimize turbulence at bottlenecks, reduce building evacuation times, produce emergent patterns, and increase the computational efficiency of an algorithm, in one case by a factor of two. Cross-validation shows that, on average, optimal parameter values generalize across scenarios that were not part of the test set. Our study includes an in-depth statistical analysis of correlations between algorithmic parameters and performance criteria; however, because of space limitations, the complete analysis can be found in Reference 4.

We also study the interesting and challenging problem of dynamically tuning the parameters of an algorithm to support interactively defined combinations of objectives. For most practical cases, it is not feasible to solve this problem in real time every time the combination changes. To address this issue, we precompute optimal trade-offs between the objectives in the form of a discrete approximation of the Pareto optimal front. During runtime, our method efficiently estimates the parameters of the algorithm that optimally support a new combination of the objectives.

11.2 Related Work

Since the seminal work of References 5 and 6, crowd simulation has been studied from many different perspectives. We refer the readers to comprehensive surveys [7–9] and present a broad review below.

Continuum-based techniques [10,11] model the characteristics of the crowd flow to simulate macroscopic crowd phenomena. Particle-based approaches [5,6] model agents as particles and simulate crowds using basic particle dynamics. The social force model [12,13] simulates forces such as repulsion, attraction, friction, and dissipation for each agent to simulate pedestrians. Rule-based approaches [14,15] use various conditions and heuristics to identify the exact situation of an agent. Egocentric techniques [16] model a local variable-resolution perception of the simulation. Data-driven methods [17–20] use existing video or motion capture data to derive steering choices that are then used in virtual worlds, and a recent work [21] demonstrates a synthetic vision-based approach to steering. The works of References 1 and 22 use predictions to steer in environments populated with dynamic threats.

Crowd evaluation: There has been a growing recent trend to use statistical analysis in the evaluation and analysis of crowd simulations. The work in Reference 23 adopts a data-driven approach to evaluating crowds by measuring its similarity to real-world data. Reference 24 proposes a compact suite of manually defined test cases that represent different steering challenges and a rich set of derived metrics that provide an empirical measure of the performance of an algorithm. Recent extensions [25] propose a representative sampling of challenging scenarios that agents encounter in crowds to compute the coverage of the algorithm and the quality of the simulations produced. Density measures [23] and fundamental diagram-based comparisons [26] use aggregate metrics for quantifying similarity. The work in References 27 and 28 measures the ability of a steering algorithm to emulate the behavior of a real crowd dataset by measuring its divergence from ground truth. Reference 29 presents a histogram-based technique to quantify the global flow characteristics of crowds. Perceptual studies rely on human factor experiments to measure the variety in appearance and motion [30], or perceptual fidelity of relaxing collisions [31] in crowds.

Parameter optimization: Parameter fitting is widely used in visual effects [32] to automate the tuning of model parameters to meet certain user-defined criteria. The resulting optimization problems tend to involve non-convex, and high-dimensional spaces. For these problems, evolutionary strategies are preferred because they generally have fewer parameters to tune and do not require the computation of derivatives. Such techniques have been successfully demonstrated on a diverse set of application domains [33,34]. By selecting the right set of parameters, researchers have shown improvements in a steering algorithm's ability to match recorded crowd data [28,35–38].

Concurrent work [39] explores parameter estimation for steering algorithms to match reference data for specific scenarios. Our method is not tied to ground truth, and can be used to optimize quantitative metrics such as the computational performance of the algorithm. Additionally, we leverage the use of different test sets, including small-scale interactions and high-density crowds, to obtain optimal parameter values that *generalize* across the space of possible scenarios. To offset the computational burden of optimizing an algorithm for different criteria, we propose a method to precompute the mapping between an algorithm's parameters and objective weights, thus allowing us to dynamically adapt the crowd behavior at real-time rates.

11.3 Parameter Fitting Methodology

We present an optimization-based framework for automatically fitting the parameters $\mathbf{v} \in \mathbb{V}$ of an algorithm, $A_{\mathbf{v}}$. Our framework automatically selects optimal parameter values $\mathbf{v}^* \in \mathbb{V}$ such that the performance of $A_{\mathbf{v}^*}$ minimizes certain performance criteria, over a set of benchmarks (test set). The next sections describe the elements involved in this problem and our approach to solving it.

11.3.1 Steering Algorithms

Our approach can be applied to any steering algorithm. For demonstration reasons, we use the following established steering approaches. (1) PPR: Reference 2 combines reactions, predictions, and planning in one single framework with 38 tunable parameters. (2) ORCA: Reference 1 uses reciprocal velocity obstacles for goal-directed collision avoidance. (3) SF: Reference 3 uses hypothetical social forces for resolving collisions between interacting agents in dense crowds. These algorithms represent the broad taxonomy of crowd approaches with mutually exclusive parameter sets that can be tuned to produce widely differing variations in the resulting crowd behavior.

11.3.2 Test Sets

We employ different benchmark sets, including local agent interactions and high-density crowds, to find the optimal values of an algorithm's parameters that generalize across the wide range of situations that agents encounter in crowds. Note that certain performance metrics may have more meaning for specific test sets. For example, computational efficiency is more meaningful for situations that involve sufficiently large numbers of agents.

Large-scale set: S contains most of the large-scale benchmarks in Table 11.1 that define large environments with many agents. S^v is a set of similar but different large-scale benchmarks that will be used to validate the results of parameter optimization on previously unseen cases (cross-validation).

TABLE 11.1

Large-Scale Benchmarks

Benchmark	# Agents	Description
Random	1000	Random agents in open space
Forest	500	Random agents in a forest
Urban	500	Random agents in an urban environment
Hallway	200	Bidirectional traffic in a hallway
Free Tickets	200	Random agents to same goal, then disperse
Bottleneck	1000	Tight bottleneck
Bottleneck evac	200	Evacuation through a narrow door
Concentric circle	250	Circle with target on opposite side
Concentric circle	500	Circle with target on opposite side
Hallway	400	Four-way directional traffic

Note: The bottom three scenario are part of S^v. All are designed to stress the steering algorithm's computational efficiency.

Representative set: The representative set includes 5000 samples from the representative space of scenarios, commonly observed in challenging steering situations. For more details, refer Reference 25.

Combined test set: The union of the large-scale set, S, and the representative set, R, $T = S \cup R$ is the main test set that we use for algorithm analysis and parameter fitting in a statistically significant general fashion. Here we use statistical significance to contrast against common practice in crowd simulation where results are demonstrated on a very limited number of test cases.

Combined validation set: Similarly, the combined cross-validation set is $T^v = S^v \cup R^v$.

Custom scenario set: A user can specify a subset of scenarios in T or even design custom benchmarks to focus the parameter fitting on application-specific requirements. Random permutations in the environment configuration and agent placement can generate multiple samples of a custom benchmark category. For example, one can create a set of test cases that capture two-way traffic in orthogonally crossing hallways as is common in large buildings.

Ground truth test set: There are few publicly available datasets of recorded crowd motion that can be used to test a steering algorithm's ability to match real-world data. We use a ground truth test set G, published by Reference 26, for our experiments.

11.3.3 Normalized Performance Measures

This section defines a variety of intuitive measures to characterize the performance of a steering algorithm on the test set T. These include (1) the fraction of scenarios that an algorithm was unable to solve in the representative set of scenarios, (2) quality measures with respect to distance traveled, total time taken, or energy consumption of an agent, (3) computational performance of the algorithm, or (4) statistical similarity with respect to ground truth. The specific metrics we use are briefly described below and we refer the reader to more detailed explanations in References 25, 27, and 40. In addition, users may define their own custom metrics to meet application-specific requirements.

Failure rate: The coverage $c(A_v)$ of a steering algorithm A_v over a test set T is the ratio of scenarios that it successfully completes in T. An algorithm successfully completes a particular scenario if the reference agent reaches its goal without any collisions and the total number of collisions among non-reference agents is less than the number of agents in the scenario. The failure rate is the complement of coverage $d(A_v) = 1 - c(A_v)$.

Distance quality: The distance quality $q^d(A_v)$ of A_v for a single scenario s is the complement of the ratio between the length of an ideal optimal path o_s^d, and the length of the path that the reference agent followed, a_s^d. It is computed as $q^d(A_v) = 1 - o_s^d/a_s^d$. The ideal optimal path is the shortest static path from the agent's initial position to its goal. If the algorithm does not successfully complete the scenario, then the associated distance quality metric is set to the worst-case value of 1.

Time quality: Similarly, $q^t(A_v)$ characterizes how much longer the reference agent took to reach its goal compared to an ideal optimal time. The ideal optimal time for a single scenario corresponds to the agent reaching its goal when moving with its desired velocity along the ideal optimal path.

Principle of least effort (PLE) quality. The PLE quality metric is computed as $q^e(A_v) = 1 - o^e/a^e$, where $o_s^e = 2 \cdot o_s^d \cdot (e_s \cdot e_w)$ is the ideal optimal effort and a^e the actual effort of the agent [40]. The distance, time, and PLE quality measures can be averaged across a large set of benchmarks to provide aggregate quality measures for a test set.

Computational efficiency: The computational efficiency $e(A_v)$ metric is the average CPU time consumed by all agents in all scenarios in a test set $\mathcal{S}$. To provide a basis for normalization, we assume that 10% of all computational resources are allocated to the steering algorithm. Hence, the maximum time allocated to a steering algorithm every frame is n_{des}^{-1} seconds for a desired frame rate of n_{des} fps. For every scenario s, the maximum time t_{max}^s allocated to every steering agent per frame is $0.1 \cdot (N \cdot n_{des})^{-1}$ seconds, where N is the number of agents in s. Let t_{avg}^s be the average time spent per frame for all agents to reach a steering decision. The average computational efficiency e over a test set $\mathcal{S}$ is computed as follows:

$$e(A_v) = 1 - \frac{\sum\limits_{s \in \mathcal{S}} e_s(A_v)}{|\mathcal{S}|}, \quad e_s(A_v) = \frac{t_{max}^s}{t_{avg}^s} \tag{11.1}$$

where $e_s(A_v)$ is the efficiency of A_v for a particular scenario s, and $|\mathcal{S}|$ is the cardinality of the test set $\mathcal{S}$. The desired frame rate, n_{des}, provides an ideal upper bound for efficiency, analogous to the ideal upper bounds of the other metrics, and allows us to define a normalized efficiency metric. Normalized metrics can be combined more intuitively into optimization objectives in the forthcoming analysis. Alternatively, we could set the desired frame rate to a very high value for all algorithms and attend to scaling issues later.

Similarity to ground truth: In addition to quantitatively characterizing the performance of a steering algorithm, we can also measure its ability to match ground truth. We compute a simulation-to-data similarity measure $g(A_v, \mathcal{G})$ [27], which computes the entropy measurement of the prediction errors of algorithm A_v relative to a given example dataset, such as the test set $\mathcal{G}$ defined in Section 11.3.2.

11.3.4 Parameter Optimization

Given a set of performance metrics such as the ones defined in Section 11.3.3, $\mathbb{M} = \langle d, q^d, q^t, q^e, e \rangle$, we can define an objective function as a weighted combination of these metrics:

$$f(A_{\mathbf{v}}, \mathbf{w}) = \sum_{m_i \in \mathbb{M}} w_i \cdot m_i \qquad (11.2)$$

where $\mathbf{w} = \{w_i\}$ contains the weights that determine the relative influence of each individual metric. By choosing different sets of metrics and associated relative weights, we can define custom objectives. For a steering algorithm $A_{\mathbf{v}}$ with internal parameters $\mathbf{v} \in \mathbb{V}$, a set of test cases, and a desired objective $f(A_{\mathbf{v}}, \mathbf{w})$, our goal is to find the optimal parameter values $\mathbf{v}_{\mathbf{w}}^*$ that minimize the objective over the test set. This can be formulated as a minimization problem:

$$\mathbf{v}_{\mathbf{w}}^* = \arg\min_{\mathbf{v} \in \mathbb{V}} f(A_{\mathbf{v}}, \mathbf{w}) \qquad (11.3)$$

This is generally a nonlinear and non-convex optimization problem for the independent parameters, $\mathbf{v} \in \mathbb{V}$. The covariance matrix adaptation evolution strategy technique (CMA-ES) [41,42] is one of the many methods that can solve such problems. We chose CMA-ES because it is straightforward to implement, it can handle ill-conditioned objectives and noise, it is very competitive in converging to an optimal value in a few iterations, and it has support for mixed integer optimization. The CMA-ES algorithm terminates when the objective converges to a minimum, when very little improvement is made between iterations, or after a fixed number of iterations. In most of our experiments, the algorithm converged within 1000 evaluations.

For practical reasons, we have to limit the range of the algorithm's parameters. The bounds are chosen separately for each parameter based on intuition, physical interpretation of the parameter, or default values provided by the algorithm's creators. Limiting the values of an algorithm's parameters transforms the problem of optimizing over an unbounded domain to a bounded one, which generally decreases the number of iterations needed for the optimization to converge.

11.4 Large-Scale Study

We study the effects of parameter fitting using the combined test sets, $\mathcal{T}$ and $\mathcal{T}^v$. Our goal is to identify whether parameter fitting has a significant effect and to understand the relation between algorithmic parameters and performance. For each of the three algorithms, PPR, ORCA, and SF, we compute the optimal parameter values for each of the five metrics, failure rate $d(A_{\mathbf{v}})$, distance quality $q^d(A_{\mathbf{v}})$, time quality $q^t(A_{\mathbf{v}})$, PLE $q^e(A_{\mathbf{v}})$, efficiency $e(A_{\mathbf{v}})$, as well as a uniform combination of these metrics $u(A_{\mathbf{v}})$, over the entire combined set $\mathcal{T}$. For comparison, we also compute the same metrics for all algorithms with their parameters set to default values. The results in Figure 11.1 show a strong increase in optimality for all metrics.

The default parameters for PPR, ORCA, and SF cannot solve 39%, 56%, and 26% of the sampled scenarios, respectively. Using the optimal parameter selection for PPR, the algorithm only fails in 9% of the scenarios, an improvement of 30% over the default settings. The significant optimization in time quality, $q^t(A_{\mathbf{v}})$, for the PPR algorithm is impressive as well. ORCA does not show significant results over the metrics with the exception of q^t.

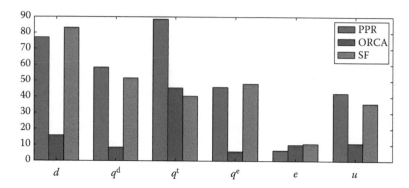

FIGURE 11.1
Relative percent improvement of failure rate d, distance quality q^d, time quality q^t, effort quality q^e, computational efficiency e, and a uniform combination of metrics u for the three steering algorithms.

On the other hand SF shows impressive improvement over most metrics, achieving the smallest failure rate d and the minimum energy expenditure, q^e.

Validation: We verify the statistical significance of the results shown in Figure 11.1 in two ways. First, we observe that for all three algorithms and for all the scenarios in the test set $\mathcal{T}$, which are more than 5000, the optimization did not time out but converged to at least a local minimum. In the context of numerical optimization, that is a sufficiently strong indication that the results are not random. Second, we perform a cross-validation study on an equally large test set of similar, but previously unseen, scenarios $\mathcal{T}^v$. Comparing the values of the objectives for the default parameters of the algorithms, and for the optimized ones, we see that the optimized parameters on average perform better even on scenarios that were not used during the optimization.

Relationship between parameters and metrics: It is interesting to identify which parameters change in relation to the objectives, and study the trade-offs that the algorithms essentially make with these changes. We present relevant data for ORCA in Table 11.2.

To optimize failure rate, $d(A_v)$, PPR chooses very high values for predictive avoidance parameters and minimal values for speed thresholds, and trades off performance by selecting higher spatial querying distances. When optimizing distance quality $q^d(A_v)$, PPR changes different speed multipliers in an attempt to minimize any extra distance covered around corners. To minimize failure rate and meet the time limit, ORCA raises its time horizon and increases its max speed. This increases the number of agents it considers in its velocity calculations and ensures agents cover as much distance as possible, respectively. For distance quality, $q^d(A_v)$, ORCA reduces max speed just like PPR. In general, SF reduces acceleration parameters to minimum values for all quality metrics to prevent agents from overreacting. Looking at the correlation coefficients for ORCA in Table 11.2, we can make the following observations:

1. For ORCA, the maximum number of neighbors considered has the highest correlation with most metrics. The max speed seems to be the second most important parameter. It affects effort quality $q^e(A_v)$ negatively and time quality $q^t(A_v)$ positively.

TABLE 11.2

Spearman Correlation Coefficients between Five Metrics and the Parameters of ORCA

Parameter	d	q^{d}	q^{t}	q^{e}	e
Max speed	0.02	0.03	−0.34	0.58	0.14
Neighbor distance	−0.094427	−0.065495	−0.1256	−0.034601	0.029667
Time horizon	−0.11981	−0.082849	0.10489	0.037645	0.073813
Time horizon obstacles	−0.08616	−0.08839	0.17168	0.041958	0.10749
Max neighbors	0.42058	0.46987	0.53814	0.28542	0.36609

Note: The maximum number of neighbors considered seems to have a significant effect on all metrics. For the effort metric, q^{e}, the maximum speed parameter has a large inverse effect.

2. For PPR, the max speed factor, which is a multiplier that increases the speed of an agent, is strongly correlated with the efficiency metric, e, and has a negative effect on all quality metrics.

3. For SF, the parameters with the highest correlation to computational efficiency, e, have to do with proximity forces. When these are increased, agents push each other away forcefully, decreasing the likelihood that they will interact again in the the next frame.

The above analysis is not meant to be definite or complete, but rather to demonstrate that the proposed methodology can be notably more effective than manual tuning. The framework is an effective way to optimize, probe, and analyze the behavior of a steering algorithm in relation to its parameters, over a small or large set of test cases.

11.5 Optimal Parameter Mapping for Multiple Objectives

Optimizing a steering algorithm's parameters across a large test set is computationally expensive. The computational complexity increases with the number of parameters and the cardinality of a test set. For example, it takes $\sim$ 20 hours to optimize the 11 parameters of SF over the representative test set $\mathcal{T}$. In a weighted multi-objective optimization application, it is desirable to model the relationship between objectives and algorithm parameters. This avoids running an expensive optimization every time we wish to change the associated weights. This can be accomplished by computing the optimal parameters for a discrete set of weighted combinations that can then be interpolated. There are two problems with this approach. First, it can waste significant amounts of computation since each sample point is a result of an independent process that could be visiting the same points in the domain. Second and most important, it is not looking at relationships between the objectives but rather at their weighted combination. Both of these problems can be addressed by computing a *Pareto optimal front*. Pareto optimality is a very important concept in optimization that has ben sparingly used in computer animation. Our method based on *Pareto optimality* not only avoids unnecessary computation but also provides a more principled model of the optimal relationships between multiple objectives.

11.5.1 Pareto Optimality

Pareto optimality (or efficiency) refers to a situation where no objective can be improved further without worsening one of the other objectives. The set of points that are Pareto optimal constitute the Pareto optimal front, a hyper-surface that captures the optimal relationships between the objectives. Computing this front is not trivial and is, in fact, an active area of research. Current state-of-the-art techniques are primarily based on genetic algorithms. We have chosen to use DEAP [43] and NSGA-II [44] to estimate the Pareto optimal front.

A standard evolutionary approach to solving a multi-objective optimization problem models the fitness of samples using a single objective function that is the weighted sum of multiple objectives, where the samples chosen in each iteration minimize the combined objective. In contrast, the goal of Pareto optimal front approximation is to maximize the hyper-volume constructed by the non-dominated samples (see Figure 11.2a). A point dominates another if it is superior in all Pareto dimensions.

Figure 11.2b through d demonstrates the Pareto optimal front for three cases. First, we optimize the ORCA steering algorithm for e and q^e over a bottleneck scenario. The process and resulting Pareto optimal front can be seen in Figure 11.2b. Second, we optimize the SF algorithm for the same scenario and three metrics, e, q^e, and $g(A_v, \mathcal{G})$ (the result

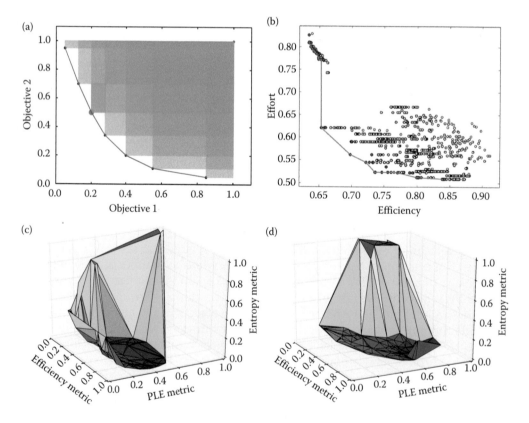

FIGURE 11.2

Each point in (a) dominates any other point in the shaded area defined by that point and adding the green point improves the Pareto front equivalent to the green patch it defines. (b) shows the final Pareto optimal front of non-dominated points (in green) for the ORCA steering algorithm over two objectives. (c and d) show the final computed Pareto optimal front for three objectives for the SF and ORCA steering algorithms.

can be found in Figure 11.2c). The ground truth set, $\mathcal{G}$, is a recording of people funneling into a small bottleneck, very similar to the scenario used. We optimize for the same objectives with the ORCA steering algorithm and the resultant Pareto optimal front can be see in Figure 11.2d. The pareto front is able to capture the nonlinear relationships between contradictory objectives and efficiently encodes the trade-offs between them. For example, optimizing q^e has an adverse effect on $g(A_v, \mathcal{G})$, as shown in Figure 11.2c and d.

The Pareto optimal front provides a principled model of the optimal relationships between the objectives. The number of dimensions is equal to the number of objectives; thus for two objectives, the result is a 2D curve and for three objectives a 3D surface. For most practical applications, three objectives should be sufficient.

11.5.2 Pareto Optimal Front Interpolation

Having an estimate of the Pareto optimal front for a set of objectives provides us with the basis to estimate optimal parameters for the associated algorithm with arbitrary combinations of the objectives.

The first step in developing an interpolation model for arbitrary combinations of the objectives is to transform the Pareto optimal front from objective space to weight space. For m objectives, the Pareto optimal front contains a set of m-dimensional points, $\mathcal{P} = \{\mathbf{b}_p | \forall p = 1, \ldots, N\}$, including a set of points $\mathcal{P}_O = \{\mathbf{b}_p^O | \forall p = 1, \ldots, m\}$, that correspond to minimizing each objective while ignoring the others. These latter points have known coordinates in weight space that correspond to the standard unit vectors, and hold the minimum value in the associated dimension.

We transform the Pareto optimal front from the m-dimensional objective space, $[b_i]$, to the m-dimensional weight space, $[w_i]$, using the following steps: (a) we normalize the Pareto optimal front so that each dimension maps to $[0, 1]$; (b) we replace each point with its distances from the normalized points in $\mathcal{P}_O$; (c) we project the points, $\mathbf{b}'$, resulting from the previous stage onto the $\sum_i b_i' = 1$ plane; and (d) we subtract them from 1. The transformed Pareto optimal front is now mapped onto a normalized simplex from which we can compute the relative weights of each original point as its barycentric coordinates (Figure 11.3).

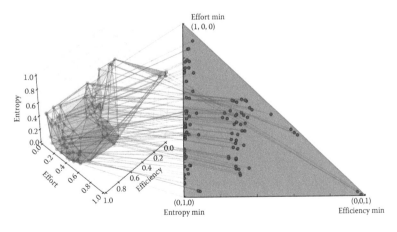

FIGURE 11.3
Projecting a 3D Pareto optimal front onto a triangular normalized weight domain.

Having the Pareto optimal front in weight space, we can now use a standard multidimensional interpolation method such as Mardy quadratics or variants of Shepard's method. A common choice within the Mardy quadratics family of methods is radial basis function interpolation. For three objectives, the associated domain forms a triangle. In this case, given a new set of weights, we can use Delaunay triangulation to compute the three points that make up the bounding simplex whose associated parameters will be interpolated with a standard inverse distance approach.

11.6 Applications and Results

Section 11.4 demonstrates that it is both beneficial and revealing to fit the parameters of a steering algorithm to performance objectives over a large set of test cases. This section presents a series of experiments that demonstrate the potential applications of parameter fitting for more specific cases.

Circular benchmark: A popular and challenging scenario, often used to test the effectiveness of a steering algorithm, distributes the agents in a circular fashion with diametrically opposite goals. Such a configuration forces dense simultaneous interactions in the middle of the circle. Using a group of 500 agents, we compare the results of ORCA with the default and optimized parameter values that minimize time quality $q^t(A_v)$. With the optimal parameters, ORCA takes 50% less time to complete the benchmark and exhibits a more organized emerging behavior. Agents seem to form groups that follow a smooth curved trajectory (Figure 11.4a and b).

Room evacuation: Evacuation benchmarks are important for a range of application domains. In this benchmark, a group of 500 agents must exit a room. For this experiment, we use the social forces, SF, method with the default as well as optimized parameter values that minimize the effort quality metric, $q^e(A_v)$. SF with optimal parameters spends 66% less energy on average per agent, exhibits tighter packing, and visibly reduces the turbulence of the crowd's behavior (Figure 11.4c and d).

Office evacuation: A more challenging evacuation scenario places 1000 agents in a complex, office-like ground floor. Optimizing ORCA for time quality, $q^t(A_v)$, reduces the average time it takes to exit the building by almost 60%. In addition, it exhibits higher crowd density and higher throughput at the exits, as seen in Figure 11.5. Here, we use ADAPT [45] to render bipedal characters.

Optimizing for ground truth: There are a few methods that use recorded crowd motion to influence and direct virtual crowds. Here, we simply show that our methodology can also support this application. We optimize the behavior of the three test algorithms to match real-world data contained in the ground truth test set, $\mathcal{G}$ (Section 11.3.2). Our experiments showed that, in most cases, the optimization was able to significantly alter the resulting steering behavior and increase the similarity to the recorded data. Figure 11.6a reports the reduction in the entropy metric, g (increase in similarity), as a result of parameter optimization for all three algorithms and two different benchmarks.

Interactive parameter blending: Using a precomputed Pareto optimal front (Section 11.5), we can automatically adapt an algorithm's parameters to provide optimal trade-offs for

(a) (b)
(c) (d)

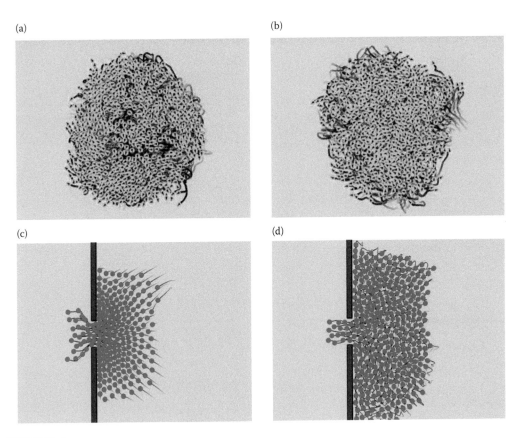

FIGURE 11.4
Comparison of simulations using optimized (a), (c) and default (b), (d) parameters. Top: Agents are initially in a circle with anti-diametric goals. The ORCA algorithm, optimized to reduce time to completion, completes the task *twice* as fast as its default configuration and exhibits a less turbulent pattern. Bottom: The SF algorithm, optimized to minimize effort, requires a third of the energy spent by its default configuration, and produces a smoother, faster, and tighter room evacuation.

(a) (b)

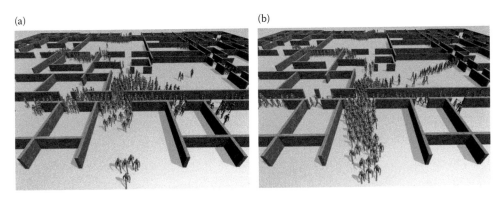

FIGURE 11.5
Office evacuation with ORCA. Simulation with parameters optimized for time quality (b) take half the time to complete as compared to the default parameters (a).

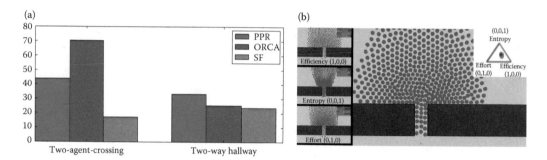

FIGURE 11.6

Relative percent improvement of entropy metric values after optimization on two benchmarks (a). Blending interactively three objectives (efficiency, entropy, and effort) using a precomputed Pareto optimal front (b).

interactively defined combinations of the associated objectives. Figure 11.6b shows a snapshot of such blending between three objectives.

11.7 Conclusion

We have presented a framework for optimizing the parameters of a steering algorithm for multiple objectives. Using cross-validation, we show that optimizing over a representative set of scenarios produces optimal parameters that generalize well to new test cases. We have also proposed a method to model trade-offs between the objectives using a Pareto optimal front. The Pareto optimal front essentially captures the optimal relationships between objectives. Although our approach can be applied to any number of objectives, three is a practical choice. Thus, we have demonstrated an interactive example that uses the computed Pareto optimal front to blend between three objectives.

Our study shows that parameter fitting can not only be used to improve the performance of an algorithm, but it can also serve as an analysis tool to produce a detailed view of an algorithm's range of behavior relative to its internal parameters. This detailed view can be the basis of a thorough introspective analysis that allows both developers and end-users to gain insights on the performance and behavior of an algorithm. Our framework and methodology are general. Most elements can be tailored to the needs of a particular application. For example, one can use different performance metrics, objectives, test sets, and optimization methods. The optimal parameter values of the three steering algorithms for the different objectives can be used by AI developers and enthusiasts to improve the performance of their crowd simulations. The computational expense of optimizations, especially for large-scale crowds, is one of the reasons why we are committed to sharing our results with the community.

11.7.1 Limitations

Optimization-based methods have certain well-known limitations. For example, it might not be easy or even possible for an optimization process to construct what is essentially a relationship between the parameters of a steering algorithm and global, or long-term, type of objectives. Furthermore, describing desired behaviors as combinations of objectives is not always straightforward and may require experimentation. Although estimating the Pareto optimal front is much more efficient and effective than naive domain sampling, it still requires significant offline computation.

11.7.2 Future Work

We would like to address heterogeneous crowds by using different parameters per agent or group of agents. We plan to thoroughly investigate the sampling and complexity issues related to the estimation of the Pareto optimal front, focusing on objectives that are common in crowd simulation.

References

1. J. van den Berg, S. J. Guy, M. Lin, and D. Manocha. Reciprocal n-body collision avoidance. *International Symposium on Robotics Research*, 70:3–19, Lucerne, Switzerland, 2011.
2. S. Singh, M. Kapadia, B. Hewlett, G. Reinman, and P. Faloutsos. A modular framework for adaptive agent-based steering. In *ACM SIGGRAPH Symposium on Interactive 3D Graphics and Games, ACM I3D*, pp. 141–150, San Francisco, California, 2011.
3. D. Helbing, I. Farkas, and T. Vicsek. Simulating dynamical features of escape panic. *Nature*, 407(6803):487–490, 2000.
4. G. Berseth, M. Kapadia, B. Haworth, and P. Faloutsos. SteerFit: Automated parameter fitting for steering algorithms. In *ACM SIGGRAPH/Eurographics Symposium on Computer Animation, SCA'14*, pp. 113–122, New York, USA, 2014. ACM.
5. C. W. Reynolds. Steering behaviors for autonomous characters. *GDC*, 1999(9602):763–782, 1999.
6. C. W. Reynolds. Flocks, herds and schools: A distributed behavioral model. In *SIGGRAPH '87 Proceedings of the 14th Annual Conference on Computer Graphics and Interactive Techniques*, pp. 25–34, Anaheim, California, 1987.
7. S. Huerre, J. Lee, M. Lin, and C. O'Sullivan. Simulating believable crowd and group behaviors. In *3rd ACM SIGGRAPH Conference and Exhibition on Computer Graphics and Interactive Techniques in Asia 2010*, pp. 13:1–13:92, Seoul, 2010.
8. N. Pelechano, J. M. Allbeck, and N. I. Badler. *Virtual Crowds: Methods, Simulation, and Control.* Morgan & Claypool Publishers, 2008.
9. D. Thalmann and S. R. Musse. Behavioral animation of crowd, In *Crowd Simulation*, Second edition. Springer, New York, 2013.
10. R. Narain, A. Golas, S. Curtis, and M. C. Lin. Aggregate dynamics for dense crowd simulation. In *2nd ACM SIGGRAPH Conference and Exhibition in Asia 2009*, pp. 122:1–122:8, Yokohama, Japan, 2009.
11. A. Treuille, S. Cooper, and Z. Popović. Continuum crowds. *ACM Transactions on Graphics*, 25(3):1160–1168, 2006.
12. D. Helbing, L. Buzna, A. Johansson, and T. Werner. Self-organized pedestrian crowd dynamics: Experiments, simulations, and design solutions. *Transportation Science*, 39(1):1–24, 2005.
13. N. Pelechano, J. M. Allbeck, and N. I. Badler. Controlling individual agents in high-density crowd simulation. In *ACM SIGGRAPH/Eurographics Symposium on Computer Animation*, pp. 99–108, San Diego, USA, 2007.
14. F. Lamarche and S. Donikian. Crowd of virtual humans: A new approach for real time navigation in complex and structured environments. *CGF*, 23(3):509–518, 2004.
15. A. Sud, R. Gayle, E. Andersen, S. Guy, M. Lin, and D. Manocha. Real-time navigation of independent agents using adaptive roadmaps. In *The ACM Symposium on Virtual Reality Software and Technology*, pp. 99–106, Irvine, California, 2007.

16. M. Kapadia, S. Singh, W. Hewlett, and P. Faloutsos. Egocentric affordance fields in pedestrian steering. In *Proceedings of the 2009 Symposium on Interactive 3D Graphics and Games, I3D '09*, pp. 215–223, New York, USA, 2009. ACM.

17. C. D. Boatright, M. Kapadia, J. M. Shapira, and N. I. Badler. Context-sensitive data-driven crowd simulation. In *Proceedings of the 12th ACM SIGGRAPH International Conference on Virtual-Reality Continuum and Its Applications in Industry, VRCAI '13*, pp. 51–56, New York, USA, 2013. ACM.

18. E. Ju, M. G. Choi, M. Park, J. Lee, K. H. Lee, and S. Takahashi. Morphable crowds. In *3rd ACM SIGGRAPH Conference and Exhibition on Computer Graphics and Interactive Techniques in Asia 2010*, pp. 140:1–140:10, Seoul, 2010.

19. K. H. Lee, M. G. Choi, Q. Hong, and J. Lee. Group behavior from video: A data-driven approach to crowd simulation. In *ACM SIGGRAPH/Eurographics Symposium on Computer Animation*, pp. 109–118, San Diego, USA, 2007.

20. A. Lerner, Y. Chrysanthou, and D. Lischinski. Crowds by example. *CGF*, 26(3):655–664, 2007.

21. J. Ondřej, J. Pettré, A.-H. Olivier, and S. Donikian. A synthetic-vision based steering approach for crowd simulation. *ACM Transactions on Graphics*, 29(4):123:1–123:9, 2010.

22. S. Paris, J. Pettré, and S. Donikian. Pedestrian reactive navigation for crowd simulation: A predictive approach. *EUROGRAPHICS 2007*, 26:665–674, 2007.

23. A. Lerner, Y. Chrysanthou, A. Shamir, and D. Cohen-Or. Context-dependent crowd evaluation. *Computer Graphics Forum*, 29(7):2197–2206, 2010.

24. S. Singh, M. Kapadia, P. Faloutsos, and G. Reinman. Steerbench: A benchmark suite for evaluating steering behaviors. *Computer Animation and Virtual Worlds*, 20(February):533–548, 2009.

25. M. Kapadia, M. Wang, S. Singh, G. Reinman, and P. Faloutsos. Scenario space: Characterizing coverage, quality, and failure of steering algorithms. In *ACM SIGGRAPH/Eurographics Symposium on Computer Animation*, pp. 53–62, Vancouver, BC, Canada, 2011.

26. A. Seyfried, M. Boltes, J. Köhler, W. Klingsch, A. Portz, T. Rupprecht, A. Schadschneider, B. Steffen, and A. Winkens. Enhanced empirical data for the fundamental diagram and the flow through bottlenecks. In *Pedestrian and Evacuation Dynamics 2008*, W.W.F. Klingsch, C. Rogsch, A. Schadschneider, and M. Schreckenberg (Eds.), pp. 145–156. Springer, Berlin, Heidelberg, 2010.

27. S. J. Guy, J. van den Berg, W. Liu, R. Lau, M. C. Lin, and D. Manocha. A statistical similarity measure for aggregate crowd dynamics. *ACM Transactions on Graphics*, 31(6):11, 2012.

28. J. Pettré, J. Ondřej, A.-H. Olivier, A. Cretual, and S. Donikian. Experiment-based modeling, simulation and validation of interactions between virtual walkers. In *ACM SIGGRAPH/Eurographics Symposium on Computer Animation*, pp. 189–198, New Orleans, USA, 2009.

29. S. R. Musse, V. J. Cassol, and C. R. Jung. Towards a quantitative approach for comparing crowds. *Computer Animation and Virtual Worlds*, 23(1):49–57, 2012.

30. R. McDonnell, M. Larkin, S. Dobbyn, S. Collins, and C. O'Sullivan. Clone attack! Perception of crowd variety. *ACM Transactions on Graphics*, 27(3):26:1–26:8, 2008.

31. R. Kulpa, A.-H. Olivierxs, J. Ondřej, and J. Pettré. Imperceptible relaxation of collision avoidance constraints in virtual crowds. In *ACM SIGGRAPH ASIA*, pp. 138:1–138:10, Hong Kong, China, 2011.

32. S. Bruckner and T. Moller. Result-driven exploration of simulation parameter spaces for visual effects design. *IEEE TVCG*, 16(6):1468–1476, 2010.

33. S. Ha, J. McCann, C. Karen Liu, and J. Popović. Physics storyboards. *Computer Graphics Forum*, 32(2pt2):133–142, 2013.

34. J. M. Wang, D. J. Fleet, and A. Hertzmann. Optimizing walking controllers for uncertain inputs and environments. *ACM Transactions on Graphics*, 29(4):73:1–73:8, 2010.

35. M. Davidich and G. Koester. Towards automatic and robust adjustment of human behavioral parameters in a pedestrian stream model to measured data. In *Pedestrian and Evacuation Dynamics*, pp. 537–546. Springer, US, 2011.

36. A. Johansson, D. Helbing, and P. Shukla. Specification of the social force pedestrian model by evolutionary adjustment to video tracking data. *Advances in Complex Systems*, 10(suppl.02):271–288, 2007.

37. S. Lemercier, A. Jelic, R. Kulpa, J. Hua, J. Fehrenbach, P. Degond, C. Appert-Rolland, S. Donikian, and J. Pettré. Realistic following behaviors for crowd simulation. *CGF*, 31(2):489–498, 2012.

38. S. Pellegrini, A. Ess, K. Schindler, and L. Van Gool. You'll never walk alone: Modeling social behavior for multi-target tracking. In *2009 IEEE 12th International Conference on Computer Vision*, pp. 261–268, Kyoto, Japan, 2009.

39. D. Wolinski, S. Guy, A.-H. Olivier, M. Lin, D. Manocha, and J. Pettré. Parameter estimation and comparative evaluation of crowd simulations. *Computer Graphics Forum*, 33(2):303–312, 2014.

40. S. J. Guy, J. Chhugani, S. Curtis, P. Dubey, M. Lin, and D. Manocha. PLEdestrians: A least-effort approach to crowd simulation. In *ACM SIGGRAPH/Eurographics Symposium on Computer Animation*, pp. 119–128, Madrid, Spain, 2010.

41. N. Hansen and A. Ostermeier. Adapting arbitrary normal mutation distributions in evolution strategies: The covariance matrix adaptation. In *IEEE International Conference on Evolutionary Computation*, pp. 312–317, Nagoya, Japan, 1996.

42. N. Hansen. A CMA-ES for mixed-integer nonlinear optimization. Technical Report RR-7751, INRIA, October 2011.

43. F.-A. Fortin, F.-M. De Rainville, M.-A. Gardner, M. Parizeau, and C. Gagné. DEAP: Evolutionary algorithms made easy. *Journal of Machine Learning Research*, 13:2171–2175, 2012.

44. K. Deb, A. Pratap, S. Agarwal, and T. Meyarivan. A fast and elitist multiobjective genetic algorithm: NSGA-II. *IEEE Transactions on Evolutionary Computation*, 6(2):182–197, 2002.

45. M. Kapadia, N. Marshak, and N. I. Badler. ADAPT: The agent development and prototyping testbed. *IEEE Transactions on Visualization and Computer Graphics*, 99(PrePrints):1, 2014.

Section IV

Applications

12

Virtual Crowds in Film and Narrative Media

Paul Kanyuk

CONTENTS

For much academic research as well as industrial applications, the goal of crowd simulation is to be maximally predictive. In film, and other narrative media, this is not even a secondary criteria: a crowd simulation is judged successful to the extent it is *believable* to the viewer, and *directable* by the creator. High levels of believability (I will not say realism—this author works more often with talking animals than humans) is the baseline standard for professional work, but ultimately, the crowd simulation must serve a specific story point. That is where directability comes in; a crowd simulation for film must be amenable to nuanced crafting to match a director's vision. This can often be in direct contradiction to believability, which is where the skill of the crowd artists and the features of the simulator are put to the test. These skills and features will be the focus of this chapter.

But first, a word on terminology. By film and other narrative media, I am referring to visual, noninteractive stories, such as feature films, short films, game cinematics, commercials, etc. The exact details of the medium, such as image format (e.g., HD or IMAX) and style of rendering (e.g., offline vs. real time), do not pertain to this discussion. The critical distinction I would like to make is that we are describing noninteractive stories. Interactive stories, such as video games, provide a fundamentally different challenge for crowd simulation, requiring persistent believability, and allowing for very limited directability.

For most noninteractive stories, crowds can be crafted specifically over a finite set of viewpoints, and limited time duration (typically the length between camera cuts), which allows for very different artistic and technological trade-offs in crowd simulation. This chapter will focus specifically on this medium, which, for simplicity, I will call film.

12.1 Why Crowds Are Important in Film

To explore the aspects of successful crowd simulation in film, it is important to understand why films call for crowds in the first place. I break the rationale down into three categories: *spectacle, realistic worlds,* and *reaction.*

It is no secret that the audience reception and commercial success of a film is often driven by the element of spectacle. This is perhaps true of mass entertainment in general, from Roman Coliseums to Broadway. Crowds such as parades, stampedes, and mass migrations are rare events, and can captivate an audience with their spectacle. In live action film, the use of human actors for crowd spectacle perhaps reached its limit in Sergei Bondarchuk's film *Waterloo* [1], which employed over 15,000 extras and failed to recoup its costs. The development of virtual crowds, however, allowed crowds of unprecedented scale and complexity at a fraction of the cost. Early examples like the wildebeest stampede in *The Lion King* [2] dazzled viewers, though the technique truly reached public awareness with the virtual armies of Middle Earth in the *Lord of the Rings* trilogy [3–5].

While spectacle is perhaps the most exciting reason to include crowds in a film, it is by no means the most common. Rather, crowds can add just another element of believability for a film set. Take a typical large city scene. Unless it is populated with a mass of pedestrians, the environment is simply not believable no matter how realistic the static elements are. Often the purpose of such crowds is not to be the center of attention, but rather to avoid drawing the viewer's attention to the artifice of filmmaking. A cost-effectively constructed film set, whether live action or virtual, may have too many cues breaking its illusion, unless it is populated with a crowd. Put succinctly, a crowd is just another part of a believable set; an important backdrop in storytelling.

A third important purpose of crowds in film is reaction. While the main characters are often assumed to have behavior reflective of their unique viewpoints and motivations, there is a film convention where the behavior of a crowd reflects the beliefs of their fictional world as a whole. For instance, when the assembled rebel soldiers cheer at the finale of *Star Wars Episode 4—A New Hope* [6], we know that all is right in the world; the crowds told us so. That is, crowd reaction is shorthand for the beliefs of entire communities in film.

12.1.1 Why Virtual Crowds Are Expensive

Despite their desirability, producers dread the use of crowds to achieve these aims due to their budgetary implications. The previously mentioned film *Waterloo*, which employed 15,000 extras, never recouped its cost [1], and the logistics of the battle scenes were no doubt a large factor. Even virtual crowds are very costly when compared to scenes without crowds, often prohibitively so. Let us briefly discuss why.

For most crowds, the ratio of time spent creating sufficient variation compared to their screen time and screen size can be very averse. That is, a month of work on a main character can have visual impacts across hours of footage, but a month spent on one background character of a cast of potentially hundreds of agent types might only affect small details of a large crowd in a limited number of shots. Most artists faced with this challenge have attempted to mitigate this cost by only focusing on the most salient axes of agent variation (scale and color), which has recently been formally supported by perceptual studies [7]. Also, repetition in the character creation pipeline can be automated, allowing for efficient variation [8].

While the cost of crowd variation is definitely a consideration in efficiency, the more significant cost of crowd simulation in film is the penalty on artistic iteration incurred by scale. This cost is felt across the pipeline, from simulation times to rendering resources, and can cause the amount of time and money required to realize a director's feedback to balloon. A specific note on a single character's acting is often less than a day's work for an animator, but a note on a crowd simulation can sometimes trigger weeks of work before an acceptable revision is ready.

12.2 Making Crowds Less Expensive: Axes of Methodological Variation

The goal of a film crowd simulation pipeline is to reduce this iteration penalty, and realize a director's vision for crowds in the most cost-effective way possible. Depending on what type of crowds a film calls for, there are a variety of trade-offs that can be made to tailor a crowd pipeline for that purpose. Similarly, depending on what the existing pipeline and talent pool of a studio looks like, very different approaches to crowd simulation may be the most efficient. For example, one might imagine a studio staffed mostly by programmers would be very comfortable relying on AI techniques to achieve a crowd simulation, whereas a studio flush with talented animators may simply apply brute force and keyframe animate a whole crowd. This section will break down the major components of the film crowd pipeline and what choices and trade-offs can be made at each level to most efficiently realize the crowd's goals.

12.2.1 Granularity

The first decision in designing a crowd pipeline is deciding the primary granularity at which a crowd is represented. For a film with exclusively "small" crowds, the wisest decision is to keep crowd agent representation as close as possible to that of primary characters. Since primary characters are typically represented as discrete "models" in a scene graph, I will call this *model-level* granularity. Choosing this granularity avoids developing custom agent representations, allows sharing of tools between hero (non-crowd) animation and crowd animation, and promotes pipeline simplicity. This approach, however, is especially susceptible to the penalties of scale, and as the number of agents grows, productivity declines at an alarming rate. Reasons include simple linear slowdown with the number of agents, or worse when exceeding the capacity of main and/or GPU memory, causing playback rates to fall off a performance cliff. Thus, the challenge in choosing this "simple" approach to crowd granularity is mitigating the performance penalty. The scale at which performance is acceptable highly depends on the computing power and software specifications. At the time of this publication, advances in software/hardware parallelism [9] , and plentiful main memory, have pushed this pain threshold to the order of 10–100 agents for the most advanced feature film animation systems.

Trade-offs can be made in other aspects of the crowd pipeline to increase the scale at which *model-level* granularity is acceptable, an example of which can be found in Section 12.3.6. Regardless, there is always a scale at which *model-level* granularity is no longer practical. At this point, it is wise to consider *aggregate-level* granularity, where an entire crowd is represented as single model or scene graph location, and the individual agents are stored as vectorized data. This allows a number of shortcuts and customizations to be deployed to improve performance at large scales. For example, the VFX studio, Industrial Light and Magic, developed a plugin for the popular animation software, Autodesk's Maya [10], to represent a crowd as a particle system. Per particle information representing an agent's state was used by the plugin to draw polygons directly in OpenGL, bypassing the overhead of Maya's scene and dependency graph [11]. Golaem Crowd [12], a popular commercial crowd simulator for films, also employs aggregate-level granularity by representing an entire crowd as a single scene graph node in Maya, reading per agent data from a highly optimized partio [13]-based data format, and drawing directly to OpenGL. The common theme among crowd pipelines using aggregate-level granularity is that far larger numbers of agents can be visualized and rendered. The trade-off is complexity: such aggregate crowd models often require specialized tools and workflows, outside the standard animation process. For truly massive crowds, say 10,000 or more agents, the decision on granularity is easy. Model-level granularity is not an option due to performance, and individual agents take up so little screen area that traditional animation tools would be of little use for manipulation anyway.

Counterintuitively, it is medium-sized crowds, of 100–1000 agents, that are the most problematic. At this scale, the trade-offs between model and aggregate granularity become more ambiguous. That is, if the crowd is large enough that performance at model-level granularity is unbearable, but small enough that agents are sufficiently large on screen to require explicit artistic manipulation, then aggregate-level granularity may fail if it cannot provide such controls. Examples of such crowds can appear complex, like battle scenes where armies are close to camera, yet stretch seamlessly into the distance [3]. Yet, even seemingly typical scenes, such a dining hall filled with revellers [14], can tread this difficult middle ground. The three main approaches to this challenge are to improve the scalability of model-level granularity, to add more sophisticated editing feature to aggregate-level granularity, and to provide a process to "promote" specific agents from aggregate granularity to model-level granularity when fine-tuned editing is demanded [15]. The feasibility of these approaches are to a large extent determined by the features and technical decisions made in the rest of the crowd pipeline.

12.2.2 Root Motion

The most user-facing (and perhaps important) decision that can be made for a crowd pipeline is how an artist creates root motion for the crowd agents. We separate root motion (overall translation and rotation), from posing (body/face motion), as for crowds, especially large crowds, this is the more salient feature. The choices here are plentiful, but the primary decision is whether or not the root motion creation should employ simulation, and if so which type. For small and highly directed crowds, agent placement and trajectories are best specified manually by artists, which need not require simulation. Sketch-based interfaces are suitable for such situations where artists can draw closed regions to place agents, and curves to define their paths [16,17]. Feedback is typically interactive as simulation is not required. However, such systems break down quickly when interagent and agent–environment interactions become complex, thus making sketching too cumbersome.

In such situations, simulation can be advantageous. One of the most common approaches is to treat agents as particles and apply forces to direct root motion. The classic "boids" flocking system may be implemented this way by applying separation, alignment, and cohesion forces to a particle system [18]. While on its own, such systems can produce pleasing trajectories, for directability, other forces are often added to guide the agents. The Industrial Light and Magic (ILM) crowd system built for *Star Wars Episodes 1–3* used additional forces from Autodesk Maya's dynamics toolkit as well as custom force plugins to guide agents and add variation [11]. Such forces include noise fields for variation, collision fields for obstacles, and "draw your own" fields that derive vector fields from user drawn splines [11], to more specifically guide behavior. The latter has proven again and again to be a simple yet powerful technique to guide crowd simulations in film, and have been used in a variety of simulators [19]. Spline-based vector fields are also a key element of Massive, and one of the primary tools for directing root motion on the film *Ratatouille* [20].

Not every crowd simulation system, however, calculates root motion by summing forces on particles. Forces are a logical choice for distant crowds where root motion is the dominant factor, and crowds appear more like a physical system such as a fluid (hence some approaches actually do use techniques inspired by fluid dynamics [21]). However, for more detailed crowds where the individual decisions of character become prominent, such approaches can undermine the illusion of sentience. While this is a hard assertion to quantify, there is an impression among crowd artists that force-based approaches often seem robotically reactive. That is, agents appear to respond too late to a mix of physical events that should have been predicated further in advance, causing artists to spend considerable time tuning forces and influence regions to compensate. Rather than tuning forces, at this level, agent-based approaches that allow a crowd artist to customize how agents respond to forces become attractive. Such techniques can both improve believability, and more importantly, improve control. It was this approach that Massive [22] brought to prominence in film crowd simulation. Users of this system design brains (small node networks shared by classes of agents) that interpret inputs from the environment, including other agents, to guild motion and animation [23]. Classic boids behavior such as "separation," rather than being a force, is a choice that an agent makes based on how the brain rules are applying to the presence of neighboring agents. In Massive, these rules, rather than resulting in Boolean trues and falses, are based on fuzzy logic, leading to truths ranging smoothly between 0 and 1, and thus often smooth behavioral transitions [19]. In addition to collision avoidance, agent-based techniques such as Massive can support a variety of environmental inputs to guide agents. Spatial timers can be used by brains to trigger behaviors in user-specified regions over time. As described earlier, sketched splines to author vector fields are particularly useful, especially with organic terrain. On *Ratatouille*, splines were sketched both to guide agents where to go, but also to annotate obstacles [20].

Sketched vector fields lose the effectiveness for more structured crowd behavior, such as traffic, where highly specific paths are required. For such situations, curve and waypoint following can be more useful. On the animated film *WALL·E* [24], crowds of robots needed to follow specific paths through corridors of space ship [25]. While layers of vector fields could have been used, annotated curves were the primary guide for the agent brains to interpret. A similar system was used for traffic on the film, *Cars 2* [26,27]. While curves and waypoints are a logical choice for man-made environments such as roads, even organic crowd simulations such as fish in the ocean, can benefit from this approach. Schools of fish have been simulated in the film, *Finding Dory* [28], that use a custom-built agent-based simulator in SideFX's Houdini [29], guided by waypoints for principal direction [30].

Brains developed for agent-based crowd simulation can ideally become sophisticated enough to generalize beyond the original scene they were developed for, and thus save labor for future crowd scenes. To achieve this generality, however, brain complexity can grow and risk becoming unintuitive for users. In particular, balancing the various behaviors in the brain, such as collision avoidance, obstacle avoidance, leader following, waypoint following, etc., can lead to such a mix of signals that control and debugging become difficult. On the animated films, *Ratatouille* [31] and *WALL·E* [24], the crowds team at Pixar used a simple weighted average of each behavior's results, and allowed the user to tune each weight to control the simulation. While intuitive and easy to emphasize or attenuate individual behaviors, creating priority between specific behaviors was difficult. By contrast, for the film *Up* [32], the same crowd team attempted to establish priority between behavior modules in the brain through weighted inhibition between behaviors prior to the weighted average [30]. That is, a high-priority behavior would inhibit a lower-priority behavior. While this leads to very accurate and controllable brains, the dense network of connections was difficult for crowd artists to reason about and reorder. On the following crowds film *Cars 2* [27], the same team decided instead to use the more traditional organizing principles of the classic robotics technique, "Subsumption Architecture" [33], not for increased control or power, but for a more transparent representation of behavior priority [26]. In Pixar's version of the model, the behaviors are organized in a linear chain, where one subsumes the next, and priority is obvious. See Figures 12.1 and 12.2 for a comparison. This has been Pixar's approach to brain design for agent-based crowd simulation ever since [30].

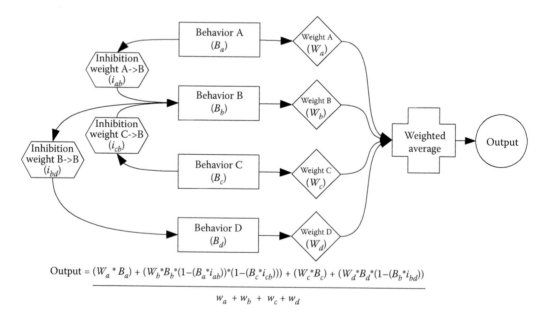

$$\text{Output} = \frac{(W_a * B_a) + (W_b*B_b*(1-(B_a*i_{ab}))*(1-(B_c*i_{cb}))) + (W_c*B_c) + (W_d*B_d*(1-(B_b*i_{bd})))}{w_a + w_b + w_c + w_d}$$

FIGURE 12.1

Diagram depicting how a weighted average and inhibition can create precise control and prioritization between behaviors (at risk of complexity). Behaviors A through D represent behavior modules in an agent brain, such as separation, leader following, waypoint following, and obstacle avoidance. The corresponding weights are controlled by the user to emphasize/attenuate behaviors via a weighted average. However, to give some behaviors priorities over others, inhibitory relationships can be established between behaviors with weights controlling the amount of inhibition. The compiled equation of this network is depicted in the output variable.

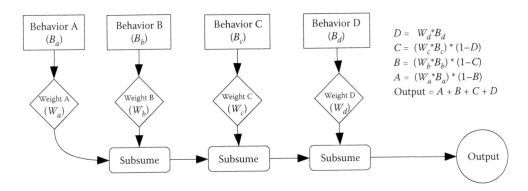

FIGURE 12.2
Diagram depicting how subsumption architecture can be used to create priority between behaviors in a simpler fashion than the weighted inhibition of Figure 12.1. Behaviors A through D represent behavior modules in an agent brain, such as separation, leader following, waypoint following, and obstacle avoidance. The more important behaviors subsume weaker behaviors, which only are expressed if the weighted result of the stronger behaviors are less than one, analogous to how alpha compositing only reveals lower layers if the higher layer has alpha less than one. The compiled equation of this network is depicted in the output variable.

There are situations where neither exclusively agent-based nor force-based simulation for root motion is ideal. For very tightly packed crowds, or crowds on physically unstable terrain, dealing with forces from impacts in an agent-based framework is cumbersome. Rather than having to code into the agent brain how to simulate and resolve these forces, it would be better to have a rigid body simulator or other system for calculating, and applying these forces. Yet, so long as the physical forces are not completely dominant, agents-based simulation still has a role in allowing artists to tune the reaction to these forces. As such, interleaving both force-based and agent-based techniques in a single crowd simulation can be an effective solution. In the film *WALL·E*, rigid body simulation guided the root motion of a crowd of falling passengers, but agent-based simulation was applied on top of this to add individual reactions [25].

There are far too many algorithms and approaches for simulating the root motion of a crowd simulation in film than I can cover in this chapter. I will refer the reader to a variety of case studies for further details [11,19,26,34–36]. While such techniques can craft almost any desired crowd trajectory, there is a major constraint to consider: how can we animate the agents' body poses over time fit this root motion? Believable solutions are not always possible, which is often dependent on the next aspect of crowd pipeline: sequencing.

12.2.3 Sequencing

While some crowds may be suitable for completely procedural animation such as spaceships and cars (the kind without eyes and faces...), the vast majority of films call for crowds that require character animation. Given the large number of agents and the variety of actions required, such animation is usually drawn from a pool of reusable and potentially retargetable animation data, created either through motion capture (e.g., orcs in *Lord of the Rings* [23]) or key framed animation (e.g., rats in *Ratatouille* [20]). A critical task of the film crowd pipeline is thus choosing animation from this pool to apply to each agent over time, a process I will call sequencing. As the name suggests, the most common approaches treat specific sections of this animation pool as discrete elements, and sequence them together.

The most basic technique is utilizing loopable clips of animation and instantiating them on each agent with temporal offsets. Despite its simplicity, a rich library of loopable clips is often all an artist needs to populate a shot with crowds, as demonstrated in Section 12.3.6. When varied behavior changes are required, however, the number and length of such clips can become burdensome. Finite-state machines (FSMs) add a level of control where loopable clips can be joined by transition clips, and triggered by spatial or temporal cues (e.g., see Section 12.3.1). Such techniques are common in games, and have been incorporated into a variety of film crowd systems [16,19,37]. While a well-designed crowd FSM system can allow directed and believable animation playback on a crowd, such sequencing may not be compatible with the desired root motion. For instance, the speeds directed by a simulation may not match that of the chosen loopable "walk cycle." Time-warping the sequence is possible, but only for limited ranges, and is rarely believable for rate increases [38]. Creating new animation clips for the desired rate is always a solution, but can be time consuming, and often unfeasible in situations where no more motion capture or animation budget is available. There are however, more advanced techniques that can help in these situations.

To more flexibly sequence a pool of animation data to believably match a desired trajectory, there is a point where it becomes necessary to apply alterations to the source data. The decision to employ such a technique should not be taken lightly as it can significantly impact the posing and rendering requirements of the crowd pipeline as we shall soon see. So, let us put a stake in the ground and name these two classes of sequencing. I will call sequencing that does not alter the source animation, but merely rearranges discrete sections, potentially with time warping: *affine sequencing*. Those techniques that alter the source animation, I will call *non-affine sequencing*. While perhaps an abuse of the term, I believe *affine* captures the intuition of structure preservation implied by affine transformations of geometry. In this case, the structure preserved by affine sequencing would be the topology of the source animation splines (only translation and scaling of the splines are permitted, so the number and relative position of knots is preserved), whereas non-affine sequencing may change these properties. Most modern character animation research falls into the latter category, such as motion graphs [39] and similar techniques, which generate transitions between clips automatically by detecting ideal connection points and using spherical linear interpolation to blend animation. While motion graphs have occasionally been used in entertainment applications, such as for crowds in the video game *Hitman Absolution* [40], for films, greater specificity requirements, and shorter shots (less need for generality), make such techniques often impractical. However, the use of spherical linear interpolation to blend between clips is commonly used in a more targeted manner for film crowds. The widely used industry tool, Massive [22], allows users to trigger blends between clips of source animation to achieve new results, and can be used to continuously blend between clips at different speeds and turning angles to believably accommodate desired trajectories. An example was the use the Massive's motion blending to convert desired velocities into a blend between a number of keyframe animated canine walks, gallops, and trots for the crowds of (talking) dogs in the Pixar film *Up* [19]. More recently, Golaem Crowd [12] has packaged this concept into its locomotion behavior system, which automatically matches and blends motion clips based on desired speed. While more sophisticated character animation techniques such as physics-based motion controllers [41] and advanced motion synthesis methods [42] show promise as tools for film crowd pipelines, targeted spherical linear interpolation of animation clips remains the most widely used non-affine sequencing technique on account of its simplicity and controllability.

12.2.4 Posing

Now that we have discussed how we may sequence animation and author trajectories on crowd agents, the next pipeline decision is how to actually pose each agent. The solution is nontrivial as feature film quality characters often require computationally intensive posing systems that struggle to maintain real-time rates even after sophisticated optimization [9], and thus fail to scale for large crowds. To complicate matters more, the software environment where characters are typically modeled, rigged, and animated may be different from the crowd simulation software environment, and executing the original posing system may not be possible. Furthermore, if the crowd is represented using aggregate granularity, the original posing system would have to be adapted to this vectorized form, a potentially costly engineering effort. For all these reasons, film crowd pipelines often take a shortcut and cache the posed geometry along with the source animation for the motion pool used by sequencing. So long as exclusively affine sequencing was used, this pre-cached geometry may be stitched together seamlessly according to the discrete motion clip choices and time warp rates. Thus, posing crowd characters can be as simple as reading mesh data from a specific frame from the data pool (or a blend between two frames' data in the case of time warping). For scalability, the pre-cached mesh data may be decimated to varying levels of detail, where each version is chosen based on the estimated screen space coverage of the agent [11,43]. Another benefit of relying on pre-cached geometry for posing and affine sequencing is that if a particular agent requires its motion to be edited by an animator post simulation, a very frequent occurrence in film where directors require nuanced control, the agent can be "promoted" to an instance of the original hero-quality character with the original source animation losslessly applied [37]. By contrast, non-affine sequencing, often results in artificially synthesized animation splines. Even when sparse, these splines can appear so foreign to animators that they "frequently comment that even if the results are '90%' correctly, fixing the remaining '10%' is almost as much work as starting from scratch" [44]. Thus, the combination of affine sequencing and pre-cached geometry posing is a simple, flexible, and appealing combination for film crowd pipelines. However, even if the control restrictions incurred by exclusively affine sequencing is acceptable, there are limitations to using pre-cached geometry for posing. While animation data is often quite compact, the same cannot be said for geometry data. Speaking from experience, a motion library of several thousand clips of roughly 100 frames each can produce several terabytes of geometry data. Streaming such scales of data for posing in interactive crowd workflows can fail due to excessive input/output (IO) and may require sophisticated data structures, level of detail, and/or compression to be feasible [16,37,45]. As such, less data-intensive posing solutions may be very advantageous for a film crowd pipeline.

Video game character posing techniques when applied to crowds in film can often achieve the desired scalability. Linear blend skinning, for example, only requires joint rotations and root transforms per frame, and is extremely fast. Moreover, such posing techniques are so common that linear blend skinning is the "lingua franca" of posing techniques, implemented in the majority of computer graphics tools, and thus amenable to most film pipelines. Commercial crowd systems such as Massive [22] and Golaem [12] perform such simplified rigging at render time with minimal overhead, as well as proprietary systems such as MPC's Alice [46] and Dreamwork's Render Time Deformation Server [15]. The challenge in using such techniques is developing a principled process for computing joints and weights that best reproduce the original high-quality posing. If the characters are exclusively for use in distant crowds, then the process need not be lossy, linear blend skinning would suffice as the primary rigging technique. For many feature film crowds, however, hero-quality rigging is required for agents that are large on screen and require some manual animation cleanup or plussing after simulation. Creating a joint hierarchy equivalent of an arbitrarily complex rig often requires identifying a subset of deformers as canonical joints and specifying mappings between animator controls and joint angles. While time consuming, if there are few character types relative to numbers of agents; this can be a worthwhile process for adapting hero-quality rigs for posing in a crowd simulator such as Massive [20]. Computing the corresponding skinning weights can be automated by using the pool of animation clips and pre-cached geometry as an exemplar database and employing optimization techniques to solve for weights that result in the least error. Recent research continues to improve such methods, and even can derive optimal joint positions [47]. However, even the best skinning weights can fail to adequately reproduce the quality of a hero rig, especially in the case of facial articulation, where the number of joints required can be intractable. Fortunately, similar to linear blend skinning, blendshapes are another computationally efficient posing technique that is widely understood by many animation and crowds tools. Computing corrective blendshapes and their corresponding weights over time can account for losses in facial articulation and other shaping quality from the linear blend skinning approximation [19]. However, such effort is only necessary if the crowd posing solution is required for final rendering, as we will discuss in the next section.

A more common solution is to use a *promotion* process to fit a hero character to each crowd agent where the quality of the linear blend skinning approximation is inadequate. Unfortunately, if non-affine sequencing techniques such as motion blending are used, this fitting process can be difficult. If in addition to defining a mapping between animation controls in the hero rig and joint rotations in the crowd rig, we define an inverse mapping, we can at least match the overall pose. Unfortunately, only a subset of original animation controls map to joint rotations, so important details such as facial animation can be lost. However, so long as any control without a mapping remains embedded in the animation data, even non-affine sequencing techniques such as motion blending can bring this data along and blend/resynthesize it. Naturally, this can be a gross simplification, using spherical linear interpolation to blend joint angles is a principled operation, but mixing arbitrary animation controls can be quite incorrect if they are nonlinear. Fortunately, in practice, most animation controls seem to be fairly linear, and simple linear interpolation and other mixing operations can be surprisingly successful in preserving animation detail when crowd agents are promoted [20]. Even when the quality is acceptable, however, the resynthesized animation splines are often too foreign for a character animator to intuitively work with them. An alternative that addresses this shortcoming is to accept a degree of posing inaccuracy when promoting an agent and use the best-fit affine sequencing, with strategic inverse kinematic offsets to correct for the differences [15]. Finding a balance between accurate posing and "animator-friendly" animation splines for simulated crowd agents remains a challenging pipeline and research problem and is a subject of ongoing effort.

12.2.5 Rendering

The final stage of the film crowd pipeline is rendering, and it is here that decisions on granularity, root motion, sequencing, and posing must be reconciled with the constraints of rendering efficiency. A typical hero-quality character for a feature film has well over 100,000 control points and gigabytes of texture data; thus simply rendering a crowd as one does hero characters is often prohibitive. The most straightforward approach to optimizing crowd rendering is instancing. Any repetition between agents that share posing and geometry may be shared in memory, with only transform and shader inputs varying. The render cost thus becomes proportional to the number of unique geometric poses rather than the number of agents. In practice, this means only affine sequencing will yield a benefit from instancing, as the restrictions on posing promotes sharing. Even when restricted to affine sequencing, however, time warping, animation pool size, and number of geometric agent variants can severely limit instancing. This means there can be a trade-off between instancing efficacy, and motion/variation quality, restricting the benefit of instancing to only large-scale and highly repetitive crowds. Human crowds seldom meet this criteria, but animals such as insects or fish may very well benefit from instancing [48].

Decimation is another frequently employed render optimization technique for crowds. As mentioned in the posing section, pre-cached geometry may be processed into discrete levels of detail, and chosen based on estimated screen space coverage, thus optimizing rendering as well as preview [11]. For pre-cached posing, the decimation can be performed after the rig has executed, decoupling decimation from rig accuracy, which is both simpler to implement and more accurate. For dynamic posing, decimated versions of the character can be explicitly rigged and retargeted, which is often more labor intensive and lossy. Alternatively, decimation can be performed per frame, per agent, at or just before render time, allowing for decoupling of decimation and posing. Such decimation would need to be sufficiently fast to not exceed the cost of rendering the original agent, and thus rules out many potential techniques. There are some, like stochastic simplification [48], and mesh streaming methods [49] that are fast enough to execute per agent per frame, and optimize render times on dynamically posed crowds.

For exceedingly large crowds of 100,000 to millions of agents, even decimation and instancing may be insufficient. At such scales, agents become so small in screen space that the aggregate shapes and colors dominate the individual details, and the crowd becomes more of an effect, like smoke or water, than a collection of agents. Thus, VFX rendering techniques, such as volumetric rendering or particle splatting, become appealing. Crowds exclusively using affine sequencing again prove beneficial to these rendering techniques as voxelization can be performed on the animation pool up front and drawn from at render time. Mip-mapped sparse voxel octrees such as brickmaps allow for only the minimum number of voxels to be read at render time [48,50]. However, even non-affine sequencing may be amenable to volumetric rendering techniques. So long as the voxelization occurs in a reference pose and a mapping between the dynamic agent pose and the reference pose is maintained, the volumetric data can be deformed into the correct shape at render time [51]. For truly enormous crowds of millions of agents with sizes of only a few pixels each, then even volumetric representations become impractical, and using fluid meshing techniques can be beneficial despite the loss of fine details [48]. However, at this scale, the motion quality restrictions that typically thwart instancing matter less and instancing can become a viable option again.

12.3 Case Studies

Now that we have discussed the methodological options available in film crowd simulation, I would like to more concretely illustrate the reasoning and processes behind the practice by exploring a number of case studies. We will start from one of the first fully animated computer graphics (CG) feature films to employ crowd simulation, *A Bug's Life*

TABLE 12.1

Methodologies Chosen in Each Crowd's Case

Film	Granularity	Root Motion	Sequencing	Posing	Rendering
A Bug's Life (1998)	Models	Sketched paths	Non-affine	Original rig	Normal
Star Wars Episodes 1–3 (1999–2005)	Aggregate	Particle simulation	Affine	Pre-posed geometry caches	Geometry archives, 3 levels of details (LODs)
Lord of the Rings trilogy (2001–2003)	Aggregate	Agent-based simulation	Non-affine	Linear blend skinning	Render time posing
Ratatouille (2007)	Models	Agent-based simulation	Non-affine	Original rig	Normal
Madagascar 3 (2012)	Models or aggregate	Agent-based simulation	Non-affine	Vectorized or original rig	Normal or render time posing
Edge of Tomorrow (2014)	Models	Sketched paths	Affine	Pre-posed geometry caches	Instanced geometry archives

(1998) [52], and finish with a modern live action sci-fi film *Edge of Tomorrow* (2014) [53]. Each case study we cover had highly different artistic requirements and resources available, and thus despite the rapid technological advances between 1998 and 2014, the crowd simulation techniques used do not always necessarily gain complexity in obvious ways. Rather, a balance is struck between the maximum possible simplicity, and the desired crowd behavior/control. Table 12.1 provides an overview.

12.3.1 *A Bug's Life*

Pixar's second animated feature *A Bug's Life* (1998) [52] was their first to feature large crowds. The main character Flik is an ant whose actions endanger his colony of thousands. To emphasize the collective nature of the colony, and Flik's failure to fit in, the ants were required to react en masse to Flik and the events he provokes (a grasshopper invasion). The crowds were required to gasp, applaud, shift gaze, and panic. Model granularity was chosen given the maximum number of ants on screen at a time was hundreds, not thousands. Much of the crowds were part of a stationary audience, so root motion did not require simulation, and where locomotion was called for, spline-based trajectories were authored by hand. To minimize the number of animation clips required, but still create the specific reactions required of the crowds, a triggered FSM system called FRED (the acronym's origin is unknown) was created. Animated geometric shapes were used to trigger state transitions where they intersected agents, so reaction could propagate spatially and temporally. However, for choreographed gaze shifting, or "look-ats," the amount of body, head, and eye rotation required of each agent is unique, and affine sequencing of a limited number of clips would be intractable. Thus, the crowd artists decided to procedurally animate gaze shifts by calculating the necessary rotation offsets for torso, neck, head, and eyes to shift gaze over time across a crowd. Doing so deviated from the source animation data (thus becoming non-affine sequencing), and prevented Pixar from using pre-cached geometry for posing. However, given the model-level granularity and the limited number of agents on screen, the cost of posing each agent uniquely at render time was acceptable. The triggered FSM sequencing approach was considered quite successful for stationary crowds, and FRED was re-implemented by Pixar in various forms for stationary crowds in later films as Barney (*Cars, Ratatouille, WALL·E, Up, Cars 2*), Wilma (*Brave*), and Elroy (*Monster's University*) [16,26,37].

12.3.2 *Star Wars Episode 1*

Six months after *A Bug's Life* premiered, the release of *Star Wars Episode 1: The Phantom Menace* [54] introduced viewers to CG crowd battle scenes, soon to be a staple for spectacle in big-budget feature films for years to come. The direction called for thousands of robot soldiers to march in tight formation and confront a less disciplined, more organic force of alien soldiers. Unlike *A Bug's Life*, individual shots called for thousands of agents, the majority of which were not stationary. Accordingly, the ILM crowds team chose an approach built upon aggregate granularity, where each agent was represented by a particle within a single particle system array [11]. Root motion was created through forces acting upon the particles and custom callback methods executing each frame per particle. Sequencing was exclusively affine, built upon a library of motion capture-based animation clips. Accordingly, ILM took advantage of the limited domain of poses and created geometry caches for all the animation clips up front, allowing for rapid posing at large scales. The full models, however, had too much geometry data for either interactive viewing or offline rendering, and two additional levels of detail were created, by manually modeling, rigging, and shading two extra versions of each character. The aggregate model used to represent the crowd would use estimated screen space size of each particle to choose the appropriate level of detail. Naturally, this approach sacrificed a degree of motion variety and control by using a restricted set of poses, but given the art direction to make the robot army seem inorganic, repetitive, and machine-like, this constraint was perfectly acceptable. Despite the simplicity, this approach of aggregate granularity, force-based particle dynamics for root motion, and affine sequenced clips/geometry caches is the basis of many professional crowd pipelines to this day. A successful recent example was the "Zerg Army" crowd from a *Starcraft 2* cinematic, which innovatively used liquid foam bubble forces to drive the motion of the swarm, on top of which geometry caches were instanced [34].

12.3.3 *Lord of the Rings*

The films to really bring crowd simulation notoriety, however, are the *Lord of the Rings* trilogy films [3–5]. Each featured dramatic, highly detailed, and extremely large battle scenes that provided engaging spectacle. It was on these films that the agent-based crowd simulator Massive was developed [22], which was so successful that many other studios have adopted and built upon this pipeline. Like the ILM approach from the previous section, Massive represents agents at aggregate granularity, fitting given *Lord of the Rings*'s battle scenes of hundreds to over a million agents. However, as discussed in Section 12.2.2, rather than applying forces to particles, Massive is built from the ground up as an agent-based simulator, where each agent type has a "brain" node graph, which interprets inputs from the environment, and sets a series of outputs. Common inputs include vector fields, point sources (called sound in Massive), guide splines, distance probes, and even artificial vision [55]. Within Massive is also an FSM sequencer called a motion tree that can define sections of loopable input motion, transitions between clips, and establish rules for triggered transitions and motion blending. The brain derives input velocities from the current animation clip and combines that with inputs from the environment to modify the velocities, agent pose, and next clip choice. Given the ability to perform motion blending and procedurally alter the pose, Massive can be used for affine or non-affine sequencing depending on the application. For the battles in *Lord of the Rings*, the motion blending was employed to create poses beyond what was afforded by the initial motion capture sessions. Linear blend skinning and occasionally blendshapes were used for rigging, and rather than sequencing caches, Massive is instrumented to run at render time to pose agents on demand. As we shall see in later case studies, these techniques continue to be used.

12.3.4 *Ratatouille*

After the completion of the *Lord of the Rings* trilogy, Massive split off from Weta to form an independent company, and became available for the rest of the industry to use. While this made it possible to replicate Weta's crowd pipeline, in practice, studios that used Massive often had very different artistic and technical needs and thus integrated the tool in divergent ways. A good case in point is the crowd pipeline developed by Pixar for the animated feature film *Ratatouille* (2007) [20,31]. The story called for scenes with complex rat locomotion and swarming, unsuitable for Pixar's traditional FSM approach, but well suited to Massive's agent-based technique. The darting scurries, gallops, and jumps of rats could be modeled through proximity-based triggers, and motion blending for accurate turn posing. Flow fields were used for primary navigations and point sources (sound) for triggering specifically choreographed behavior changes.

Unlike *Lord of the Rings*, however, the shots included tens to many hundreds of agents (but never thousands), which featured far closer to camera. Also, being fully animated, there were never actors in the foreground plates, and thus exacting scrutiny was required for crowds that extended into the foreground. As a result, the crowds team on *Ratatouille* chose a model-level granularity and full hero-quality rigging to maintain posing fidelity and the ability for animators to override the simulation where needed. Unfortunately, such an approach ran counter to the non-affine sequencing employed by Massive, and required significant engineering effort to reconcile. Mappings between animation controls of the original rig, and joint angles in a simplified skeleton were derived by hand, and allowed animation to flow to Massive agents, and back into the hero models in Pixar's proprietary animation software. All animation controls that did not map to joint angles "went along for the ride" as translations on "fake bones," to be linearly interpolated during motion blending. While such a system could adequately preserve animation fidelity in simulation output, the resulting animation splines were not simple for animators to work with, as alluded to in Section 12.2.4. So, while the *Ratatouille* crowd pipeline was successful in achieving higher agent quality by adapting Massive to model-level granularity, post-simulation fixes did admittedly require more re-animation than would have been ideal.

12.3.5 *Madagascar 3*

The animated film *Madagascar 3: Europe's Most Wanted* [56], released in 2012, required a similar degree of scrutinized crowd animation as *Ratatouille* for human audiences and pedestrians, but at scales into the thousands and sometimes tens of thousands. The crowds team at Dreamworks Animation, like Pixar, had integrated Massive into their pipeline, but given the scale, aggregate- rather than model-level granularity was chosen. All of Massive's tools for behavioral animation and motion blending were employed, and thus non-affine sequencing ruled out the use of prebaked geometry caches for posing/rendering. Instead of limiting posing to the linear blend skinning and blendshapes supported by Massive, however, the Dreamworks crowds team created an implementation of their full-quality rigging system in a form that could consume the limited data simulated from Massive, and generate the full-quality geometry on demand at render time. Dubbed the "render time deformation" system, the full range of geometry variation and LODs for an agent type was loaded in memory, and then posed by request at render time [15]. According to the authors, this was a 50× savings in IO and diskspace compared to the closest equivalent of geometry caching, and permitted the benefits of non-affine sequencing. However, like the *Ratatouille* pipeline, such motion blending yielded very unworkable motion splines when agents were promoted for cleanup by an animator. To address this, the Dreamworks crowds team created a "hero promotion" process that used IDs embedded in the motion clips to track which clips were played when, per agent, to find the best-fit affine sequencing to approximate the simulated non-affine sequencing. Thus, the original animation data could be applied, and resulted in much more animator-friendly motion splines. Where motion blending was significant, the animation splines were blended, degrading the quality. Thus, unlike the *Ratatouille* pipeline, these approximations could result in loss of posing accuracy, but the improved animator productivity was highly beneficial for post-simulation fixup, and proved complementary to the strengths of their simulation pipeline.

12.3.6 *Edge of Tomorrow*

So far, the case studies we have discussed each shows a steady increase of technology and complexity in the film crowd pipeline, each solving new artistic challenges. However, it is not necessarily the case that such technological evolutions were uniformly beneficial to all film crowds challenges. That is, some studios, given their specific constraints, have used simpler approaches to great artistic effect, at a fraction of the resources. An excellent example is the sci-fi film *Edge of Tomorrow* [53]. The film depicts numerous crowd scenes of futuristic soldiers and invading aliens, some of which required complex behavioral simulation, but the majority of which involved either stationary crowds or simple formations. While the studio, Sony, had built a Massive pipeline similar to that used by Weta in *Lord of the Rings*, there was a significant resource cost to employing these techniques in both the up-front work required to adapt a character type for crowd simulation, and in the time required by the small number of skilled crowd artists trained in the pipeline. Thus, the Sony crowds team determined that a simpler tool, with a more limited set of features, based in their common animation platform, Autodesk's Maya, could improve productivity for shots where complex behavioral simulation was not required. Dubbed CrAM (Crowd Asset Manager) [17], the new system used model-level granularity, simple animation cycle affine sequencing, sketch-based root motion authoring, and geometry cache posing/rendering. Exclusive use of geometry caches allows model-level granularity to scale well beyond the typical pain threshold from 10–100 agents to 100–1000. Because of its simplicity and intuitive user interface, CrAM is now a common tool at Sony, used alongside its Massive pipeline. Other studios have similarly discovered that simpler crowd tools can improve productivity and control where such constraints are acceptable. Another notable example is Pixar's sketch-based Crowd Placement Editor, and "Elroy" motion-clip/geometry-cache sequencing used for the ambient student crowds in *Monster's University* [16].

12.4 Future Directions

Despite the impressive work done by crowd artists in the aforementioned case studies, the set of tools employed by these pipelines still fall short in a number of situations. Highly constrained simulations where agents must accurately contact one another, or a complex environment, are difficult to achieve. Examples include acrobatic formations, like a "Castell" or "Human Tower," adaptation to highly irregular terrain, like a boulder quarry, or a number of agents sharing the weight of a large object carried among them. All these activities require unique, environment-specific, poses per agent, and thus rule out affine sequencing. Motion blending and motion graphs can help achieve arbitrary trajectories, but not such pose constraints. While Ad Hoc IK and constraint-based solutions are often used by animation studios to handle these situations, a more general approach would be desirable. The computer graphics research community offers some enticing solutions in the form of motion controllers, which can be trained on animation input, and incorporate physics to adapt to novel situations [41,42]. While there are some promising directions, the performance limitations, overhead, fragility of training the controller, and levels of expertise required have so far precluded their use in feature film crowd simulation. I fully expect in the coming years that this will evolve to be a fruitful avenue for improved artistic capabilities in crowd spectacle. However, even if motion controllers become feasible to deploy in a crowd pipeline, it is highly unlikely any simulation will be customizable enough to meet all the nuanced demands of a director. Thus, it always becomes necessary for animators to work with the results of a simulation and further improve upon it. While the "hero promotion" pipeline of *Madagascar 3* provides a principled approach for accommodating motion blending, no such approach exists for producing animator-friendly splines from the arbitrary posing performed by motion controllers. Promising work simplifying motion captured facial blendshapes into "human-readable" splines inspired by animator workflow [44] shows that such process should be possible, but as of now, this is an unsolved problem. Finally, even with further technological progress, as the success of the streamlined CrAM [17] workflow indicates, intuitive and controllable user interfaces can often trump features in terms of efficiently creating crowd simulations. Thus, it remains an ongoing challenge to adapt the powerful crowd pipelines that have been and are being developed into a form that more artists can use to best meet the demand of feature film crowds.

References

1. S. Bondarchuk. *Waterloo*, 1970.
2. R. Allgers and R. Minkoff. *The Lion King*, 1994.
3. P. Jackson. *The Lord of the Rings: The Fellowship of the Ring*, 2001.
4. P. Jackson. *The Lord of the Rings: The Two Towers*, 2002.
5. P. Jackson. *The Lord of the Rings: The Return of the King*, 2003.
6. G. Lucas. *Star Wars: Episode IV—A New Hope*, 1977.
7. R. McDonnell, M. Larkin, B. Hernández, I. Rudomin, and C. O'Sullivan. Eye-catching crowds: Saliency based selective variation. *ACM Transactions on Graphics*, 28(3):55:1–55:10, July 2009.
8. M. Planck and S. V. Bugaj. Shading the many: Solutions for shading crowd characters on *WALL·E*. In *ACM SIGGRAPH 2008 Talks, SIGGRAPH '08*, pp. 24:1–24:1, New York, USA, 2008. ACM.

9. M. Watt, E. Coumans, G. ElKoura, R. Henderson, M. Kraemer, J. Lait, and J. Reinders. *Multithreading for Visual Effects*. A. K. Peters, Ltd., Natick, MA, USA, 1st edition, 2014.

10. Autodesk. Company website: http://www.autodesk.com/products/maya/overview.

11. D. Thalmann, C. Hery, S. Lippman, H. Ono, S. Regelous, and D. Sutton. Crowd and group animation. In *ACM SIGGRAPH 2004 Course Notes, SIGGRAPH '04*, New York, USA, 2004. ACM.

12. G. Crowd. Company website: http://golaem.com.

13. P. Project. Project website: http://www.disneyanimation.com/technology/partio.html.

14. M. Andrews, B. Chapman, and S. Purcell. *Brave*, 2012.

15. N. Dirksen, J. Fischer, J.-H. Kim, K. Vassey, and R. Vogt. Improving crowd quality through interdepartmental collaboration on *Madagascar 3: Europe's Most Wanted*. In *Proceedings of the Digital Production Symposium, DigiPro '12*, pp. 15–20, New York, USA, 2012. ACM.

16. H. Arumugam, M. Frederickson, and J. D. Northrup. Crowds at *Monster's University*. In *ACM SIGGRAPH 2013 Talks, SIGGRAPH '13*, pp. 51:1–51:1, New York, USA, 2013. ACM.

17. J. Hood. Cram: Artist-friendly crowds on "edge of tomorrow." In *ACM SIGGRAPH 2014 Talks, SIGGRAPH '14*, pp. 5:1–5:1, New York, USA, 2014. ACM.

18. C. W. Reynolds. Flocks, herds and schools: A distributed behavioral model. In *Proceedings of the 14th Annual Conference on Computer Graphics and Interactive Techniques, SIGGRAPH '87*, pp. 25–34, New York, USA, 1987. ACM.

19. M. Cioroba, P. Kanyuk, S. Regelous, T. Yoshida, C. Halperin, and M. Salvati. Crowd animation: Tools, techniques, and production examples. In *ACM SIGGRAPH ASIA 2009 Courses, SIGGRAPH ASIA '09*, New York, USA, 2009. ACM.

20. D. Ryu and P. Kanyuk. Rivers of rodents: An animation-centric crowds pipeline for *Ratatouille*. In *ACM SIGGRAPH 2007 Sketches, SIGGRAPH '07*, New York, USA, 2007. ACM.

21. A. Treuille, S. Cooper, and Z. Popović. Continuum crowds. *ACM Transactions on Graphics*, 25(3):1160–1168, July 2006.

22. Massive Software. Company website: http://www.massivesoftware.com.

23. M. Aitken, G. Butler, D. Lemmon, E. Saindon, D. Peters, and G. Williams. *The Lord of the Rings*: The visual effects that brought Middle Earth to the screen. In *ACM SIGGRAPH 2004 Course Notes, SIGGRAPH '04*, New York, USA, 2004. ACM.

24. A. Stanton. *WALL·E*, 2008.

25. P. Kanyuk. Brain springs: Fast physics for large crowds in *WALL·E*. *IEEE Computer Graphics and Applications*, 29(4):19–25, July 2009.

26. T. Crow, S. Gustafson, M. Lorenzen, J. Merrell, B. Moyer, and J. D. Northrup. Crowds on *Cars 2*. In *ACM SIGGRAPH 2011 Talks, SIGGRAPH '11*, pp. 43:1–43:2, New York, USA, 2011. ACM.

27. J. Lasseter and B. Lewis. *Cars 2*, 2011.

28. A. Stanton and A. MacLane. *Finding Dory*, 2016.

29. SideFX. Company website: http://sidefx.com.

30. P. Kanyuk and S. Gustafson. AI in feature film animation: How crowds artists use AI techniques at Pixar. In *SIGGRAPH Asia 2015 Courses, SA '15*, pp. 2:1–2:1, New York, USA, 2015. ACM.

31. B. Bird and J. Pinkava. *Ratatouille*, 2007.

32. P. Docter and B. Peterson. *Up*, 2009.

33. R. A. Brooks. A robust layered control system for a mobile robot. *IEEE Journal of Robotics and Automation*, 2(1):14–23, Mar 1986.

34. M. Cordner and B. La Barge. Zerg rush hour: Simulating swarms for *Starcraft 2* cinematics. In *ACM SIGGRAPH 2013 Talks, SIGGRAPH '13*, pp. 30:1–30:1, New York, USA, 2013. ACM.

35. T. Dervieux-Lecocq, D. Gatenby, M. Adams, and J. Bisceglio. Bats, birds, and boggans: The simulated armies of epic. In *ACM SIGGRAPH 2013 Talks, SIGGRAPH '13*, pp. 4:1–4:1, New York, USA, 2013. ACM.

36. B. Herman, J. Gibson, and E. Gamache. A.I. cars for speed racer. In *ACM SIGGRAPH 2008 Talks, SIGGRAPH '08*, pp. 27:1–27:1, New York, USA, 2008. ACM.

37. P. Kanyuk, L. J. W. Park, and E. Weihrich. Headstrong, hairy, and heavily clothed: Animating crowds of scotsmen. In *ACM SIGGRAPH 2012 Talks, SIGGRAPH '12*, pp. 52:1–52:1, New York, USA, 2012. ACM.

38. M. Pražák, R. McDonnell, and C. O'Sullivan. Perceptual evaluation of human animation time-warping. In *ACM SIGGRAPH ASIA 2010 Sketches, SA '10*, pp. 30:1–30:2, New York, USA, 2010. ACM.

39. L. Kovar, M. Gleicher, and F. Pighin. Motion graphs. In *Proceedings of the 29th Annual Conference on Computer Graphics and Interactive Techniques, SIGGRAPH '02*, pp. 473–482, New York, USA, 2002. ACM.

40. M. BÃttner. Project website: http://aigamedev.com/ultimate/presentation/hitman-reinforcement/.

41. S. Coros, A. Karpathy, B. Jones, L. Reveret, and M. van de Panne. Locomotion skills for simulated quadrupeds. In *ACM SIGGRAPH 2011 Papers, SIGGRAPH '11*, pp. 59:1–59:12, New York, USA, 2011. ACM.

42. S. Levine, J. M. Wang, A. Haraux, Z. Popović, and V. Koltun. Continuous character control with low-dimensional embeddings. *ACM Transactions on Graphics*, 31(4):28:1–28:10, July 2012.

43. B. Hiebert, J. Dave, T.-Y. Kim, I. Neulander, H. Rijpkema, and W. Telford. *The Chronicles of Narnia*: The lion, the crowds and rhythm and hues author video presentations are available from the citation page. In *ACM SIGGRAPH 2006 Courses, SIGGRAPH '06*, New York, USA, 2006. ACM.

44. Y. Seol, J. Seo, P. H. Kim, J. P. Lewis, and J. Noh. Artist friendly facial animation retargeting. *ACM Transactions on Graphics*, 30(6):162:1–162:10, December 2011.

45. A. Gneiting. Realtime geometry caches. In *ACM SIGGRAPH 2014 Talks, SIGGRAPH '14*, pp. 49:1–49:1, New York, USA, 2014. ACM.

46. J. Haddon and D. Griffiths. A system for crowd rendering. In *ACM SIGGRAPH 2006 Sketches, SIGGRAPH '06*, New York, USA, 2006. ACM.

47. B. H. Le and Z. Deng. Robust and accurate skeletal rigging from mesh sequences. *ACM Transactions on Graphics*, 33(4):84:1–84:10, July 2014.

48. P. Kanyuk. Level of detail in an age of GI: Rethinking crowd rendering. In *ACM SIGGRAPH 2014 Talks, SIGGRAPH '14*, pp. 6:1–6:1, New York, USA, 2014. ACM.

49. M. Limper, Y. Jung, J. Behr, and M. Alexa. The pop buffer: Rapid progressive clustering by geometry quantization. *Computer Graphics Forum*, 32(7):197–206, 2013.

50. P. H. Christensen and D. Batali. An irradiance atlas for global illumination in complex production scenes. In *Proceedings of the Fifteenth Eurographics Conference on Rendering Techniques, EGSR'04*, pp. 133–141, Aire-la-Ville, Switzerland, Switzerland, 2004. Eurographics Association.

51. S. Palmer, E. Maurer, and M. Adams. Using sparse voxel octrees in a level-of-detail pipeline for *Rio 2*. In *ACM SIGGRAPH 2014 Talks, SIGGRAPH '14*, pp. 70:1–70:1, New York, USA, 2014. ACM.

52. J. Lasseter and A. Stanton. *A Bug's Life*, 1998.

53. D. Liman. *Edge of Tomorrow*, 2014.

54. G. Lucas. *Star Wars: Episode I—The Phantom Menace*, 1999.

55. J. Ondřej, J. Pettré, A.-H. Olivier, and S. Donikian. A synthetic-vision based steering approach for crowd simulation. *ACM Transactions on Graphics*, 29(4):123:1–123:9, July 2010.

56. E. Darnell, T. McGrath, and C. Vernon. *Madagascar 3: Europe's Most Wanted*, 2012.

13

Real-Time Micro-Modeling of Millions of Pedestrians

Rainald Löhner, Muhammad Baqui, Eberhard Haug, and Britto

CONTENTS

13.1 Summary

A first-principles model for the simulation of pedestrian flows and crowd dynamics capable of computing the movement of millions of pedestrians in real time has been developed. The model is based on a series of forces, such as will forces (the desire to reach a place at a certain time), pedestrian collision avoidance forces, obstacle/wall avoidance forces, pedestrian contact forces, and obstacle/wall contact forces. In order to allow for general geometries, a so-called background triangulation is used to carry all geographic information. At any given time, the location of any given pedestrian is updated on this mesh. The code has been ported to shared and distributed memory parallel machines. The results obtained show that the stated aim of computing the movement of millions of pedestrians in real time has been achieved. This is an important milestone as it enables faster-than-real-time simulations of large crowds (stadiums, airports, train and bus stations, concerts) as well as evacuation simulations for whole cities. This may enable the use of validated, micro-model-based pedestrian simulation for design, operation, and training within the context of large crowds.

13.2 Introduction

The accurate prediction of pedestrian motion can be used to assess the potential safety hazards and operational performance at events where many individuals are gathered. Examples of such situations are sport and music events; cinemas and theatres; museums; conference centers; places of pilgrimage and worship; street demonstrations; emergency evacuation during natural disasters; and evacuation from airplanes, ships [1], trains, and buildings [2]. The PED series of conferences [3] gives a good summary of the state of the art in this emerging field.

For cases where the prediction of many ($>10^6$) individuals over a long time is considered (e.g., pilgrimage centers or evacuation during natural disasters), optimal, scalable algorithms and data structures must be used in order to carry out a simulation in a reasonable time. The objective of the present effort is to achieve *highly realistic simulations for $>10^6$ pedestrians in real time*. The hardware architectures targeted at present are large multicore clusters. Previous experience with graphics processing units (GPUs) in the field of computational fluid dynamics indicates that for memory-bound applications such as pedestrian simulation, at present, the difference between GPUs and central processing units (CPUs) is at most a factor of 1:5 [4,5]. Given the rapid increase in the number of cores, as well as the widespread availability of CPU-based clusters, it seemed prudent to pursue this road rather than recode a large, validated code in a GPU-specific language.

The aim is to obtain validated, micro-modeling-based simulation tools that can be used for architectural and civil engineering design (safety, comfort, overall customer experience), operation (security officers), and training (first responders, security officers). Particularly for operational decisions, it is important to achieve faster than real-time speeds so that security officers can obtain accurate predictions of future crowd states in a time where preventive measures can still be taken (Figure 13.1).

The modeling of pedestrian motion has been the focus of research and development for more than two decades. If one is only interested in average quantities (average density, velocity), continuum models [6] are an option. For problems requiring more realism, approaches that model each individual are required [7,8]. Among these, discrete space models (such as cellular automata [9–17]), force-based models (such as the social force model [18–21]), and agent-based techniques [7,22–28] have been explored extensively. Together with insights from psychology and neuroscience (e.g., [28,29]), it has become clear that any pedestrian motion algorithm that attempts to model reality should be able to mirror the following empirically known facts and behaviors:

- Newton's laws of motion apply to humans as well: from one instant to another, we can only move within certain bounds of acceleration, velocity, and space.

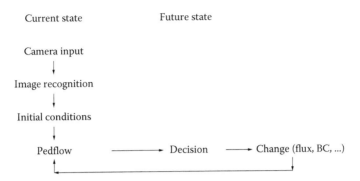

FIGURE 13.1
Use of pedestrian modeling within operational environment.

- Contact between individuals occurs for high densities; these forces have to be taken into account.

- Humans have a mental map and plan on how they desire to move globally (e.g., first go here, then there, etc.).

- In even moderately crowded situations ($O(1\,\mathrm{p/m^2})$), humans have a visual horizon of $O(2.5\text{–}5.0\,\mathrm{m})$, and a perception range of $120°$; thus, the influence of other humans beyond these thresholds is minimal.

- Humans have a "personal comfort zone"; it is dependent on culture and varies from individual to individual, but it cannot be ignored.

- Humans walk comfortably at roughly 2 paces per second (frequency: $\nu = 2\,\mathrm{Hz}$); they are able to change the frequency for short periods of time, but will return to $2\,\mathrm{Hz}$ whenever possible.

We remark that many of the important and groundbreaking work cited previously took place within the animation/computer graphics/gaming/visualization community, where the emphasis is on "looking right." Here, the aim is to answer civil engineering or safety questions such as maximum capacity, egress times under emergency, or comfort. Therefore, comparisons with experiments and actual data are seen as essential [30–32].

13.3 PEDFLOW Model

The PEDFLOW model [32] incorporates these requirements as follows: individuals move according to Newton's laws of motion; they follow (via will forces) "global movement targets"; at the local movement level, the motion also considers the presence of other individuals or obstacles via avoidance forces (also a type of will force) and, if applicable, contact forces. Starting from Newton's laws:

$$m \frac{d\mathbf{v}}{dt} = \mathbf{f}, \quad \frac{d\mathbf{x}}{dt} = \mathbf{v}. \tag{13.1}$$

where $m, \mathbf{v}, \mathbf{x}, \mathbf{f}, t$ denote, respectively, mass, velocity, position, force, and time, and the main modeling effort is centered on $\mathbf{f}$. One should note that many force models have been developed in the past (see, e.g., [3,8,18–21,25,33,34]). We have tried many of these, but, in the end, have found the following ones to work best for our purposes.

PEDFLOW separates the forces into internal (or will) forces (I would like to move here or there) and external forces (I have been hit by another pedestrian or an obstacle). For the sake of completeness, and in order to clarify the techniques used for parallelization, we briefly review the main forces and data structures used. For more information, as well as verification and validation studies, see References 30 through 35 and 32.

13.3.1 Will Force

Given a desired velocity $\mathbf{v}_d$ and the current velocity $\mathbf{v}$, this force will be of the form

$$\mathbf{f}_{will} = g_w \left(\mathbf{v}_d - \mathbf{v} \right). \tag{13.2}$$

The modeling aspect is included in the function g_w, which, in the nonlinear case, may itself be a function of $\mathbf{v}_d - \mathbf{v}$. Supposing g_w is constant, from dimensional analysis, we obtain

$$[g_w] = \frac{[m]}{[t_r]}. \tag{13.3}$$

One can see that the crucial parameter here is the "relaxation time" t_r, which governs the initial acceleration and "time to desired velocity." Typical values are $v_d = 1.35\,\mathrm{m/s}$ and $t_r = O(0.5\,\mathrm{s})$. The "relaxation time" t_r is clearly dependent on the fitness of the individual, the current state of stress, desire to reach a goal, climate, signals, noise, etc. Slim, strong individuals will have low values for t_r, whereas fat or weak individuals will have high values for t_r. Furthermore, scaling by the mass of the individual allows all other forces (obstacle and pedestrian collision avoidance, contact, etc.) to be scaled by the "relaxation time" as well, simplifying the modeling effort considerably. The *direction* of the desired velocity

$$\mathbf{s} = \frac{\mathbf{v}_d}{|\mathbf{v}_d|} \tag{13.4}$$

will depend on the type of pedestrian and the cases considered. A single individual will have as its goal a desired position $\mathbf{x}_d(t_d)$ that he/she would like to reach at a certain time t_d. If there are no time constraints, t_d is simply set to a large number. Given the current position $\mathbf{x}$, the direction of the velocity is given by

$$\mathbf{s} = \frac{\mathbf{x}_d(t_d) - \mathbf{x}}{|\mathbf{x}_d(t_d) - \mathbf{x}|}. \tag{13.5}$$

For members of groups, the goal is always to stay close to the leader. Thus, $\mathbf{x}_g(t_g)$ becomes the position of the leader. In the case of an evacuation simulation, the direction is given by the gradient of the perceived time to exit τ_e to the closest perceived exit:

$$\mathbf{s} = \frac{\nabla \tau_e}{|\nabla \tau_e|}, \tag{13.6}$$

or by the motion of neighbors ("social" or "herd behavior"). The magnitude of the desired velocity $|\mathbf{v}_d|$ depends on the fitness of the individual, and the motivation/urgency to reach a certain place at a certain time. Pedestrians typically stroll leisurely at 0.6–0.8 m/s, walk at 0.8–1.0 m/s, jog at 1.0–3.0 m/s, and run at 3.0–10.0 m/s.

13.3.2 Pedestrian Avoidance Forces

PEDFLOW models the desire to avoid collisions with other individuals by first checking if a collision will occur. If so, forces are applied in the direction normal and tangential to the intended motion. The forces are of the form

$$f_i = f_{max}/(1 + \rho^p); \quad \rho = |\mathbf{x}_i - \mathbf{x}_j|/r_i, \tag{13.7}$$

where $\mathbf{x}_i, \mathbf{x}_j$ denote the positions of individuals i, j; r_i the radius of individual i; and $f_{max} = O(4) f_{max}(will)$. Note that the forces weaken with increasing non-dimensional distance ρ. For years we have used $p = 2$, but, obviously, this can (and probably will) be a matter of debate and speculation (perhaps a future experimental campaign will settle this issue). In the far range, the forces are mainly orthogonal to the direction of intended motion: we tend to move slightly sideways without decelerating. In the close range, the forces are also in the direction of intended motion, in order to model the slowdown required to avoid a collision.

13.3.3 Wall Avoidance Forces

Any pedestrian modeling software requires a way to input geographical information such as walls, entrances, stairs, escalators, etc. In PEDFLOW, this is accomplished via a triangulation (the so-called background mesh; those more familiar with animation or computer graphics should think of the background mesh as something similar to a navigation mesh). A distance to walls map (i.e., a function $d_w(x)$ is constructed using fast marching techniques on unstructured grids), and this allows to define a wall avoidance force as follows:

$$\mathbf{f} = -f_{max}\frac{1}{1 + \left(\dfrac{d_w}{r}\right)^2} \cdot \nabla d_w, \quad p = 2. \tag{13.8}$$

Note that $|d_w| = 1$. The default for the maximum wall avoidance force is $f_{max} = O(8) f_{max}(will)$. The desire to be far/close to a wall also depends on cultural background.

13.3.4 Contact Forces

When contact occurs, the forces can increase markedly. Unlike will forces, contact forces are symmetric. Defining

$$\rho_{ij} = |\mathbf{x}_i - \mathbf{x}_j|/(r_i + r_j), \tag{13.9}$$

these forces are modeled as follows:

$$\rho_{ij} < 1 : f = -[f_{max}/(1 + \rho_{ij}^p)]s; \quad p = 2 \tag{13.10}$$

$$\rho_{ij} > 1 : f = -[2f_{max}/(1 + \rho_{ij}^p)]s; \quad p = 2 \tag{13.11}$$

and $f_{max} = O(8) f_{max}(will)$.

13.3.5 Motion Inhibition

A key requirement for humans to move is the ability to put one foot in front of the other. This requires space. Given the comfortable walking frequency of $v = 2$ Hz, one is able to limit the comfortable walking velocity by computing the distance to nearest neighbors and seeing which one of these is the most "inhibiting."

13.3.6 Psychological Factors

PEDFLOW also incorporates a number of psychological factors that, among the many tried over the years, have emerged as important for realistic simulations. Among these, we mention

- Determination/pushiness: It is an everyday experience that in crowds some people exhibit a more polite behavior than others. This is modeled in PEDFLOW by reducing the collision avoidance forces of more determined or "pushier" individuals. Defining a determination or pushiness parameter p, the avoidance forces are reduced by $(1 - p)$.
- Comfort zone: In some cultures (northern Europeans are a good example), pedestrians want to remain at some minimum distance from contacting others. This comfort zone is an input parameter in PEDFLOW, and is added to the radii of the pedestrians when computing collisions avoidance and precontact forces.
- Right/left avoidance and overtaking: In many Western countries, pedestrians tend to avoid incoming pedestrians by stepping toward their right, and overtake others on the left. However, this is not the norm everywhere, and one has to account for it.

13.4 Data Structures

In order to achieve a real-time modeling for pedestrian simulations with more than 10^6 pedestrians, it is of paramount importance to devise proper data structures that minimize CPU and memory requirements. In fact, it may be argued that after the proper behavioral phenomena have been identified, the realization of real-time modeling hinges on these data structures.

13.4.1 Data Carried by the Individual

These data, which include, among others, items such as the pedestrian's height, width, fitness, nationality, familiarity with surroundings, objectives, current physical and mental state, as well as the current motion data (location, velocity, etc.), are stored in arrays attached directly to the pedestrians. In this way, these data become easily accessible at any time. In order to save storage, the individual's height, width, and fitness are taken from a database, that is, through a table lookup. In this table, the data belonging to a limited number of representative groups are stored, and the individual is tagged as belonging to one of these groups. In order to enhance realism, a random variation number for personal data is also attached to each individual.

Typical pedestrians will follow a path that requires them to reach a certain place at a certain time, with loiter intervals in between. A table of paths is devised before or during the simulation, and each pedestrian is assigned a path according to some statistical distribution. For museums, basilicas, or other places of interest, the number of possible paths can be considerable. In some cases, it may be better to input destinations and loiter time, and obtain the possible paths through a combinatorial assignment of the stations, with due care for conflicting paths (zig-zag, reverse, etc.). For evacuation simulations, this does not have to be done, as pedestrians will move in the direction of the closest perceived exit.

13.4.2 Geographic Data

Under geographic data, we consider, among others, items such as terrain data (inclination, soil/water, escalators, obstacles, etc.), climate data (temperature, humidity, sun/rain, visibility), signs, the location and accessability of guidance personnel, as well as doors, entrances, and emergency exits. These data are stored in a so-called background grid consisting of triangular elements. This background grid is used to define the geometry of the problem, and is generated automatically using the advancing front method [36]. All geometrical and environmental data are attached to this grid. This implies that the amount of data stored and used for the pedestrian movement depends only on the level of detail stored in this mesh, and is proportional to the number of elements in it. For obvious reasons, the size of this mesh (number of elements and points) should be limited to the necessary and available amount of information required for the simulation. In general, the elements of the background grids are of size $O(2\,m)$, but the size is adjusted automatically to define properly curved columns, corners, or other features that are smaller. At every instance, a pedestrian will be located in one of the elements of the background grid. This "host element" is updated continuously using a nearest-neighbor tracking procedure [37]. Given the host element, the geographic data, stored in the nodes of the background grid, are interpolated linearly to the pedestrian.

The closest distance to a wall δ_w for any given point is evaluated via a fast $O(N \log N)$ nearest-neighbor/heap list technique [36].

13.4.3 Neighbor Data

By far, the most time-consuming portion of pedestrian simulations is the evaluation of the interaction between nearest neighbors. These nearest neighbors of every pedestrian must be identified and accounted for at every timestep. A possible way of solving this task efficiently is via optimal spatial data structures, such as bins or octrees [38–42]. These approaches will find the neighbors, but will not be able to identify if walls or other obstacles separate close pedestrians. Thus, they require subsequent spatial searches. In the present case, a different approach, based on the Delauney triangulation, was followed. Assuming an arbitrary cloud of points, a Voronoi tesselation, or its dual, the Delauney triangulation, uniquely defines the nearest neighbors of a point. The Delauney criterion states that the circumcircle of any triangle does not contain any other point. In two dimensions, this is equivalent to minimizing the maximum angle for any combination of triangles adjacent to an edge. For dynamically moving points, the Delauney or min–max criterion will be violated in parts of the mesh. Every so often (e.g., after every timestep), the mesh must be modified in order to restore it. For two-dimensional grids like the ones contemplated here, this is best achieved by flipping diagonals until the Delauney or min–max criterion has been restored. In this way, no boundary recovery is required, and the procedure is guaranteed to yield a valid mesh unless pedestrians stray outside the domain. This last situation can be easily detected, as it would produce elements with negative areas. An edge-based data structure that is well suited for this purpose stores the two points of the edge, the neighbors on either side of the edge, as well as the four edges that enclose the edge (see Figure 13.2). For boundary edges, some of these items will be missing, making it easy to identify them.

In order to expedite the search, a first pass is performed over all edges, storing those that require a modification. After flipping these diagonals, the neighboring diagonals are stored for further inspection. The procedure is then repeated until no edges remain in the list.

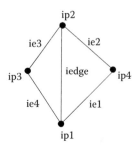

FIGURE 13.2
Edge-based nearest-neighbor data.

In order to identify possible collisions or crossings, a loop over the *edges* of the present pedestrian "mesh" is performed. With the data stored for each edge iedge as shown in Figure 13.2, the nearest neighbors of points ip1, ip2, as well as the next layer of neighbors for points ip3, ip4 can be obtained immediately and processed further.

13.5 Shared-Memory Parallelization

Given the emergence of multi-core machines, the first step in parallelizing PEDFLOW was via shared-memory parallelization, that is, at the loop level via !$omp-directives. In the sequel, we describe the main types of loops and how they were treated.

The first type of loop is a loop over points or edges that only affect points or edges, respectively. This type of loop is trivially parallelized via a simple !$omp-directive. Given that we have many pedestrians and many edges, the efficiency obtained is acceptable.

The second type of loop is over edges, computing forces at the end-points of the edges (i.e., for the pedestrians). These loops are characterized by a series of applicability tests (distance, velocity, orientation, ...) that is then followed by the actual force calculation. These two parts are separated so as to have all local cores working all the time. The first part (filtering) obtains a list of edges that need to be treated. The second part obtains the forces at the edge level. These forces are then added to the pedestrians in scalar mode.

The third type of loop is also over edges, swapping diagonals and reestablishing the edge data structures in the vicinity of a flipped edge. As before, this operation is divided into a test as to whether the edge should be flipped. This list is then processed in scalar mode. As it turns out, the number of edges flipped per timestep is very low, and the (parallel) test for flipping is much more expensive than the flipping itself. This implies that the diagonal flipping scales well in shared-memory mode, and consumes less than 10% of the overall CPU time.

A fourth type of loop is encountered when searching for the host element of a pedestrian in the background mesh. The number of operations required can vary greatly, as some pedestrians do not change host element while others jump into another one. By working with a list of "pedestrians that have not found their host element yet" [37], the work can be evenly distributed across cores.

We remark that the alternative of using general GPUs, currently the "ultimate shared-memory option," has been proposed by several authors; see, for example, Reference 43. We have considered this option, but have opted for the more conservative OpenMP multicore solution in order to be able to run on more systems.

13.6 Distributed-Memory Parallelization

While shared-memory parallelization yields speedup factors of about an order of magnitude, the requirement of $>10^6$ pedestrians in real time necessitates the use of distributed-memory parallelization. This option has been explored in the past by several groups [20,24,44].

The aim of any parallel code must be to preserve, as much as possible, the deterministic result of the original scalar code. While this is relatively simple for shared-memory parallelization, the distributed-memory case is much more difficult. This is because the parallelization is done via some form of domain-splitting, and the whole aim is to arrive at algorithms and codes that operate as much as possible on the local level, that is, need as little knowledge as possible about the pedestrians in regions that are far away. Given that the inter-pedestrian movement is influenced mainly by the near vicinity, and that spatially relevant information (e.g., distance and gradient to walls) is stored on the background grid, one can parallelize the pedestrian update algorithm by invoking a distance argument. However, one cannot simply subdivide space and proceed: in order to arrive at a scheme that is as close as possible to the original scalar code, an overlap region between the domains must be introduced. This has been shown diagrammatically for a case with four distributed-memory processors in Figure 13.3. Around each original element partition (the so-called core elements of each domain), a layer of distance d of neighbor elements is added (the so-called buffer zone). This then defines the domain treated by each processor. In this way, the forces (and hence the movement) of pedestrians that are close to the boundary of the core region of each domain are still computed properly. We remark that a similar argumentation and approach has been employed by Quinn et al. [20].

For the spatial subdivision, a number of techniques have been implemented. Among these, the advancing front, moment recursive bisection, and Computer Aided Design (CAD)-surface based [36] have seen the most use. For a comparison of these methods, see References 24 and 44.

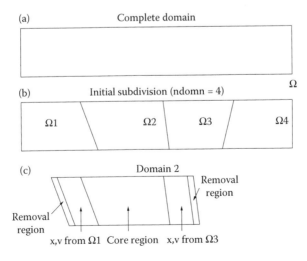

FIGURE 13.3
Domain partitioning with overlap and removal regions.

As a pedestrian can now exist in several processors/extended domains, one has to define which one is the "dominant" or "true" one. The obvious choice is to assign this to the pedestrian whose host element is inside the core elements of one of the processors/domains. After each timestep, the pedestrians that are in elements of the core zones and that are part of the buffer zones in other processors are sent to them. The pedestrian information (position, velocity, state, etc.) is then updated accordingly.

13.6.1 Efficiency Considerations

Before proceeding, it may be beneficial to estimate if the proposed scheme will lead to a scalable technique that can compute more than a million pedestrians in real time.

Denoting by A_1 the area computed by a single processor, and by A_p the area computed for multiple processors and overlapping domains, an estimation of the loss of efficiency can be obtained by assuming square domains of length l with overlap distance d and a uniform distribution of pedestrians. Then $A_1 = l^2$ and $A_p = (l + 2d)^2$, implying that the ratio of work is given by

$$r = \frac{A_p}{A_1} = \left(1 + \frac{2d}{l}\right)^2.$$ (13.12)

Thus, for a desired ratio of work, the required length l is given by

$$l = \frac{2d}{\sqrt{r} - 1}.$$ (13.13)

The number of pedestrians in each processor is given by

$$p_p = A_p \rho = (l + 2d)^2 \rho.$$ (13.14)

Table 13.1 shows the lengths, areas, and required pedestrians for different densities as a function of the ratio of work for an overlap distance of $d = 5\,\text{m}$. As expected, the ratio of parallel-to-scalar work increases with decreasing length l (or area). However, even for $l = 25\,\text{m}$, the ratio is only of order $r = O(2)$. Assuming that one can update $O(10^3)$ pedestrians in real time per core, the number of cores needed to obtain a real-time update for $O(10^6)$ pedestrians is only $O(2 \times 10^3)$, that is, well within the possibilities of commodity hardware.

13.6.2 Further Improvements

The parallel domain decomposition procedure described above can be improved in several ways. We mention the most important of these:

TABLE 13.1

Size of Domain as a Function of Ratio of Parallel-to-Scalar Work

r	l (m)	l^2(m^2)	Peds($\rho = 1$)	Peds($\rho = 2$)	Peds($\rho = 4$)
1.20	105	10,977	10,977	21,954	43,909
1.40	55	2979	2979	5958	11,916
1.60	38	1425	1425	2850	5700
1.80	29	857	857	1714	3427
2.00	24	583	583	1166	2331

- *Less frequent exchange of information*: The amount of information exchanged between domains can be considerable. An immediate way to have less communication overhead is by performing the data exchange only every n_{xch} steps. This number clearly depends on the timestep chosen, the forces present, etc. Experimentation has shown that values up to $n_{xch} = 4$ are acceptable for PEDFLOW.
- *Update host table via global host element index*: Once a pedestrian has been migrated from one domain to the next, the host element in this domain must be found. In order to save unnecessary CPU expense, a table of the relationship between the element numbers in each domain and the original complete (global) mesh is kept. One can then obtain immediately the host number in all other domains.
- *Update in list via universal number index*: A slow-moving pedestrian may be migrated from one domain to the next many times. This implies that one has to test if a pedestrian just received from another domain is already present in the current domain. This test is accomplished by assigning to each pedestrian a so-called unique universal number. The unique universal number index array can then be queried to see if a pedestrian received already exists in the domain.

13.6.3 Dynamic Load Balancing

During the course of a simulation, pedestrians may crowd into certain regions, while emptying from other zones. Given that computational work is proportional to the number of pedestrians, this can lead to large load imbalances. These may be alleviated via dynamic load balancing.

A complete dynamic load balancing consists of the following steps:

- Evaluate the work required in each element of the background grid.
- Re-split the background grid (e.g., using recursive orthogonal moment bisection).
- Determine the new processor number of each element and pedestrian.
- Send the elements of the background grid (together with all other spatial information) and pedestrians to their respective new processors.
- Assemble the elements of the background grid (together with all other spatial information) and pedestrians in the new (updated) processors.

While this list is easily drawn, the bug-free realization is far from trivial.

13.7 Examples

For all examples, the following standard pedestrian parameters were chosen:

- Desired velocity: $1.2 \pm 0.1\,\text{m/s}$
- Relaxation time: $0.50 \pm 0.1\,\text{s}$
- Pedestrian radius: $0.25 \pm 0.02\,\text{m}$
- Min/max ellipticity: $0.00 : 0.50$
- Min/max pushiness: $0.00 : 0.80$
- Comfort zone: $0.05 \pm 0.00\,\text{m}$

In the sequel, we denote by `ndomn` the number of spatial domains used to distribute the work (i.e., the number of `mpi` processes running), and by `nprol` the number of shared-memory threads used. Thus, the total number of cores used for a run is given by `ncore=ndomn*nprol`.

We also denote by efficiency loss the measured maximum ratio over the domains of the number of pedestrians, including overlap versus the number of pedestrians in the core region:

$$e = max_i \left[\frac{N_t^i}{N_c^i} - 1 \right], \quad i = 1, ndomn. \tag{13.15}$$

All timings were performed on the SGI-ICEx Cluster at SL Rasch. This SGI machine is composed of 108 nodes. Each node has two Intel Xeon CPU E5-2680 (Sandybridge) processors with 8 cores each running at 2.7 GHz, and 64 GB of RAM. Thus, one can run up to 16 cores in shared-memory mode. The interconnection network is composed of two InfinibBand interconnect (10/20 Gb/s), one interconnect is dedicated to I/O and the other to MPI traffic. The operating system is Red Hat Enterprise Linux 6.5.

13.7.1 Cross-Flow Case

This case combines cross-streams as well as obstacle avoidance. The geometry is composed of 196 segments of 200×200 m (Figure 13.4a) (note: there is nothing special about this

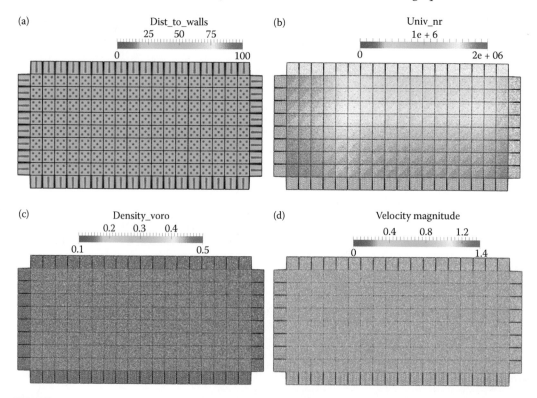

FIGURE 13.4

(a, b) Cross-flow: Distance to walls and universal pedestrian numbers at time $T = 6000$ s. (c, d) Cross-flow: Density and velocity at time $T = 6000$ s. (e, f) Cross-flow: Velocity and universal numbers (detail). (g) Cross-flow: Number of pedestrians exchanged with neighbors in each domain.   (*Continued*)

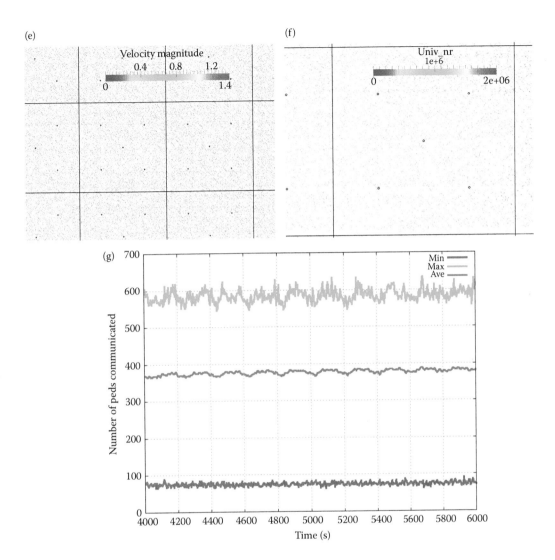

FIGURE 13.4 (Continued)
(a, b) Cross-flow: Distance to walls and universal pedestrian numbers at time $T = 6000$ s. (c, d) Cross-flow: Density and velocity at time $T = 6000$ s. (e, f) Cross-flow: Velocity and universal numbers (detail). (g) Cross-flow: Number of pedestrians exchanged with neighbors in each domain.

geometry: the machine on which the timings were done had only a limited number of cores available, and it happened that 196 segments was the limit).

In each of the segments, five circular obstacles are present (Figure 13.4a through f). A steady flux of $f_p = 160$ p/s is coming in from the left and $f_p = 360$ p/s from the bottom. The pedestrians entering through the left aim at exiting at the right, while those entering through the bottom aim at exiting at the top. Figure 13.4b through f shows the density and velocity at time $T = 6000$ s. The number of pedestrians in the domain reaches a stable number of $O(1.2\,\mathrm{M})$ after approximately $T_0 = 4000$ s. The timing studies considered the time from $T_0 = 4000$ s to $T_1 = 6000$ s. The number of pedestrians communicated between domains/processors over time may be inferred from Figure 13.4g. The measured loss of efficiency was of the order of $O(0.25)$, that is, negligible (Table 13.2).

TABLE 13.2

Cross-Flow

ndomn	nprol	ncore	Time (s)	µs/Ped/Step	Mpeds/s	Peds/s/Core
196	1	196	2662	1.07	0.93	6326
196	2	392	1503	0.61	1.65	3163
196	4	784	1117	0.45	2.22	1582

13.7.2 Large-Scale Evacuation

In order to give a more complete picture as to how the proposed procedure works for more realistic cases, a large-scale evacuation simulation is included. The case is a hypothetical evacuation scenario of a possible extension of the Holy Mosque complex in Mecca, Saudi Arabia. The geometry assumed here is shown in Figure 13.5a and b. One can see that it is quite extensive, consisting of several levels, many passages, staircases, etc. The final surface where pedestrians/pilgrims could move (shown in gray in Figure 13.5a and b) was defined by 1731 surface patches. The background mesh consisted of approximately

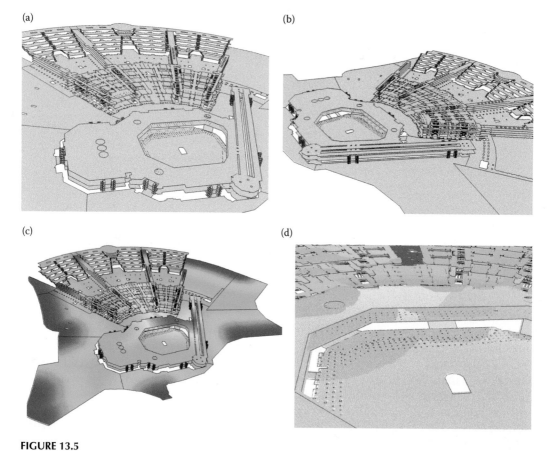

FIGURE 13.5

(a, b) Large-scale evacuation: Geometry. (c, d) Large-scale evacuation: Distance to exits and initial position of pilgrims (detail). *(Continued)*

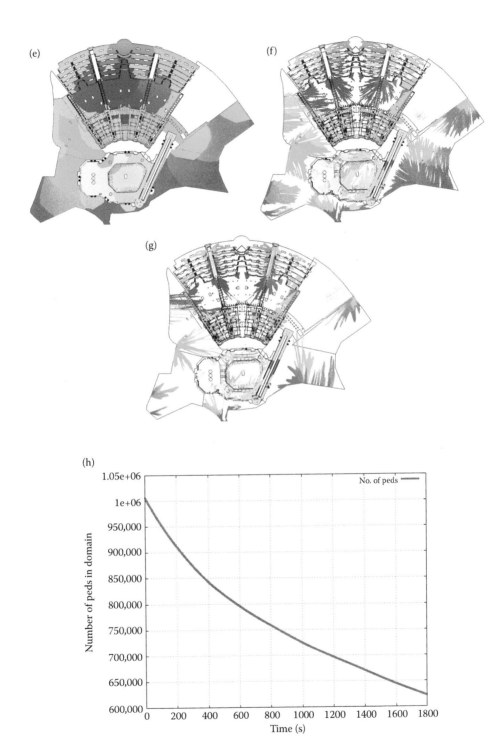

FIGURE 13.5 (Continued)
(e, f, g) Large-scale evacuation: Pilgrim distribution at time $T = 0, 2, 5\,\text{min}$. (h) Large-scale evacuation: Number of pedestrians over time. *(Continued)*

(i)

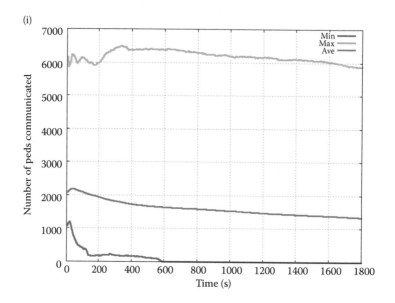

FIGURE 13.5 (Continued)
(i) Large-scale evacuation: Number of pedestrians exchanged with neighbors in each domain.

3 M triangles. We remark that this is not an actual geometry, as it does contain architectural imprecisions. In particular, the size and arrangement of the stairs as well as the exits leading to the surrounding neighborhoods were based on incomplete information. Some of the internal passages between different levels also had to be guessed. As such, it is a simulation that is carried out for demonstration purposes only in order to see if cases with millions of pedestrians/pilgrims can be handled.

At the beginning of the simulation, the pedestrians/pilgrims were all placed in the usual prayer locations. It was assumed that the prayer rows emanate from the Kaaba, and are separated radially by 1.2 m and circumferentially by 0.6 m. These figures are consistent with the guidelines of the mosque's authority (Riassa). This led to a total of 1,007,771 pedestrians/pilgrims. Details of the resulting rows of pedestrians are shown in Figure 13.5d.

In order to get a first estimate of the evacuation time, all pedestrians/pilgrims were "released" at the beginning of the calculation. Their paths followed the "shortest time to exit," shown in Figure 13.5c. Figure 13.5e through g shows the pedestrians at times $T = 0, 2, 5$ min. The coloring is according to the unique universal pedestrian number in order to be able to trace the origin of the pedestrians exiting. Note that "rows" or "striations" occur close to the exits. This seldomly occurs in reality, and is due to the fact that the "time to exit" was not recalculated during the run. The timing studies considered the time from $T_0 = 0$ s to $T_1 = 1800$ s. The number of pedestrians, as well as the amount of pedestrians communicated over time, may be inferred from Figure 13.5h and i. The measured loss of efficiency was of the order of $O(1.25)$, that is, no longer negligible. The run took 4865 s (1 h and 21 min) using 32 domains, with 4 cores for each domain, that is, a total of 128 cores. This translates to an update speed of approximately 0.3 Mpeds/s. We remark that the total evacuation time for a building of this size can be more than an hour. However, given that the geometrical details were not all correct, it was decided to perform these demonstration runs to $T = 1800$ s.

13.8 Conclusions and Outlook

A first-principles model for the simulation of pedestrian flows and crowd dynamics capable of computing the movement of a million pedestrians in real time has been developed. The model is based on a series of forces, such as will forces (the desire to reach a place at a certain time), pedestrian collision avoidance forces, obstacle/wall avoidance forces, pedestrian contact forces, and obstacle/wall contact forces. In order to allow for general geometries, a so-called background triangulation is used to carry all geographic information. At any given time, the location of any given pedestrian is updated on this mesh. The code has been ported to shared- and distributed-memory parallel machines. The results obtained show that the stated aim of computing the movement of million pedestrians in real time has been achieved. This is an important milestone, as it enables faster-than-real-time simulations of large crowds (stadiums, airports, train and bus stations, concerts) as well as evacuation simulations for whole cities.

Future work will center on the following topics:

- Treatment of larger groups when moving across domain boundaries
- Further increases in realism for pedestrian behavior modeling, such as
  - Queuing at certain locations
  - Aleatoric stopping
- Fast input and initialization from multiple camera images
- Detailed comparison of results with video footage obtained from large-scale pilgrimage events

Furthermore, a considerable burden awaits when trying to produce realistic avatar-based displays of the results obtained. A recent 5-min film with more than 10^5 pedestrians visualized with sophisticated raytracing and scenery required days on more than 300 cores. There is a clear opportunity (and requirement) for improvement here.

Acknowledgments

It is a pleasure to acknowledge the many collaborators who helped to bring to fruition this effort: Bodo Rasch, whose visionary ideas started this work; Achmed Rasch, Mohammed Khaled Gdoura, Timo Leucht, Stefan Haenlein, and Iris Treffinger from the visualization department at SL Rasch; Juergen Bradatsch, Bernhard Gawenat, and Prabhudev Dambalmath from the engineering department at SL Rasch; and Fernando Camelli and Michelle Isenhour from the CFD Center at GMU.

References

1. E.R. Galea, S.J. Deere and P.J. Lawrence. A systematic methodology to assess the impact of human factors in ship design. *Appl. Math. Model.*, 33(2):867–883, 2009.

2. T. Zhong, X. Zheng and M. Liu. Modeling crowd evacuation of a building based on seven methodological approaches. *Build. Environ.*, 44:437–445, 2009.

3. *The Conference on Pedestrian and Evacuation Dynamics*, A bi-annual conference, Delft, The Netherlands. Transportation Research Procedia, 2014.

4. R. Löhner, A. Corrigan, F. Camelli and F. Mut. Semi-automatic porting of a large-scale Fortran CFD code to GPUs. *Int. J. Num. Meth. Fluids*, 69(2):314–331, 2012.

5. R. Löhner, A. Corrigan, F.F. Camelli and J. Wallin. Running unstructured grid based CFD solvers on modern graphics hardware. *Int. J. Num. Meth. Fluids*, 66:221–229, 2011.

6. R.L. Hughes. The flow of human crowds. *Annu. Rev. Fluid Mech.*, 35(1):169–182, 2003.

7. J. Allbeck, M. Kapadia, N. Pelechano and N. Badler. *Virtual Crowds: Steps toward Behavioral Realism*. Morgan & Claypool Publishers, San Rafael, California, 2015.

8. D. Thalmann and S.R. Musse. *Crowd Simulation*. Springer-Verlag, London, 2007.

9. J. Wahle, A. Kessel, H. Klüpfel and M. Schreckenberg. Microscopic simulation of pedestrian crowd motion. In *Pedestrian and Evacuation Dynamics* (M. Schreckenberg and S.D. Sharma, eds.), pp. 193–202. Springer, New York, 2002.

10. V.J. Blue and J.L. Adler. Emergent fundamental pedestrian flows in cellular automata microsimulation. *Transport. Res. Rec.*, 1644:29–36, 1998.

11. V.J. Blue and J.L. Adler. Flow capacities from cellular automata modeling of proportional splits of pedestrians by direction. In *Pedestrian and Evacuation Dynamics* (M. Schreckenberg and S.D. Sharma, eds.), Springer, New York, 2002.

12. N. Courty and S. Musse. Simulation of large crowds including gaseous phenomena. In *Proceedings of IEEE Computer Graphics International 2005*, pp. 206–212, New York, June 2005.

13. J. Jesurun, J. Dijkstra and H. Timmermans. A multi-agent cellular automata model of pedestrian movement. In *Pedestrian and Evacuation Dynamics* (M. Schreckenberg and S.D. Sharma, eds.), pp. 173–180, Springer, New York, 2002.

14. Y. Takeyama, K. Teknomo and H. Inamura. Review on microscopic pedestrian simulation model. In *Proceedings of Japan Society of Civil Engineering Conference*, Morioka, Japan, March 2000.

15. H.L. Klüpfel. *A Cellular Automation Model for Crowd Movement and Egress Simulation*. University of Duisburg-Essen. Ph.D. dissertation: Falkutät, 2003.

16. R. Masling, P.A. Langston and B.N. Asmar. Crowd dynamics discrete element multi-circle model. *Safety Sci.*, 44:395–417, 2006.

17. A. Schadschneider. Cellular automaton approach to pedestrian dynamics—Theory. In *Pedestrian and Evacuation Dynamics* (M. Schreckenberg and S.D. Sharma, eds.), pp. 75–86. Springer, New York, 2002.

18. P. Molnár, D. Helbing, I.J. Farkas and T. Vicsek. Simulation of pedestrian crowds in normal and evacuation situations. In *Pedestrian and Evacuation Dynamics* (M. Schreckenberg and S.D. Sharma, eds.), pp. 21–58. Springer, New York, 2002.

19. D. Helbing and P. Molnar. Social force model for pedestrian dynamics. *Phys. Rev. E*, 51:4282–4286, 1995.

20. R.A. Metoyer, M.J. Quinn and K. Hunter-Zaworski. Parallel implementation of the social forces model. In *Proceedings of the 2nd International Conference in Pedestrian and Evacuation Dynamics*, pp. 63–74, The University of Greenwich, London, 2003.

21. D.J. Kaup, T.I. Lakoba and N.M. Finkelstein. Modifications of the Helbing-Molnár-Farkas-Vicsek social force model for pedestrian evolution. *Simulation*, 81(339), 2005.

22. E. Andersen, S. Guy Ming Lin, A. Sud, R. Gayle and D. Manocha. Real-time navigation of independent agents using adaptive roadmaps. In *ACM Symposium on Virtual Reality Software and Technology*, Newport Beach, CA, November 2007.

23. S. Curtis and D. Manocha. Pedestrian simulation using geometric reasoning in velocity space. In *Pedestrian and Evacuation Dynamics* (U. Weidmann, U. Kirsch, and M. Schreckenberg, eds.), pp. 875–890. Springer, New York, 2012.

24. J.M. Ordun, G. Vigueras, M. Lozano and F. Grimaldo. A comparative study of partitioning methods for crowd simulations. *Appl. Soft Comput.*, 10:225–235, 2010.

25. N. Pelechano and N.I. Badler. Modeling crowd and trained leader behavior during building evacuation. *IEEE Comput. Graph. Appl.*, 26(6):80–86, 2006.
26. C. Kim, N. Satish, M. Lin, D. Manocha, S.J. Guy, J. Chhugani and P. Dubey. Clearpath: Highly parallel collision avoidance for multi-agent simulation. In *Proceedings of ACM SIGGRAPH/Eurographics Symposium on Computer Animation* (D. Fellner and S. Spencer, eds.), pp. 177–187. Association of Computing Machinery, 2009.
27. S. Curtis, P. Dubey, M. Lin, S.J. Guy, J. Chhugani and D. Manocha. Pledestrians: A least-effort approach to crowd simulation. In *Eurographics/ACM SIGGRAPH Symposium on Computer Animation*, pp. 119–128. Association of Computing Machinery, 2010.
28. P.M. Torrens. Moving agent pedestrians through space and time. *Annals of the Association of American Geographers*, 102(1):35–66, 2011.
29. P.M. Vishton and J.E. Cutting. Wayfinding, displacements, and mental maps: Velocity fields are not typically used to determine one's aimpoint. *J. Exp. Psychol.*, 21(5):978–995, 1995.
30. M. Isenhour and R. Löhner. Verification of a pedestrian simulation tool using the NIST recommended test cases. In *The Conference in Pedestrian and Evacuation Dynamics*, pp. 237–245, Delft, The Netherlands. Transportation Research Procedia, 2014.
31. M. Isenhour and R. Löhner. Verification of a pedestrian simulation tool using the NIST stairwell evacuation data. In *The Conference in Pedestrian and Evacuation Dynamics*, pp. 739–744, Delft, The Netherlands. Transportation Research Procedia, 2014.
32. R. Löhner. On the modeling of pedestrian motion. *Appl. Math. Model.*, 34(2):366–382, 2010.
33. D. Helbing and P. Molnar. Self-organization phenomena in pedestrian crowds. In *Self-Organization of Complex Structures: From Individual to Collective Dynamics* (F. Schweitzer, ed.), pp. 569–577. Gordon and Breach, London, 1997.
34. J. Allbeck, N. Pelechano and N.I. Badler. *Virtual Crowds: Methods, Simulation and Control*. Morgan & Claypool, 2008.
35. M. Chraibi, R. Löhner, E. Haug, J. Zhang, D. Britto and B. Gawenat. Qualitative validation of pedflow for description of unidirectional pedestrian dynamics. In *The Conference in Pedestrian and Evacuation Dynamics 2014 (PED2014)*, pp. 733–738, Delft, The Netherlands. Transportation Research Procedia, 2014.
36. R. Löhner. *Applied CFD Techniques*, Second Edition. John Wiley & Sons, Chichester, 2008.
37. R. Löhner and J. Ambrosiano. A vectorized particle tracer for unstructured grids. *J. Comp. Phys.*, 91(1):22–31, 1990.
38. E. Rougier, A. Munjiza and N.W.M. John. MR linear contact detection algorithm. *Int. J. Num. Meth. Eng.*, 66:46–71, 2006.
39. D.E. Knuth. *The Art of Computer Programming*. pp. 1–3. Addison-Wesley, Reading, Massachusetts, 1973.
40. R. Löhner. The empty bin: A data structure for spatial search of time-varying data. *Comm. Num. Meth. Eng.*, 23(12):1111–1119, 2007.
41. A. Munjiza and K.R.F. Andrews. NBS contact detection algorithm for bodies of similar size. *Int. J. Num. Meth. Eng.*, 43:131–149, 1998.
42. R. Sedgewick. *Algorithms*. Addison-Wesley. 1983.
43. P. Richmond, T. Karmakharm and D.M. Romano. Agent-based large scale simulation of pedestrians with adaptive realistic navigation vector fields. In *EG UK Theory and Practice of Computer Graphics* (J. Collomosse and I. Grimstead, eds.), 2010.
44. A. Steed and R. Abou-Haidar. Partitioning crowded virtual environments. In *Proceedings of the ACM Symposium on Virtual Reality Software and Technology (VRST'03)*, pp. 7–14, 2003.

Section V

Conclusions

14

Conclusions from the Editors

In this book, we have covered a large number of topics that are needed to simulate heterogeneous crowds. The goal throughout was to give a good introduction to different simulation techniques, always keeping in mind that we are aiming at microscopic models that should exhibit heterogeneity.

In order to examine the sorts of variety expected in heterogeneous crowds, we have included chapters on enhancing realism, improving believability, adding psychological and personality models, exploiting data-driven techniques, and creating visual variety though pre-joint impostors.

Each of the chapters in this book gives a good overview of future work and challenges in each specific area, which can provide a good source of ideas for future research. In addition to all the ongoing research on each of the topics covered in this book, we would like to address the importance of the integration of all these different matters to achieve believable heterogeneous crowds, especially toward immersive environments.

With recent advances in virtual reality technology and its multiple applications, the need for believable, populated immersive virtual environments is increasing. Even though current computer graphics methods allow us to develop highly realistic virtual worlds, the main element failing to convince the user is autonomous groups of human inhabitants. A great number of crowd simulation techniques have emerged in the last decade, but critical details in the crowd's movements and appearance do not meet the standards necessary to convince virtual reality (VR) participants that they are present in a real crowd.

In this book, we have dedicated a full section to provide a deep overview of a variety of quantitative approaches for the evaluation of crowd simulation. Alternatively, qualitative methods can also be used for evaluation from a perceptual perspective or even from an immersive point of view. The power of presence and plausability illusion in VR open the doors to a large amount of unexplored research in immersive crowds for both the evaluation and extraction of human behavior information. The data extracted under controlled immersive experiments can then be used to further enhance crowd simulation methods.

One of the biggest challenge in crowd simulation is that the uncanny valley issues escalate. Not only are there more virtual humans, but there is also added complexity that appears from the interactions between them. It is well known that when participant expectations are not met, presence can be broken. If participant expectations are set too high by one aspect of the simulation, lower quality in another aspect can break presence. Along these lines, there are areas of active research that need continued improvement for crowd simulations in VR to be successful. We need better animation and blending tools, better rendering for large crowds, and better stepping and navigation algorithms (particularly in cluttered environments). In fact, animation bugs and glitches tend to be very noticeable in VR and are very distracting. We also need to calibrate the speed of characters when placed in VR, as we have observed that they tend to be perceived as moving more quickly than they should be.

Another challenge is enabling people naive to programming to create and modify environments. Current software frameworks like game engines have begun addressing this challenge. They provide tools for importing models, designing levels, blending animations, designing simple AIs, etc. They do not, however, provide tools for the creation and control of virtual human populations. While there has been some work explored toward authoring the behaviors of populations from a limited number of easy-to-author-action types, additional research is needed.

Social presence would be increased through better communication and social actors. Certainly, this is an element of crowd simulation that could use additional research. Characters in crowds tend to be expressionless and largely nonreactive. While they may respond to avoid collisions and to a few scripted events, they tend to appear rather lifeless. They possess limited communication models and few social features. Even the addition of models of attention would provide more lifelike qualities. Characters should look where they are going and at interesting objects and events in the world. Individuals in crowds that meet the eye of the participant from time to time could help to increase social presence. Characters should react to each other and to the participant in a natural manner. Work in presence shows that even in a rather primitive crowd simulation and VR setup, participants can be positively influenced by even unintentional character actions. To increase social presence, characters should exhibit surprise, curiosity, and even anger. They should exhibit different personalities and attitudes. They should appear. . .human.

Index